The Discourse on F[

Ji Yun and Eighteenth-Cent[

Leo Tak-hung Chan

UNIVERSITY OF HAWAI'I PRESS
HONOLULU

Published in North America by
  University of Hawai'i Press
  2840 Kolowalu Street
  Honolulu, Hawai'i 96822

First Published in Hong Kong by
  The Chinese University Press
  The Chinese University of Hong Kong
  Sha Tin, N.T., Hong Kong
  E-mail address: cup@cuhk.edu.hk
  Web-site: http://www.cuhk.edu.hk/cupress/w1.htm

Printed in Hong Kong

Library of Congress Cataloging-in-Publication Data

Chan, Tak-hung Leo, 1954–
    The discourse on foxes and ghosts: Ji Yun and eighteenth-century
  literati storytelling / Leo Tak-hung Chan.
        p.   cm.
    Includes bibliographical references and index.
    ISBN 0-8248-2051-7 (alk. paper).
    1. Chinese fiction — Ch'ing dynasty, 1664–1912 — History and
  criticism.   2. Chi, Yün, 1724–1805. Yüeh wei ts'ao t'ang pi chi.
  3. Ghost stories, Chinese — History and criticism.   4. Fantastic
  fiction, Chinese — History and criticism.   I. Title.
  PL2437.C43   1998
  895.1'348 — dc21   97-41698
                                                                          CIP

For my wife
Sandy

Contents

Acknowledgements

This book grew out of a doctoral thesis I wrote under the supervision of Eugene Eoyang from 1989 to 1991, and it is to him that I owe my greatest intellectual debts. He has continued to be a source of inspiration and support after I left Indiana, went to conduct research at Ann Arbor, and then taught in Washington D.C. Our paths have once again crossed because of his recent move to Hong Kong. I would like to acknowledge a special debt, too, to Robert Eno who, always more than just a teacher, has shown great enthusiasm about my research on the literature of the strange, an area quite different from his own. Others at Bloomington, Indiana, who have offered guidance include David Arkush, Judith Berling, Robert Campany, Irving Lo, Susan Nelson, Margaret Sung, and Lynn Struve. In particular, Judith Berling helped set the direction for my academic career by instilling in me a "fondness for the strange" before she left for the Graduate Theological Union.

Among those who read portions of the manuscripts I would like to express my gratitude to Kenneth DeWoskin and David Rolston, whose comments and criticisms are especially invaluable since their research focuses on related fields — Chinese classical tales and vernacular fiction, respectively. The year I spent at Ann Arbor was especially memorable, and I will always recall the stimulating discussions I had with Chang Chun-shu, Paul Forage, Lin Shuen-fu, and Marshall Wu. I take this opportunity to thank the Center for Chinese Studies, University of Michigan, for the post-doctoral fellowship that enabled me to devote a full year's time to my research and to avail myself of the excellent resources at Ann Arbor.

For reading part or all of the manuscript and giving valuable advice, I am grateful to my colleagues at Lingnan College, Ma Yau-woon and Barry Asker. A very special debt is owed to Laurence Wong, Head of the Department of Translation, Lingnan College, whose unstinting support made the past few years of my work-life most fruitful, when administrative and teaching duties rendered it almost impossible to carry on any research. For expert editing, I would like to thank Esther Tsang, Editor of the Chinese University Press; for preparation of the index and going through the initial manuscript, Robert Battistini; for the Chinese calligraphy on the cover, my former student Kuan Ling; and for recommending my manuscript for publication, the anonymous reviewers.

Portions of this book have previously appeared in a slightly different form: Chapter Three as "Narrative as Argument: The *Yuewei caotang biji* and the Late Eighteenth-Century Elite Discourse on the Supernatural" in *Harvard Journal of Asiatic Studies* and Chapter Two as "Text and Talk: Classical Literary Tales in Traditional China and the Context of Casual Oral Storytelling," in *Asian Folklore Studies*. For permission to reprint them, thanks are due to the publishers.

While wives always get their share in acknowledgements of this sort, Sandy deserves more than casual recognition. She has from the start listened sympathetically to the tales that I retold, was convinced that many were didactic in implication, and encouraged me in my endeavours by narrating a few of the old wives' tales that she heard while working in Southern Taiwan some years ago. To her this book is dedicated.

Abbreviations

LZZI	*Liaozhai zhiyi*
LYWB	*Liuya waibian*
SKQSZM	*Siku quanshu zongmu*
YTSL	*Yetan suilu*
YWCTBJ	*Yuewei caotang biji*
ZBY	*Zi bu yu*

The editions used for the above are found in the section "Bibliography." Citations from the *Yuewei caotang biji* are indicated by the following abbreviations for the separate volumes, as well as the chapter number and entry number:

GW	*Guwang tingzhi* (4 volumes)
HX	*Huaixi zazhi* (4 volumes)
LY	*Luanyang xiaoxialu* (6 volumes)
LX	*Luanyang xulu* (6 volumes)
RS	*Ru shi wo wen* (4 volumes)

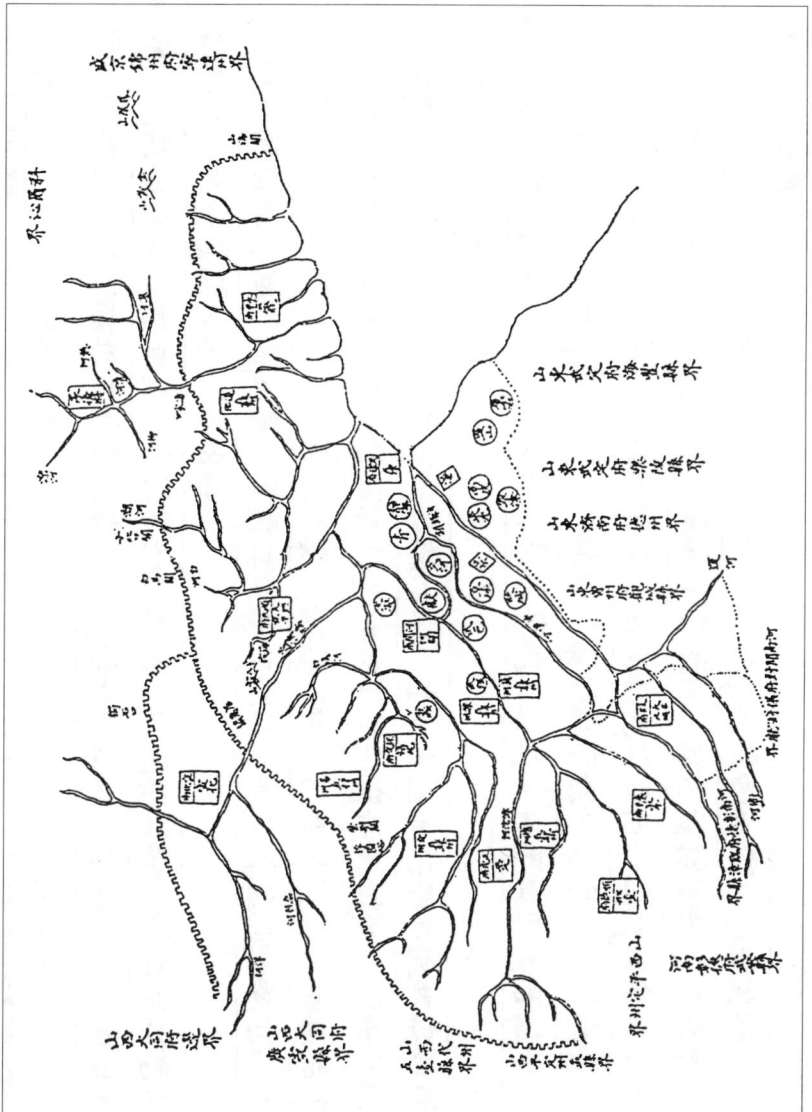

Figure 1. Location map for stories in the *Random Jottings at the Cottage of Close Scrutiny*

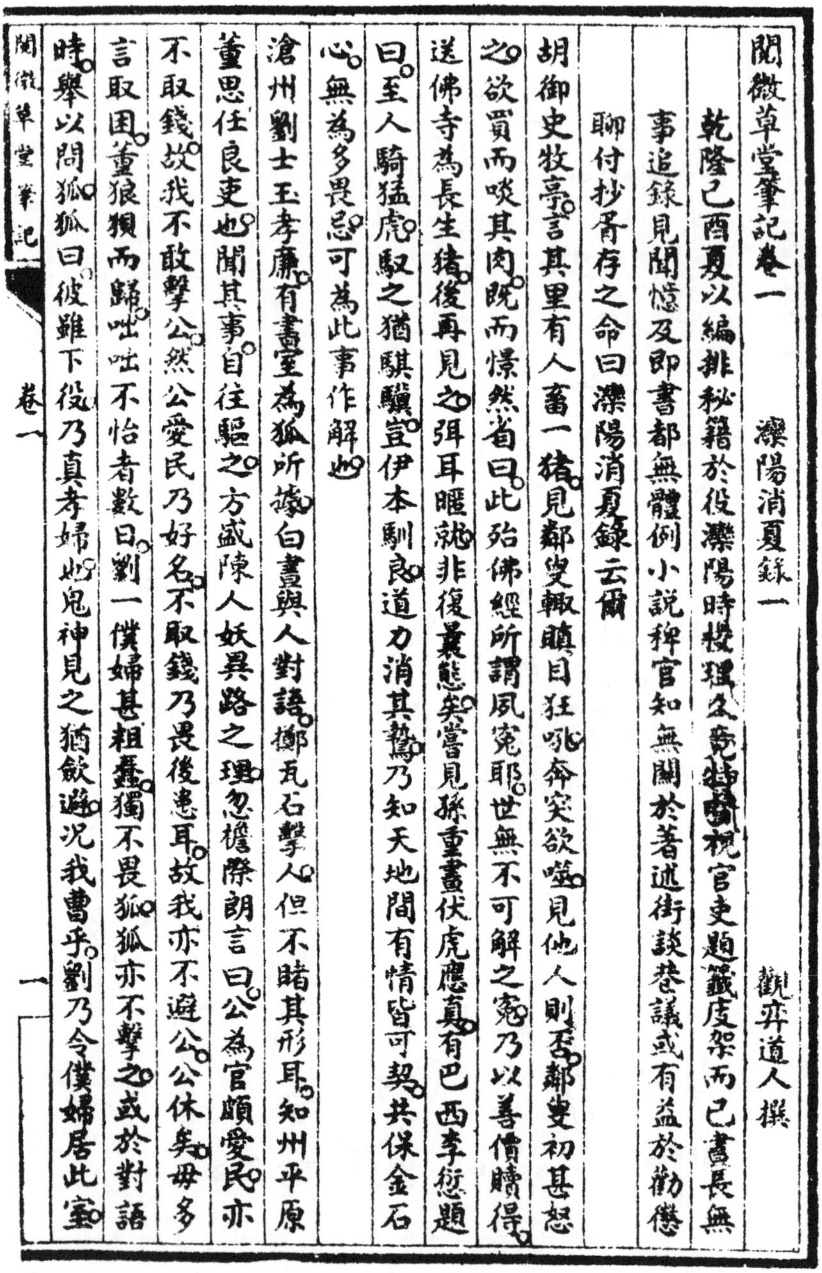

閱微草堂筆記卷一　灤陽消夏錄一

觀弈道人撰

乾隆己酉夏以編排秘籍於灤陽時校理久竟而諸君視官吏題籤庋架而已晝長無

事追錄見聞憶及即書都無體例小說稗官知無關於著述街談巷議或有益於勸懲

聊付抄胥存之命曰灤陽消夏錄云爾

胡御史牧亭言其里有人畜一豬見鄰叟輒瞋目狂吼奔突欲噬見他人則否鄰叟初甚恚

之欲買而啖其肉既而憬然省曰此殆佛經所謂夙冤耶世無不可解之冤乃以善價贖得

送佛寺為長生豬後再見之弭耳暱就非復曩態矣嘗見孫重畫伏虎應真有巴西李衍題

曰至人騎猛虎馭之猶騏驥宣伊本馴良道力消其鷙乃知天地間有情皆可契共保金石

心無為多畏忌可為此事作解也

滄州劉士玉孝廉有書室為狐所據白晝與人對語擲瓦石擊人但不睹其形耳知州平原

董思任良吏也聞其事自往驅之方盛陳人妖異路之理忽簷際朗言曰公為官頗愛民亦

不取錢故我不敢擊公然公愛民乃好名不取錢乃畏後患耳故我亦不避公公休矣毋多

言取困董狼狽而歸咄咄不怡者數日劉一僕婦甚粗蠢獨不畏狐狐亦不擊之或於對語

時舉以問狐狐曰彼雖下役乃真孝婦鬼神見之猶斂避況我曹乎劉乃令僕婦居此室

Figure 2. An early edition of *Random Jottings at the Cottage of Close Scrutiny*

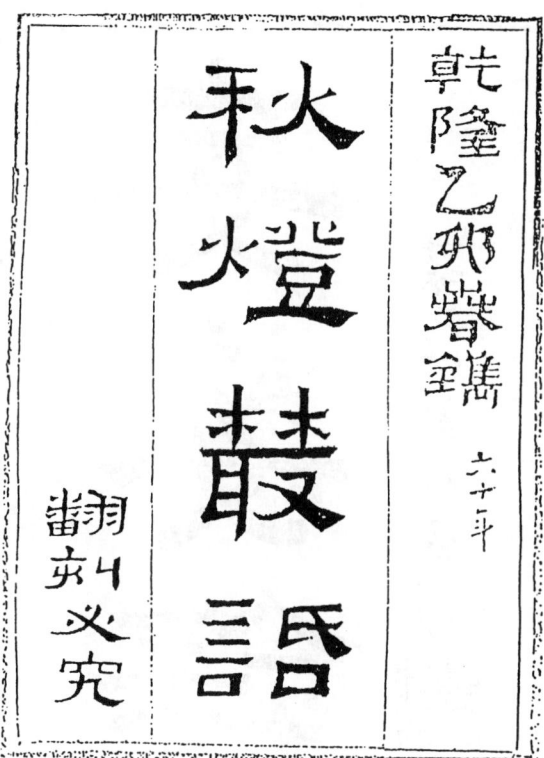

Figure 3. Title page of the Qianlong edition of *Miscellaneous Discourses under the Autumn Lamp*

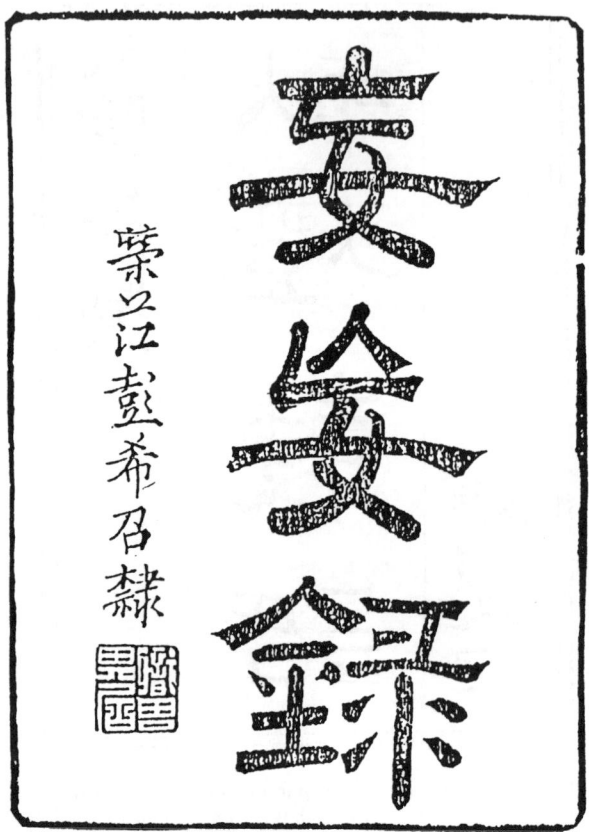

Figure 4. Earliest extant edition of *Hearsay Accounts*, in the
Rare Books Collection, The Chinese University of
Hong Kong

高坡異纂二卷採進本

明楊儀撰儀有蠙頭密語已著錄是編乃志怪之

書前有自序謂高坡者京邸之寓名粲明張爵坊巷術衛集

東城有高坡術衛蓋卽所居也錢希言獪園稱楊

儀禮部素不信元怪之談因閱王維賢親見仙人騎鶴事始

遂傾心著有高坡異纂行於世然書中所記往往誕妄如黃澤為元末通儒趙

汸之所師事本以經術名家而

儀謂劉某入石壁得天書從澤講投真可謂齊東之語至閩織女渡河文星私窺其媒狎織女褻牽文曲星衣

上帝醜之手批牽牛頹傷眉流血竟公然敢於侮天矣小說之誕妄未有如斯之甚者也

冶城客論二卷浙江范懋柱家天一閣藏本

明陸采撰采字子元長洲人棨之弟也是編乃其肄業南雍時記所聞見大抵妖異不根之言其胡銓後身一條

云閩之祝允明又云初聞祝子之言以為祝好奇必記此不暇詳叩因近閱語怪兩編無之追書於冊是允明有

所不記而采記之其誕妄甚於允明矣乃護沈周作座新聞多信門客妄言何也卷末駕鴦記一篇述施氏婦

閩閫幽會之事淫媟萬狀如身歷目睹此同時士大夫家也誰見之而誰言之乎九有乖名教矣

祐山雜說一卷兩淮鹽政採進本

明馮汝弼撰汝弼字惟良平湖人嘉靖壬辰進士官工科給事中以言事謫濬山縣丞遷知太倉州調揚州府同

知不赴隆慶中追贈布政司參政是書自記生平瑣事率涉卜禊祥其所記他人事亦多不出此末載種植數

方尤與全書不類

Figure 5. Three reviews from *An Annotated Catalogue of the Complete Library of Four Treasuries*

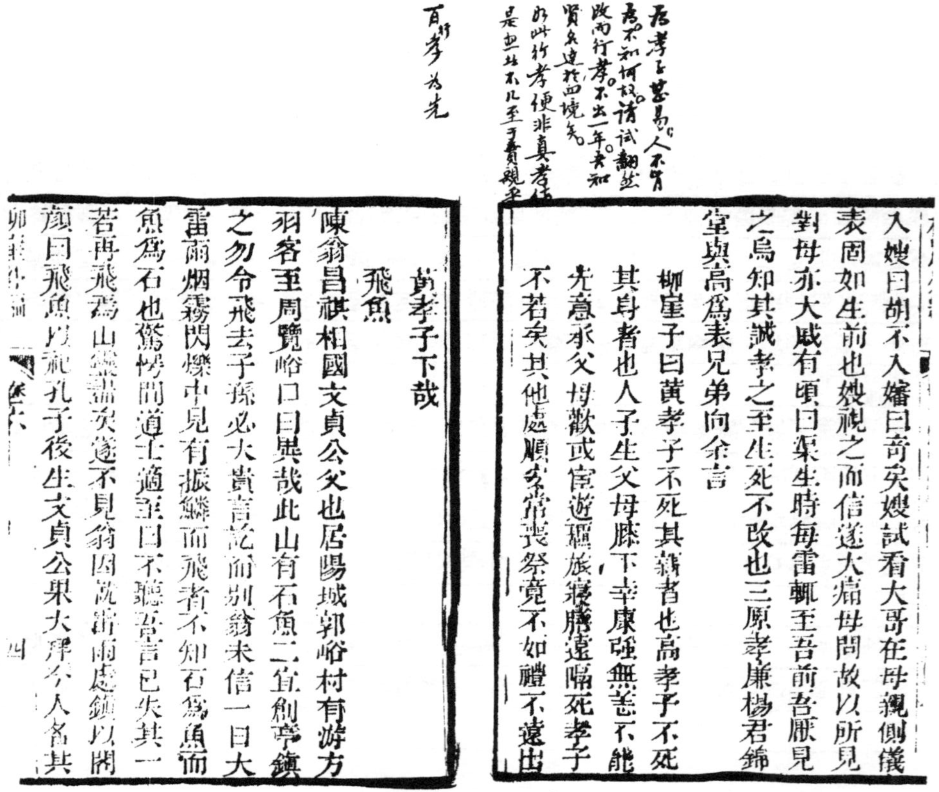

Figure 6. Pages from Xu Kun's *Unauthorized Compilations of Willow Cliff* with "eyebrow" comments

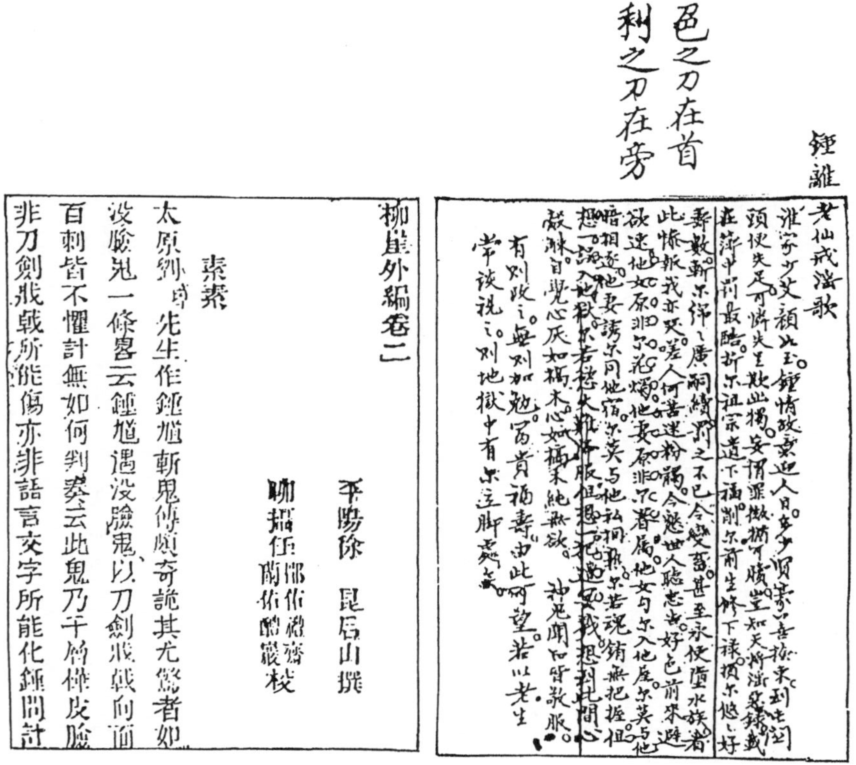
色之刀在首
利之刀在旁
鍾離
老仙戒淫歌

柳崖外編卷二
平陽徐　昆后山撰
太原劉　先生作鍾馗斬鬼傳頗奇詭其尤警者如
沒臉鬼一條畧云鍾馗遇沒臉鬼以刀劍戕戟向面
百刺皆不懼計無如何判授云此鬼乃千層樺皮臉
非刀劍戕戟所能傷亦非語言文字所能化鍾問計

Figure 7. Pages from Xu Kun's *Unauthorized Compilations of Willow Cliff* with end-of-chapter comments

Chapter 1

Ji Yun and the Eighteenth-Century Zhiguai

> Devote yourself earnestly to the duties due to men, and respect
> spiritual beings but keep them at a distance.
>
> — *Confucius*

There seems to be general consensus that few of the *zhiguai* 志怪
(stories of the strange) after the Six Dynasties (*Liuchao* 六朝) are worth
much serious attention: the later *zhiguai* collections have fared poorly
at the hands of present-day critics and readers. This immediately raises
the question why the late eighteenth-century examples of this genre
should merit extended analysis, not to mention the choice of Ji Yun's
紀昀 (1724–1805) *Random Jottings at the Cottage of Close Scrutiny* (*Yuewei
caotang biji* 閱微草堂筆記) as the focus for the present study. As a first
step toward formulating an answer, it needs to be noted that the *zhiguai*
has rarely been approached as it ought to be — as a distinct category
of narrative that is socially situated and that cannot be divorced from
the actual contexts of its occurrence. Relating the *zhiguai* to the world
in which it finds itself is the key to unravelling the dynamics of this
genre. Lu Jintang 盧錦堂, a critic of *Close Scrutiny*, was right in more
senses than one when he described the collection as a "book of the
gentry."[1]

---

[1] Lu Jintang, "Ji Yun shengping jiqi *Yuewei caotang biji*" 紀昀生平及其閱微草堂筆記 (The
Life of Ji Yun and His *Yuewei caotang biji*) (M.A. thesis, National Chengchi University 政治大
學, 1974), p. 112a.

The magnitude of *zhiguai* production in traditional China simply cannot be exaggerated. This whole tradition, rooted in various forms of pre-Han 漢 literature, continued uninterrupted until the end of the Qing 清 .[2] A representative catalogue like *A Comprehensive Catalogue of Chinese Collectanea* (*Zhongguo congshu zonglu* 中國叢書綜錄) lists over one hundred items in its *zhiguai* section, beginning with *The Classic of Spirits and Anomalies* (*Shenyi jing* 神異經) of the Han and concluding with *Forest of Talk* (*Shuo lin* 説林) of the late Qing.[3] There is

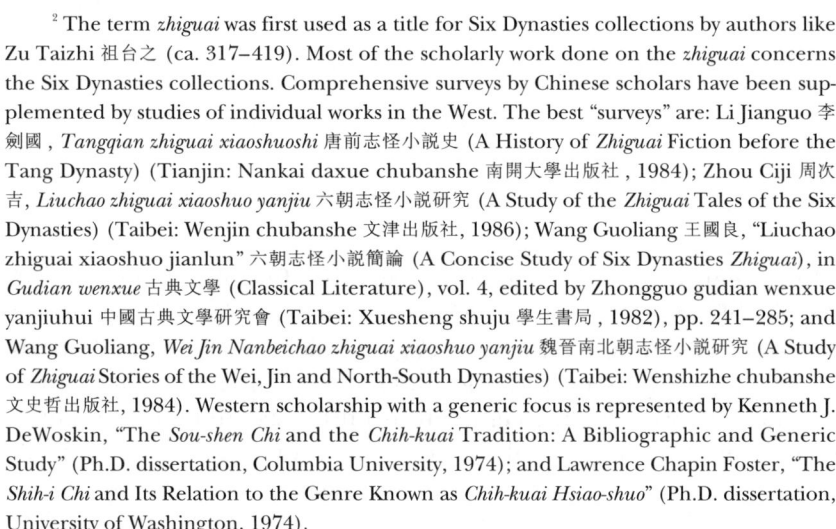

---

[2] The term *zhiguai* was first used as a title for Six Dynasties collections by authors like Zu Taizhi 祖台之 (ca. 317–419). Most of the scholarly work done on the *zhiguai* concerns the Six Dynasties collections. Comprehensive surveys by Chinese scholars have been supplemented by studies of individual works in the West. The best "surveys" are: Li Jianguo 李劍國 , *Tangqian zhiguai xiaoshuoshi* 唐前志怪小説史 (A History of *Zhiguai* Fiction before the Tang Dynasty) (Tianjin: Nankai daxue chubanshe 南開大學出版社 , 1984); Zhou Ciji 周次吉 , *Liuchao zhiguai xiaoshuo yanjiu* 六朝志怪小説研究 (A Study of the *Zhiguai* Tales of the Six Dynasties) (Taibei: Wenjin chubanshe 文津出版社, 1986); Wang Guoliang 王國良, "Liuchao zhiguai xiaoshuo jianlun" 六朝志怪小説簡論 (A Concise Study of Six Dynasties *Zhiguai*), in *Gudian wenxue* 古典文學 (Classical Literature), vol. 4, edited by Zhongguo gudian wenxue yanjiuhui 中國古典文學研究會 (Taibei: Xuesheng shuju 學生書局 , 1982), pp. 241–285; and Wang Guoliang, *Wei Jin Nanbeichao zhiguai xiaoshuo yanjiu* 魏晉南北朝志怪小説研究 (A Study of *Zhiguai* Stories of the Wei, Jin and North-South Dynasties) (Taibei: Wenshizhe chubanshe 文史哲出版社, 1984). Western scholarship with a generic focus is represented by Kenneth J. DeWoskin, "The *Sou-shen Chi* and the *Chih-kuai* Tradition: A Bibliographic and Generic Study" (Ph.D. dissertation, Columbia University, 1974); and Lawrence Chapin Foster, "The *Shih-i Chi* and Its Relation to the Genre Known as *Chih-kuai Hsiao-shuo*" (Ph.D. dissertation, University of Washington, 1974).

[3] Shanghai tushuguan 上海圖書館 , ed., *Zhongguo congshu zonglu* (Beijing: Zhonghua shuju 中華書局 , 1959), pp. 1082–1094. The chronological listing given in this catalogue is far from comprehensive. But unlike some major catalogues and the *yiwen zhi* 藝文志 (bibliographies) of the dynastic histories, it devotes a single section to the *zhiguai* (and another to the *chuanqi* 傳奇 [stories of marvels]). Cf. Yuandong tushu bianjibu 遠東圖書編輯部 , ed., *Zhongguo lidai yiwen zhi* 中國歷代藝文志 (Bibliographies in the Standard Histories through the Chinese Dynasties) (Taibei: Yuandong tushu gongsi 遠東圖書公司, 1956). The *zhiguai* is also often listed as *yiwen* 異聞 (anomalous accounts). See *SKQSZM*, vol. 5, pp. 140–144; Sun Dianqi 孫殿起 , *Fanshu ouji* 販書偶記 (Occasional Records of the Book Trade) (Beijing: Zhonghua shuju 中華書局 , 1959); and Dongfang wenhua shiye weiyuanhui 東方文化事業委員會 , ed., *Xuxiu siku quanshu zongmu tiyao* 續修四庫全書總目提要 (A Continuation to the Annotated General Catalogue of the *Complete Library of Four Treasuries*) (Taibei: Commercial Press, 1971–1972). Still useful as general catalogues of fiction in the classical language are Cheng Yizhong 程毅中 , *Gu xiaoshuo jianmu* 古小説簡目 (A Brief Catalogue of Old

ample evidence that an especially large number of *zhiguai* collections were produced in the late imperial era, particularly in the late eighteenth and early nineteenth centuries. In addition to *zhiguai* collections which identified themselves as such, there was also at the time plenty of *biji* 筆記 (random jottings) literature in which one finds stories of strange events.

The general neglect accorded this genre of writing can be attributed to its close links with popular superstitions and folk beliefs and to its divorce from the mainstream of imaginative literature. Apart from the Six Dynasties *zhiguai*, which garner interest as the earliest specimens of Chinese narrative, most *zhiguai* collections invite interest only as documents from which information about religious beliefs in certain localities can be culled.[4] But the denigration of the eighteenth-century varieties of this genre — which for purposes of convenience we shall term the "late *zhiguai*" — must also be explained with reference to that pinnacle in the tradition of classical tales in the literary language,[5] *Tales of Anomalies from the Studio of Leisure* (*Liaozhai zhiyi* 聊齋志異) of Pu Songling 蒲松齡 (1644–1715). Though not all *zhiguai* tales as such, Pu Songling's stories are recognized for having brought to a remarkable end the entire classical-story tradition, and

---

Fiction) (Beijing: Zhonghua shuju 中華書局 , 1981); and Yuan Xingpei 袁行霈 and Hou Zhongyi 侯忠義, *Zhongguo wenyan xiaoshuo shumu* 中國文言小説書目 (A Catalogue of Chinese Fiction in the Classical Language) (Beijing: Beijing daxue chubanshe 北京大學出版社, 1981).

[4] In their article "Topics for Research in Ch'ing History," *Late Imperial China*, 8.1 (1987), pp. 187–203, Susan Naquin and Evelyn S. Rawski suggest that the *zhiguai* of the eighteenth century could be studied for popular beliefs in particular cultural regions, though "it is more problematic to decide *whose* beliefs these stories actually reflect" (p. 203). A study applying such an approach to popular religions in the Southern Song is Valerie Hansen, *Changing Gods in Medieval China, 1127–1276* (Princeton: Princeton University Press, 1990).

[5] Critics have generally adhered to a strict separation of classical Chinese fiction into the *wenyan* 文言 and *baihua* 白話 streams. For instance, Lu Xun 魯迅 alternates discussions of vernacular fiction with discussions of the literary tale. See Lu Xun, *A Brief History of Chinese Fiction*, translated by Yang Hsien-yi and Gladys Yang (Beijing: Foreign Language Press, 1959). The two "streams" can be distinguished, however, not so much on the basis of the language used as by their formal features, intended readership, and authorial characteristics. It is noteworthy that these two categories of Chinese fiction also share themes and concerns. The supernatural, for one, has found its way into both. *Wenyan* tales, too, were often recreated in the vernacular.

their brilliance has overshadowed all that came in their wake. In the opinion of many critics, all the major eighteenth-century collections were written either under Pu's influence or as a reaction against *Studio of Leisure*.[6]

A more devastating condemnation of the *zhiguai* of the late imperial era attacks the blatant didacticism displayed in almost every collection. Ever since its beginnings, the *zhiguai* has betrayed a tendency towards the didactic. Simply put, didacticism in literature occurs when the author articulates ethical messages that could have been conveyed just as well in non-literary forms. Thus, some extrinsic, ulterior purpose propels the literary enterprise, and determines every strategic move undertaken by the writer. In the context of narrative literature, the success of the didactic author depends less on his ability to make a story "come to life" than on the degree to which he manages to communicate his intended message. This kind of approach is consequently author-centred as well as reader-centred, with the text serving as no more than the medium in a communicative process.

Early *zhiguai* writers resorted to the didactic for religious reasons. Many were engaged in what should more appropriately be called proselytizing efforts. Notable examples of the didactic *zhiguai* are those by Wang Yan 王琰 (active during the late fifth and the early sixth centuries), who wrote *Records of Miraculous Omens* (*Mingxiang ji* 冥祥記) to promote Buddhism, and by Ge Hong 葛洪 (283–343), whose *Biographies of Immortals* (*Shenxian zhuan* 神仙傳) propagated the Daoist immortality cult. Much of the later *zhiguai*, on the other hand, evinces a radical transformation in the didactic strain: shedding its ties to partisan conflicts between different religious faiths, it promoted morality of a more secular nature and demonstrated a particular interest in the rectification of unethical behaviour unacceptable to society.

Typifying such trends is Ji Yun's *Close Scrutiny*, which is important not just because of its immense popularity as a Qing *zhiguai* collection, but also because it exemplifies most vividly the dynamics of

---

[6] Maeno Naoaki 前野直彬, *Chūgoku shōsetsushi kō* 中國小説史考 (Researches into the History of Chinese Fiction) (Tokyo: Akiyama shoten 秋山書店, 1973), pp. 256–347.

didacticism in the eighteenth-century *zhiguai*.[7] Its significance in this context is underlined, first, in the contrasts with *Studio of Leisure* set up by Ji Yun himself, who implicitly considers his work as *zhiguai* couched in the didactic mode, whereas Pu Songling's collection is in the aesthetic mode.[8] Secondly, although one can talk of resemblances among the dozen or so *zhiguai* collections roughly contemporaneous with *Close Scrutiny* only up to a certain point, there is no doubt that the didactic patterns in the latter are discernible in a number of these texts. In fact, Ji Yun's approach to writing the *zhiguai* created an influence that lasted well into the late nineteenth century.

For some generations didacticism has been consistently disparaged among Western literary theorists, and readers have generally found unpalatable the de-emphasis of representation, as well as the moralistic use of narrative. According to René Wellek and Austin Warren, works with a "non-aesthetic" purpose should not count as literature at all.[9] It is also said that, when didacticism occurs, "the thing to be communicated takes precedence as an act of communication over the artistic qualities of the form through which it is communicated."[10] It is doubtless for this reason that the *chuanqi* 傳奇 (stories of marvels), with their better-rounded characters and fuller exploitation of narrative plots, have for long been held by Western-trained scholars in higher regard than the majority of the *zhiguai*. *Studio of Leisure,*

---

[7] According to Cai Yuanpei 蔡元培 (1867–1940) in his preface to an edition of *YWCTBJ,* Ji Yun's collection was among the three most widely read fictional works of the Qing dynasty. Quoted in Liu Zhaoyun 劉兆雲, comp., *Yuewei caotang biji xuanzhu* 閱微草堂筆記選註 (Selected Stories from the *Yuewei caotang biji,* with Annotations) (Beijing: Remnin wenxue chubanshe 人民文學出版社, 1982), p. 5. The other two works were *Dream of the Red Chamber* (*Honglou meng* 紅樓夢) and *LZZI*. See also Iizika Akira 飯塚朗 and Imamura Yoshio 今村与志雄, trans., *Chūgoku koten bungaku zenshū* 中國古典文學全集 (An Appreciation of Classical Chinese Literature) (Tokyo: Heibonsha 平凡社, 1958), vol. 20, p. 348.

[8] See Sheng Shiyan's 盛時彥 colophon, in which Ji Yun is quoted, at the end of *GW*. *YWCTBJ,* pp. 471–473.

[9] René Wellek and Austin Warren, *Theory of Literature* (New York: Harcourt Brace, 1949), p. 25.

[10] William F. Thrall and Addison Hibbard, *A Handbook to Literature* (New York: Odyssey Press, 1962), p. 145.

generally considered to be the masterpiece of Chinese short-story collections, happens to be, as Ji Yun would have put it, *zhiguai* in the *chuanqi* mode.[11]

While the didacticism of *Close Scrutiny* will be a primary focus of this study, it needs to be emphasized that the moral imperatives there were voiced in a context of: (1) a belief that the supernatural realm of ghosts, deities, and other spirits did indeed exist, in spite of contentions to the contrary; and (2) an understanding of the way such supernatural beings worked, as revealed in the analysis of factual evidence from witnesses of the strange. While the insistence that the world of spirits does exist is a recurrent feature throughout *zhiguai* literature, the understanding of the nature of spirits demonstrated by *Close Scrutiny* is characteristic of Ji Yun's time. Both elements, however, are essential to the structure of arguments leading up to the expression of a didactic viewpoint in *Close Scrutiny*.

The *Zhiguai* as a Genre

To set the stage for the ensuing discussion on *Close Scrutiny* and other eighteenth-century *zhiguai* collections, the meanings of several terms ought to be determined with some degree of precision. The most unwieldy and enigmatic problem is how to define the generic term *zhiguai*, especially as it relates to the *xiaoshuo* 小説 (loosely translated as "fiction"), the *biji*, and the *chuanqi*. A proper understanding of what the *zhiguai* is necessarily begins with the origin of the word *xiaoshuo*, first used by Zhuangzi 莊子 (369–286 B.C.) when he talked of "winning honour and renown by means of *xiaoshuo*."[12] Lu Xun 魯迅 (1881–1936) accordingly interpreted it to mean "chit-chat of no great importance."[13] The standard bibliographic definition is, however, given by Ban Gu 班固 (32–92) in *History of the Han Dynasty* (*Han shu* 漢書), where the

---

[11] See chap. 3. For a recent attempt to compare the terms *chuanqi* and *zhiguai*, see Zheng Huijing 鄭惠璟, "Tangdai zhiguai xiaoshuo yanjiu" 唐代志怪小説研究 (A Study of the Tang *Zhiguai*) (M.A. thesis, National Taiwan University 國立台灣大學, 1989), pp. 1–17.

[12] See *Zhuangzi jishi* 莊子集釋 (Annotated Collected Edition of *Zhuangzi*), edited by Guo Qingfan 郭慶藩 (Beijing: Zhonghua shuju 中華書局, 1961), chap. 26 ("Waiwu pian" 外物篇), p. 15.

[13] *A Brief History of Chinese Fiction*, p. 1.

writing of *xiaoshuo* was said to have been modelled on the activity of the minor Zhou 周 officials (*baiguan* 稗官), quasi-historians who collected street gossip for the guidance of the ruling government.[14]

This meaning of the term *xiaoshuo* can be further elaborated. A careful look at the listing of fifteen *xiaoshuo* works in the bibliographies of *History of the Han Dynasty* reveals that none of these works are narratives pure and simple.[15] They are primarily discursive in nature and show an affinity with the argumentative writings of the philosophers, information which partly explains why the works were classified in the "Philosophers" section in the first place. In fact, it was not until *New History of the Tang Dynasty* (*Xin Tang shu* 新唐書) that an abundance of narrative works came to be included amongst the *xiaoshuo*. Thus, we can fairly conclude that both the post-Six Dynasties understanding of *xiaoshuo* as, simply, "tales" and the twentieth-century identification of *xiaoshuo* with "fiction" can be misleading, for neither definition takes into account one central aspect of this genre. The word *xiaoshuo* may also be rendered into English as "inconsequential conversations" or "minor persuasions."

What does this tell us about the *zhiguai*, itself a type of *xiaoshuo*? The modern emphasis on the written text, as well as the strict segregation of fiction from history and philosophy, has perhaps blinded us to certain significant characteristics of a genre like the *zhiguai*. One must recall that a lot of *zhiguai* stories began with writers recording the "strange" events told to them by relatives and friends in their own circle.[16] Since no pre-existent form of writing was available at first for such stories, *zhiguai* writers like Gan Bao 干寶 (fl. 320) borrowed the

---

[14] *Han shu* (Beijing: Zhonghua shuju 中華書局, 1964), vol. 4, p. 1745.

[15] For an excellent discussion of the discursive nature of the *zhiguai*, see Kenneth J. DeWoskin, "The Six Dynasties *Chih-kuai* and the Birth of Fiction," in *Chinese Narrative: Critical and Theoretical Essays*, edited by Andrew H. Plaks (Princeton: Princeton University Press, 1977), pp. 21–52.

[16] As an offshoot of an undifferentiated body of Han and Pre-Han narrative, the *zhiguai* has, from a very early stage, partaken of a wayward and unorthodox character. Its lack of respectability (compared to, say, the histories), as well as the disregard in which it was held among the elite, is traced by Kenneth J. DeWoskin in his entry "Chih-kuai," *The Indiana Companion to Traditional Chinese Literature*, edited by William H. Nienhauser, Jr. (Bloomington: Indiana University Press, 1986), pp. 280–284.

styles of history-writing. His compilation of *In Search of Spirits* (*Soushen ji* 搜神記) must be considered analogous to his writing of *History of the Jin Dynasty* (*Jin shu* 晉書). Another form of borrowing is seen in the use made by other writers of the anecdotal tradition in philosophical discourse, exemplified in such works as *Zhuangzi* and *Liezi* 列子. The consequences of these two kinds of generic borrowing are found here and there in the *zhiguai*. For instance, the evaluation of historical personages (demonstrated, say, by *Records of History* [*Shi ji* 史記]), as well as the use of anecdotes to illustrate arguments, have left their mark on *zhiguai* stories. These characteristics set the *zhiguai* apart from the type of imaginative narrative divorced from history and fact that is generally defined as fiction in the West.[17]

Similarly, the task of defining the *biji*, which carry the bulk of *zhiguai* materials, is beset with difficulties. Its name literally meaning "notes casually jotted down," the genre first flourished during the Six Dynasties and was characterized in particular by entries on a wide range of topics — tales of the supernatural, notes on barbarian lore and customs, incidents of historic significance, brief remarks on literature and art, short treatises on geography, and so on. Hybrid as it already was, the *biji* continued to expand its scope in later dynasties, and while some collections evince a certain degree of thematic specialization, the typical *biji* often turns out to be no more than a smorgasbord of historical, literary, and philological writings.[18] It is partly for this reason that the *biji* has been described (albeit in a rather exaggerated way) as an "anti-genre" that flaunts the established, more clear-cut categories. However, one ought to bear in mind that, despite the diversity in content, *biji* collections all share one common formal feature: the brevity of the entries.

That tales of the supernatural should figure as the main category in *biji* writings (in fact, these tales outnumber historical accounts,

---

[17] Fiction is "a term often used inclusively for any literary narrative, whether in prose or verse, which is feigned or invented, and does not purport to be historical truth." M. H. Abrams, *A Glossary of Literary Terms* (New York: Holt, Rinehart and Winston, 1981), p. 61.

[18] For discussions of the *biji* as a generic term, see Joseph S. M. Lau and Y. W. Ma, eds., *Traditional Chinese Stories: Themes and Variations* (New York: Columbia University Press, 1978), pp. xx–xxi; and Y. W. Ma, "Pi-chi," in *The Indiana Companion to Traditional Chinese Literature*, edited by William H. Nienhauser, Jr., pp. 650–652.

humorous sayings, and literary notes) goes a long way towards showing the suitability of the *biji* genre as a vehicle for the *zhiguai*. In the first place, the *zhiguai* itself displays diverse subject-matter: typical juxtapositions are tales of miraculous or portentous omens against biographies of immortals, and accounts of fantastic creatures against stories of encounters with ghosts and spirits. Indeed, the *zhiguai* is as much a hodgepodge of hybrid elements as the *biji*. Second, the ideal form of most *zhiguai* items is also a prevalent form in the *biji* — the anecdote or "very short story," which often lacks an extended plot and usually centres on a single action.[19] Of course, as the *zhiguai* developed, they were adapted to a full range of forms, and even the novella figures rather prominently in a collection like *Studio of Leisure*.

The presence of an abundance of *zhiguai* materials in *biji* collectanea makes imperative the distinction between "*zhiguai* collections" and "individual *zhiguai* stories." While much of the current critical discussion focuses primarily on the better known *zhiguai* collections like those from the Six Dynasties and the Tang 唐 -Song 宋 period, there is a staggering amount of *zhiguai* material in virtually untouched *biji* collections. Some, like Huang Wei's 黃暐 (b. 1438) *Categorized Records at an Overgrown Window* (*Pengchuang leiji* 蓬窗類記), incorporate separate *zhiguai* sections.[20] In many others the accounts of supernatural events are simply dispersed in the text, as in Xue Yongruo's 薛用弱 (Tang dynasty) *Records of Anomalies Compiled* (*Jiyi ji* 集異記). Even the so-called "*zhiguai* collections" may contain subject matter with no relation to the supernatural. In *Close Scrutiny*, for instance, Ji Yun occasionally digresses on archaeological matters or indulges in personal reminiscences. This would be perfectly natural in a *biji* context.

Yet another aspect of the nature of the *zhiguai* emerges when it is juxtaposed against the genre long considered to be diametrically opposed to it in the Chinese narrative tradition, the *chuanqi*. Although the term *zhiguai* had gained currency in the Six Dynasties and was made the title of at least six different collections, it was not until the

---

[19] The anecdote, not the short story, must be considered the primary form of the *zhiguai*. The short story is the form of many *chuanqi* tales.

[20] The two sections containing *zhiguai* materials are: "Records of Retribution" ("Guobao ji" 果報記) and "Records of the Weird" ("Guaiyi ji" 怪異記).

Ming 明 that it became established as a generic designation. Hu Yinglin 胡應麟 (fl. 1590) divided *xiaoshuo* into six categories and provided a number of examples of each. They are

(1) miscellaneous records (*zalu* 雜錄);
(2) collected anecdotes (*congtan* 叢談);
(3) documented sources (*bianding* 辨訂);
(4) exhortatory writings (*zhengui* 箴規);
(5) *zhiguai;* and
(6) *chuanqi.*

For the first time, *zhiguai* and *chuanqi* were introduced into the realm of critical discourse.

Hu Yinglin has often been chastised for setting up critical distinctions that are blurry and confusing. One may well wish that he had made finer distinctions. But he provided, as nobody before him had, useful genre discriminations based essentially on a consideration of content. He insisted on distinguishing between the *zhiguai* and the *chuanqi,* even though the two modes overlap and co-exist not just in one book but in the same tale.[21] Most traditional scholars, including Ji Yun who struggled with the problem in his work as a bibliographer, had little difficulty working with such categories. The two must remain vaguely defined; Hu Yinglin implied that they were two stylistic forms that exist at two ends of a continuum, and that if placed on a scale, each tale would "weigh heavily" either in one direction or the other.[22]

For the purposes of the present study, however, it seems best to locate the distinction between the *zhiguai* and the *chuanqi* in the characters *qi* 奇 and *guai* 怪 , which are translatable, respectively, as "marvellous" and "strange." The emphasis on human events in the *chuanqi* and on the supernatural in the *zhiguai* further illuminates the

---

[21] See Hu Yinglin, "Jiuliu xulun" 九流緒論 (An Introductory Discussion of the Nine Schools), in his *Shaoshi shanfang bicong* 少室山房筆叢 (Collected Writings from the Retreat at Mount Shaoshi). Collected in Hou Zhongyi 侯忠義 , *Zhongguo wenyan xiaoshuo cankao ziliao* 中國文言小説參考資料 (Reference Materials on Chinese Classical Tales) (Beijing: Beijing daxue chubanshe 北京大學出版社 , 1985), pp. 25–29.

[22] Hou Zhongyi, *Zhongguo wenyan xiaoshuo cankao ziliao,* p. 27.

difference between the forms: any event that gives rise to feelings of wonder or marvel can be the stuff of the *chuanqi*, but only uncanny phenomena not explicable with reference to natural laws are the proper domain of the *zhiguai*. In view of this, I have followed accepted practice in adhering to "narratives of the strange" as a translation for *zhiguai*, but in addition I freely talk about tales "of the otherworld" or "of the supernatural." One needs, however, to bear in mind with regard to the last that this phrase may evoke a Western cosmology not entirely appropriate in the case of the Chinese. I have chosen not to use "tales of the contra-natural," a phrase coined by Everett F. Bleiler,[23] though it must be noted that his phrase pinpoints very nicely the ontological qualities of the *zhiguai* narratives, which are the focus of my analysis. Yet on the whole, as the reader has noticed by now, my preference is for the direct, unambiguous transliteration, *zhiguai*.

The Eighteenth-Century *Zhiguai*

The eighteenth century is generally considered the great age of Chinese narrative literature, although that judgement is based essentially on the achievements of full-length vernacular novels like Cao Xueqin's 曹雪芹 (d. 1764) *Dream of the Red Chamber* (*Honglou meng* 紅樓夢) and Wu Jingzi's 吳敬梓 (1701–1754) *Unofficial History of the Scholars* (*Rulin waishi* 儒林外史). The quality of the *xiaoshuo* in the classical language, it seemed, had been declining since the Tang and Ming tales. Interestingly enough, the celebrated novels, noted for their pointed critique of traditional morality and for espousing a new set of personal and public values, stand in sharp contrast to the vast collections of eighteenth-century *zhiguai* tales, which seem to lean towards more conventional ethics.[24] Especially worthy of note is the fact that

---

[23] See Everett F. Bleiler, *The Guide to Supernatural Fiction* (Kent, Ohio: Kent State University Press, 1983), p. vii.

[24] The subversive nature of vernacular narratives, especially those of the late Ming, has been documented in Keith McMahon, *Causality and Containment in Seventeenth-century Chinese Fiction* (Leiden: E. J. Brill, 1988). In McMahon's view, "the argument is between the orthodox tradition and the heterodox form of literature that the *xiaoshuo* has grown to be" (p. 1).

most of the *zhiguai* collections of that era were written and circulated at about the same time as the monumental vernacular novels — in the latter half of the century.[25] Add to this the difference in subject-matter: one focuses on supernatural matters and the other on the realm of human activity. The polarization can hardly be more extreme.

By sheer quantity the stories of the strange written during this period make it one of the high points in *zhiguai* production in Chinese literary history.[26] Within about a decade, Ji Yun brought out five *zhiguai* collections, beginning with *Record of Spending the Summer at Luanyang* (*Luanyang xiaoxialu* 灤陽消夏錄) in 1789 and ending with *A Sequel to the Luanyang Record* (*Luanyang xulu* 灤陽續錄) in 1798. These were brought together and published in 1800 by Sheng Shiyan 盛時彥, a disciple of Ji Yun. Entitled *Close Scrutiny*, the compilation was a voluminous collection containing, according to one count, 1,074 entries in twenty-four chapters.[27] One of the literary doyens of the eighteenth century, Yuan Mei 袁枚 (1716–1797), whose fame was

---

[25] The 120-chapter version of *Dream of the Red Chamber* came out in 1791, and the first extant edition of *Unofficial History of the Scholars* is that of 1803. It must also be noted that the late eighteenth century was an age of large-scale publishing activities sparked off by imperially sponsored projects and fuelled by a rapidly developing book trade. For a description of the book production scene of the time, see Benjamin A. Elman, *From Philosophy to Philology: Intellectual and Social Aspects of Change in Late Imperial China* (Cambridge, Mass.: Harvard University Press, 1984), pp. 151–160.

[26] It can be argued that the high point of *zhiguai* compilation in the Qing should be located in the late seventeenth century. Wu Zhenfang's 吳震方 (seventeenth century) *Bell-talk, Second Collection* (*Shuoling houji* 説鈴後集) anthologized about ten early Qing *zhiguai* collections, but none was more than three chapters in length. *LZZI* thus stood alone as a substantial collection in the early Qing. The early nineteenth century saw another flurry of *zhiguai* works, including Xu Yuanzhong's 許元仲 (b. 1755) *Strange Talk from the Three Brushes* (*Sanbi yitan* 三筆異談) and Xu Qiuzhai's 徐秋垞 *Accounts of Anomalies Heard and Seen* (*Wenjian yici* 聞見異辭), but no major work appeared until late in the 1870s, when Xuan Ding 宣鼎 (1832–1880?) brought out *Records of Rainy Nights under the Autumn Lamp* (*Yeyu qiudeng lu* 夜雨秋燈錄).

[27] Kakinuma Chizuko 柿沼千鶴子, "*Etsubi sōdō hikki* ni okeru shippitsu taido no henka ni tsuite" 閲微草堂筆記における執筆態度の變化について (On the Evolution of [Ji Yun's] Writing Attitude in the *Yuewei caotang biji*), *Ochanomizu Joshi Daigaku bungaku kaihō* 御茶の水女子大學文學會報, vol. 3 (1984), p. 61.

linked with Ji Yun's in the epithet "nan Yuan bei Ji" 南袁北紀 (Yuan in the South and Ji in the North),[28] came out in 1788 with his own twenty-four-chapter *zhiguai* collection, *What the Master Would Not Discuss* (*Zi bu yu* 子不語). To the 742 stories he included in this collection, Yuan Mei later added several hundred more in his *A Sequel to What the Master Would Not Discuss* (*Xu Zi bu yu* 續子不語). There is evidence to suggest that Yuan's collections, circulated both singly and in conjunction with his other "Garden of Contentment" (*Suiyuan* 隨園) writings, enjoyed wide popularity at the end of the eighteenth century.[29]

While some of the collectanea of *zhiguai* stories actually became available to readers slightly earlier, when manuscripts were circulated among friends and relatives, the last ten years of the eighteenth century no doubt marked a high point in *zhiguai* writing. The prefaces, postfaces, and colophons now appended to modern reprints help date the collections with some degree of precision. Wang Xian's 王樾 (*juren* 舉人 [provincial graduate], 1736)[30] *Collected Discourses under the Autumn Lamp* (*Qiudeng conghua* 秋燈叢話) was prefaced by a friend, Hu Gaowang 胡高望 (*juren*, 1753), in 1777, and the earliest extant edition is that of 1791, with eighteen chapters and 645 entries. 1791 saw the completion not only of the second of Ji Yun's *zhiguai* collections, *Thus Have I Heard* (*Ru shi wo wen* 如是我聞), but also of Xu Kun's 徐昆 (b. 1715) eight-chapter *Unauthorized Compilations of Willow Cliff* (*Liuya waibian* 柳崖外編). Xu's mentor added to the latter work a preface

---

[28] Yuzi 愚子, "Fengliu caizi Yuan Zicai" 風流才子袁子才 (Yuan Mei, the Hedonist), in *Yuan Zicai yanjiu ziliao huibian* 袁子才研究資料匯編 (A Compilation of Research Materials on Yuan Mei) (Hong Kong, n.d.), vol. 1, p. 1.

[29] The popularity of *ZBY* is attested by the controversy some of its tales aroused. The censorship imposed on it in 1836 by Emperor Daoguang 道光 may in fact be an attempt to check its influence. See Wu Yuhui 吳玉惠, "Yuan Mei *Zi bu yu* yanjiu" 袁枚子不語研究 (A Study of Yuan Mei's *Zi bu yu*) (M.A. thesis, Tunghai University 東海大學, 1988), pp. 53–54.

[30] Information about Wang Xian's life can be gleaned from the local gazetteer of Fushan 福山 prefecture in Shandong 山東 and Hu Gaowang's 胡高望 (*juren*, 1753) preface to *Collected Discourses under the Autumn Lamp*. Among the dates that can be ascertained is 1736, when Wang Xian was granted the title of *juren* by imperial favour. Ji Yun might have been acquainted with him, as he included a tale narrated by Wang Xian's nephew, Wang Depu 王德圃, in *HX*. See *YWCTBJ*, p. 305.

explaining the unusual reason behind Xu's fondness for the weird
and uncanny: Xu was purportedly a reincarnation of Pu Songling.[31]

In that same year the Manchu writer He Bang'e 和邦額 (b. 1748)
finished and prefaced his own compilation, *Occasional Accounts of Conversations at Night* (*Yetan suilu* 夜談隨錄), which features strange events
of North China, in a setting in sharp contrast to that of Yuan Mei's
tales. At least one modern critic, showing enthusiasm for this collection, has considered it equal to the best of the Qing classical tale collections, namely *Studio of Leisure* and *Close Scrutiny*. The accomplished
lyricist and dramatist from Jiangsu 江蘇, Shen Qifeng 沈起鳳 (b. 1741),
also brought out his miscellany of anecdotes on the strange and marvellous, *Words of Humour from an Ancient Bell* (*Xie duo* 諧鐸), in 1791.
Many of Shen Qifeng's tales, with their fuller plot development and
lack of emphasis on supernatural elements, are of course only tan-
gentially related to the *zhiguai*, but a sizeable portion of this collection
consists nonetheless of straightforward, unadulterated records of
strange events that purportedly occurred.[32]

The preface to *Hearsay Accounts* (*Ershi lu* 耳食錄) by Yue Jun 樂鈞
(1766–1814), a descendant of the renowned *chuanqi* writer Yue Shi 樂
史 (930–1007) of the early Song, dates this collection to 1792.[33] A
sequel to this 112-entry collection was compiled two years later. Again
a full range of narrative forms, from the verbal report of less than fifty
words to the short novella that extends over several folio pages, can
be seen in this compilation. A relative of Ji Yun's, Zhang Jingyun 張景

---

[31] See Li Jinzhi's 李金枝 1791 preface to *LYWB*, quoted in Maeno Naoaki, *Chūgoku
shōsetsushi kō*, p. 323.

[32] On He Bang'e, see Fang Zhengyao 方正耀, "He Bang'e *Yetan suilu* kaoshi" 和邦額夜
談隨錄考釋 (An Explication of He Bang'e's *Yetan suilu*), *Wenxue yichan* 文學遺產, no. 3
(1988), p. 110. On Shen Qifeng, see Leo Tak-hung Chan, "Chinese Animal Fables of the
Eighteenth Century: Translations from Shen Qifeng's *Words of Humour from an Ancient Bell*,"
Asian Culture Quarterly, 23(1995), pp. 29–36.

[33] "Preface" to *Ershi lu* (dated "the summer of 1792"), edited by Shi Jichang 石繼昌
(Changchun: Shidai wenyi chubanshe 時代文藝出版社, 1986), p. 1. For brief biographies
of Yue Jun, see Zhao Erxun 趙爾巽, *et al.*, eds., *Qing shi gao* 清史稿 (Drafts of Qing History)
(Shanghai: Lianhe shudian 聯合書店, 1942), and Qingshi bianzuan weiyuanhui 清史編纂委
員會, ed., *Qing shi* 清史 (A History of the Qing Dynasty) (Taibei: Guofang yanjiuyuan 國防研
究院, 1961).

運 (*gongsheng*貢生 [tribute student], 1777), was the author of *New Words on Autumnal Plains* (*Qiuping xinyu* 秋坪新語), completed also in 1792, according to the prefaces by Zhang himself and three of his friends.[34] Finally, *Records of the Wildly Improbable* (*Wangwang lu* 妄妄錄) bears a preface by the compiler, Zhu Hai 朱海 (fl. late eighteenth century), noting that it was compiled in 1794, although thirty years elapsed before the collection eventually appeared in print.[35]

There can be little doubt that during the years 1788–1798, more *zhiguai* were published than at any other time during the Qing dynasty. It may further be argued that perhaps more *zhiguai* literature appeared in those years than ever before in Chinese history. Beginning with Yuan Mei's *What the Master Would Not Discuss* and ending with the last instalment of Ji Yun's *Close Scrutiny*, fifteen collections came out, containing a total of 128 chapters and tens of thousands of *zhiguai* tales. The list of *zhiguai* works from the late seventeenth century up to the early nineteenth on the next page shows, by way of figures, the flurry of *zhiguai*-writing activity through the greater part of the Qing, though production peaks in the late eighteenth century.[36]

The rich crop of stories of the strange published near the close of the eighteenth century was found not only in *zhiguai* but also in *biji* collections of the time. Such stories were sometimes scattered in various places and sometimes inserted as a special section of a collection. A notable example of the latter is Yu Jiao's 俞蛟 (b. 1744?) *Miscellaneous Comments at the Hut of Dreams* (*Meng'an zazhu* 夢庵雜著) — datable to 1801 — in which two of the ten chapters are devoted to the recording of strange events, the rest being travelogues, short pieces of

---

[34] As Ji Yun makes clear in the last entry to his *YWCTBJ*, Zhang Jingyun was connected to him through marriage. *YWCTBJ*, p. 562.

[35] No modern edition or reprint of *Records of the Wildly Improbable* is available. The Daoguang edition of 1830 referred to in this book is presently housed in the Chinese collection of the Chinese University of Hong Kong.

[36] The dating of these works is mostly determined by reference to the earliest preface extant. *Yingchuang yicao* 螢窗異草 (*Exotic Grass at the Glow-worm Window*) has been proved to be a work of the late eighteenth century, although the earliest preface we have dates it to the early nineteenth century. Works marked with an asterisk are found in Wu Zhenfang's *Shuoling houji*; those marked with a dagger have sequels: for *Gusheng* 觚賸 (*Leftover [Wine] in the Goblets*), a sequel of four chapters; for *ZBY*, ten chapters; and for *Ershi lu*, eight chapters.

IMPORTANT COLLECTIONS OF QING *ZHIGUAI* (UP TO 1850)

Date	Title	Author	Chapter(s)
1661	*Mingbao lu* 冥報錄 *	Lu Qi 陸圻	2
1664	*Nuogao guangzhi* 諾皋廣志	Xu Fang 徐芳	1
1671	*Xianguo suilu* 現果隨錄 *	Shi Jiexian 釋戒顯	1
1671	*Yin'an suoyu* 蚓庵瑣語 *	Wang Bu 王逋	1
1681	*Guobao jianwenlu* 果報見聞錄 *	Yang Shifu 楊式傅	1
1686	*Jianwen lu* 見聞錄 *	Xu E 徐岳	1
1696	*Chunxiang suibi* 蓴鄉隨筆 *	Dong Han 董含	3
1700	*Gusheng* 觚賸 *†	Niu Xiu 鈕琇	1
1701	*Xinzheng lu* 信徵錄 *	Xu Qing 徐慶	1
1701	*Shuyi ji* 述異記 *	Dongxuan zhuren 東軒主人	3
1703	*Kuangyuan zazhi* 曠園雜志 *	Wu Chenyan 吳陳琰	2
1766	*Liaozhai zhiyi* 聊齋志異	Pu Songling 蒲松齡	12
1788	*Zi bu yu* 子不語 †	Yuan Mei 袁枚	34
1789	*Luanyang xiaoxialu* 灤陽消夏錄	Ji Yun 紀昀	6
1791	*Qiudeng conghua* 秋燈叢話	Wang Xian 王棫	18
1791	*Yetan suilu* 夜談隨錄	He Bang'e 和邦額	12
1791	*Xie duo* 諧鐸	Shen Qifeng 沈起鳳	12
1791	*Rushi wowen* 如是我聞	Ji Yun 紀昀	4
1791	*Liuya waibian* 柳崖外編	Xu Kun 徐昆	8
1792	*Ershi lu* 耳食錄 †	Yue Jun 樂鈞	20
1792	*Huaixi zazhi* 槐西雜志	Ji Yun 紀昀	4
1792	*Qiuping xinyu* 秋坪新語	Zhang Jingyun 張景運	12
1793	*Guwang tingzhi* 孤妄聽之	Ji Yun 紀昀	4
1794	*Wangwang lu* 妄妄錄	Zhu Hai 朱海	12
1795	*Xiaodoupeng* 小豆棚	Zeng Yandong 曾衍東	16
1796	*Kechuang suibi* 客窗隨筆	Jin Bangchang 金棒閶	5
1798	*Luanyang xulu* 灤陽續錄	Ji Yun 紀昀	6
179–	*Yingchuang yicao* 螢窗異草	Changbai Haogezi 長白浩歌子	12
1800	*Yingtan* 影談	Guan Shihao 管世灝	4
1801	*Meng'an zazhu* 夢庵雜著	Yu Jiao 俞蛟	10
1827	*Sanbi yitan* 三筆異談	Xu Yuanzhong 許元仲	4
1843	*Zhiwen lu* 咫聞錄	Yongna jushi 慵訥居士	12
1847	*Wenjian yici* 聞見異辭	Xu Qiuzhai 徐秋垞	4
1849	*Yisi baibian* 異駟稗編	Tang Yongzhong 湯用中	8

historical research, comments on paintings, or records of folk customs in Guangdong 廣東.[37] Another example is Qian Yong's 錢泳 (1759–1844) *Discourses at Footwear Garden* (*Lüyuan conghua* 履園叢話), its earliest preface dated 1825. Chapters 14 to 17 of this collection are devoted to accounts of supernatural events which were reported during the Qianlong 乾隆 (r. 1736–1796) period. All in all, the unprecedented scale at which *zhiguai* writing was carried on in these years simply cannot be exaggerated. To end with yet one more comparison: more *zhiguai* was written from 1788 to 1798 than was collected in *Extensive Gleanings from the Taiping Reign* (*Taiping guangji* 太平廣記), the encyclopaedic Song compendium which contains most of the *zhiguai* prior to the Song and is the most voluminous *zhiguai* compilation of all time.

The Compilers' Motives

The proliferation of records of the supernatural at this time is particularly intriguing: the *zhiguai* evinced a fascination with the bizarre which was, apparently, not consonant with the spirit of the age. The problematic nature of *zhiguai* writing being carried on at this time can be highlighted with reference to two background factors: the optimism of the age and the advent of critical scholarship.

The final decades of the eighteenth century — the late Qianlong era — were characterized by an unbridled optimism, an irrepressible sense of confidence, and a concern with the here-and-now, with everyday practicalities.[38] Thus the turmoil of the previous century had

---

[37] Fang Nansheng 方南生 writes of the difficulty of accurately dating the text and identifying the author, but there seems little doubt that *Miscellaneous Comments at the Hut of Dreams* belongs to the late Qianlong and early Jiaqing 嘉慶 (r. 1796–1820) era. See Yu Jiao, *Meng'an zazhu*, edited by Fang Nansheng (Beijing: Wenhua yishu chubanshe 文化藝術出版社, 1988); and Liu Yeqiu 劉葉秋, "Qing Yu Jiao *Meng'an zazhu*" 清俞蛟夢庵雜著 (The *Meng'an zazhu* of Yu Jiao of the Qing Dynasty), in his *Gudian xiaoshuo biji luncong* 古典小説筆記論叢 (Critical Essays on Classical *Xiaoshuo* and *Biji*) (Tianjin: Nankai daxue chubanshe 南開大學出版社, 1985), pp. 191–195.

[38] For survey-studies of the political and social climate of the mid-Qing period, see Albert Feuerwerker, *State and Society in Eighteenth-century China: The Ch'ing Empire in Its Glory* (Ann Arbor: Center for Chinese Studies, University of Michigan, 1976); Susan Naquin and

become a thing of the past. The uncertainties of the Yongzheng 雍正
(r. 1723–1735) reign were resolved as Emperor Qianlong not only
tightened ideological and administrative control over the entire country, but also made successful forays into China's outlying regions to
expand her boundaries as no emperor had before. The Han Chinese
seemed on the whole to have acquiesced to Manchu rule, and the
occasional revolts at the border were quickly quelled and caused
little stir.[39] As a number of scholars have put it, this period is "a golden
era in [Chinese] history."[40] The predominant concern among most
was very much to uphold what had been achieved rather than, say, to
venture into the unknown.

On the other hand, it was — intellectually — the heyday of Confucianism, especially of a variety of Confucian thinking that was antithetical (perhaps even inimical) to any impulse to speculate on otherworldly
phenomena. While the state enshrined Zhu Xi's 朱熹 (1130–1200)
ideology, in academic circles practical learning triumphed over metaphysical investigation, the dominant mode of intellectual discourse
in previous centuries.[41] Empirical research in the form of evidential
studies (*kaozheng* 考證) was carried out in diverse fields of inquiry,
including archaeology, palaeography, and phonology. A product of
such efforts is the compilation of the *Complete Library of the Four Treasuries* (*Siku quanshu* 四庫全書), completed and presented to Qianlong

---

Evelyn S. Rawski, *Chinese Society in the Eighteenth Century* (New Haven: Yale University
Press, 1987); and Richard J. Smith, *China's Cultural Heritage: The Ch'ing Dynasty, 1644–1911*
(Boulder, Colorado: Westview Press, 1983).

[39] The late eighteenth-century Qing state was relatively free from major domestic disturbances; these became more frequent only later in the next century, with Qing dynastic
decline. *YWCTBJ* makes repeated references to the Jichang 吉昌 incident in 1768, which was
no more than a case of disorder caused by vagabonds and convicts in a peripheral region —
Xinjiang 新疆. See *YWCTBJ*, pp. 214, 419, and 492. The peasant revolt at Shandong in 1774,
led by Wang Lun 王倫 , was quickly put down by Qing forces. Personal experiences in this
uprising were recorded by Yu Jiao in his *Meng'an zazhu*, pp. 205–230.

[40] See, for instance, Immanuel C. Y. Hsu, *The Rise of Modern China* (New York: Oxford
University Press, 1995), p. 41.

[41] For a summary of the different views of the shift to an emphasis on scholasticism and
kaozheng 考證 (evidential studies) methods in the Qing intellectual scene, see Chow Kai-
wing, *The Rise of Confucian Ritualism in Late Imperial China: Ethics, Classics, and Lineage
Discourse* (Stanford: Stanford University Press, 1994), pp. 2–14.

in 1782. The system of imperial and regional academies, as well as the examination system, stood firm as the pillars of Confucianism.

The emphasis on pragmatics and verifiable knowledge, as well as the "scientific" slant in research methods, conformed with the centuries-long orthodox Confucian attitude towards the supernatural that made writing *zhiguai* a dubious enterprise. Well-known to the traditional scholar was Confucius' injunction against talking of prodigies, feats of strength, disorder, and spirits.[42] Confucius may have expressed neither belief nor disbelief with regard to the issue of the existence of the supernatural, but his attitude of avoidance is unambiguous. Else-where in *Analects* (*Lun yu* 論語) he is reported to have said: "Devote yourself earnestly to the duties due to men, and respect the spirits but keep them at a distance."[43] It is precisely for this reason that the *zhiguai* has long struggled to gain acceptability. The history of *zhiguai* writing is, from one angle at least, a record of the perennial efforts it makes to create for itself a place in the order of things, in a cosmos determined primarily by a Confucian worldview.

The eighteenth-century *zhiguai* compilers, like some of their pre-decessors, discovered in moralization the best means of removing the stigma attached to this genre from its beginnings. By claiming to serve a moral function, by stressing a positive impact on the social hier-archy, the compilers justified the recording and compiling of super-natural events at the same time that they validated the *zhiguai* as a genre. In what follows, disregarding *Close Scrutiny* for the moment, we shall look at the prefaces to five collections of this period for what the prefaces reveal of their compilers' stated and unstated motives. The urge to moralize, as might be expected, provided the main line of defense for most, and indeed its utility as a form of rationalization was demonstrated in disclaimers by others, who felt it incumbent upon themselves to assert that moralizing was the last thing on their minds.

---

[42] See *The Analects,* book 7 ("Shu'er pian" 述而篇), no. 22. D. C. Lau, trans., *The Analects* (Hong Kong: The Chinese University Press, 1983), p. 61.

[43] For a clear account of Confucius' views on ghosts and deities as seen in *The Analects,* see Yamashita Ryūji 山下龍二 , "Rongo ni okeru kishin ni tsuite" 論語における鬼神について (*Analects* on Ghosts and Gods), in *Nagoya Daigaku Bungakubu nijushūnen kinen ronshū* 名古屋大學文學部二十周年紀念論集 (Commemorative Essays on the Twentieth Anniversary of the Literature Department of University of Nagoya) (Nagoya, 1968).

Hu Gaowang's preface to the 1791 edition of Wang Xian's
Collected Discourses under the Autumn Lamp begins by criticizing Tao
Zongyi's 陶宗義 (1316–1403) *Precincts of Talk* (*Shuo fu* 説郛), a huge
compendium of selected and abridged extracts culled from writings
stretching from the Han to the Yuan 元 dynasties. Impressive as
this work is, to Hu Gaowang it includes "vain and flighty words"
which a Confucian gentleman should hold in low regard. To correct
such wrong-headedness, he then states the twin principles of *xiaoshuo*
composition:

> *Xiaoshuo* writers seek a similar sort of significance as that expounded by
> the Histories; they share the same aims of expression as embodied in *The
> Classic of Poetry* [*Shijing* 詩經]. To distinguish truths from falsehoods, in
> order that laws and prohibitions be clarified — this is the purport of the
> Histories. To discriminate between chastity and licentiousness, so as to
> convey admonitions and instructions — this is the aim of *The Classic of
> Poetry.*[44]

Hu Gaowang thus elevated the status of the rank and file of *xiaoshuo*
writers by comparing them to the historian and the poet, both of whom
fulfil their social responsibilities by creating a positive influence on
morals.

After giving a brief biographical account of Wang Xian, Hu
Gaowang proceeds to adumbrate the reasons behind the compilation
of *Collected Discourses*. Far from trying to stimulate his readers' imagination with accounts of the weird and exotic, Wang Xian avails himself of their fondness for tales of the supernatural in order to impart a
serious message. But it was not only the compiler's intentions that
were utilized to justify the compilation; Hu Gaowang also assures the
reader of the almost immediate effect that the collection could have:

> When inside a tiny chamber, on a cold rainy day, [one reads the collec-
> tion] under a solitary lamp by the window that is hidden from view, one
> might find one's emotions deeply engaged, or turn quite serious as en-
> lightenment dawns on oneself. Imperceptibly the feelings mount; one
> becomes serious, aware of what should be feared.[45]

---

[44] "Preface" to Wang Xian, *Qiudeng conghua* (Taibei: Guangwen shuju 廣文書局, 1968),
pp. 1–2.

[45] Ibid., p. 2.

According to Hu, this power to fully engage the reader and then to induce in him fear and understanding should be reason enough to rid the *zhiguai* of charges of triviality and superficiality. He even proposes, by way of conclusion, that Wang Xian's collection, being no different from the histories or *The Classic of Poetry*, should "not be regarded as *xiaoshuo*."

The justification of *zhiguai* writing by recourse to its moral function was enunciated at greater depth in Ye Shishuo's 葉世倬 (*juren*, 1774) preface to Zhu Hai's *Records of the Wildly Improbable*. Ye Shishuo asserts that Zhu Hai, his old schoolmate, was a dilettante in his youth, was much given to loose living, and was an eccentric who planted (through his misconduct, presumably) "karmic seeds" that were to last three lives. The only deed to his credit was compiling these stories of the strange which, straddling the realms of illusion and reality, fiction and fact, convey messages of warning and impending punishment to those who have gone astray. Once again the point is stressed that the apparent superficiality covered up an underlying seriousness of purpose:

> Through accounts that are at times frivolous, at times vituperative, [the author] conveys his intent — to admonish and exhort. Empty and vacuous as they are, fictions can turn out to be reality. Truths become distinguishable from falsehoods if one scrutinizes them closely enough. There are spirits and monsters who wield not a trace of mercy, ox-headed devils and serpent gods who laugh and are merry all the time. In the midst of all this, the principles of cause-and-effect as well as karmic retribution are clear, vivid, and inexorable.[46]

Particularly noteworthy is Ye Shishuo's emphasis on retributive logic in *zhiguai* texts: it is the *raison d'etre* of a great proportion of *zhiguai* stories as well as — in the present context — the saving grace of a *zhiguai* collection. Like Hu Gaowang, Ye Shishuo describes the effect of the *zhiguai* on the reader, which he crystallizes into two images: the nodding of the obdurate rock in response to the preaching of the *dharma*, and the reaching of the yonder shore (in Buddhist terms) after crossing of the sea of "bitterness" — of unenlightened human experience. Ye Shishuo's concluding statement is that *Records of the*

---

[46] "Preface" to Zhu Hai, *Wangwang lu* (1830), p. 1b.

Wildly Improbable contains anything but "wild and far-fetched talk" and is as far removed as can be imagined from the meaningless gossip and idle conversations associated with the *baiguan* of ancient times. Hence "they should definitely not be grouped together."[47]

A special feature of these two prefaces is that their writers, while doing all they can to promote the works in question, show a special awareness of the *zhiguai* tradition in which the collections found themselves. Hu Gaowang notes a Ming antecedent as an example of how the *xiaoshuo* — and by extension, the *zhiguai* — should not be written; Ye Shishuo points to the roots of the genre in Zhou times but insists that *zhiguai* compilers and gossip-mongers be differentiated. Both, in other words, were ostensibly setting up new criteria for understanding the *zhiguai* and seeking to salvage it from its ignoble status with an argument based on its didactic function. They were, however, not advocating a new mode of reading for the Qing *zhiguai*. Judith Zeitlin has delineated, with insight, the prevalent habit in the eighteenth century of reading other "meanings" into the tales of strange events, an activity partly encouraged by *Studio of Leisure*.[48] Such an approach implies that the *zhiguai* writers were not really concerned with the unusual events themselves, but with their allegorical potential. As we shall see, a fine line has to be drawn between the didactic and the allegorical. While an ulterior purpose on the part of the author is discernible in both, the relations established between the writer, the text, and the reader in either case are radically different.

The recourse to the didactic was by no means the sole strategy mustered to defend the reporting of supernatural events. In two other prefaces one glimpses the formulation of another argument that puts a premium on the knowledge imparted by such collections. The argument for *boxue* 博學 (knowledge-broadening) functionality has as old

---

[47] Ibid., p. 2a.

[48] Judith Zeitlin, *Historian of the Strange: Pu Songling and the Chinese Classical Tale* (Stanford: Stanford University Press, 1993), pp. 15–42. Zeitlin also gives an excellent definition of the "strange": rather than a genre or a literary mode, the strange is to her both a cultural construct and a psychological effect. She chooses not to equate the strange with the supernatural. However, in order to emphasize the epistemic realities that the *zhiguai* tales are essentially about, I have focused more on the elements of the supernatural embodied therein.

a history as the argument for didactic utility, but its relevance to *zhiguai* reporting is more convoluted and achieved at times only through twists of logic. In his extended statement on historiography, *Generalities on History* (*Shi tong* 史通), Liu Zhiji 劉知幾 (661–721) considers the various schools of historical writing and castigates the miscellaneous narratives and gossip of the streets (which he labels "heterodox") for their unreliability. Nevertheless, he argues that, if one reads with enough caution, perusing such materials might serve to extend one's knowledge. Taking heed of Confucius' dictum that "knowledge follows from broad learning and the discrimination of what is good," Liu even goes so far as to suggest that the pseudo-histories do have some value for historians.[49]

It must be remembered that among the works labelled as unorthodox in Liu Zhiji's discussion is the representative Six Dynasties *zhiguai* collection, *In Search of Spirits.* And so, with its avowed contribution (albeit dubious) to the broadening of knowledge, the *zhiguai* makes its entry into the ranks of respectability. In fact, throughout much of the imperial period, as Kenneth DeWoskin has noted, "broadening of knowledge" became an epithet of praise for the *zhiguai* writer, for the phrase denotes research into materials outside the Confucian canon.[50] Following this line of reasoning, Yuan Mei, in the preface to his *What the Master Would Not Discuss,* seeks justification for the compilation by arguing that the documentation of the strange enables one "to exhaust the transformations of Heaven and Earth" and to see "all the principles in their unerring operation."[51]

While Yuan Mei simply excuses himself by stressing that he was reporting facts from which universal principles can be adduced, He Bang'e, the Manchu *zhiguai* writer, goes a step further and challenges the arbitrary distinction between what is strange and what is not.

---

[49] See the "zashu" 雜述 (miscellaneous topics) section, in Huang Lin 黃霖 and Han Tongwen 韓同文, eds., *Zhongguo lidai xiaoshuo lunzhu xuan* 中國歷代小說論著選 (A Selection of Studies of *Xiaoshuo* Theory through the Dynasties) (Nanchang: Jiangxi renmin chubanshe 江西人民出版社, 1982), vol. 1, pp. 33–35.

[50] Kenneth J. DeWoskin, "Chih-kuai," *The Indiana Companion to Traditional Chinese Literature,* edited by William H. Nienhauser, Jr., p. 281.

[51] "Preface" to *ZBY,* p. 1.

Anomalous phenomena are as worthy of investigation as supposedly normal ones. He Bang'e admits that he never had any personal experience of a bizarre kind and he begins his own preface to *Occasional Accounts of Conversations at Night* in this way:

> The Master [Confucius] would not speak of the strange, but here nothing that is not strange will be recorded. Outlandish indeed, though this is not meant to be so. For Heaven and Earth are broad indeed, the myriad things most varied. There are principles behind everything that happens. If principles exist, how can anything be strange? The sages have exhausted the principles of Heaven and Earth and of the myriad things. What is strange to man is but the normal order of things for the sages.[52]

He laments the stupidity of those who are filled with awe at phenomena they see only rarely. Instead of subjectively categorizing phenomena as strange or not, one should aim — according to He Bang'e — to broaden one's insights into the principles that inhere in such phenomena. By thus arguing for the autonomy of every phenomenon, he successfully counters the view that the "strange" does not deserve to be talked about and creates a rationale for his own compilation.

Over and against those who insisted on the functionality of the *zhiguai*, either by virtue of its usefulness as a vehicle for moral messages or by dint of its contribution to knowledge, were a distinct group of *zhiguai* compilers who disclaimed any ulterior motive behind their collections — a group to which Yue Jun and Yuan Mei belonged. Stating quite unequivocally that his reports were "hearsay and gossip" (*wangyan wangting* 妄言妄聽), Yue Jun notes in the 1792 preface to *Hearsay Accounts* the fad for seeking the spirits and documenting bizarre occurrences. He speaks of how his own compilation came about:

> I am a man of humble origins. When I was at rest after my wild wanderings, I braced myself and, on my writing tablets, recorded what I had previously heard — wild words not worth attending to. I do not believe in them at all; others do. . . . This is no different from what the Grand Historian [Sima Qian 司馬遷] referred to as "fodder for the ears."[53]

---

[52] "Preface" to *YTSL*, p. 6177.
[53] "Preface" to *Ershi lu*, p. 1.

"Fodder for the ears" is a literal translation of *ershi* 耳食 in the title of his collection and is a metaphor for over-credulousness employed by Sima Qian (ca. 145–ca. 85 B.C.) in the preface to "Chronological Table of the Six States" ("Liuguo nianbiao" 六國年表) of *Records of History*. In the above passage Yue is specifically referring to the tendency of many to accept what they are told as true, without giving it much thought. The kind of low profile that Yue Jun strikes is especially noticeable, as is his apologetic tone: it was almost as though he had acquiesced in the popular perception of *zhiguai* collecting as a negligible pursuit.

Although Yuan Mei does present his *What the Master Would Not Discuss* as a repository of reported phenomena that merits close investigation, his position with regard to *zhiguai* writing is fundamentally anti-didactic. He disowns even the slightest hint of moral seriousness in his compilation by asking his readers to take it as "wild words" — a move that might reasonably be expected from somebody as well-known for leading an unconventional life as Yuan Mei was. Unlike Yue Jun, however, he makes it plain that he revels in the frivolity of the enterprise:

> Hobbies have never been very much part of my life. I do not indulge in any of the activities that are enjoyed in groups, including drinking wine, making music, and gambling. There was nothing that I can entertain myself with, other than literature and history. So I collected pleasurable as well as shocking events from a variety of sources — wild words hardly worth attending to. Now I am putting them down just as a record, not in order to lead people astray.[54]

Indeed, beneath the title of *What the Master Would Not Discuss* is added the note: "Compiled for fun in the Garden of Contentment" ("*Suiyuan xibian*" 隨園戲編). The fact is, he not only adopted a flippant attitude to the narratives he collected, but also adamantly refused to have his stories interpreted as if they had significance. Unlike the other major *zhiguai* collections of the same period, *What the Master Would Not Discuss* and its sequel did come very close to a kind of "pure recording." As a raconteur of tales Yuan Mei resembles a modern folklorist, as he

---

[54] "Preface" to *ZBY*, pp. 1–2.

takes field trips in the Jiangnan 江南 region, and records stories of the supernatural in which he has taken much pleasure.[55]

The preface to *What the Master Would Not Discuss* thus contains clues to a largely unstated dimension in the protestations of most *zhiguai* compilers: an interest in, and fascination with, the supernatural. To better understand such a preoccupation with strange phenomena, it has to be placed in the context of the oral transmission of the narratives.

For some time the oral origins of *Studio of Leisure* have been the focus of scholarly attention. According to Zou Tao 鄒弢, a nineteenth-century scholar, during his writing of the book, Pu Songling set up a stall at the roadside of a thoroughfare and provided free tea to passersby.[56] He listened to, and reported, their stories of unusual events. Though doubts have been cast on this theory, there are critics, mostly from Mainland China, who subscribe to it and insist that this "nourishment by the commonfolk" is essential to the greatness of *Studio of Leisure*.[57]

As a matter of fact, the oral and written transmissions of *zhiguai*, which reveal a tremendous interest in the supernatural, have always gone hand in hand. Many of the accounts in the early *zhiguai* compilations, especially those of a legendary nature, were combed from written sources then in circulation. *In Search of Spirits*, for one, duplicates stories recorded in Ge Hong's *Biographies of Immortals*, in the dynastic histories, and in other *zhiguai*. As time progressed, however, *zhiguai* collecting became centred predominantly on stories that were orally circulated. Extensive contact with such stories, transmitted in

---

[55] For a study of the background to the compilation of *ZBY*, see Wu Yuhui, "Yuan Mei *Zi bu yu* yanjiu," pp. 67–75.

[56] Zou Tao, *Sanjielu bitan* 三借廬筆談 (Sketches and Notes at Thrice-Loaned Lodge) (Qingdao: Guocui tushushe 國粹圖書社, 1912), 6:13a–b.

[57] Wang Panling 汪玢玲 has unravelled much of the folklore (now recoverable mainly from Ming-Qing *biji* collections) that provided sources of inspiration for Pu Songling when he created his *LZZI* tales. Through a detailed comparison of four of Pu's texts with selected *biji*, she concludes that Pu managed to capture the essence of the folk stories he worked with and, siding with the common people, exposed the reality of peasant-landlord conflicts. See Wang Panling, *Pu Songling yu minjian wenxue* 蒲松齡與民間文學 (Pu Songling and Folk Literature) (Shanghai: Wenyi chubanshe 文藝出版社, 1985), pp. 94–126.

the South, was instrumental to the creation of Hong Mai's 洪邁 (1123–1202) *Records of Yijian* (*Yijian zhi* 夷堅志). For over fifteen years, it must be noted, Hong Mai worked as a provincial administrator in parts of modern Zhejiang 浙江, Fujian 福建 and Jiangxi 江西, where he had the opportunity of listening to many of the stories that were to appear in his work. The originality of many of the stories is often noted — "originality" not in the sense that they were imaginative creations of the author, but that they did not appear in other written sources.[58]

Among current approaches to the *zhiguai* collections is one that reads them as treasure-houses of folktales. This has most likely been encouraged by two recent developments. First, insights gained through a deepened understanding of the evolution of the great vernacular novels like *Water Margin* (*Shuihu zhuan* 水滸傳) and *Journey to the West* (*Xiyou ji* 西遊記) have fuelled arguments for some sort of "folk" genius or consciousness that underlies the creation of fictional master-pieces. Then, the advent of modern folklore studies has tilted the scale still further: the scenario of a folktale collector tracking down all the gossip and rumour in remote localities and out-of-the-way places, writing down the lore that he gathers almost verbatim, and analysing the motifs and folk patterns discernible therein, seems apt as a description of the processes of *zhiguai* collecting. No wonder that collections of this type have appealed to anthropologists and religious historians as soil to be ploughed for information on popular attitudes and folk beliefs of special periods.[59]

What Yuan Mei points to in his preface is a tradition of oral *zhiguai* storytelling *among the elite*. The Chinese expression for this sort

---

[58] Materials in many of the Six Dynasties *zhiguai* collections were duplicated. For example, some stories in *In Search of Spirits* appeared also in *Biographies of Immortals*. Even *LZZI* shared several stories with Wang Shizhen's 王士禛 (1634–1711) *Casual Talks by the North Side of the Pond* (*Chibei outan* 池北偶談), which led to accusations of plagiarism against the latter. Undoubtedly different criteria of "originality" are applicable with respect to the *zhiguai*.

[59] Sandra K. D. Stahl has drawn a fine distinction between "folklore in literature" and "folklore as literature," although she does not dwell at length on the latter, no doubt owing to "the inevitable confusion when oral texts are written down — whether verbatim or not — and thus appear to be literature rather than folklore." Sandra Stahl, "Studying Folklore and American Literature," in *Handbook of American Folklore,* edited by Richard M. Dorson (Bloomington: Indiana University Press, 1983), p. 426.

of activity is "discourse on fox-spirits and ghosts" (*tanhu shuogui* 談狐
說鬼). In this discourse the time-worn fascination with the supernatural, pervasive in a social stratum other than the "folk," expresses
itself. In the second half of the preface, Yuan Mei remarks that,
instead of trying to emulate the strengths of the "Four Worthies," he
has succumbed to the temptations to which they were prone. These
"Worthies" included Yan Hui 顔回 (521–490 B.C.), a disciple of Confucius, and Li Mi 李密 (722–789), the mid-Tang prime minister, both of
whom were said to be fond of talking about spirits and unusual occurrences, even though they were eminent intellectual and political
figures. Han Yu 韓愈 (768–824), the advocate for the orthodox transmission of the Way, also dabbled in "absurd and eccentric talk" in his
day. There is, finally, Xu Xuan 徐鉉 (917–992) of the Southern Song
and author of *Records Examining Spirits* (*Jishen lu* 稽神錄), who, though
denouncing Buddhism and Daoism, liked to hear of the wayward
and unusual; some of his protegés even forged accounts of the supernatural to curry favour with him.

It seems that, though the triviality of such "small talk" (oral or
written) was commonly acknowledged, conversing on the strange was
extremely popular among elite members of society. A close look
at the *zhiguai* prefaces in question will bear this out. Never having
encountered fantastic events himself, He Bang'e has this to say:

> I often like to get together with a couple of friends. While we are either
> inebriating ourselves with wine, or drinking tea at a low table, we extin-
> guish candles and talk of ghosts, or converse on fox-spirits under the
> moonlight. The wild and bizarre often enter into such conversations. To
> please myself I jot down all of these stories and over time have collected
> chapters full of them.[60]

Wu Shanxi 吳山錫 , in his 1824 foreword to *Hearsay Accounts*, notes a
similar phenomenon in his time: learned scholars, travellers, eminent
statesmen and ministers, poets and men of letters all were constantly
engaged in enthusiastic conversations on the supernatural. Additionally, in his preface to *Miscellaneous Comments at the Hut of Dreams*, Yu

---

[60] "Preface" to *YTSL*, p. 6177.

Jiao mentions that he recorded the "wild words" of peasants in Eastern Qi 齊 (an allusion from Mencius) because these could be raw material for popular songs and fanciful conversations.

It seems, then, that in all likelihood the eighteenth-century *zhiguai* compilations were to a certain degree a by-product of this fad, in which writers jotted down what they had heard in anecdotal or more extended forms. But the reverse is just as true. Hu Gaowang said the accounts in *Occasional Accounts of Conversations at Night* could help "stimulate conversation" (*she tan zhu* 奢談助). He implies that readers got material for their conversations from such collections.[61] Further support for this hypothesis is given by the fact that many of the stories were circulated in manuscript form for a long time prior to their eventual publication. There can be little doubt that during this process the stories entered the daily conversations of readers, accrued comments, and perhaps were substantiated with additional information. This partly explains why the writing of *Occasional Accounts* was temporarily halted after Chapter 12 and why the first dozen chapters underwent some revision before they were printed in their present form.[62] *Studio of Leisure*, too, was read, discussed, criticized, and evaluated for almost a century before it finally became available to the general reader in the first edition of 1766. In light of all this, the relationship between the written texts and the oral conversations can be said to be two-way, roughly analogous to the double use of the Tang transformation texts (*bianwen* 變文) as "prompt-book" and as "recording."[63]

To summarize, the undercurrents of thinking related to the compilation of *zhiguai* narratives were complex, especially because apparent motives must be distinguished from real ones and what was stated must be supplemented by what remained hidden. Most compilers alluded in their prefaces to one of two reasons for their compilation's existence: either to encourage ethical behaviour or to broaden

---

[61] Ibid.

[62] It is Maeno Naoaki who discusses this possibility. See Maeno Naoaki, *Chūgoku shōsetsushi kō*, p. 292.

[63] See Eugene Eoyang, "Oral Narration in the *Pien* and *Pien-wen*," *Archiv Orientalni*, vol. 46, no. 3 (1978), pp. 232–252.

knowledge. To be sure, these arguments had a long history. For instance, Li Zhao 李肇 (fl. 820) noted, centuries ago in his preface to *A Supplement to the History of the Tang* (*Tang guoshi bu* 唐國史補), several aims of anecdote-collecting, the most important of which were

(1) exploring the principles of things (*tan wuli* 探物理);
(2) clarifying doubts and misgivings (*bian yihuo* 辨疑惑); and
(3) giving guidance and admonitions (*shi quanjie* 示勸戒).[64]

But what several eighteenth-century *zhiguai* prefaces hint at is a reason not mentioned by Li Zhao: an interest in the wayward and bizarre among the elite. By this explanation, the collections become a repository of information drawn on in the elite's conversations to sustain this interest. This theory undermines the validity of the didactic and "intellectualist" imperatives and raises the question of whether, as well as to what extent, these were rationalizations used to justify *zhiguai* discourse in the face of orthodox Confucian prohibitions against it. The case of *Close Scrutiny*, however, shows that a *zhiguai* collection could be compiled with multiple motives which were not mutually exclusive. While there was an evident need to legitimize the compilation of *zhiguai* against a generally pejorative attitude toward the genre, Ji Yun was genuinely didactic, sought to explore and expand the boundaries of the supernatural, *and* was writing out of a love for things that were bizarre. Of these motivations, however, the didactic seemed to be paramount. And to have a fuller view, we shall now turn to his collection.

Ji Yun and His Collection

Perhaps the last thing that might be expected of *Close Scrutiny*, the most influential *zhiguai* collection of the eighteenth century, is that it should have been written by Ji Yun. A prominent scholar and official during the last twenty years of the Qianlong period, Ji Yun was particularly noted for his contribution to a major compilation project,

---

[64] Li Zhao, *Tang guoshi bu* (Taibei: Yiwen shuju 藝文書局 , 1965), p. 1.

the *Complete Library of the Four Treasuries*, formally inaugurated by an imperial edict in 1773.[65] The significance of the project, according to many Qing historians, was twofold. It was in part an effort at censorship by enabling the government to remove from general circulation submitted works that were deemed treasonous or offensive to the ruling Manchu dynasty. It was also a way for adherents of Han Learning (*Hanxue* 漢學) in the era to assert the primacy of their own empiricist approach to learning over and against the methods of the more speculative, less textually-oriented methods of the neo-Confucian or Song school. The *Complete Library* project helped, in other words, to define "orthodoxy" from two perspectives — the political as well as the intellectual.

Despite a few minor setbacks, Ji Yun's career was very much a success story, for it charted a sequence of promotions after he passed the *jinshi* 進士 (metropolitan graduate) examinations in 1754. The many anecdotes circulated about Ji Yun up to the present day describe the imperial favours bestowed on him time and again by the Qianlong

---

[65] For accounts of Ji Yun's life, see Li Zongfang's 李宗昉 (1779–1846) biographical essay and *nianpu* 年譜 (bibliography) in his *Wenmiaoxiangshi wenji* 聞妙香室文集 (Collected Writings from the Studio of Fragrant Smell), 14:1a; the epitaph by Zhu Gui 朱珪 (1731–1806) in his *Zhizuzhai wenji* 知足齋文集 (Collected Essays at the Studio of Self-contentment), 5:23b–28b, in *Baibu congshu jicheng* 百部叢書集成 (Collectanea of a Hundred Categories of Works) (Taibei: Yiwen shuju 藝文書局, 1966), vol. 94; Wang Lanyin 王蘭蔭, "Ji Xiaolan xiansheng nianpu" 紀曉嵐先生年譜 (A Chronology of Ji Xiaolan [Ji Yun]), *Shida yuekan* 師大月刊, vol. 1, no. 6 (1933), pp. 77–106; Qingshi bianzuan weiyuanhui, ed., *Qing shi*, vol. 6, p. 4250; Li Huan 李桓, ed., *Guochao qixian leizheng chubian* 國朝耆獻類徵初編 (Classified Collection of Biographies of Famous Men of the Qing Dynasty) (Taibei: Wenhai chubanshe 文海出版社, 1966); Li Yuandu 李元度, *Guochao xianzheng shilue* 國朝先正事略 (Brief Accounts of the Worthies of the Qing Dynasty), in *Jindai Zhonguo shiliao congkan* 近代中國史料叢刊 (Collectanea of Historical Documents on Early Modern China) (Taibei: Wenhai chubanshe 文海出版社, 1967), chap. 20, pp. 992–995; and Zhou Jiming 周積明, *Ji Yun pingzhuan* 紀昀評傳 (A Critical Biography of Ji Yun) (Nanjing: Nanjing daxue chubanshe 南京大學出版社, 1994), pp. 1–100. Book-length biographical treatments include: Dongguo xiansheng 東郭先生, *Ji Xiaolan chuanqi* 紀曉嵐傳奇 (The Legend of Ji Xiaolan) (Taibei: Shishi shuju 時事書局, 1978); Xu Tao 徐濤, *Ji Xiaolan waizhuan* 紀曉嵐外傳 (An Unofficial Chronicle of Ji Xiaolan) (Taibei: Shijie wenwu chubanshe 世界文物出版社, 1981); and Zhu Chuanyu 朱傳譽, ed., *Ji Yun shengping gaishu* 紀昀生平概述 (A Brief Account of Ji Yun's Life) (Taibei: Tianyi chubanshe 天一出版社, 1982).

Emperor.[66] Nevertheless, there were three occasions on which his career was in a precarious state. First, in 1768 he was exiled to Urumqi for secretly informing his in-law, Lu Jianzeng 盧見曾 (1690–1768), of the latter's being implicated in the bribery case of the Yangzhou 揚州 salt commissioners.[67] In 1774 he was demoted because of his son's involvement in a tax fraud case. Finally, in 1790, he was chastened by being ordered to revise parts of *An Annotated Catalogue of the Complete Library of Four Treasuries* (*Siku quanshu zongmu tiyao* 四庫全書總目提要) that contained editorial errors. But none of these events had more than a temporary impact on his career. In the first, for instance, he was quickly recalled after spending one year in Urumqi, and later he was speedily restored to his original post when he wrote for the emperor a poem celebrating the return of the Tunguts from Russia.[68]

While functioning in official positions of authority at the top of the civil bureaucracy, Ji Yun also maintained ties in the intellectual world. In the project on the *Complete Library* he had as editorial assistants some of the leading scholars of the day, including Dai Zhen 戴震 (1724–1777), Zhou Yongnian 周永年 (1730–1791), Shao Jinhan 邵晉 涵 (1743–1796) and Weng Fanggang 翁方剛 (1733–1818). With Dai Zhen, foremost proponent of the philological movement, Ji Yun had a particularly close relationship — for years Dai Zhen stayed as a guest in Ji Yun's house, and the two men had similar views on Han Learning and an abhorrence for the neo-Confucian moralists. The truth seems

---

[66] These are found in innumerable anecdotal accounts scattered through *biji* collections of the nineteenth century. See, in particular, Xiaohengxiangshi zhuren 小橫香室主 人, comp., *Qingchao yeshi daguan* 清朝野史大觀 (An Unofficial History of the Qing Dynasty) (Taibei: Zhonghua shuju 中華書局, 1959); Xu Ke 徐珂, ed., *Qingbai leichao* 清稗類鈔 (Miscellaneous Notes from the Qing Dynasty) (Taibei: The Commercial Press, 1966); Chen Kangqi 陳康祺, *Langqian jiwen* 郎潛紀聞 (Records of Things Heard by the Lowly Official) (Taibei: Wenhai chubanshe 文海出版社, 1970); and Li Boyuan 李伯元, *Nanting biji* 南亭筆記 (Random Jottings at Southern Pavilion) (Shanghai: Shanghai guji chubanshe 上海古籍出版 社, 1983).

[67] For a brief account of the incident, see Arthur W. Hummel, ed., *Eminent Chinese of the Ch'ing Period (1644–1912)* (Washington D.C.: Government Printing Office, 1943), pp. 541–542.

[68] See Arthur M. Hummel, ed., *Eminent Chinese of the Ch'ing Period (1644–1912)*, pp. 120–121.

to be that, with the impressive public figure that he struck, Ji Yun was one of the best spokesmen for the dominant school of intellectual thought of his day, a school that was at the time gaining official support.

Under such circumstances the writing of a collection like *Close Scrutiny*, which represented a departure from the "Great Way" with which Ji Yun was — understandably — associated, is nothing short of surprising. It is more so when one takes into consideration the fact that Ji Yun compiled *Close Scrutiny* during the last decade of the eighteenth century, when he was at the pinnacle of his career. In the years after the completion of the project on the *Complete Library* (in 1782), Ji Yun was promoted to several important government positions, including President of the Censorate, President of the Board of Ceremonies, as well as President of the Board of War. Strange as it may seem, during this time he actively devoted his energy to writing tales of anomalous and untoward events. There can hardly be a more extreme contrast than the one between this picture of Ji Yun and that of Pu Songling as a frustrated scholar who, after repeated failures at the examinations, attempted to vent his "solitary rage" (*gufen* 孤憤) through his collection of *zhiguai*.

The search for the reason why *Close Scrutiny* came to be compiled must of necessity begin with Ji Yun's statements of intentions, namely the five prefaces to the collection. Time and again Ji Yun points out the haphazard nature of the undertaking, as if he wants to counter the possible charge that he is engaged in an activity ill-befitting a Confucian gentleman. This is how he describes the background to his writing of *Record of Spending the Summer at Luanyang*:

> In the summer of the *jiyou* 己酉 year of the Qianlong reign [1789], I was dispatched to Luanyang 灤陽 [present-day Chengde 承德, in Hebei 河北] to reorganize the special library. Having finished the collating and the revising, I only had to supervise my subordinates, sign documents and stock the bookshelves. Since the days were long and there was not anything worth doing, I recorded what I remembered hearing and seeing.[69]

---

[69] *YWCTBJ*, p. 1.

Zhiguai writing was thus, according to him, a pastime, permissible because it does not take up time that could be utilized more fruitfully. A similar argument, that *zhiguai* collecting was a diversionary activity, is presented in the 1793 preface to volume four of *Close Scrutiny, Listen in a Rough Way* (*Guwang tingzhi* 姑妄聽之):

> Before I was thirty I indulged in evidential research. Wherever I sat, I was surrounded by books set out like fish left on the bank by the otter. When I was past thirty I competed with all under Heaven with my essays. I frequently spent sleepless nights preparing and structuring my writings. After the age of fifty I took charge of editorial work on rare texts, thereby reverting to evidential investigations. Now that I am old, the enthusiasms of days gone by are no more. With ink on paper I write of old recollections, just to pass the idle moments.[70]

Ji Yun justifies writing stories of the strange on the grounds that it takes place not only at his leisure, but also in his old age.

A second distinctive feature of Ji Yun's prefaces, related to the question of how he viewed his own work, is his frequent reference to literary antecedents. In the preface to volume three, *Miscellaneous Accounts West of the Locust-tree* (*Huaixi zazhi* 槐西雜志), he notes two well-known Song compilations to which his own could be compared, the afore-mentioned *Records of Yijian* and Wang Mingqing's 王明清 (1127–ca. 1215) *Waving a Chowry* (*Huichen lu* 揮塵錄). In the preface to *Listen in a Rough Way*, in a self-deprecating gesture, Ji Yun also remarks that neither does he have the breadth of knowledge of a Wang Chong 王充 (27–91) or a Ying Shao 應劭 (active 165–ca. 204),[71] who discussed with fervour social issues of their time, nor has he achieved the stylistic simplicity of Six Dynasties *zhiguai* writers like Tao Qian 陶潛 (365–427), Liu Jingshu 劉敬叔 (386?–467), and Liu Yiqing 劉義慶 (403–444). Through these references Ji Yun was apparently suggesting not only a practical purpose that *zhiguai* collections could fulfil,

---

[70] Ibid., p. 359.

[71] At first glance, the comparison with Wang Chong and Ying Shao here seems as oddly out of place as the comparison with the three Six Dynasties *zhiguai* writers is singularly appropriate. But Ji Yun characterized the former two as writers who "drew on the ancient classics and showed their breadth of knowledge, able to distinguish the real from the specious" — men of the *boxue* type.

but also the presence of a set of formal and stylistic parameters that characterize the *zhiguai* as an established and viable genre of writing.

However, the third and strongest argument justifying the compilation effort, one that presumably can rescue it from the charge of superficiality, is that the compilation is educational and has moral value. The issue is broached in the first preface:

> Zhou officials assigned to the collection of *xiaoshuo* realized that these things had no connection with genuine composition. Nevertheless, the anecdotes and opinions of the back streets and alleys may still be useful in encouraging good and discouraging evil.[72]

Here the marriage of the *zhiguai* with didacticism is effected through the ancient example of the Zhou *baiguan*, who collected chit-chat circulated among the populace for the "admonition" and "edification" of the emperors. The view, put simply, was that accounts of the strange could have an ethical value in censuring evil and promoting correct behaviour. Ji Yun made it even clearer in the preface to *Listen in a Rough Way*. There, after noting the superiority of the works of men like Tao Qian, Ji Yun defines the moral bearings of his collection: "Although I dare not presume that I could emulate these former masters, [my collection] will not run counter to public morals and customs."[73]

Naturally, the question of whether Ji Yun was earnest in his declaration of didactic intent is answerable in the final analysis only through a close study of *Close Scrutiny* itself. But on the whole it seems that, while didactic intent may have been a guise assumed by some *zhiguai* writers, there is little reason to question Ji Yun's sincere intentions stated in his prefaces. Further, genuine moral didacticism was not unknown, nor was it unfamiliar to the *zhiguai* reader of the time. Seventeenth-century precedents are plentiful. An instance is Lu Qi's 陸圻 (fl. 1661) *Records of Recompense in the Next Life* (*Mingbao lu* 冥報錄), in which the author aims, as he says, to "show goodness rewarded and evil punished."[74] Moral didacticism was also entirely in keeping

---

[72] *YWCTBJ*, p. 1.

[73] Ibid., p. 359.

[74] "Preface" to Lu Qi, *Mingbao lu*, p. 1b. Anthologized in Wu Zhenfang 吳震方, ed., *Shuoling* 説鈴 (Bell-talk) (Juxiutang 聚秀堂, 1825), vol. 23.

with the role Ji Yun played as an intellectual and as a public figure. He would no doubt have seen the didactic potential of *zhiguai* narratives, which could be placed at the service of the custodians of the culture.

In fact, besides being earnest, the didacticism of *Close Scrutiny* is double-edged, serving two purposes for Ji Yun. It emerges first as a line of defense against those who might suggest that he should attend to matters more commensurate with a man of his position, rather than indulge in what serious-minded Confucian scholar-bureaucrats would denigrate. But more significantly, this didacticism is also a strategic deployment of narrative elements to persuade readers to act morally, a skilful use of anomalous events and phenomena to effect moral edification of the masses — which indeed was Ji Yun's concern as a man of letters influential in the late eighteenth century. This is a powerful explanation of why Ji Yun favoured the didactic mode in spite of a predilection in the eighteenth century for the aesthetic mode exemplified by *Studio of Leisure*. *Close Scrutiny* is indeed a most revealing instance of didacticism displacing aesthetics as a principle of literary expression.

Given the complexity of the context in which *Close Scrutiny* is written, however, we cannot simply conclude that the didactic impulse alone accounted for Ji Yun's compilation effort. Another motivation is a fondness for narratives concerning the supernatural. To be precise, Ji Yun's prefaces indicate a widespread interest in the supernatural among people of his social group. He notes how, after his early *Close Scrutiny* collections were printed, his friends and acquaintances gathered to tell him tales meant for inclusion in the later volumes.[75] Their fondness for talking about ghosts and fox-spirits is amply documented by the collection itself, for Ji Yun gives, in almost every entry, detailed and authentic information about the informant, the place and time of the reported strange occurrence, and sometimes even different versions of the same story by different narrators.

Through the storytellers, bizarre happenings were reported to have been witnessed by important scholars and notable government officials. Among the more famous storytellers were Dai Zhen, Jiang

---

[75] In the "Preface" to *HX. YWCTBJ*, p. 228.

Shiquan 蔣士銓 (1725–1785), famous poet and dramatist, and Wang Huizu 汪輝祖 (1731–1807), author of books on local administration that continued to be indispensable guides until 1912. Regarded as the last master of traditional Chinese painting and the youngest of the Eight Eccentrics of Yangzhou (Yangzhou baguai 揚州八怪), Luo Pin 羅聘 (1733–1799) was yet another storyteller who was said to have an ability to see ghosts in broad daylight: he excelled with his many drawings of ghosts. Included in such a world of discourse on the strange were people like Zhu Yun 朱筠 (1729–1781), who was credited with having suggested the project on the *Complete Library* to the Qianlong Emperor, as well as *zhiguai* writers like Yuan Mei and Zhang Jingyun. All of them derived great pleasure in discussing the supernatural in their own socially cohesive group, and this must be considered as one of the basic motivating forces which gave rise to the collection. Viewed thus, *Close Scrutiny* can be regarded as an eighteenth-century version of *A New Account of Tales of the World* (*Shishuo xinyu* 世説新語),[76] although demons, wraiths, spirits, and ghosts are addressed rather than major battles of the age or the rise and fall of notable families.

---

[76] *A New Account of Tales of the World,* as a record of noteworthy conversations and re-marks, has of course been classified in the *zhiren* 志人 ("describing men," a term first in-vented by Lu Xun) genre of the traditional *biji*, in contrast to the *zhiguai*. However, in its depiction of the values of an elite class at a time of peace and prosperity, *YWCTBJ* does bear a striking similarity to the portrayal of the gilded lives and values of aristocrats living in an epoch of turmoil and instability in *A New Account of Tales of the World.*

Chapter 2

Close Scrutiny *and Oral Storytelling*

> Their powers of conversation were considerable. They could
> describe an entertainment with accuracy, relate an anecdote with
> humour, and laugh at their acquaintance with spirit.
>
> — *Jane Austen*

Since *Close Scrutiny* originates in the overwhelming interest among
the elite in events weird and unusual, it seems best in our task of
understanding the text, to begin with the late eighteenth-century oral
discourse on the supernatural. The "discourse on fox-spirits and
ghosts," centring on reported events and facts, has had a long history,
and direct evidence of this is discoverable in the voluminous literature of tales in the classical language, in the twin categories of the
zhiguai and the *chuanqi*. The oral element in these tales merits greater
attention than it has hitherto been given, for it throws light on the
nature of composition, the authors' intended meaning, and intricate
intertextual relationships (when, for instance, different written versions manipulate materials provided by the same oral tale).

A recognition of orality in the story of the strange enables us to
better understand the structural configuration of the *zhiguai* — in
particular, its two elements: the story proper and the dialogic frame.
The relationship of the oral to the written *zhiguai* probably has no
parallel at all in traditional Chinese writing. The *zhiguai* story, consisting of a narrative as well as a discursive component, needs to be
seen as a reflection of features in the informal social conversations of
people in everyday life.

Two critical issues are brought to our attention by this consideration of the *zhiguai* against the oral context in which it first
occurred. In the first place, because of its genesis in personal or
hearsay testimony, any *zhiguai* narrative straddles the realms of fact
and fiction, and thus its authenticity is constantly questioned. The
perennial insistence by the storytellers as well as the authors that what
is narrated did indeed happen moves the stories precariously close to
objective reportage, to journalistic accounts. Secondly, since the *zhiguai*
originates with oral discourse, the forms and styles of the latter have
been imported almost imperceptibly into the written *zhiguai*. The
result is that *zhiguai* narratives often have to be understood in terms
of the gestures and manoeuvres of oral communication, of which
one of the most noticeable is a certain expository tendency, a wish to
"make a point." This once again explains why the *zhiguai*, by its very
nature, seems to militate against being considered as ordinary fictional
narrative.

Appreciating the oral origins of the *zhiguai* in *Close Scrutiny* is
essential to our understanding of the collection as well as of its
didacticism. The variety of concerns conveyed by the oral discourse
on the strange reveals the potentials of narratives of the strange and
shows how they can become a vehicle for the expression of personal
preferences and opinions. One of the aims of the present chapter is
to delineate the oral features of the *zhiguai* in *Close Scrutiny*, but in
order to view such features in the proper perspective, we need to sketch
the complicated and long-standing relationship between oral tales and
the written story in both the *chuanqi* and *zhiguai* forms.

"Casual Fiction"

In his distinguished study of the Song-Yuan-Ming vernacular short
story, Patrick Hanan mentions a class of oral "casual fiction" which
differs substantially from the much better-known oral fiction narrated
by professional storytellers. The latter, often designated as "telling
books" (*shuoshu* 說書) literature, has formed a continuous tradition
of its own lasting well up to the present. Its beginnings can be traced
to a time as old as the Zhou dynasty, though clearly written references
to the activities of the professional artists are found only by Tang times.
To an overwhelming number of literary scholars, the vernacular short

story, which reached its full flowering in the late Ming, was linked to such storytelling activity. However, Hanan draws attention to an alternative tradition of oral storytelling, to which classical literary tales (or "classical tales" for short) like those by Hong Mai were indebted. Hong's *Records of Yijian* shows that his stories originated in a variety of contexts, not the least important of which were occasions of amateur storytelling, which gave rise to the so-called "casual fiction."[1]

Hanan remains one of the few critics to stress the importance of these casually narrated tales and to note their impact on the development of Chinese narrative. Jaroslav Průšek, another acknowledged authority on the colloquial short story in China, also makes brief reference to these two kinds of oral storytelling in traditional China, one of which gave rise to an "epic folk literature" and the other to an "upper class folklore" recorded in miscellaneous writings and anecdotal literature.[2] His bias, however, is reflected in his choosing to regard only the former as "true" folklore, and his scholarly work is devoted in the main to elaborating the contributions of the professional storytellers to the narrative tradition.[3] Such privileging of professional storytelling in fact explains why some literary historians treat the classical tales only as sources for the colloquial story, yet also argue for the nearly pervasive influence of the professional storytellers' tales on all varieties of classical Chinese fiction, including the full-length novel.[4] Thus we need to reconsider the intricate relationship between narratives in the literary language (*wenyan* 文言) and

---

[1] Patrick Hanan, *The Chinese Short Story: Studies in Dating, Authorship, and Composition* (Cambridge, Mass.: Harvard University Press, 1973), pp. 186–187.

[2] Jaroslav Průšek, *The Origins and the Authors of the Hua-pen* (Prague: Oriental Institute in Academia, 1967), pp. 9–10.

[3] See, for instance, Jaroslav Průšek, "Researches into the Beginnings of the Chinese Popular Novel," in *Chinese History and Literature: Collection of Studies* (Dordrecht: D. Reidel Publishing Co., 1970), pp. 228–302.

[4] It is this simplified view of the Ming novels as little more than accretions of popular lore that Andrew H. Plaks sets out to reconsider in his *The Four Masterworks of the Ming Novel* (Princeton: Princeton University Press, 1987).

those in the colloquial language (*baihua* 白話), as well as the link of both to oral storytelling traditions, casual and professional.[5]

It can well be argued that casual fiction undergoes great changes when written down, making its form and style difficult to detect and thus rendering any reconstruction of its influence sketchy at best.[6] It can also be argued that the contexts for amateur storytelling were invented, as is the case for colloquial fiction, to provide the occasion for literary creations. Or, one can even argue that the original oral elements were superseded by literary elements as the tales assumed lives of their own later. The point to be stressed, however, is not that all classical tales need to be studied from this oral perspective, but that few of the contextual references can be dismissed simply as literary constructs. In fact, a special value of the oral approach to the classical tale is that it facilitates a consideration of narrative as more than just a pure literary or aesthetic form. The close relationship that amateur storytelling bears to historical reality — whether it be the rivalry of political factions in the mid-Tang or the literary inquisitions of the Manchu government in the Qing period — permits a renewed understanding of *xiaoshuo*. This relationship requires the literary critic to pay attention to the element of referentiality in a tale and renders the need to contextualize as important as the need to textualize.

As Hanan has remarked, more often than not such casual narrative (or conversational narrative, when it is embedded in conversations) is represented as the "actual experience" of the narrator, of an acquaintance, or of the acquaintance of an acquaintance. This raises once again the much debated issue of the presentation of experience in Chinese narratives.[7] A close look at Chinese collections of "tales"

---

[5] For a theoretical discussion of the use of the classical literary language and the vernacular by fiction-writers, see Patrick Hanan, *The Chinese Vernacular Story* (Cambridge, Mass.: Harvard University Press, 1981), pp. 1–16. Jaroslav Průšek illustrates the recasting of a *wenyan* story in the colloquial in his "The Creative Methods of Chinese Medieval Storytellers," in Průšek, *Chinese History and Literature*, pp. 366–384.

[6] "Fiction" is a term that can be misleading when used as a translation for Chinese *xiaoshuo*; it is not even inclusive enough to be an adequate concept. But I am simply following Hanan here.

[7] The understanding of Chinese narratives has suffered under a rather limiting view of generic categorization, and nowhere is this seen more clearly than in the strict separation

makes one thing clear: the fact-or-fiction issue is not to be solved by collapsing the distinction itself and asserting the primacy of fictiveness, as some recent Western theorists have done.[8] Of special importance is an awareness of the unreliability of everything reported — of what is essentially an ultimate epistemological uncertainty. The fact that the bulk of the tales were in the first place *orally* transmitted on occasions of amateur storytelling creates the need to claim facticity.

Evidence of the oral provenance of a sizable proportion of classical tales is provided by the titles of the collections themselves. While we are accustomed — erroneously — to considering *xiaoshuo* as fiction, what was uppermost in the minds of compilers or writers was the element of "talk," of conversational interchange.[9] That much is suggested by the following list of *xiaoshuo* titles:

(1) *Records of the Eyes and Ears* (*Ermu ji* 耳目記), by Zhang Zhuo 張鷟 (ca. 657–730);

(2) *Records of Conversations* (*Jutan lu* 劇談録), by Kang Pian 康駢 (fl. 875–886);

(3) *Conversations of the Minister of State Affairs* (*Shangshu tanlu* 尚書談録), by Li Chuo 李綽 (late ninth century);

(4) *Guest-talk at the Thatched Pavilion* (*Maoting kehua* 茆亭客話), by Huang Xiufu 黃休復 (fl. 1006);

(5) *Records of Events Heard in the Southeast* (*Dongnan jiwen* 東南記聞), by an unknown Yuan author;

---

of "historical" from "fictional" narratives. More recently, Western historiographers have noted the overlapping between the two and suggested that the latter may provide a conceptual model for analysing sequences of historical events.

[8] See Wallace Martin, *Recent Theories of Narrative* (Ithaca: Cornell University Press, 1986), pp. 31–56. To a large extent this can be attributed to the ascendancy of the novel — fiction created essentially for its own sake — since the eighteenth century in Europe and to its consequent impact on criticism. Martin notes how the narrative (as opposed to the novel) has regained the centre of the stage through the work of theorists in the past few decades.

[9] For the origin of the term *xiaoshuo*, referred to in the Bibliographies section of the *Han shu* as "street talk and alley gossip" gathered by minor officials as intelligence about ordinary people in their own locales, see Lu Xun, *A Brief History of Chinese Fiction*, p. 1, and Kenneth J. DeWoskin, "The Six Dynasties *Chih-kuai* and the Birth of Fiction," in *Chinese Narrative: Critical and Theoretical Essays*, edited by Andrew H. Plaks, pp. 21–52.

(6) *Admonitory Records of What Was Heard and Seen (Jianwen jixun* 見聞紀訓), by Chen Liangmo 陳良謨 (1482–1572);

(7) *Bell-talk (Shuoling* 説鈴), edited by Wu Zhenfang 吳震方 (seventeenth century);

(8) *Collected Discourses under the Autumn Lamp,* by Wang Xian;

(9) *Hearsay Accounts,* by Yue Jun; and

(10) *Records of Events Heard in the Vicinity (Zhiwen lu* 咫聞錄), by Yongna jushi 慵訥居士 (fl. 1843).

What was told (and heard) was, in effect, the stuff of which the stories were made. In this light, the narrative tradition in China ought to be seen as much in the context of the transmission of events and occurrences by word of mouth as it is in terms of the gradual maturity in imaginative mastery of narrative material.[10]

Bearing in mind the impossibility of tracking down actual oral discourse of the past — no recording facilities were then available — we can do no more than comb literary and historical documents for whatever vestiges of casual storytelling that remain. The corpus of literature classified as the *chuanqi* and the *zhiguai* contains most of the casual fiction needed for our analysis, although one must necessarily be wary of treating every story for which the author indicates a source as a conversational narrative.[11] The defining characteristics of these tales are their referential elements as well as their discourse-oriented nature. Being embedded in conversations where, as recent folklore studies have revealed, both the tellers and the listeners contribute to the story puts casual fiction in distinct contrast to *shuoshu,* for the professional storytelling situation involves an active performer and his rather passive audience.[12]

---

[10] The latter approach is typified by Victor Mair, who stresses the impact of Indian Buddhist tales in enabling Chinese authors in the Six Dynasties to deal imaginatively with narrative material. Mair, "The Narrative Revolution in Chinese Literature: Ontological Presuppositions," *Chinese Literature: Essays, Articles, Reviews,* vol. 5, nos. 1–2 (1983), pp. 1–28.

[11] Hong Mai, for instance, says that he heard some of the stories he eventually included in his collection, *Records of Yijian,* but many were sent to him by friends, and others he copied from published works.

[12] Gary R. Butler has noted how little attention is paid in folklore studies to the casual story, in contrast to the *märchen* of professional artists, often considered the narrative genre *par excellence.* Butler, *Saying Isn't Believing: Conversation, Narrative and the Discourse of Belief in*

Orality and the Tang *Chuanqi*

We turn first to the Tang *chuanqi*, in which, in contrast to the *zhiguai*, traces of oral storytelling are less easily discernible. Much recent criticism of the Tang tale of marvels, in the form of thematic, structural, and archetypal analysis, has focused on its supposedly literary merits or timeless significance at the expense of topicality and relevance to then-contemporary political and social life.[13] Part of this critical trend is due to the widely-held view, spread by critics like Lu Xun, that the *chuanqi* is to be considered the first "consciously artistic" specimen of Chinese narrative and that it needs to be sharply distinguished from its antecedent, the Six Dynasties *zhiguai*.[14] Yet both, in fact, share the same oral roots.

That many tales of marvels are later renditions of stories narrated in elite gatherings suggests the possibility of approaching these tales less as aesthetic phenomena than as social discourse. The implicit claim for authenticity made at the beginning or the end of these tales is, therefore, more than just a convention borrowed from official historiography. Instead, it is a sign of the tales' oral provenance. An insistence on a tale being a true and accurate account, which is seen in a number of Tang *chuanqi*, is a feature common to many narratives and reveals how much the narrator would like to be believed. Other than considering the *chuanqi* tales as literary creations,[15] we do well to also take a look at why they were told in the first place and what contexts originally informed the storytelling. To cite one of the best-known

---

a French Newfoundland Community (St. Johns: Memorial University of Newfoundland, 1990), p. 32.

[13] In the category of archetypal analysis is Curtis P. Adkins, "The Hero in Tang *Ch'üan-ch'i* Tales," in *Critical Essays on Chinese Fiction*, edited by Winston Yang and Curtis P. Adkins (Hong Kong: The Chinese University Press, 1980), pp. 17–46. A structural-thematic study is Sarah Yim's "Structure, Theme, and Narrative in T'ang *Ch'uan-ch'i*" (Ph.D. dissertation, Yale University, 1979).

[14] This distinction is echoed by Sarah Yim when she remarks on the "expressive" quality of the *chuanqi*. See Yim, "Ch'uan-ch'i," in *The Indiana Companion to Traditional Chinese Literature*, edited by William H. Nienhauser, Jr., p. 358.

[15] Moderns assume "artistic value" as the primary reason for literacy composition, but often, in the past, other motives were cited: self-vindication (*Records of History*), revenge (*Plum in the Golden Vase* [*Jin Ping Mei* 金瓶梅]), and moral teaching (in the *zhiguai*).

examples: "The Chronicle of the White Gibbon" ("Baiyuan zhuan" 白
猿傳), an early *chuanqi* about the abduction of Ouyang He's 歐陽紇
(538–570) wife by a white gibbon, was read in its time as containing a
veiled attack directed, possibly by an ally of the political clique of
Zhangsun Wuji 長孫無忌 (ca. 600–659), against Ouyang He's son,
Ouyang Xun 歐陽詢 (557–641).[16] The attack consisted of implying
that the wife was said to have slept with the gibbon and eventually
gave birth to Xun (who reportedly had the face of a monkey). That
the author chose to remain anonymous — much as a scandal-monger
would, to protect himself — is a telling fact. It does not matter in this
case whether the rumour was spread by the written story or whether
the *chuanqi* was a record of orally transmitted rumours.

A rather similar case of a *chuanqi* being involved in the spread of
an elaborate libel against a political adversary is seen in "The Chronicle
of Li Wa" ("Li Wa zhuan" 李娃傳) by Bai Xingjian 白行簡 (775–826),
a tale datable to the closing years of the eighth century. This story of a
Chang'an 長安 courtesan who falls in love with a young scholar from a
reputable family coming to the capital to take examinations is the
subject of considerable critical controversy. Much of it revolves around
the question of whether the tale originated with a sophisticated professional storyteller who performed it in front of a scholar-official group
consisting of Bai Xingjian, his brother the famed poet Bai Juyi 白居易
(772–846), and another *chuanqi* writer Yuan Zhen 元稹 (793–831),
or whether the three friends simply told the tale among themselves
one night in the year 795.[17] The latter position, while giving rise to

---

[16] All citations below of the Tang *chuanqi* are taken from Wang Du 王度 , *et al.*, comp.
Tangren xiaoshuo 唐人小説 (Tang Narratives) (Taibei: Wenguo shuju 文國書局 , 1984).

[17] Glen Dudbridge has summed up the arguments of the opposing sides in his book-
length study of the tale. See Dudbridge, *The Tale of Li Wa: Study and Critical Edition of a
Chinese Story from the Ninth Century* (London: Ithaca Press, 1983). In addition to the critics he
cited, Seo Tatsuhiko 妹尾達彦 is also of the opinion that "The Chronicle of Li Wa" was
derived from a story in the Chang'an professional storytellers' repertoire. See Seo, "Tōdai
kōhanki no Chōan to denki shosetsu — Ri Ai Den no bunseki o chūshin toshite" 唐代後半期
の長安と傳奇小説 — 李娃傳 の分析を中心として (Chang'an in the Latter Half of the Tang and
the *Chuanqi* Tale: Concerning the Focus of Analysis in "The Chronicle of Li Wa"), in *Ronshū
Chūgoku shakai seido bunkashi no shimondai: Hino Kaisaburō Hakushi shōju kinen* 論集中國社會、
制度、文化史の諸問題：日野開三郎博士頌壽記念 (China, Society, Institution and Culture),

certain dating problems, is nevertheless based very clearly on evidence in the text itself — the last paragraph of the story:

> Once during the Zhenyuan 貞元 years (785–805) I was talking with Li Gongzuo 李公佐 (ca. 778–ca. 848) of the Longxi 隴西 clan about women's firm and unbending character, and in that context told him the affairs related to the "Duchy of Qian" [i.e. Li Wa 李娃]. Clapping his hands as he respectfully listened, Gongzuo persuaded me to chronicle the story. Accordingly I took up my brush, dipped it in ink, and recorded down the story in its broad outline.[18]

This account of the background to the composition of the Li Wa narrative becomes even more persuasive when viewed against the informal storytelling habits of literati friends in their gatherings at home, on their trips, or when they were merely off duty. Such activities reflect not only the leisure life of the elite class, but also the unity — as well as inner divisions — among its members. Other than the author's remarks, there is evidence from readers showing that the story was a rumour being circulated as political satire by people with an axe to grind. Two views of the origin of "The Chronicle of Li Wa" that must have been current after it was written are mentioned by the Southern Song poet Liu Kezhuang 劉克莊 (1187–1269).[19] According to Liu, some read the tale as an attack on Zheng Ya 鄭亞 (?–ca. 848) and his son, the renowned minister Zheng Tian 鄭畋 (825–883), for the tale makes insinuating parallels between the protagonist and Zheng Ya. These readers could not have been unaware of the hidden suggestion in this tale that Zheng Tian was the son of a prostitute (Li Wa). Others thought that since Bai Minzhong 白閔中, an elder member of the Bai clan, was engaged in a factional feud with Li Deyu 李德裕 (787–849) and the two Zhengs, "The Chronicle of Li Wa" by Bai Xingjian was meant as a scurrilous attack on the latter group.

---

edited by Hino Kaisaburō Hakushi shōju kinen ronshū kankōkai 日野開三郎博士頌壽記念論集刊行會 (Fukuoka: Chūgoku shoten 中国書店 , 1987), pp. 476–505.

[18] Wang Du, *et al.*, ed., *Tangren xiaoshuo*, p. 104. Translation adapted from Dudbridge, *The Tale of Li Wa*, p. 185.

[19] Liu Kezhuang, *Houcun xiansheng daquanji* 後村先生大全集 (The Complete Works of Liu Kezhuang), in *Sibu congkan* 四部叢刊 (Collectanea in Four Divisions) (Shanghai: The Commercial Press, 1922), 173:18a–18b. Translated in Dudbridge, *The Tale of Li Wa*, p. 187.

Although Glen Dudbridge has largely discredited these "political interpretations" of the tale, the fact remains that such views are in perfect keeping with what we know of the likely background to the tale's transmission.[20] In the study of oral narratives of everyday life, the need to approach them within the human context cannot be over-emphasized. Two components are essential to the structure and meaning of such a narrative: what happened and why it is worth telling. The latter, this element of "tellability," ties the tale to its immediate context, for the tale simply would not have been recounted unless it was storyworthy, unless it made a point relevant to the speaker, the audience, and the world in which they found themselves.[21] An awareness of the amateur storytelling background to the Li Wa story, therefore, works as a powerful corrective against the modern predilection to dissociate the Li Wa story from its historical context and to discount the fact that the scandal surrounding the Zhengs must have been of fresh and immediate interest to Bai Xingjian's circle of friends. The contemporary Tang and the later Song readers were, to say the very least, a surer guide than present-day readers.

A number of other Tang tales of marvels were obviously also derived from similar oral contexts. Interestingly enough, two more originated in conversations in the Bai-Yuan literary circle — Chen Hong's 陳鴻 (fl. 805) "The Song of Everlasting Sorrow" ("Changhenge zhuan" 長恨歌傳) and Yuan Zhen's "The Story of Yingying" ("Yingying zhuan" 鶯鶯傳). At the end of "The Chronicle of Old Woman Feng of Lujiang" ("Lujiang Feng'ao zhuan" 廬江馮媼傳), which concerns the chance meeting of an old woman with a certain Dong Jiang's 董江

---

[20] Dudbridge on the whole underplays the importance of topical references and highlights instead intertextual relationships (between "The Chronicle of Li Wa," "The Song of Everlasting Sorrow" ["Changhenge zhuan" 長恨歌傳], and "The Chronicle of Ms. Ren" ["Renshi zhuan" 任氏傳], among others) and generic properties (of the *chuanqi*). The argument here aims to counterbalance the social and historical context against the role of intertextuality and other factors in the creation of the "The Chronicle of Li Wa."

[21] Livia Polanyi, for example, treats such stories as "cultural texts" and notes that "people do not talk to each other at length *about* matters which are not of some interest to them." Polanyi, *Telling the American Story: A Structural and Cultural Analysis of Conversational Storytelling* (Norwood: Ablex Publishers, 1985), p. 1.

dead wife and parents the night before Dong remarries, is the following colophon:

> On the fifth month of the sixth year of the Yuanhe 元和 reign [i.e. 811], in the summer, Li Gongzuo, the Retainer of the Jianghuai 江淮 region, went to the capital Chang'an on official business. On his return trip he put up at Hannan 漢南, and at the inn happened to meet Gao Yue 高鉞 of Bohai 渤海, Zhao Zan 趙儹 of Tianshui 天水, and Yuwen Ding 宇文鼎 of Henan 河南. Through the night they conversed on strange events, exhausting all that they had heard and seen. This [tale] was narrated by Gao Yue, and Li Gongzuo has duly written it down.[22]

Shen Jiji 沈既濟 (ca. 740–ca. 800) also gave details concerning the oral origins of his tale of the virtuous female fox-spirit, "The Chronicle of Ms. Ren" ("Renshi zhuan" 任氏傳).

While it is possible for one to list other *chuanqi* inspired by conversational narratives, the above examples are sufficient to allow us to delineate an alternative approach to the *chuanqi*.[23] Obviously, a serious literary intent behind *chuanqi* tales cannot be denied in all cases, but neither can the vestiges of oral transmission be regarded as mere conventions. In the alternative approach being proposed, one crucial concern is with the reasons for telling a story, and a consideration of the "point" of a story is more pertinent than a look at the "theme." Another concern is with the possible communicative function to be served by the narrative. It is likely that practical or

---

[22] Wang Du, *et al.*, comp., *Tangren xiaoshuo*, p. 97. The story is found in Duan Chengshi's 段成式 (fl. 843) *Sundry Anecdotes at the Youyang Caves* (*Youyang zazu* 酉陽雜俎), among other places.

[23] A few other examples where the processes of oral transmission are expressly indicated include: "The Betrothal Shop" ("Dinghun dian" 定婚店) (in Li Fuyan's 李復言 [fl. 820–840] *A Sequel to Records of the Hidden and Wayward* [*Xu Xuanguai lu* 續玄怪錄]), Shen Yazhi's 沈亞之 (ca. 770–ca. 830) "The Chronicle of Feng Yan" ("Feng Yan zhuan" 馮燕傳), Wang Zhu's 王洙 (*jinshi*, 818) "Record of the Night-Demon at Dongyang" ("Dongyang yeguai lu" 東陽夜怪錄), and Sun Xun's 孫恂 "Record of Fox-Hunting" ("Liehu ji" 獵狐記). With regard to the first of these, Karl S. Y. Kao notes that the story is "surely *constructed* for the purpose of illustrating the notion of predestination." Kao, *Classical Chinese Tales of the Supernatural and the Fantastic: Selections from the Third to the Tenth Century* (Bloomington: Indiana University Press, 1985), p. 274. One can surmise that it could have been constructed by more than one man and circulated orally before it was put down in writing.

pragmatic functions like persuasion, indictment, justification, rebuttal, and exemplification are more to the fore than the presentation of
abstract truths or ethical values. A third concern is with topical relevance; critical energies can be directed to explicating the "rhetoric
of reference" — the techniques relating the tale to history.

Orality and the *Zhiguai*

The oral storytelling behind the Tang *chuanqi* belongs to a continuous tradition of casual narration of strange events involving ghosts,
demons, deities, and fox-spirits. However, a close look at the orality of
zhiguai tales reveals an important difference between the *zhiguai* and
the *chuanqi*: the links of the *zhiguai* to oral discourse are often more
clearly documented than they are in the case of the *chuanqi*. Beginning with Su E's 蘇鶚 (*jinshi*, 886) Tang collection *Collection of Miscellanea at Duyang (Duyang zabian* 杜陽雜編), in which the compiler takes
care to name the informants, the practice of indicating the source of
stories has become standard for *zhiguai* collections.[24] This is again a
clear response to disbelief and an effort to lend greater credibility to
the transmitted tales.[25]

In tracing *zhiguai* literature from the Six Dynasties to the end of
the Qing, one discovers that, while the content of the ghost and fox-
spirit stories remains generally unchanged throughout the entire
tradition, tales of each historical period speak to their own time. The
same chains of motifs, in other words, serve different functions; they
evolve over time. To take an example, the Qing *zhiguai* raconteurs'
use of stories to express views on prostitution, homosexuality, and
master-servant relationships would have been unthinkable to the Six
Dynasties storytellers. The Six Dynasties narrators' primary concern

---

[24] See Liu Yeqiu 劉葉秋 , *Lidai biji gaishu* 歷代筆記概述 (A Survey of Random Jottings
through the Dynasties) (Beijing: Zhonghua shuju 中華書局 , 1980), p. 37.

[25] The *chuanqi* has also been said to be more "literary." Karl Kao's discussion of the
literariness of the Tang *chuanqi* remains the most incisive treatment of the issue to date, but
his analysis is largely author-centred. Kao, "Introduction," *Classical Chinese Tales of the Supernatural and the Fantastic,* pp. 1–53. Literariness also consists of the application by the reader
of a special regime of reading to a certain text.

was simply that of reporting contemporary responses to a new epistemological category called the "strange." Hence, oral narratives at the
time of wayward events and bizarre phenomena did no more than
reveal the responses of proponents of different religious affiliations
(Buddhist, Daoist, and Confucian) to the upsurge of local reports of
anomalies.[26] The desire to offer interpretive schemes that supposedly
would continue to buttress the old order helps account for the sense
of urgency and imminent threat in these Six Dynasties stories.

The proliferation of *zhiguai* narratives in the Tang has received
much less attention than it deserves. Tales of supernatural events are
abundantly present not only in *zhiguai* collections, but also in miscellaneous histories of the time. Additionally, the tales are re-worked
as *chuanqi*.[27] The oral background to these tales was often noted by
their authors: Li Chuo's *Conversations of the Minister of State Affairs*,
a record of trivial events including much that is magical and supernatural, was derived from conversations that its author had with a
minister while a guest at the latter's house. Strange occurrences also
abound in Wang Renyu's 王仁裕 (b. 880) *Reminiscences of Events in the
Kaiyuan and Tianbao Reigns* (*Kaiyuan Tianbao yishi* 開元天寶遺事), a
collection of what were orally circulated stories related to Emperor
Xuanzong 玄宗 (r. 712–756). The fad at the time for collecting oral
tales is perhaps best indicated by Wei Xuan 韋絢 (mid-ninth century).
He jotted down stories told by Liu Yuxi 劉禹錫 (772–842), a poet related to the Bai Juyi circle discussed above, in his *Enchanting Tales Told
by Master Liu* (*Liugong jiahua lu* 劉公嘉話錄), and he compiled as well
Casual Conversations in the Military Quarters (*Rongmu xiantan* 戎幕閑
談), a record of conversations with Li Deyu.

As time passed, however, the attitude of the literati towards the
strange gradually changed. At the risk of over-simplification, we might

---

[26] See, in particular, Robert F. Campany, "Chinese Accounts of the Strange: A Study in
the History of Religions" (Ph.D. dissertation, University of Chicago, 1988), pp. 337–456.

[27] As Charles Hammond has pointed out, a lot more *zhiguai* than *chuanqi* were written
during Tang times. After all, there was no clear distinction at the time between what we
today recognize as two genres; the term *chuanqi* was first used as such by Yin Zhu 尹洙 (1001–
1046) of the eleventh century. See Hammond, "T'ang Stories in the *T'ai-p'ing kuang-chi*"
(Ph.D. dissertation, Columbia University, 1987), p. 16.

say that the fear and curiosity towards the supernatural of earlier times gradually gave way to a more relaxed and dispassionate approach. Su Shi 蘇軾 (1037–1101) can be taken as a representative figure for this trend in Song times. His habit of soliciting bizarre stories from his guests typifies the interest among the literati for tales of the unusual, which served to enliven social conversations. Ye Mengde 葉夢得 (1077–1148), a contemporary of Su Shi's, gave an account of the amateur storytelling activities associated with Su's circle. In Ye Mengde's *Record of Talk While Taking a Summer Retreat* (*Bishu luhua* 避暑錄話), he says that while in exile to Huangzhou 黃州, Su Shi frequently invited guests to his home or went to visit them to indulge in "conversations on practically any topic." Su Shi would force the reticent to talk of ghosts; he suggested that one could "listen in a rough way" and not take the stories seriously. He, too, eventually recorded many of these stories in books two and three of his collection of random notes, *Records of Eastern Slope* (*Dongpo zhilin* 東坡志林).[28] In noting that Su Shi's friends "laughed to their hearts' delight on hearing the ghost stories," Ye Mengde was underscoring the jovial mood in which the stories were told and taken. It is not surprising that Su Shi, popularly known for his convivial character and his fondness for socializing, has become associated by tradition with this mode of *zhiguai* narration.

This more light-hearted and inconsequential kind of oral storytelling which took the supernatural as its subject continued to be an important facet of literati life, as evidenced by many collections of random jottings in Ming times. There is evidence for such activities among literati groups in the Jiangnan region which centred around the famed poet-painters Tang Yin 唐寅 (1470–1524) and Zhu Yunming 祝允明 (1461–1527). One of the outcomes of such discourse is the *zhiguai* collection put out by Zhu Yunming, *Record of Strange Events* (*Zhiguai lu* 志怪錄).[29]

---

[28] Chapters 2 and 3 of *Records of Eastern Slope*, entitled "Anomalous Affairs," contain thirty-two anecdotes of strange events. See Su Shi, *Dongpo zhilin* (Shanghai: Huadong shifan daxue chubanshe 華東師範大學出版社 , 1983), pp. 72–99.

[29] *Discourses by Guests at Yecheng* (*Yecheng kelun* 冶城客論) by Lu Cai 陸采 (ca. 1495–1540) also contains anecdotes circulated in the conversations among such literary and artistic luminaries of the mid-Ming as Shen Zhou 沈周 (1427–1509) and Zhu Yunming.

In contrast to those who narrated *zhiguai* stories out of an intrinsic interest in the strange, there were tellers for whom these stories served ulterior purposes. For instance, in times of political and social turmoil, stories of untoward events must have been told as reflections of the disintegration of the old order. An example concerns the renowned poet and literary critic Yuan Haowen 元好問 (1190–1257), whose collection of stories of the strange called *A Sequel to the Records of Yijian* (*Xu Yijian zhi* 續夷堅志) records the many wayward occurrences which were reported when Northern China was overrun by the Mongols.

Similar circumstances informed the narration of stories of ghosts and fox-spirits in the final years of the Ming. In the poem "I Believe" ("Zixin" 自信), Wu Weiye 吳偉業 (1609–1672) describes the very real presences of ghosts in an age when hundreds of thousands died amidst the perpetual warfare:

Convinced I am of my lifelong indolence,
Exhausting it is for me to make my way over spring dust.
Seeing ruins, I am worried about battles,
Yet I hear the wind and waves speaking of ghosts and spirits.
Let me be drunk today with a cup of unstrained wine.
Lovely flowers will bring spring to my old garden tomorrow.
Who knows how many high officials there are at Chang'an?
The white-haired idler travels to the lakes and rivers.[30]

The indulgence in *zhiguai* storytelling was a way of escaping from the harsh reality brought by years of strife and political instability. Having withdrawn from public service and leading a reclusive life after the collapse of the Ming, the loyalist Wan Tai 萬泰 (1598–1657) was said to have frequented a tea-shop near his cottage to engage enthusiastically in casual conversations on the supernatural.[31]

---

[30] Wu Weiye, *Wushi jilan* 吳詩集覽 (Collected Digest of Wu Weiye's Poetry), in *Sibu beiyao* 四部備要 (Comprehensive Compilation of Works in Four Divisions), vols. 2130–2140 (Taibei: Zhonghua shuju 中華書局, 1965–1966), 12:9b.

[31] According to Huang Zongxi 黃宗羲 (1610–1695), in his "Epitaph for Wan Hui'an" (Wan Hui'an muzhiming 萬悔庵墓誌銘), collected in Huang Zongxi, *Nanlei ji* 南雷集 (Writings of Huang Zongxi), in *Sibu congkan*, vols. 1610–1617, 6:1a–3a.

On the other hand, the fondness for *zhiguai* stories in social talk during the first century or so of Manchu rule needs to be explained with reference to the repressive political measures adopted by that government. In the early years of the dynasty, there were the legal prohibition against meetings of more than ten members of the elite, the famous Jiangnan Tax Arrears Case and the censorship of Zhuang Tinglong's 莊廷鑨 (ca. 1600) writings.[32] In the mid-eighteenth century, there was a whole series of literary inquisitions, and the compilation of the *Complete Library of Four Treasuries* served to further the goal of controlling the scholar-elite. Since seditious statements could be made in speech just as in writing, it seems conceivable that, under the fear of impeachment, the literati turned to ghosts and fox-spirits in their conversation because these were apolitical and trouble-free subjects. The penchant for telling stories involving ghosts and fox-spirits is, then, a reflection of the general political situation.

Be that as it may, stories of supernatural occurrences could still be manipulated as vehicles for the expression of anti-Manchu sentiments. That the character for fox (*hu* 狐) is homophonous with that for non-Han or foreign tribes (*hu* 胡) makes possible the use of tales about fox-spirits for concealed attacks on the Manchus. For instance, a tale recorded in He Bang'e's *Occasional Accounts of Conversations at Night* can be interpreted this way. The homophonous parallel was obviously well-known at the time: it came as a surprise to Zhaolian 昭槤 (1780–1833), a distant descendant of the Qing founder Nurhaci 努爾哈赤 (1559–1626), that He's collection was not proscribed by the Qianlong Emperor.[33] It would not be unreasonable to suppose that there were

---

[32] A great deal has been written about the repressiveness of the Qing, but for special reference to that of the Kangxi 康熙 reign, including the two cases mentioned here, see Lawrence D. Kessler, *K'ang-hsi and the Consolidation of Ch'ing Rule 1661–1674* (Chicago: University of Chicago Press, 1976). For general surveys of the mid-Qing literary inquisitions, see Wang Youli 王有立 , ed., *Qingdai wenziyu dang* 清代文字獄檔 (Archival Records of the Literary Cases in the Qing Dynasty) (Beijing: Huawen shuju 華文書局, 1934); and L. C. Goodrich, *The Literary Inquisition of Ch'ien-lung* (Baltimore: Waverly Press, 1935).

[33] The tale in question is "Lu of the Water Works" ("Lu shuibu" 陸水部), in *YTSL*, pp. 199–203. For Zhaolian's comment on the story, see his *Xiaoting zalu* 嘯亭雜錄 (Miscellaneous Recordings at the Whistles Pavilion) (Taibei: Wenhai chubanshe 文海出版社 , 1967), p. 453.

diatribes against Qing practices, rebuttals of its legitimacy, and expressions of pent-up hatred of the Manchu ruling class hidden in many fox-spirit stories.

Thus once again we see a link, observed earlier in regard to certain *chuanqi* tales, between conversational narratives and political allegorizing. Further, the storytellers were all too aware of the way in which tales of the strange could furnish a pretext not only for political satire, but also for discourses on the relationship between the sexes and socio-economic issues of the storytellers' time. For one thing, the belief in female fox-demons' ability to nurture themselves spiritually through the absorption of male sexual energy was turned to good use by those who wished to condemn prostitution. For another, the dishonest practices of hypocrisy and double-dealing among the general public — the prevalence of which was often linked to the corruptive influence of money and wealth that arose with the development of an embryonic capitalism in the late imperial era — were criticized in stories where such vices were conveniently attributed to ghosts and fox-spirits.

Oral Storytelling as a Literati Pastime

Against this backdrop we shall attempt a reconstruction of the world of casual *zhiguai* storytelling in the Qing dynasty by focusing on the contexts of its occurrence and the conscious and unconscious uses to which it was put. The sources available being as they are, this would primarily be the world of conversational give-and-take of the elite of the mid-Qing in the lower Yangtze region and at the capital, Beijing 北京 . These two areas played a distinguished role as nuclei of elite activity: in cities and commercial towns in the Jiangnan region, literati members frequently gathered to compose and exchange poetry, and to partake of food and drink, while in Beijing (and the capitals of the provinces, too) the periodic examinations provided opportunities for candidates from different parts of the country to meet each other and to socialize with government officials.

In what follows, drawing on examples from *Close Scrutiny*, we will analyse five kinds of relationship networks — the first four can be subsumed under the broad rubric of Qing systems of patronage — that furnished occasions for discourse on foxes and ghosts. Instances will be cited to show the specific concerns of individual raconteurs, the relevance of the narratives to the social situation, and the characteristically "elite" response underlying the narration. Taken together, these accounts will help paint a picture not only of the *zhiguai* storytellers of Ji Yun's circle, but also of the late eighteenth-century fascination with the "strange." The table on pages 58 to 59 shows the way in which eminent figures in elite society at the time make their appearance in the collection.

Participants in Compilation Projects.   One of the important networks of elite relationships at the time was provided by the system of national and local patronage created to support large-scale compilation projects. The earliest example is the project on *History of the Ming Dynasty* (*Ming shi* 明史) during the Kangxi 康熙 era (r. 1662–1722), which encouraged collaboration of scholars under an officially approved institutional framework. Ultimately, the deployment of large groups of scholars on imperial projects reached its culmination with the *Complete Library of the Four Treasuries*. In the Bureau of the Four Treasuries, over three hundred scholars worked full time on the project. A group of eminent scholars including Dai Zhen, Hong Liangji 洪亮吉 (1746–1809), Zhang Xuecheng 章學誠 (1738–1801), Huang Jingren 黃景仁 (1749–1783) and Shao Jinhan formed the core of the editorial staff there.[34]

Many of the *zhiguai* collected in *Close Scrutiny* originated with these editors. As Chief Editor of the project,[35] Ji Yun, quite naturally, worked very closely with the other editors of the *Complete Library*. He was on close terms with Dai Zhen, who not only worked as one of the compilers under him, but also managed to publish one of his books with Ji Yun's sponsorship. Dai Zhen figures prominently in *Close Scrutiny* as a

---

[34] The nature of the relationship among the members of this group is discussed in Kawata Teichi 河田悌一 , "Shindai gakujutsu no ichi sokumen — Shu In, So Shinkan, Kō Ryokichi to Shō Gakusei" 清代學術の一側面：朱筠、邵晉涵、洪亮吉、章學誠 (One Aspect of Qing Scholarship: Zhu Yun, Shao Jinhan, Hong Liangji and Zhang Xuecheng), *Tōhō gakuhō* 東方學報 , vol. 57 (1979), pp. 84–105.

[35] Ji Yun was appointed, along with Lu Xixiong 陸錫熊 (1734–1792), as Chief Editor of the project on the *Complete Library* in 1773. For details of the inauguration of the project, see R. Kent Guy, *The Emperor's Four Treasuries: Scholars and the State in the Late Ch'ien-lung Era* (Cambridge, Mass.: Harvard University Press, 1987), chap. 4.

narrator of supernatural events. His contribution includes four anecdotes: one concerns a ghost-hermit (*LY* VI:10); in another, a fox-spirit solicits the help of a Daoist priest, and by means of an amulet exorcizes a ghost who, for years, has been haunting his house (*GW* IV:2); in a third, a spirit cuts short an evidential debate by two licentiates concerning *The Spring and Autumn Annals* (*LY* V:27); and in yet another, a man living in a deserted house stubbornly refuses to be coaxed or cajoled by a ghost into leaving (*LX* V:1). While the second and the fourth anecdotes are ostensibly accounts without a political agenda, the other two do reveal concerns that were appropriate to Dai Zhen — the difficulty of staying truly aloof from politics in one, and the proper use of philological methods in the other.

Another project compiler, who was at the same time a raconteur of bizarre tales in *Close Scrutiny*, was Cheng Jinfang 程晉芳 (1718–1784), who came from one of the most famous merchant families of Yangzhou.[36] One of his stories takes the form of a classic retribution tale, and the interesting response of a listener justifies citing the story in full (*HX* III:46):

> Cheng Yumen 程魚門 [Cheng Jinfang] also told of a certain traveller who took a concubine in Guangling 廣陵 [present-day Yangzhou, Jiangsu]. She was rather refined, being an adept at literary pursuits. The two, being extremely close to one another, enjoyed much nuptial harmony in the boudoir. One day the traveller returned from a drinking bout, only to find the maids and servants already asleep, with not a candle lit in the darkness. There was a deep silence in the inner chambers, and he found a letter on the table, which read:
>
> "I was originally a vixen leading a solitary life amidst mountains and forests. For half a year I stayed with you to repay a debt I owed you previously. My karmic destiny having been fulfilled, I would not dare to linger any further. At first I intended to stay behind temporarily to take care of

---

[36] Li Dou's 李斗 *Records of the Painted Boats at Yangzhou* (*Yangzhou huafang lu* 揚州畫舫錄) contains detailed descriptions of the wealthy merchant families at Yangzhou who provided patronage to literati in the eighteenth century. Li Dou, *Yangzhou huafang lu* (Beijing: Zhonghua shuju 中華書局, 1960), chap. 15. A study of the importance of such patronage networks to painters and artists can be found in Vicki F. Weinstein, "Painting in Yang-chou 1710–1765: Eccentricity or the Literati Tradition?" (Ph.D. dissertation, Cornell University, 1972), pp. 41–97.

PROMINENT EIGHTEENTH-CENTURY PERSONALITIES FIGURED IN *CLOSE SCRUTINY* (SELECTED)

Person Figured	Alias*	Relationship to Ji Yun	Role in *Close Scrutiny*
Akedun 阿克敦 (1685–1756)	Wenqin 文勤	Examiner at 1747 exam	Commentator
Cao Xuemin 曹學閔 (1719–1787)	Mutang 慕堂	*jinshi* of 1754	Raconteur and character
Cheng Jinfang 程晉芳 (1718–1784)	Yumen 魚門	Editor of the *Complete Library*	Raconteur
Dai Zhen 戴震 (1724–1777)	Dongyuan 東原	Tutor at Ji Yun's home	Raconteur
Dong Bangda 董邦達 (1699–1769)	Wenke 文恪	Ji Yun's teacher	Raconteur and character
Dong Yuandu 董元度 (fl. 1752)	Qujiang 曲江	Candidate at 1747 provincial exam	Raconteur and character
Fan Jiaxiang 范家相 (fl. 1754)	Hengzhou 蘅洲	*jinshi* of 1754	Raconteur
Ge Tao 戈濤 (fl. 1751)	Jiezhou 芥舟	From same subprefecture	Raconteur# and character
Ge Yuan 戈源 (fl. 1165)	Xianzhou 仙舟	*jinshi* of 1754	Raconteur
He Xiu 何琇 (*jinshi*, 1733)	Li'an 勵菴	Ji Yun's teacher	Character and commentator
Jiang Bingzhang 姜炳璋 (fl. 1754)	Baiyan 白巖	*jinshi* of 1754	Raconteur
Jiang Shiquan 蔣士銓 (1725–1785)	Xinyu 心餘	Candidate at 1747 provincial exam	Raconteur
Li Youdan 李又聃 (fl. 1752)	—	Ji Yun's teacher	Raconteur and character
Liu Tongxun 劉統勳 (1699–1773)	Wenzheng 文正	Examiner at 1747 exam	Commentator
Lu Xixiong 陸錫熊 (1734–1792)	Ershan 耳山	Co-editor of the *Complete Library*	Commentator
Luo Pin 羅聘 (1733–1799)	Liangfeng 兩峰	Got acquainted with Ji Yun (on his trip to Beijing)	Raconteur and character
Ming Sheng 明晟 (fl. 1723)	—	From the same county as Ji Yun	Character and commentator

Name	Style name	Role	Category
Ni Chengkuan 倪承寬 (1712–1783)	Yujiang 餘疆	*Jinshi* of 1754	Character and commentator
Nie Jimau 聶際茂 (1700–?)	Songyan 松巖	Introduced to Ji Yun by Song Bi in 1752	Raconteur and character
Qian Daxin 錢大昕 (1728–1804)	Xinmei 辛楣	*Jinshi* of 1754	Name mentioned
Qian Weicheng 錢維城 (1720–1772)	Wenmin 文敏	*Hanlin* scholar and one of Ji Yun's mentors	Commentator
Qiu Rixiu 裘日修 (1712–1773)	Wenda 文達	Ji Yun's teacher	Raconteur and character
Shao Jinhan 邵晉涵 (1743–1796)	Nanjiang 南江	Editor of the *Complete Library*	Character
Shen Dan 申丹 (fl. late 18th c.)	Cangling 蒼嶺	Youthful friend of Ji Yun	Raconteur and character
Song Bi 宋弼 (1703–1768)	Mengquan 蒙泉	Close friend	Raconteur
Wang Huizu 汪輝祖 (1731–1807)	Longzhuang 龍莊	Student of Ji Yun	Raconteur#
Wu Shaoding 胡紹鼎 (1713–1776)	Muting 牧亭	*Jinshi* of 1754	Name mentioned
Wu Zhongqiao 吳鍾僑 (fl. late 18th c.)	—	Student of Ji Yun	Raconteur#
Yi Bingshou 伊秉綬 (1754–1815)	Zusi 組似	Student of Ji Yun	Raconteur
Zhou Yongnian 周永年 (1730–1791)	Shuchang 書昌	*Complete Library* compiler	Raconteur
Zhu Yun 朱筠 (1729–1781)	Zhujun 竹君	*Jinshi* of 1754	Name mentioned
Zhu Xiaochun 朱孝純 (1735–1801)	Ziying 子穎	Student of Ji Yun	Raconteur and character
Zhuang Peiyin 莊培因 (1723–1759)	Benchun 本淳	*Jinshi* of 1754	Character

* Usually the name as used in *Close Scrutiny*.
# Stories originally in written form.

you, and to reveal why we were parting for good. Fearing, however, that our intense mutual devotion would make separation extremely difficult, in excruciating pain I decided to depart, rather than see you one more time. I looked back, bracing the wind; a thousand emotions beset me. Who knows if, with such thoughts, I will not find my destiny further intertwined with yours on the Rock-of-Three-Lives?[37] You should take good care of yourself, and not let your pure spirit be tarnished for the sake of one woman. If so, though I have to leave, I will feel slightly consoled."

On reading the letter, the traveller was much distressed. When shown the letter, friends and old acquaintances all sighed with emotion. As similar events could be seen in ancient books and records, no one cast any doubt on the incident. A month or so later, the concubine and her lover showed their identities as they went north in a boat and were robbed. They reported the matter to government officials and waited for the robbers to be caught. While the two were detained for months in this way in the Huai 淮 River area, the truth came out: the concubine's mother had sold her off at a high price, and so the concubine had to extricate herself by claiming to be a vixen.

Zhou Shuchang 周書昌 [Zhou Yongnian] noted: "She *was* a vixen; how could there be talk of her being *disguised* as one? Many stories of the strange tell of human encounters with female fairies and immortals who eventually took their leave. I suspect that some of these might have belonged to the same category as this incident."[38]

There is nothing unique about a story concerning a concubine who cheats her husband by saying that she is a fox-spirit in human form, so that she can leave him. What is remarkable is the comment of Zhou Yongnian, another project compiler, for whom the concubine was, by virtue of her treacherous nature alone, indeed nothing less than a fox-spirit. This displacement of the spiritual into an ethical metaphor effectively raises doubt concerning the reliability of many similar stories of the supernatural then in circulation. Zhou Yongnian is

---

[37] This alludes to a Tang tale about the monk Yuan Guan 圓觀 , who arranges to meet his younger friend, Li Yuan 李源, after his death at a temple at Hangzhou 杭州. He appears as a shepherd boy singing the line: "The spiritual essence returns to the Rock-of-Three-Lives."

[38] Two other tales by Cheng Jinfang are found in *LY* III:21 and *LX* III:6.

making a moral point, and Cheng Jinfang's story happens to suit his purpose.[39]

Examiners and Candidates.   The traditional examination system as it functioned in Qing times fostered special relationships between examiners and candidates of the same examination. These relationships lasted, in most cases, for life. Among candidates for the same examination — whether it be at the provincial, metropolitan, or palace levels — a bond also existed. Scholars who owned *jinshi* titles would address their examiners as "teachers," humbling themselves as "disciples." Degree holders of the same year called each other "classmates." According to his biographer, Zhu Yun had close to one thousand "disciples" in his lifetime.[40] Among the disciples of Ji Yun were Li Wenzao 李文藻 (1730–1778), Zhu Ziying 朱子穎 (1735–1801) and Hong Liangji — the first two figured in *Close Scrutiny*, while the last took a stance nearly antithetical to Ji Yun's regarding the existence of the supernatural, as we shall see in the next chapter.

R. Kent Guy regards both the relationship between masters and disciples and that among the "classmates" themselves as one of "congeniality." It is not unlikely that at the parties and feasts where these candidates and bureaucrats socialized, the topic of conversation turned to topics like spirits and anomalies. Ji Yun's teachers (including those connected through examinations) who narrated stories, responded to them, or offered comments in *Close Scrutiny* include Li Youdan 李又聃 (fl. 1752), Qian Weicheng 錢維城 (1720–1772) and Liu Tongxun 劉統勳 (1699–1773).

Li Youdan was responsible for five of the recorded items, and his accounts are very specific in giving actual names of people involved.[41] He tells of a pair of macabre poems he saw (*LY* I:4), a continuing

---

[39] *YWCTBJ*, p. 496. Two other narratives attributed to Zhou Yongnian are *HX* IV:8 and *HX* II:13. Ji Yun suspected Zhou of having invented them to support his belief in the supremacy of Han learning (in the first story) and to criticize the feuding and bickering among intellectuals at the time (in the second).

[40] See Yao Mingda 姚名達, *Zhu Yun nianpu* 朱筠年譜 (Chronological Biography of Zhu Yun) (Shanghai: The Commercial Press, 1933), pp. 129–141.

[41] See *HX* II:16, *LX* V:5 and *LX* V:6.

friendship between a learned ghost and a scholar with only superficial knowledge of the classics (*HX* II:17), a special concoction prepared by aborigines with centipedes (*GW* I:15), and a fox-spirit who
dashes all her male lovers to death after having sexual intercourse
with them (*LX* V:6).

While Li Youdan seems mainly interested in reporting events involving the supernatural, Liu Tongxun, examiner for the provincial
examination of 1747 when Ji Yun received his *juren* degree, added to
zhiguai reportage a certain argumentative edge. In a notice in *Spending the Summer at Luanyang* (*LY* I:44), Qian Weicheng, chief examiner
at the 1754 *jinshi* examination, refutes the superstitious belief in
auspicious and inauspicious sites.[42] That seems to have occasioned
some fierce arguments on the efficacy of geomancy (*fengshui* 風水).
These arguments (including Liu's), along with several strange
incidents used as supporting examples, are described in full by Ji Yun
(*LY* I:44):

> Qian Wenmin 錢文敏 [Qian Weicheng] said, "As for the blessings and
> calamities dispensed by Heaven — aren't they comparable to the rewards
> and penalties administered by the emperor? As for ghosts and deities in
> their supervision of human actions — aren't they like government offi-
> cials who put their heads together in consultation?
>
> "Suppose a document were presented for the impeachment of an
> official. According to it, his behaviour is spotless and he has achieved
> much in his tenure, but because the door of his house was built on an
> inauspicious day and opens to influences from a malefic direction, he
> ought to be punished by being sent off and demoted. Would the person
> in charge of the case act accordingly, or would he refute such a pro-
> posal? Suppose a letter was submitted for the commendation of an offi-
> cial. According to it, his behaviour falls short of perfection and he has
> achieved nothing during his tenure, but since the door of his house was
> built on an auspicious day and faces a beneficent direction, he ought to
> be promoted to a higher position. Would the person in charge of this
> case act accordingly or refute the proposal? He will definitely refute it.

---

[42] While inveighing against geomancy, Qian Weicheng reasserts the ability of spirits to
dispense rewards and punishments. *YWCTBJ*, p. 18. Qian typifies the attitude of many mid-
Qing intellectuals who denounced certain aspects of popular belief but condoned others.

Could we say that the ghosts and deities permitted this? I continue to find it impossible to acquiesce in the theory of auspicious *yang* 陽 abodes."

This argument by analogy is most enlightening, and even the geomancers, when questioned on it, could put up no defense. Yet in truth I did see inauspicious abodes: in the capital [Beijing], diagonally across from the Temple of Giving-to-the-Fatherless and to the south of the road, was a house where I mourned five deaths; at another house on the western portion of the northernmost road in the Powder Lane and Coloured-Glaze Street area, I mourned the deaths of seven. Cao Xuemin 曹學閔, the Assistant Director of the Court of the Imperial Clan, once lived in the house by the Temple. Shortly after moving in, two servants died on the same night, and Cao, becoming apprehensive, moved out. Shao Dasheng 邵大生, the Instructor, once took up his residence in a house in Coloured-Glaze Street. Time and again he witnessed anomalies in the daytime. Adamant and fearless, he eventually died in the house. How can that be explained?

Liu Wenzheng 劉文正 [Liu Tongxun] said, "*Book of History* records divination with reference to elements in the landscape while *Book of Rites* discusses divination with reference to the sun. Were there no signs of blessings and calamities, how could the sages foretell the future? That, however, is probably unknown to the diviners of today."

Liu's opinions appear to be most balanced and fair.

Here one finds some of the strongest defenses put up for geomancy, which is known to have been widespread among the elite and commoners alike in late imperial times. It needs to be pointed out here how easily storytelling activity merged with casual talk among the examiners and candidates, each of whom had his own concerns and preoccupations.

Among those mentioned in the above entry is Cao Xuemin (1719–1787), who belonged to the *jinshi* class of 1754.[43] In addition to Cao, this class consisted of prominent Qing scholar-officials and literary men (besides Ji Yun) such as Qian Daxin 錢大昕 (1728–1804), Zhu Yun, Wang Mingsheng 王鳴盛 (1722–1798), and Jiang Bingzhang 姜

---

[43] Cao Xuemin continued to be a close friend of Ji Yun's while both served in the Hanlin 翰林 academy. Lu Jintang documented an incident in 1761 when Cao supported Ji Yun against rumours spread by rival members in the academy. Lu Jintang, "Ji Yun shengping jiqi *Yuewei caotang biji*," p. 40a.

炳璋 (fl. 1754).[44] Several of them, as could be expected, are "voices" in *Close Scrutiny*,[45] but it is Dong Yuandu 董元度 (fl. 1752), Ji Yun's 1747 provincial examination "classmate," who seems, of all informants, to have contributed the greatest number of stories to the collection.[46]

Dong Yuandu's stories were mostly first-hand encounters with the supernatural.[47] He recounts how in 1747, at a Buddhist temple in Ji'nan 濟南 (in Shandong 山東), a female ghost, formerly the concubine of a local official, appeared to him and begged that she be reburied since her coffin had rotted away.[48] He also describes how he received from a spirit-writing deity (*jixian* 乩仙) a poem, which surprised everyone by containing accurate characterizations of his personality.[49]

Other stories reveal aspects of the real-life relationships among those who came for the same examination. One story was used to spread a scandalous rumour concerning Dong Yuandu and his scholar-friend. Narrated by some unidentified person, it involved a fox-spirit who preferred Dong, characterized as an upright and cultivated person, to his conceited and vulgar friend. This might accurately reflect

---

[44] Among the others in this class with whom Ji Yun was closely associated were Li Feng 李封 (1723–1796), Ge Yuan 戈源 (1738–1761), Wang Chang 王昶 (1724–1806) and Wang Youzeng 王又曾 (1706–1761). For a complete listing of the *jinshi* of 1754, see Fang Zhaoying 房兆楹 and Du Lianzhe 杜聯喆, eds., *Zengjiao Qingchao jinshi timing beilu fu yinde* 增校清朝進士題名碑錄附引得 (Collated Lists, as Inscribed in Stone, of Successful *Jinshi* Candidates in the Examinations of the Qing Dynasty) (Taibei: Chinese Materials and Research Aids Service Centre, 1966), pp. 101–102.

[45] For instance, Jiang Bingzhang narrated a scholar's meeting with the Mountain-god, who explained how the universe and spiritual beings came into existence at the same time. The Mountain-god also faulted Zhu Xi for replacing the spirits with his Heavenly principle. See *RS* I:44.

[46] Among the other "classmates" of Ji Yun who took the provincial examination in 1747 were the famed literary theorist Weng Fanggang, the poet Jiang Shiquan, and the statesman Zhu Gui 朱珪.

[47] The importance of distinguishing first-person from third-person conversational narratives, though it does not form part of my discussion here, cannot be overstated. The classic formulation of narratorial strategies in fictional texts is, of course, provided by Wayne C. Booth, but for a study of orally recounted first-person stories, see Richard Anderson, "*Taiken*: Personal Narratives and Japanese New Religions" (Ph.D. dissertation, Indiana University, 1988).

[48] See *HX* I:22.

[49] See *LY* V:34.

what was a general perception of Dong's character in his circle. Nevertheless, the story soon engendered intense bitterness on the part of the "vulgar friend" against the storyteller.[50] The tale suggests that certain stories were circulated as disguised expressions of personal rancour, perhaps even as "weapons" in the intrigues amongst members of the elite, for they were in competition with one another.

Low Level Functionaries.   A third aspect of the Qianlong social scene that relates to the vogue for "ghost-and-fox talk" is the emergence, in late imperial times, of a new group of administrative experts employed by local officials and commonly referred to as private secretaries (*muyou* 幕友). This group was generally made up of scholars who had failed in the higher examinations and were thus barred from higher bureaucratic positions in the government. With special technical knowledge and skills, they performed secretarial functions, kept accounts, enforced tax collection in the area under the jurisdiction of the magistrate they served, and acted as advisors in legal matters. Quite a few scholars have studied the spectacular expansion of this stratum in the Qing period. This expansion was said to be related to the drastic increase in the number of government student (*shengyuan* 生員) since the beginning of the dynasty, as well as to the essential part these low level secretaries and functionaries played in the smooth operation of the government machinery.[51] Socially, one might add, they belonged to the class of literati non-elites wedged between the well-defined traditional elite and the commoner classes.[52]

---

[50] See *LY* IV:29.

[51] For a detailed treatment of the *muyou* in the Qing dynasty, see Miao Quanji 繆全吉, *Qingdai mufu renshi zhidu* 清代幕府人事制度 (The System of Private Secretaries in the Qing) (Taibei: Zhongguo renshi xingzhengshe 中國人事行政社, 1971); and Chü T'ung-tsu, *Local Government in China under the Ch'ing* (Cambridge, Mass.: Harvard University Press, 1962), chap. 4.

[52] David Johnson has dealt with the role of the class of literate non-elite at some length in two articles: "Chinese Popular Literature and Its Contents," *Chinese Literature: Essays, Articles, Reviews*, vol. 3, no. 2 (1981), pp. 225–233; and "Communication, Class and Consciousness in Late Imperial China," in *Popular Culture in Late Imperial China*, edited by David Johnson, Andrew J. Nathan and Evelyn J. Rawski (Berkeley: University of California Press, 1985), pp. 34–72.

Prominent eighteenth-century figures like Zhang Xuecheng and Wang Zhong 汪中 (1745–1794) were, at one time, low level functionaries.[53] But the best-known of them all was Wang Huizu, who for thirty-four years worked as private secretary under sixteen different officials in Jiangsu and Zhejiang. There are not many studies of the lifestyle of this group, but on the whole it must have resembled that of the elite. Besides going to theatricals, collecting rubbings, seals, and other rarities, writing *biji*, and taking part in various artistic pursuits,[54] they also indulged in religious practices, including divination by spirit-writing and alchemical self-cultivation. Above all, however, as extant *biji* show, they spent much time in the quarters of their patrons discoursing on the strange.

Miao Quanji 繆全吉 has scoured important Qing anecdotal collections for accounts of the strange narrated by private secretaries and subordinate clerks;[55] *Close Scrutiny* contains the greatest number. Though many of these accounts are reported by an intermediary, quite a few detail direct, first-hand encounters of the private secretaries with supernatural beings or their descents into the realm of the dead. Zhong

---

[53] Wang Zhong served under Shen Yefu 沈業富 (1732–1807), Zhu Yun, and Feng Tingcheng 馮廷丞 (1728–1784). See Arthur W. Hummel, ed., *Eminent Chinese of the Ch'ing Period (1644–1912)*, p. 814.

[54] The leisure life of low level functionaries was depicted in various Qing documents, the most notable of which are: Gong Weizhai 龔未齋, *Xuehongxuan chidu* 雪鴻軒尺牘 (Letters Written at the Study of the Wild Goose in the Snow) (Hong Kong: Guangzhi shuju 廣智書局, 1956?); and Lu Changchun 陸長春, *Xiangyinlou bitan* 香飲樓筆談 (Sketches and Notes at the Pavilion of Fragrant Drinks), in *Biji xiaoshuo daguan erbian* 筆記小說大觀二編 (Comprehensive Collection of *Biji* Tales, Second Compilation), vol. 10 (Taibei: Xinxing shuju 新興書局, 1978). The best first-hand accounts of the life of private secretaries are Wang Huizu's handbooks on local administration, published in the 1780s and 1790s, which aim to give advice and instructions to civil servants. See Wang Huizu, *Zuozhi yaoyan ji qita yizhong* 佐治藥言及其他一種 (Medicinal Words to Aid Good Governance, with One Other Essay), in *Congshu jicheng chubian* 叢書集成初編 (Collectanea Assembled, First Compilation) (Shanghai: The Commercial Press, 1937); and his *Xuezhi yishuo ji qita erzhong* 學治臆說及其他二種 (Unfounded Opinions on Learning to Govern, with Two Other Essays), also in *Congshu jicheng chubian* (Changsha: The Commercial Press, 1939). A description of these works, with translations of parts of them, is provided by Etienne Balazs, *Political Theory and Administrative Reality in Traditional China* (London: School of Oriental and African Studies, University of London, 1965), pp. 50–75.

[55] Miao Quanji, *Qingdai mufu renshi zhidu*, chap. 8.

Xinhu 鍾忻湖 , private secretary for Ji Yun, tells of a friend, another private secretary, overhearing the complaints of two ghosts. They spoke against ineffectual officials whom they could not rely on to settle their grievances (*LY* V:11).[56] Sun Yushan 孫漁珊, an apprentice private secretary in Fujian, narrates the story of a "ghost of refinement," which leads to speculations among listeners on whether ghosts are able to drink wine (*LY* I:28).

Indeed, the interest in telling *zhiguai* tales may simply indicate the general superstitiousness of the private secretaries as a class. An in-depth look, however, reveals more intricate dynamics at work. An account narrated by Ji Lianfu 季廉夫 (active late eighteenth century) is more than merely a tale of vengeful ghosts offering judgement on the carelessness of private secretaries who undertook legal work. Two private secretaries, one in charge of statistical records and the other of signing and dispatching documents, are aroused one night by a ghost (*HX* III:40):

> Ji Lianfu also said that when Zhong Guangyu 鍾光豫 was a magistrate at Jiangning 江寧 [in present-day Jiangsu], there were two subordinate administrative officials who were cousins. One was in charge of statistical records, the other of the signing and dispatch of documents, and they constantly slept in the same room, on the same bed. One night, one of them went to sleep first. Whilst still holding a candle, the other saw a woman in a red dress seated by the table. He was greatly alarmed and woke up his cousin. Wiping their eyes and then staring in fear, they found that it was not a woman, but a deformed ghost. They went forward and wrestled with it, and both fell unconscious. The next day, curious that the door could not be opened, the people there broke it, and entered their room. The first one they saw was dead already, and the one discovered later still had the faintest of breaths. When given water and proper treatment, he was brought back to life. Thereupon he described the coming of the ghost the night before in detail.
>
> There may be instances of ghosts coming to disturb men for no reason at all, but for a ghost to appear in its real form and come to seek human lives, there must be a reason behind it. Private secretaries and assistant functionaries are not officially appointed but they have the authority

---

[56] Zhong Xinhu was also engaged in a conversation about poems on ghost-encounters. See *HX* I:29 (p. 240).

of officials. They decide on matters of life and death with a flourish of
their brushes. Easy enough it is for them to do good as well as do harm.
Obviously it was a wronged soul seeking vengeance, and a catastrophe
was the result. It is just that the reason is unknown to us.

Ji Yun's view, as expressed in the final paragraph, is that though their
duty simply involves drawing up documents for court cases, private
secretaries often play a crucial role;[57] thus, some grave wrong must
have been committed by the two.

Once this perspective is considered, the stories of the strange
circulated among private secretaries may be seen as reflections of the
fears of a group who shouldered heavy legal responsibilities. They
lived in the households of patrons far away from their families, and
they justified their lifestyles solely by skills acquired through practical
trial and error, rather than by the comfortable certification of a degree. The fears created by the special situation the private secretaries
found themselves in are portrayed in yet another tale (*RS* III:53). Here,
according to the raconteur, a private secretary on the verge of death
is summoned as a witness to hell to testify about a lawsuit that he was
involved in over fifty years before. He is found to have obstructed the
course of justice and has to pay for it with his own life.[58]

If one were to speak of different types of *zhiguai* narratives, then
undoubtedly the type most closely associated with private secretaries
in *Close Scrutiny* would be tales of crime and punishment in which the
supernatural realm intercedes to defend the innocent whenever human
justice is not meted out. The six stories in *Close Scrutiny* narrated by
Wang Huizu, all lifted verbatim from his *Medicinal Words to Aid Good
Governance* (*Zuozhi yaoyan* 佐治藥言), are telling examples of how this
otherworldly scheme of justice is brought to bear on human affairs.
All the stories are purportedly actual happenings and some are recorded with the greatest precision, with details about the time and
location of the spectral events. In one, a Zhejiang magistrate narrates

---

[57] The legal duties of private secretaries were essentially restricted to the preparation
of written documents. They were not allowed to preside in court cases tried at the *yamen*
衙門.

[58] Tales in the *YWCTBJ* involving private secretaries are plentiful. Besides those considered here the reader is also referred to: *LY* II:13, *LY* II:43, *LY* III:12, *LY* VI:11, *RS* I:17, *RS*
II:20, *HX* II:17, *HX* II:51, *GW* II:26, and *GW* IV:23.

a personal-witness account that took place in the autumn of 1755: he saw two ghosts appear to an official and demand the right verdict to be conferred on the perpetrators.[59] In another, a private secretary acting as judge is possessed by the ghost of a woman he had wrongfully sentenced to death, and he stabs himself to death.[60] Both tales, in which the supernatural intervenes to promote justice, provide an interesting foil for the prototypical hell-tale, in which it is only after a victim's death that injustices are redressed and miscreants condemned. These two tales reflect the concern of legal personnel with justice being carried out in the here and now.[61]

Cumulatively, conversational narratives concerning the supernatural by the marginal group of private secretaries embody belief in a morally active universe which punishes them for their errors, yet assists them in making correct legal decisions. The intercession of supernatural forces assures private secretaries of the intimate connections between human and suprahuman laws, and provides no little psychological comfort as the private secretaries venture their occasionally wayward judgements. At the same time, these narrative remind them that they need to take their vocation seriously and that they will always be held responsible for their own mistakes. Oral storytelling in this context is therefore as much a diversionary activity as it is a response to the exigencies of daily life. In these apparently inconsequential tales the most subtle psychological processes of folk psychology are revealed. We witness, in other words, an example of what Jerome Bruner has called the "narrative construction of reality," in which the tales help the tellers to make sense of their world, to organize experience in comprehensible ways.[62]

---

[59] The tale is derived from Wang Huizu, *Xu zuozhi yaoyan* 續佐治藥言 (A Sequal to Medicinal Words to Aid Good Governance), in *Zuozhi yaoyan ji qita yizhong*, p. 8.

[60] Ibid., pp. 7–8. The name of the raconteur that Ji Yun gave, however, is different from the one in Wang Huizu's account.

[61] In the eighteenth-century discourse on spirits, parallels were drawn between judges in the human and sublunary worlds. Ji Yun once wondered whether judges in hell could help settle four intriguing cases he knew of. See *RS* I:21.

[62] According to Jerome Bruner, "It was perhaps a decade ago that psychologists became alive to the possibility of narrative as a form not only of representing but of constituting reality." Jerome S. Bruner, "The Narrative Construction of Reality," *Critical Inquiry*, vol. 18, no. 1 (1991), p. 5.

Belletristic Friends.   Eighteenth-century elite social life is relevant to
zhiguai collections in yet another context besides those outlined
above — that of the informal coteries where literati members could
give expression to their literary and artistic talents. Forms of patronage figured in such coteries, though presumably not all their gatherings would include patrons and protégés. A great deal of talking about
ghosts and fox-spirits must have taken place when members met. The
sample of stories given below reveals a variety of concerns expressed
by the literati. One recurrent theme, interestingly enough, is the relation of young scholars to fox-spirits.

Biographies of Ji Yun in official histories and local gazetteers,
together with commemorative essays written by friends upon his
death, supplement what we can glean from *Close Scrutiny* about life in
his "world." A literary coterie is known to have been formed in 1748
consisting of Ji Yun, Qian Daxin, Lu Wenchao 盧文弨 (1717–1796),
and Zhang Tan 張坦 (1723–1795). For several years they met and
exchanged poems, and some of the tales recorded later in *Close
Scrutiny* could have been transmitted in their gatherings. One informal gathering of friends of Ji's literary circle yielded four of the
stories in *Close Security*. First, Ji's friend Nie Songyan 聶松巖 (Nie Jimau
聶際茂, 1700?–) told a story about a certain scholar Ji 紀 who possesses
tremendous strength of will — he wants to terminate his liaison with
a female fox-spirit, though he realizes the difficulty of extricating
himself (*HX* II:18):

> In the seventh month of the *renshen* 壬申 year [1752] we were informally
> gathered at the home of Song Mengquan 宋蒙泉 [Song Bi 宋弼, 1703–
> 1768]. Quite by accident affairs related to foxes became the topic of the
> conversation. Nie Songyan said: "An incident concerns a member of your
> clan, which I wonder if you know of. Previously, when I was in Ji'nan for
> the provincial examinations, I heard of a certain Licentiate Ji. His story
> might have taken place in Shouguang 壽光 or Jiaozhou 膠州 [both in
> present-day Shandong] — I have forgotten which."
>
> One evening Ji came across a woman who was smeared with mud,
> trudging along unsteadily and stumbling. He offered to help and held
> her up by her armpits. While quite certain that she must be a fox, Licen-
> tiate Ji believed that, by being intimate with her, he could nevertheless
> learn something of the nature and the character of demonic creatures.
> To her he said:

"I know what you are; don't seek to deceive me. It is wonderful for me to have a woman like you, though. Come to my studio when all is quiet. For us to flirt here is to court trouble and invite complications."

Smiling, the woman left. Indeed she returned in the middle of the night, and for several nights Licentiate Ji indulged in indecent liberties with her. Feeling that he was increasingly bewitched by the woman, however, he tried to stop her from visiting him further. Vituperative and bitter, the vixen refused to go away. Licentiate Ji said, assuming a stern expression:

"Don't act like that. Men carry full authority in matters pertaining to men and women. A man desirous of a woman can force her to satisfy him against her will, but for the woman in pursuit of a reluctant man whose heart is iron-cold, even resorting to force will be futile. What's more, you have come to sap my vital energies. I do not owe you an emotional debt, for we are never united by feelings. You've been with so many men that it would be hard to talk of chastity: I was not the cause of your fall. The gentleman derides the practice of abusing a woman and in the end abandoning her, but that holds true for humans, not for creatures of your type. Why linger around here? What good does that do you?"

The vixen, at a loss for words, went off.

Hence it is clear that those who, once enticed, become entangled in relationships with fox-spirits that cannot be expelled even with Daoist magical figures and talismans, are in the last analysis trapped in the fetters of their own passions, unable to extricate themselves. If they were tranquil and unmoved by desires, would these foxes, with no advantage to gain, not leave?

This entry is of interest on two counts. First, it has an almost prototypical quality; like many other *zhiguai* of this and earlier periods, its plot centres around the liaison between the young, aspiring scholar and the beautiful fox-spirit. The sheer quantity of this type of tale has led to the suggestion that it was a channel for the release of sexual desires in repressed, traditional China — presumably through writing or reading the tales.[63] But this theory needs to be qualified. One notes the wonderful twist to Nie Songyan's story: there is a piece

---

[63] According to C. K. Yang, writing ghost stories involving the seduction of poverty-stricken scholars provided an outlet for sexual energies in a society governed by strict moral codes. C. K. Yang, *Religion in Chinese Society: A Study of Contemporary Social Functions of Religion and Some of Their Historical Factors* (Berkeley: University of California Press, 1961), pp. 56–57.

of well-intentioned advice on extricating oneself from such situations, whether human or supernatural beings are involved. While the narrative is not explicitly allegorical, the comments at the end on the proper control of one's passions seem momentarily to reach beyond the specific story about a fox-spirit.

Besides containing a clue to dealing well with amorous fox-spirits (and their human counterparts as well), this entry also reveals one aspect of the internal dynamics governing oral discourse in the *zhiguai*. Nie Songyan's story was told in 1752 at the house of Song Bi, and it occasioned three others also collected in *Close Scrutiny*. Fa Nanye 法南野, Tian Baiyan 田白巖, a friend, and Song Qingyuan 宋清遠, the brother of Song Bi, responded by giving their fox-tales variants: one is about a fox-spirit's revenge on her assailants, one about another fox-seductress, and the last about a fox-spirit reincarnated as a maid to repay debts owed her master in a previous life (*HX* II:19–21). Such chain or serial storytelling must have been a prominent feature in *zhiguai* narration in whichever historical period.

The belletristic friendships depicted here abounded in elite society of the time, one other example being the circle of Yuan Mei. Retiring from office in 1752, Yuan Mei moved to his estate called Suiyuan in Nanjing 南京 and spent the rest of his life entertaining friends and guests from all over the country. Besides participating in the rich cultural life of the Yangtze region, he, together with his friends, made trips to places as far off as Guangdong (in 1784) and Fujian (in 1786), and these trips yielded a rich crop of *zhiguai* stories.[64] Opulent families in Yangzhou, especially those of the wealthy salt merchants, also provided venues for literary coteries to meet.[65] Besides making excursions to scenic spots, discoursing on literature, and engaging in other traditional amusements like gazing at plum blossoms, such literary men no doubt exchanged stories about the supernatural.

---

[64] See Arthur Waley, *Yuan Mei: Eighteenth-Century Chinese Poet* (Stanford: Stanford University Press, 1970), especially chap. 4.

[65] See Ho Ping-ti, "The Salt Merchants of Yang-chou: A Study of Commercial Capitalism in the Eighteenth Century," *Harvard Journal of Asiatic Studies*, vol. 17 (1954), pp. 130–148.

Elite Household Members.   Finally, a sizable proportion of eighteenth-century "talk of the strange" was transmitted within the elite household by family members and relatives, maids and servants. Ji Yun's father Ji Rongshu 紀容舒 (1685–1764), referred to by his honorary title "Master Yao'an'" 姚安公, is the source for some thirty stories in *Close Scrutiny.*[66] His comments, appended to tales he told himself as well as to those of other raconteurs, creates a voice that resounds throughout the collection.[67] His voice was especially authoritative: none of his remarks was ever contradicted. Adjudicating human actions and dispensing standards of what was right and wrong, his remarks posit a moral norm. As we shall have occasion to observe more closely later, his was the didactic model upon which Ji Yun fashioned his own. The fact that Ji Rongshu tirelessly offers his remarks also highlights an important distinction between two kinds of raconteurs — those who simply narrate the supernatural occurrences and those who look for meaning or significance in the tales.

The raconteurs of even earlier generations in Ji Yun's household include, first, Master Aitang 愛堂 (d. 1637), who was evidently interested in magical formulae and amulets, and befriended Daoist priests. He was even said to have once journeyed to hell, though he survived the trip (*LY* VI:28).[68] Then, Ji Runsheng 紀潤生 (d. 1716), a great-grandfather of Ji Yun's, provided a story of a foolhardy man in Shandong who vowed to tie up one ghost each night. His tale was transmitted by Ji Rongshu (*RS* II:47). And finally, there are Zhang Jianting 張健亭 and Zhang Mengzheng 張夢徵, Ji Yun's maternal

---

[66] For a brief account of Ji Rongshu's life and his works, see Lu Jintang, "Ji Yun shengping jiqi *Yuewei caotang biji,*" p. 36.

[67] See *LY* I:3, *LY* II:4, *LY* II:8, *LY* II:20, *LY* II:32, *LY* II:46, *LY* III:5, *LY* IV:6, *LY* V:10, *LY* V:30, *LY* V:31, *LY* V:39, *LY* VI:4, *RS* I:33, *RS* I:34, *RS* I:61, *RS* II:24, *RS* II:33, *RS* II:45, *RS* II:46, *RS* II:51, *RS* IV:21, *RS* IV:27, *HX* I:17, *HX* I:43, *HX* I:59, *HX* IV:15, *HX* IV:40, *LX* III:14, and *LX* IV:6.

[68] There was evidently a similar interest on the part of Ji Yun himself. An anecdote showing the power of incantations is *HX* II: 29; a proto-scientific interpretation of how they functioned is given in *HX* II:27. Tricks were played on two flippant scholars by means of Daoist amulets (*LY* I:31). Ji Yun also theorized about how spirits could be ordered about by incantations and amulets. See *LY* I:20.

uncles. This succession of family storytellers broadens the scope of the narratives to include supernatural events that happened as far back as the late Ming.[69] It also reveals a strain of superstition handed down from one generation to another in a typical elite family in seventeenth- and eighteenth-century China.

We can enumerate the belief in the supernatural revealed by Ji Yun and his closest kin through *zhiguai* storytelling and discussion. Trust is placed in geomantic theories when the family looks for a propitious site for the burial of Ji Rongshu (*HX* II:11). Ji Yun also recalls that portents forewarned him of his banishment to Urumqi in 1768. This background of family superstition obviously encouraged the spread of stories of strange events in the household. Ji Yun's cousins (like Liu Xiangwan 劉香畹 and An Zhongkuan 安中寬) and nephew (Ji Rulun 紀汝倫 [b. 1738]) are together responsible for over a dozen accounts. His eldest son, Ji Ruji 紀汝佶 (1744–1786), was said to have been completely captivated by *Studio of Leisure*, and his infatuation with Pu Songling's tales was linked to his early death at the age of forty-two.[70] *Close Scrutiny* also contains instances in which Ji Yun asserts the efficacy of divinatory methods like spirit-writing, astrological calculation, geomancy, and glyphomancy (*chaizi* 拆字 , or ideographic analysis).

In fact, whether carried on among relatives or in friendly circles, conversations on ghosts and fox-spirits reveal superstitious beliefs and practices as an integral part of eighteenth-century elite culture.[71] Other sources supplement the stories from *Close Scrutiny* to prove that one of the favourite pastimes of the elite at that time was divination by means

---

[69] The vast majority of the anecdotes narrated in *YWCTBJ* are roughly contemporaneous with Ji Yun's life. Only about twenty-eight of the entries can be identified as events that occurred in the Ming.

[70] Six of the *zhiguai* stories written by Ji Ruji are appended, with an introduction by Ji Yun, to the *YWCTBJ*. *YWCTBJ*, pp. 562–565.

[71] In the section on the arts of the necromancer, Xu Ke records all the varieties of Qing fortune-telling practices. He also includes a brief history of such beliefs from the Han to the Ming. Xu Ke, comp., *Qingbai leichao*, vol. 9, pp. 1–150. A good source on superstitions in the Qing is the nineteenth-century poetry collection by Zhang Yingchang 張應昌 , which has a section devoted to "Shen gui" 神鬼 (deities and ghosts). See Zhang Yingchang, ed., *Qing shiduo* 清詩鐸 (Qing Bell-poetry) (Beijing: Zhonghua shuju 中華書局 , 1960).

of spirit-writing. Ji Yun mentions at least two experts in this form of divination who were known to his father. One was able to invoke an immortal called "Hermit-of-the-Reclining-Tiger" who composed poetry and painted (*LY* III:30).[72] The other could invoke a certain "Man-Amidst-the-Reeds" who diagnosed illnesses and cured the sick (*RS* II:22). Ji's father was able to tell whether the apparition conjured was an immortal or a ghost.[73] Incidents of séances, naturally, find their way into *zhiguai* narratives. Much like stories of descents into hell, they document a form of communication between the human world and the supernatural realm, though the communication is accomplished in this case through a spirit-medium, who invites the spirit to the world of man.

In the above survey of the circumstances surrounding the circulation of *zhiguai* stories in *Close Scrutiny,* we discern a diversity of motives for the storytelling. While we cannot be absolutely certain of motivation in all cases, a few possibilities suggest themselves. Some (like Dai Zhen) wished to make a political point, others a moral point (as in the stories by Cheng Jinfang and Nie Songyan). Some used the narratives as satire or as a means of taking a jab at a personal enemy (the story circulated about Dong Yuandu), others wanted to vent grievances (the stories by the private secretaries) or solicit emotional support (the narratives of private secretaries). Some (like Li Youdan and most members of the Ji household) were interested in no more than the narration, while others were concerned about giving their own opinions (on geomancy, for instance). In a vast number of cases, the discourse on the strange evinces a fascination with the supernatural *per se,* which is understandable in the context of the so-called "superstitiousness" of eighteenth-century elite culture.

---

[72] Ji Yun recorded numerous poems (some of them composed by spirit-writing deities) that contained hidden clues to future events that had to be deciphered. A poem by Ji Yun himself that portended the exile to Urumqi is noted in *LY* I:35. A landscape painting by Dong Bangda 董邦達 (1699–1769) was also said to have portrayed an Urumqi scene that Ji Yun saw later (*LY* I:35, pp. 14–15).

[73] Among the most popular spirit-writing deities to be summoned at the time were the warrior-spirit Guan Yu 關羽, the bodhisattva Guanyin 觀音, and Lü Dongbin 呂洞賓, one of the eight legendary immortals.

The description of multifarious amateur storytelling activities among the Qing elite and semi-elite presented here is of necessity incomplete. Not the least significant reason for this is the dearth of dependable records. Available sources of evidence are written, not oral. What I have attempted is simply to show that the casual narratives of the strange from the Qing, as much as those from earlier periods, must be interpreted first and foremost with reference to social contexts of occurrence.

To summarize, this chapter has sought to relate both the *zhiguai* and the *chuanqi* through their conversational frames to the world of the "amateur" storytellers and their audiences. General contours are delineated for earlier periods, which provides the backdrop for an extended analysis of tales from *Close Scrutiny*. Specifically, each tale or group of tales from this collection can be said to serve a special purpose related to the particular circumstances of its telling. By attending to elements of orality, readers can see the tales in *Close Scrutiny* as speech acts that derive meaning from actual contexts. The storytelling impulse is of course as old as language itself and is observable in the use of stories to prove a point, to solicit sympathy or approval, to generate laughter, or simply to provide amusement. Conversational storytelling, in *Close Scrutiny* and elsewhere, is essentially a communicative act that speaks to its own time and age.

Chapter 3

Questions of Belief and Disbelief

> Beliefs, like values and attitudes, normally find their expressions
> either in action or descriptions of action, that is, narratives.
>
> — *David Hufford*

> The first condition for exploiting our credulity is to believe.
>
> — *Prosper Merimée*

As a repository of tales transmitted among the late eighteenth-century elite, *Close Scrutiny* offers invaluable information on the mentality of this group. Among other things, it documents the group's attitude concerning the existence of spirits.[1] Though some of the narration that took place in social conversations also occurred within the elite family, the majority of tales seem to have flowed along the various patronage networks. One must concede, however, that the dividing line between family talk and social chit-chat may at times be hard to draw. Servants, maids, actors, and Buddhist monks and

---

[1] Although the term "supernatural" as derived from Western concepts of the "natural" cannot be applied without qualification to the Chinese context, it is used here to denote categorically that which relates to the otherworldly realm. The Chinese have numerous terms for what is considered to be "supernatural," and the ontological realities that could be designated as such are referred to individually as *shen* 神, *gui* 鬼, *guai* 怪, *yi* 異, and so on. The *guai* — the "strange" or the "anomalous" — denotes a category of spiritual beings and is the coinage for uncanny phenomena not explicable with reference to natural laws. But the term "supernatural" is useful, in any case, because it covers the entire range of otherworldly activities and phenomena as they figured in pre-modern discourse.

nuns figure in the narratives too, but they play an insignificant part and, in any case, they are rarely the raconteurs.

One might begin with the observation that most *zhiguai* raconteurs appearing in Ji Yun's collection are believers: they tell stories either to provide empirical confirmation of their belief or to persuade disbelievers of the reality of the supernatural. Likewise, Ji Yun used *Close Scrutiny* to demonstrate the existence of the otherworldly realm, and the collection contains ample clues as to where he stood on the issue of the supernatural. In fact, in its approach to the narratives of the strange, *Close Scrutiny* resembles *In Search of Spirits*, which is generally considered the most influential of the early *zhiguai* collections. According to its author Gan Bao, *In Search of Spirits* was written to prove that "the Way of the Spirits is no lie." Throughout the traditional period the literati continued to compile *zhiguai* stories in the classical language, and this may be interpreted as an attempt to disprove the arguments of the sceptics. In this sense, then, Ji Yun is another interlocutor in the "tradition of belief."

The debate over the issue of spirits was carried on among the literati for centuries and admits of no simple resolution. On the one hand, critics of supernaturalism continually dismissed sightings of ghosts, deities, and demons as hallucinatory. They tried to advance rational explanations for the sightings, and they even pointed out logical fallacies in believers' understanding of causes and effects. On the other hand, the believers defended themselves by referring to actual experiences and even by appealing to reason. Therefore it cannot be argued that believers consisted only of those who lacked judgment or sound critical thinking. The debate between the supernaturalists and the sceptics is a confrontation between two traditions; each has its own set of explanations.[2] A more fruitful approach to such a debate as it informed the telling, retelling, and compiling of *Close Scrutiny* stories is to view the debate as an activity that is ideological (related to beliefs) and rhetorical (connected with persuasion). Such an approach

---

[2] These are the "traditions of belief and disbelief," according to Gillian Bennett. Bennett pits the rationalist tradition of disbelief against the supernaturalist tradition in the post-Enlightenment period in the West, but she cautions against polarizing the two camps. Gillian Bennett, *Traditions of Belief: Women and the Supernatural* (London: Penguin Books, 1987), pp. 23–29.

seeks to understand the opposed parties in terms of the discourse through which they present their views. The narratives mustered by the raconteurs to validate, support, and defend arguments need not be judged on the basis of their truth-value. They need to be understood in terms of the verbal combat between the believers and the sceptics.[3]

Scepticism and its Proponents

While some members of the elite in Ji Yun's time were fascinated with the supernatural and sought to vindicate it before the sceptics, other members disapproved of supernatural beliefs and fiercely attacked popular superstitions. Their scepticism had a long tradition, and they quoted Confucius's dictum against "speaking of prodigies, feats of strength, disorders, and spirits" time and again as proof that Confucius was a sceptic — even though Confucius had hardly argued for disbelief. Over the course of centuries various thinkers openly challenged the widespread belief in supernatural occurrences. Among the earliest sceptics were the Han philosopher Wang Chong and the Han scholar-historian Ying Shao. In the Six Dynasties, with the spread of Buddhist ideas of hell, karma, and transmigration, partisan religious groups often heatedly debated the reality of the supernatural. The arch-sceptic at the time was Ruan Zhan 阮瞻 (281–310, nephew of the Daoist thinker and poet, Ruan Ji 阮籍 [210–263]), whose trenchant denial of the existence of ghosts made him a household name for the "no-ghost theory" (*wugui lun* 無鬼論).[4] The frequency with which

---

[3] David Hufford expresses a similar point when he notes that, rather than reducing supernatural beliefs to physical explanations or constructing an argument for a supernatural reality, he aims to show the processes of reasoning behind the disputes for and against those beliefs. David J. Hufford, *The Terror That Comes in the Night: An Experience-centered Study of Supernatural Assault Traditions* (Philadelphia: University of Pennsylvania Press, 1982), pp. ix–xxiv.

[4] For Ruan Zhan's biography, see Fang Xuanling 房玄齡, *et al.*, eds., *Jin shu* 晉書 (History of the Jin Dynasty) (Beijing: Zhonghua shuju 中華書局, 1974), vol. 5, pp. 1363–1364, where Ruan Zhan is said to have died after meeting a ghost who attempts to convert him. This anecdote is also recorded in Gan Bao, *Soushen ji* (Shanghai: The Commercial Press, 1931), p. 116. An even earlier advocate of the "no-ghost theory" is Xunzi 荀子 (ca. 313–238 B.C.), who refutes the existence of ghosts epistemically by saying that they are simply tricks played on us by the senses.

he was referred to in eighteenth-century debates concerning ghosts indicates his continued popularity as a spokesman for scepticism.

Clues from *Close Scrutiny* suggest that in late imperial times Zhu Xi had become almost exclusively associated with the sceptics; he took on a role very much like Ruan Zhan's. His case was, however, far more ambiguous, and in one long entry Ji Yun sets out, with quotations from *Classified Sayings of Zhu Xi* (*Zhuzi yulei* 朱子語類), to correct the misconception that Zhu Xi denied the existence of spirits. To Ji Yun, Zhu Xi had only said that spirits were not of the "natural order."[5] What appears to have been the case is that Zhu Xi believed that spirits could be relegated to a realm of *qi* 氣 (material force). Ji Yun concludes that the connection between Zhu Xi and the "no-ghost theory" is untenable and presumably attributable to the neo-Confucians' insistence that "nothing exists outside of principle" (*li wai wu wu* 理外無物). This conclusion is compatible, in fact, with twentieth-century views expressed by scholars like Wing-tsit Chan 陳榮捷, who has shown that Zhu Xi accepted some strands of popular thinking and even believed in certain superstitions.[6] Furthermore, what Ji Yun has done reflects the late eighteenth-century debate on the reality of spirits — like the other debaters, he drew upon the stated or implied views of Confucius, Ruan Zhan, and Zhu Xi. Both the attack on and the defense of supernaturalism at the time focused on these three figures. The sceptics cited them as authorities in the debate, and the believers either challenged or re-interpreted the viewpoints of the trio in their own favour.

The debate was usually carried on in essays, but for the believers as for the sceptics, accounts of firsthand experience or hearsay evidence must also have provided strong support for their arguments. In any case, it must be conceded that the late eighteenth century saw

---

[5] Ji Yun corrected the misconception that the "no-ghost" theory originated with Zhu Xi: "The Master Zhu regarded the ascent of the *hun* 魂-soul and the descent of the *po* 魄-soul as part of the natural order, to which the varieties of spirits and demons do not belong. He did not say [the latter] do not exist." (*HX* VI:12)

[6] For his discussion of Zhu Xi's attitudes towards dreams, divination, and popular beliefs, see Wing-tsit Chan, *Chu Hsi: New Studies* (Honolulu: University of Hawaii Press, 1989), pp. 110–125.

some of the most vehement attacks on supernatural beliefs in traditional China. Indeed, some scholars, taking the critique of popular superstition and the remarkable transformations in intellectual outlook as signs of a new *Zeitgeist*, have spoken of the eighteenth century as the dawn of a Chinese "Enlightenment."[7] It was the "last wave" before the advent of anti-superstitious iconoclasm in the early twentieth century under the influence of the West.[8] Interestingly enough, the attacks occurred when *zhiguai* storytelling was extremely popular. Just when *Close Scrutiny* was compiled, staunch critics of supernatural beliefs and practices appeared. They included Yuan Mei, Qian Daxin, and Hong Liangji.

Two of them — Qian Daxin and Hong Liangji — actually belonged to Ji Yun's circle; Yuan Mei was indirectly connected to him. Hong Liangji, who was probably the most outspoken among the sceptics, topped the list of successful candidates chosen by Ji Yun for the metropolitan examination in 1784. Qian Daxin is referred to as a close friend more than once in *Close Scrutiny*. As for the link between Ji Yun and Yuan Mei, on three occasions in *Close Scrutiny* Ji Yun alludes to episodes in Yuan Mei's *What the Master Would Not Discuss*, and Yuan cites twelve of Ji's notices in his *A Sequel to What the Master Would Not Discuss*.[9] Both Yuan Mei and Ji Yun compiled *zhiguai* stories, though their views are never completely similar.

Any line between sceptics and proponents of supernatural beliefs becomes difficult to draw when we look closely at the eighteenth-

---

[7] See Hou Wailu 侯外廬, *Zhongguo zaoqi qimeng sixiangshi* 中國早期啟蒙思想史 (An Intellectual History of Enlightenment in Its Formative Period in China) (Beijing: Remin chubanshe 人民出版社, 1956). Gao Qihua 高琦華 sees Ji Yun as a precursor of Enlightenment ideas who critiques social injustices. See Gao Qihua, "*Yuewei caotang biji* yanjiu zongshu" 閱微草堂筆記研究綜述 (A Survey of Studies on the *Yuewei caotang biji*), *Yuwen daobao* 語文導報, no. 8 (1985), pp. 10–12.

[8] A discussion of the movement against popular superstitions in the early twentieth century is found in Prasenjit Duara, "Knowledge and Power in the Discourse of Modernity: The Campaign against Popular Religion in Early Twentieth-Century China," *Journal of Asian Studies*, vol. 50, no. 1 (1991), pp. 67–83.

[9] References are to Yuan Mei's anecdotes about eggs laid by cocks (*GW* II:3), a needleman's encounter with a ghost (*GW* III:21), and the judgment in hell received by Lü Liuliang 呂留良 (1628–1683), who was noted for his anti-Manchuism (*GW* IV:21).

century debate. Disbelievers at times admitted their limits in providing rational explanations for strange events, and those who appeared to be supernaturalists often shifted positions and could, paradoxically, accede to the views of sceptics. The sceptics were a minority within the elite, but in the eighteenth century their voices were clearly discernible. Thus the storytellers who reported strange events to support their viewpoints were keenly aware of an alternative, sceptical position regarding the supernatural.

Yuan Mei went far in condemning supernatural practices, though he still did not go all the way. In his *Random Jottings from the Garden of Contentment* (*Suiyuan suibi* 隨園隨筆), he enumerates countless historical instances of the unreliability of fortune-telling, physiognomy, geomancy, magical calculations, dreams, and astromancy.[10] He shows, for example, that the same signs that portended the ascendancy of Shi Huangdi 始皇帝 (259–210 B.C.) also signaled the demise of the "Han hegemon," Xiang Yu 項羽 (233–202 B.C.), and that what held true for the late Ming rebel leader Li Zicheng 李自成 (1605?–1645) (namely, the belief that the desecration of the gravesites of ancestors is inauspicious) did not hold for the first emperor of the Tang.[11] Yuan Mei also catalogues the actual cases in which prognostication failed. Again citing works of the past, he shows that portents like the sweet dew, which is supposedly sent down from Heaven, generated conflicting interpretations.[12]

Although Yuan Mei castigates superstitious practices, he does not altogether doubt the existence of spirits. Rather, in some of the instances cited he finds evidence that "the spirits fool men" (*guishen nongren* 鬼神弄人), and he seems comfortable asserting that the occult arts could prove efficacious.[13] When arguing against the belief that dreams are portents, he stops short of denying the existence of spirits: "Once one believes in what one dreams of, one renders oneself vulnerable to the tricks of deities and ghosts."[14] When suggesting

---

[10] Yuan Mei, *Suiyuan suibi* (Taibei: Mingming chubanshe 明明出版社 , 1955), 28:3b.

[11] Ibid., 28:2a.

[12] Ibid., 28:4a–4b.

[13] Ibid., 28:2b–3a.

[14] Ibid., 28:3a.

that real spirits are no more than spectres originating in the human heart, he does not clearly deny their existence.

The famed Qing historian, Qian Daxin, was similarly ambivalent in his scepticism. He notes that some forty years before, Zhu Yun — the scholar who helped initiate the project on the *Complete Library* by memorializing the Qianlong emperor — had asked him for his horoscopes and predicted his future career. But, Qian Daxin observes, events since then had proved Zhu Yun wrong. Also Qian Daxin lamented the absurdity of fortune-telling. He calculated that only 518,400 variations are possible with the horoscopes and that people with different fortunes therefore must have shared the same *bazi* 八字 (horoscope). He further argued that little attention ought to be paid to divinatory methods because "sages find contentment in their lot, seek to direct their own fate, and remain untouched by either blessings or calamities."[15]

However, Qian Daxin's vacillation is manifested in his essay "On Reincarnation" ("Lunhui lun" 輪迴論), which he wrote ostensibly to attack Buddhist beliefs in rebirth and hell.[16] He ridicules the Buddhist notion of reincarnation by levelling charges of unfiliality and selfishness against those who follow the Buddhist path. Comparing the life of a human to that of a flower, he asserts that a person's spiritual essence will disperse at his death, much as the scent fades when a flower withers. Yet almost in the same breath he adds: "The ancient kings knew of the nature and character of spirits, and thus instituted the sacrificial rites in order that they could return to their own proper places and not cause violence."[17] And so, while rebirth and hell are viewed as fictitious, ghosts and deities are not. On the whole, Qian Daxin's views are neither striking nor original — his

---

[15] Qian Daxin, "Xingming shuo" 星命説 (Astrology and Human Fate), in *Qianyantang wenji* 潛研堂文集 (Collected Prose Writings from the Hall of Devotion to Studies), in *Sibu congkan*, vols. 1838–1853 (Shanghai: The Commercial Press, 1922), 3:11b–12b.

[16] Ibid., 2:22a–24b.

[17] Ibid., 2:23a. The allusion is to an incident described in the *Zuo's Commentary* (*Zuozhuan* 左傳) in which the ghost of Boyou 伯有 returns to carry out his revenge. See "The Seventh Year of Duke Zhao" in *Chunqiu Zuozhuan jijie* 春秋左傳集解 (*Chunqiu Zuozhuan,* Collectively Annotated) (Beijing: Wenxue guji kanxingshe 文學古籍刊行社 , 1955), pp. 38–39.

anti-Buddhist sentiments are little more than cliché-ridden platitudes that had long characterized the Confucian attack on Buddhism[18] — and his dabbling in divinatory practices, as noted in a Qing miscellany, weaken his arguments.[19]

In a series of essays in *Writings from Juanshi Pavilion, First Collection* (*Juanshige wen jiaji* 卷施閣文甲集), Hong Liangji expresses a slightly more radical standpoint than that of either Yuan Mei or Qian Daxin.[20] He deals not only with superstitious practices, but also with notions concerning the working of spirits and ideas of predestination and fate that are grounded in a belief in the interrelatedness of the human and supernatural realms. In "Principles of Destiny" ("Mingli pian" 命理篇), he debunks the popular belief in predetermined fate by saying that it is forged and perpetuated by Buddhists. The manipulation of such a belief was for Hong comparable to the sages' promotion of self-cultivation among mediocre people. Though having pedagogical value for inducing the masses to do good and avoid evil, ideas of fate were, for Hong Liangji, nonetheless fabricated.

In "Immortals" ("Xianren pian" 仙人篇), Hong Liangji compared human ageing to the onset of night — death "must follow" old age — and concludes that immortality is simply make-believe. In "Good and Bad Fortune" ("Huofu pian" 禍福篇), Hong also argues against the belief that spirits have the power to administer rewards and punishments for human deeds. Here he raises the question of whether unfilial

---

[18] The eighteenth century did not produce groundbreaking Buddhist thinkers comparable to those in the late Ming. It was basically a "Confucian period." Interest in Buddhism on the part of the intelligentsia was evidenced by only a few men, like Peng Shaosheng 彭紹昇 (1740–1796), Luo Yougao 羅有高 (1733–1778), and Wang Jin 汪縉 (1725–1792).

[19] Xu Ke, comp., *Qingbai leichao*, vol. 9, p. 109.

[20] Hong Liangji, *Juanshige wen jiaji*, in *Hong Beijiang shiwenji* 洪北江詩文集 (Collected Poems and Prose Writings of Hong Liangji) (Shanghai: The Commercial Press, 1935), pp. 5b–18a. Studies of Hong Liangji's agnosticism are: Jin Chunfeng 金春峰 , "Qingdai jiechu de wushenlun sixiangjia Hong Liangji" 清代傑出的無神論思想家洪亮吉 (Hong Liangji, a Renowned Agnostic of the Qing), in *Zhongguo wushenlun wenji* 中國無神論文集 (Essays on Agnosticism in China), edited by Zhongguo wushenlun xuehui 中國無神論學會 (Hubei: Hubei renmin chubanshe 湖北人民出版社 , 1982), pp. 272–287; and Paul S. Ropp, *Dissent in Early Modern China: Ju-lin wai-shih and Ch'ing Social Criticism* (Ann Arbor: University of Michigan, 1981), pp. 186–190.

people who worship the deities would be spared when misfortune strikes. A consequence of supernatural beliefs, according to Hong Liangji, is that man fears deities and ghosts more than his fathers and elder brothers. He concludes: "There are no beneficent deities of the sun, moon, and stars. Just as deceptive are the cataclysmic thunderbolts that supposedly wreck destruction on men. Therefore I say: Heaven does not send thunder to strike men; neither can deities and ghosts bring blessings and calamities."[21]

In "Ghosts and Divinities" ("Guishen pian" 鬼神篇), Hong Liangji addresses the issue of whether spirits are real, but the validity of his arguments is marred by inconsistencies. Rather than thoroughly denouncing belief in the supernatural, he tacitly accepts certain spirits and, in particular, a category of "anomalous spirits." His central aim in the essay, in fact, is to distinguish anomalous spirits from ghosts and deities. For him, the current talk about deities and spirits is misguided. The only "real" spirits are those of remote antiquity — those of mountains, rivers, and ancestors. Besides them, there are the anomalous spirits that have plagued man since the decline of the three most ancient dynasties. Early examples are the Heaven-god who descended on the ancient Shen 莘 Kingdom and the River God who caused much disruption in the state of Chu 楚. According to Hong, the spirits that his contemporaries fear so much are of this "anomalous" category, for "real" deities and ghosts (like ancestors and gods of the soil and crops) have never been known to be harmful. He then gives advice on how to handle the anomalous spirits: "[They] are not to be feared. [Control over them] is entirely a matter of the potency of one's *qi*. One can wrestle with them when one's *qi* is strong, or be cowed when one's *qi* is weak."[22] Thus, while Hong Liangji opposed *indulgence* in ghosts and spirits, he is once again not against belief in their *existence*.

Scepticism in the eighteenth century, though brilliantly expounded by these three well-known literary and intellectual figures, was far from broadly conceived. First of all, the majority of them focused on excoriating the popular religious practices then rampant

---

[21] Hong Liangji, *Juanshige wen jiaji*, p. 47.
[22] Ibid., p. 52.

among the commonfolk. Yuan Mei, for instance, exposed the unreliability of astrology and fortune-telling, and other men of letters derided geomancy, not only in essays, but in popular fictional works. One example is *Unofficial History of the Scholars*. The critics of popular religion indirectly confirm what the *zhiguai* stories themselves have indicated: it was an age of superstitions.[23]

Secondly, where the existence of spirits is concerned, the critiques are neither markedly original, nor systematic or thoroughgoing. Qian Daxin's argument against rebirth and karmic retribution echoes the views of earlier Confucian apologists, and Hong Liangji's demonstration of the illogicality of beliefs in the ability of spirits to mete out retribution likewise has precedents. The habit of disproving superstitious practices by citing individual examples — clearest in Yuan Mei's writings — undercuts, rather than augments, the forcefulness of the critiques expressed. The eighteenth-century sceptics failed to move beyond the condemnation of specific elements of popular belief to a consistent, well-reasoned attack on supernatural concepts. Perhaps few writers at the time were prepared to reject supernaturalism outright; such reluctance was a pronounced characteristic of the sceptical tradition not just in the eighteenth century, but throughout the pre-modern era. Hong Liangji went farthest in his critiques, yet he accepts spirits as real.[24]

Supernaturalism and Its Adherents

As prominent as the tradition of scepticism was a tradition of belief amongst the Chinese elite. The *zhiguai*, as a unique category of literary writing, flourished in the context of these clashing traditions.

---

[23] See, for example, Meng Chaoran 孟超然 (1731–1797), *Chengshi lu* 誠是錄 (For Certain), a work in one chapter condemning *fengshui* 風水 , in *Mengshi balu* 孟氏八錄 (Eight Records of Meng Chaoran) (1815), vol. 3. For the critique of geomancy in *Unofficial History of the Scholars*, see the incident involving the two Yu brothers.

[24] One must, of course, qualify this statement by adding that, from a modern perspective, the rationalistic scepticism of eighteenth-century intellectuals appears limited. Although the sceptics revealed the irrationality of beliefs in spirits, they could not possibly have gone far enough to point out (as, for instance, Freud did) that religion is a cultural institution that serves to reconcile men to things beyond their control.

Although Anthony Yu perceptively notes the paradox of the continued proliferation of *zhiguai* tales in the face of strong disbelief,[25] a more comprehensive view needs to recognize an underlying link between these compilations and the promotion of belief in the supernatural. Could the argumentative rhetoric of the narratives themselves be an expression of belief? Might the supernaturalist viewpoint have been buttressed by the tales of anomalous events and phenomena? Furthermore, if the *zhiguai* stories are thus tied to their intellectual milieu, what sort of background informed Ji Yun's *Close Scrutiny*?

Some of the views expressed through the stories of *Close Scrutiny* are detectable outside the compilation in the writings of contemporaries. Many wrote in defense of spirits in the late Qianlong and early Jiaqing 嘉慶 (r. 1796–1820) periods, and in order to put into sharper focus Ji Yun's own beliefs regarding the supernatural, we should briefly sketch the views of believers in Ji Yun's time.[26] A brief overview of their arguments will show that it does not appear preposterous at all to suggest that Ji Yun was in the camp of the "believers."

One trenchant advocate in Ji Yun's circle was the renowned painter and last of the Eight Eccentrics of Yangzhou, Luo Pin. Luo argues in his essay "Ghosts and Deities" ("Guishen" 鬼神) for the reasonableness of the belief in ghosts and demons. He begins by quoting the

---

[25] Anthony C. Yu, "Rest, Rest, Perturbed Spirit: Ghosts in Traditional Chinese Prose Fiction," *Harvard Journal of Asiatic Studies*, vol. 47, no. 2 (1987), pp. 397–434.

[26] Other essays written slightly later (in the early and mid-nineteenth century) that argued in varying degrees for the existence of ghosts and deities include: Fang Dongshu 方東樹 (1772–1851), "Yuan shan" 原善 (An Inquiry into Goodness) and "Yuan tiandao lun" 原天道論 (An Inquiry into the Heavenly Way), in *Yiweixuan quanji* 儀衛軒全集 (Collected Writings from the Study of the Civil and Military), chaps. 1 and 2; Cheng Hongzao 程鴻藻 (1820–1874), "Shi fei wu gui" 是非無鬼 (For and against the No-ghost Theory), in *Youhengxinzhai ji* 有恆心齋集 (Collected Writings at the Studio of Perseverance), 1:26b; Pan Deyu 潘德輿 (1785–1839), "Guishen lun" 鬼神論 (On Ghost and Deities), in *Yangyizhai ji* 養一齋集 (Collected Writings at the Studio of Cultivating Unity), 12:4a; Jiang Xiangnan 蔣湘南 (fl. 1835), "Guishen" 鬼神 (Ghosts and Deities), in *Qijinglou wenchao* 七經樓文鈔 (Collected Literary Works at the Pavilion of the Seven Classics), 4:3a; and Yu Yue 余樾 (1821–1907), "Gui shuo" 鬼説 (Discourse on Ghosts) and "Shen shuo" 神説 (Discourse on Deities), in *Binmeng ji* 賓萌集 (Records of Guests and Commoners), in *Chunzaitang quanshu* 春在堂全書 (Complete Writings at Hall of the Presence of Spring), 2:23b, 24b. Hence the tradition of belief can be seen to have been carried on with rigour by men of letters into China's modern age.

Song neo-Confucian Zhang Zai 張載 (1020–1077), who used a theory of *qi*, conceived as a fundamental substance of the universe, to explain all natural processes. For Luo Pin, all the ghosts, deities, demons, and monsters are also products of this *qi* in its multifold manifestations. Therefore nothing under Heaven is too weird or outlandish to be believed. The rationalists are only blinded by their limited view of what is reasonable.

Another of Luo Pin's arguments is that because ghosts and deities existed in the past, they must also exist in the present. In both "Ghosts and Deities" and "Ghosts" ("Gui" 鬼), he cites from *The Rites of Zhou* (*Zhouli* 周禮), *Zuo's Commentary* (*Zuo zhuan* 左傳), and other classical works numerous references to spirits and discussions of their nature. He challenges the reader to peruse the twenty-one standard histories, *A Comprehensive Survey of Literary Documents* (*Wenxian tongkao* 文獻通考), *Extensive Gleanings from the Taiping Reign,* and *Imperial Digest of the Taiping Reign* (*Taiping yulan* 太平御覽) for further evidence of supernatural beings.[27] He constantly turns to ancient authorities for support: the legendary king Yu 禹 of the Xia 夏 dynasty reputedly carved demons like sprites and elves on his nine tripods to make them familiar to his subjects;[28] Confucius allegedly once indicated his belief in ghosts who "enjoyed" (*xiang* 享) human offerings;[29] and the Buddhist scriptures refer to sixty-four types of *preta* (hungry ghosts).[30] This catalogue of examples includes even the folk practices at the Buddhist ghost festival.

Luo Pin, of course, would not end without countering the widely propagated view that Confucius warned against supernatural beliefs. In a third essay, "The Strange" ("Guai"), he says: "Confucius would not speak of anomalies. Not that they do not exist. He simply refused to talk about them. For if he did, men would be bewildered; their intelligence would be dimmed; they would abandon what is normal and go after what is bizarre and absurd."[31] He also pokes fun at the

---

[27] Luo Pin, *Wo xin lu* 我信錄 (Records of My Beliefs), in *Huaibin zazu* 懷邠雜俎 (Miscellany in Remembrance of Bin Subprefecture), vol. 3 (1911), 1:13a–16b.

[28] Ibid., 1:14a.

[29] Ibid., 1:14b.

[30] Ibid., 1:15a.

[31] Ibid., 1:16b.

arch-proponent of disbelief, Ruan Zhan, who, in an incident recorded
in the history of the Jin 金 dynasty (1115–1234), was himself rebuked
by a ghost.

Luo Pin also painted ghosts. One painting worth mentioning is
the scroll "Ghost Amusement" ("Guiqu tu" 鬼趣圖), composed of a
series of eight paintings of ghosts interacting with men. The scroll
also contains close to a hundred colophons, brief notes, poems, and
short essays, all dealing with the subject of ghosts. The contributors
include the most eminent scholar-officials and literary men of the late
Qianlong era — Ji Yun, Yao Nai 姚鼐 (1732–1815), Lufei Chi 陸費墀
(d. 1790), Jiang Shiquan, Qian Daxin, Zhang Dunren 張敦仁 (1753–
1834), Yuan Mei, Qian Zai 錢載 (1707–1793) and so on.[32] Luo Pin
came to know many of these members of the elite from 1783 to 1798,
when he was in Beijing displaying his paintings. His "Ghost Amusement" scroll must have served to draw the literati together by providing an occasion for discourse on ghosts — perhaps as much as the
zhiguai collections through the centuries had.[33]

Luo and the contributors to the handscroll show a relaxed, even
jovial, attitude to the subject of ghosts. The lightness and inconsequen-
tiality of their discourse stands in sharp contrast, on the one hand, to
the slightly more sombre tone of *Close Scrutiny*, and, on the other, to
the dry, astute argumentation of the essays disputing or affirming the
supernatural. Admittedly, the *zhiguai* genre allows for jokes, satire,
wit, and wordplay; in fact, *What the Master Would Not Discuss* by the
sceptic-iconoclast Yuan Mei shows an obvious affinity with the "Ghost

---

[32] Lufei Chi was a noted Hunan 湖南 official who was fond of poetry, Zhang Dunren
was famous for his studies of the *Book of Rites* (*Li ji* 禮記) scholar, and Qian Zai was a poet-
painter and a connoisseur of painting and calligraphy. See Arthur W. Hummel, ed.,
Eminent Chinese of the Ch'ing Period (1644–1912), pp. 542–543, 417, 156–157, respectively.

[33] The painting is reproduced in its entirety in Luo Pin, *Luo Pin guiqu tu juan* 羅聘鬼趣
圖卷 (The Ghost Amusement Scroll of Luo Pin) (Hong Kong: Cafa Company, 1970); and
Kei Suzuki, comp., *Comprehensive Illustrated Catalogue of Chinese Paintings* (Tokyo: University
of Tokyo Press, 1982), vol. 2, pp. 89–91. Several of the poems written on this scroll appear
in Gu Linwen 顧麟文, ed., *Yangzhou bajia shiliao* 揚州八家史料 (Historial Documents Related
to the Eight Artists at Yangzhou) (Shanghai: Renmin meishu chubanshe 人民美術出版社 ,
1962), pp. 179–184. Luo Pin was obviously at the centre of an elite circle with artistic
interests. See Leo Tak-hung Chan, "In Dalliance with Ghosts: Humor and the Fantastic in
Luo Pin's *Ghost Amusement* Scroll," *Journal of Oriental Studies* (forthcoming).

Amusement" painting, and many of Yuan Mei's stories are virtually
zhiguai in the "comic" mode. But the stories in Ji Yun's *Close Scrutiny*
are rarely lighthearted or humorous; in contrast to the stories in *What
the Master Would Not Discuss* (which Yuan Mei described as "frivolous"),
the *Close Scrutiny* stories express a seriousness of purpose more
characteristic of the essays.

Also writing in defense of supernaturalism was Mei Zengliang 梅
曾亮 (1786–1856), a disciple of Yao Nai, the founder of the Tongcheng
桐城 school of scholarship. Mei Zengliang, while accepting the supernatural as real, looks beyond specific manifestations of the spiritual
realm to a cosmic order which dispenses blessings and calamities.
Mei Zengliang's view contrasts clearly with Hong Liangji's. For the
latter, men are simply fooling themselves with the belief that spirits
administer rewards and punishments for human actions. In his treatise "On Graves" ("Mu shuo" 墓說), Mei Zengliang laments the disre-
spect paid to deities and ghosts, particularly in the neglect of graves
and in the abandonment of various rituals. He stresses that one should
be honest when dealing with the spirits, for "man's fortune, good or
ill, is determined by the deities."[34]

Another disciple of Yao Nai's, Guan Tong 管同 (1780–1831), argues in "An Inquiry into Ghosts" ("Yuan gui" 原鬼) for the existence
of ghosts with the metaphor of smoke coming from burnt plants. To
him ghosts are departed human souls that are invisible, just as smoke
is invisible until plants are burnt and turned into ashes. On this basis,
he upbraids both Ruan Zhan for denying the existence of ghosts and
Han Yu for erroneously suggesting that ghosts lack sound, shape, and
breath.[35] For Guan ghosts are of two kinds: those of Heaven and Earth,

---

[34] Mei Zengliang, "Mo shuo," in *Bojian shanfang wenji* 柏梘山房文集 (Collected Literary
Writings from the Retreat at Mount Bojian) (Taibei: Huawen shuju 華文書局, 1969?), 1:4b.

[35] To Han Yu, "Of the myriad things the earth and stones have shape but no sound; the
wind and thunder have sound but no shape; men and beasts have both sound and shape;
ghosts have neither shape nor sound." See Han Yu's essay, "Yuan gui" 原鬼 (An Inquiry into
Ghosts), in *Han Changli wenji jiaozhu* 韓昌黎文集校注 (Annotated and Collated Edition of
the Literary Works of Han Yu), edited by Ma Tongbo 馬通伯 (Shanghai: Gudian wenxue
chubanshe 古典文學出版社 , 1957), pp. 15–16.

born of the *yin* 陰 element, and those of men, created from the souls of the deceased.[36]

Yet another exponent of a theory of spirits at about the same time is Yao Ying 姚瑩 (1785–1853), who is associated with the revival of the Song school of learning in the early nineteenth century. Yao's theory resembles Luo Pin's, but it is more elaborate and is developed in three stages in "On Ghosts and Deities" ("Guishen pian" 鬼神篇).[37] First, he takes issue with the notion that ghosts and deities are distinct entities, the former originating with human beings and the latter created by Heaven. To him both are created from *qi*, the basic stuff of the universe. When the physical body decays, *qi* is left, marauding as ghosts in vast, empty space.[38] When activated, *qi* becomes wind, rain, thunder, and hail; when in its tranquil state, it takes the form of mountains and streams, which can be worshipped as deities.

Having established this point, Yao Ying proceeds to spell out the activities of *qi* in terms of *yin* and *yang*, its bright/dark and purposive/passive modes. He stresses that *yin* and *yang* are two facets of the same thing. Through the patterns of activity and non-activity to which the primal *qi* is subject, the sundry phenomena of the physical world emerge. Along these lines Yao Ying characterizes the individual categories of animate and inanimate beings: deities of mountains and rivers, as well as ghosts, partake of *yin*, while human beings and growing plants partake of *yang*.

In summing up his arguments, Yao Ying elaborates the mechanism of "metamorphosis" (*huaji* 化機) that these phenomena, in coming into existence, reveal: "All physical matter undergoes transformation. Things are self-transformed, and they also transform into

---

[36] Guan Tong, *Yinjixuan wen chuji* 因寄軒文初集 (Essays from the Study of Taking up One's Residence, First Collection) (1879), 1:2b–3a.

[37] Yao Ying, *Dongming wenji* 東溟文集 (Essays of Yao Ying), in *Zhongfutang quanji* 中復堂全集 (Collected Writings from the Hall of Reviving the Doctrine of the Mean), in *Jindai Zhongguo shiliao congkan xuji* 近代中國史料叢刊續集 (Sequel to the Collectanea of Historical Documents on Early Modern China) (Taibei: Wenhai chubanshe 文海出版社, 1974), 1:19a–20a.

[38] Ibid., 1:19a.

each other. For a while one is human, then one is a ghost. A deity can turn into wind and rain, then thunder and hail, and then also mountains and rivers."[39] The logical conclusion to his line of thought is that "there is a oneness in the multiplicity of phenomena, and all is one"[40] — a unitary, monistic interpretation of the world that is the hallmark of the "materialist" thoughts of Chinese philosophy.[41]

The last eighteenth-century supernaturalist to be discussed here is Yu Zhengxie 俞正燮 (1775–1840), outspoken critic of repressive ethical codes. In his "Against Disbelief in Ghosts" ("Fei wugui" 非無鬼), Yu rebuts sceptics on the basis of extensive evidence from the Six Classics, the nine schools of Chinese philosophy, the rituals of the emperor, animal behaviour, miscellaneous ceremonies, and even Catholic beliefs.[42] He begins with a quotation from *The Book of Changes* (*Yijing* 易經) and ends by noting the Catholic belief in saints. According to Yu Zhengxie, because the Confucian scholar is able to penetrate the three spheres of existence (heaven, earth, and man), the affairs related to ghosts should be a domain of his concern.[43] This is virtually a rebuttal of Confucius's injunction against indulging in talk on ghosts and deities.

Yu Zhengxie ventures further to suggest that, when they are old enough, objects (like cloth) are transformed into "ghosts." Similarly, the *hun* 魂-soul of man can be understood with reference to two analogies — the sharpness of a knife and the flame of a candle. Both of those are believed to have an existence independent of the objects to which they are temporarily attached. In his conclusion, Yu Zhengxie decries the sceptics' notion that the spirits were fabricated by the sages in order to buttress their moral teachings. As he reasons: "How can one teach if ghosts do not exist? If there are no ghosts this amounts to

---

[39] Ibid., 1:19b–20a.

[40] Ibid., 1:20a.

[41] Yao Ying also discussed the relationship of ghosts to man in a short essay, "Shuo gui" 説鬼 (On Ghosts), in *Dongming waiji* 東溟外集 (The Other Collection of Yao Ying), in his *Zhongfutang quanji*, 1:2a.

[42] Yu Zhengxie, *Guisi leigao* 癸巳類稿 (Classified Writings in the *Guisi* Year) (1833), 14:35a–36b.

[43] Ibid., 14:35a.

deception. And observing the proper rituals [for ghosts] would be self-deception. If we worship our ancestors' ghosts while at the same time not believing that they exist, then we are making fun of our own forebears."[44]

Those who defended the existence of the supernatural thus countered the arguments of the sceptics point by point. To dismiss the charge that believing in spiritual manifestations is irrational, they offered their own proto-scientific explanation, which drew upon theories of *qi* and *yin-yang*. The representative polemicist in this regard is Yao Ying. His system, though a far cry from modern scientific rationalism, is nevertheless consistent and inclusive, and it is firmly grounded in a philosophical discourse centred on ancient texts like *The Book of Changes*. His arguments, as well as Luo Pin's, show that distinctions between "supernatural" and "rational" views are arbitrary. In fact, he successfully refutes the accusation that supernatural beliefs are a grave error in logic.

In their debate, believers and their opponents used similar strategies. Both sides, for instance, argued by way of metaphors. Guan Tong and Yu Zhengxie used metaphors for presenting their belief in the separability of the soul from the human body; Qian Daxin utilized his metaphor of the withered flower to argue for almost the reverse. Both sides cited Confucius and Ruan Zhan, although both disagreed about what their predecessors *actually* said. Discussion between the two sides was possible, after all, because they shared a common discourse.

Proponents of either viewpoint amassed supporting evidence with great earnestness. In contrast to the contemporary *zhiguai* stories in *Close Scrutiny*, however, the evidence was culled largely from the past. The two main sources were the classics and the standard histories, though some reference was also made to random jottings. By refraining from the use of personal witness accounts, these formidable debaters increased the credibility of their arguments, for there can be little dispute over supernatural occurrences encountered by real historical personalities and recorded in printed texts, while living witnesses can more easily be charged with observational or interpretive

---

[44] Ibid., 14:36a.

errors. In contrast to the narrative accounts, these essays rest on an underlying assumption that textual evidence wields greater authority than contemporary reports — an assumption that no doubt reflects the evidential trend in research of the late eighteenth century.

The adherents of the two positions clashed fiercely on numerous fronts, but at times what fueled the debate were issues other than whether spirits exist. The debate often turned on the role of supernatural beings as regulators of retributive justice or as agents of a cosmic machinery punishing misdeeds and rewarding virtuous behaviour. Guan Tong and Yao Ying do not explicitly deal with questions of retribution, but if one is to judge solely by their arguments, then it is clear that they cannot conceive of a scenario in which ghosts, deities, and demons did not exist. Hence Hong Liangji discovered that in denouncing popular beliefs in spirits, he simultaneously had to jettison the notion of supernatural retribution. Mei Zengliang, in contrast, found it necessary to defend both the existence of spirits and the moral order they reinforced. Yu Zhengxie resorts to a different tactic: he denies that the elite fabricated supernatural beliefs to promote morality among the masses by threatening them with retribution. It must have been obvious to him, as to many a defender of supernaturalism at the time, that when doubts are cast on the existence of spirits — even when there is the slightest suspicion that they are fabricated — an entire moral/cosmic order is challenged.

Stories as Accumulated Evidence

The *zhiguai* tales of *Close Scrutiny* must be seen as engaging in the eighteenth-century debate on the supernatural on two levels. In the eyes of many of the storytellers themselves, the tales offer concrete, firsthand evidence that spirits exist. But for Ji Yun the purpose of his collection is to bolster belief and thus to lend force to his moral exhortation.

Of course, many stories of the strange may have been narrated for other reasons, and *Close Scrutiny* may be read from other perspectives. The keen interest in supernatural phenomena was obviously multifaceted. Some storytellers and *zhiguai*-compilers were concerned first and foremost with satirizing various intellectual and social positions. Others took delight in developing allegories. Imitators of Pu Songling's *Studio of Leisure* were exploring the potential for romance and fictionalizing in tales of the supernatural. But Ji Yun was decidedly against putting *zhiguai* tales to such uses. One of Ji Yun's fundamental concerns, understood in the context of the conflicting views of the supernatural, is to present spirits as they have been seen, observed, and commented upon. From one perspective at least, the cumulative effect of the collection is to induce the reader to consider the supernatural seriously.

The tales in *Close Scrutiny* represent an approach to the question of the supernatural markedly different from that of the essays. Ostensibly the compilation is an accumulation of facts, but the facts are significant as evidence for supernatural beliefs. Interestingly, Ji Yun does not use "evidence" from the ancient texts — a favourite source in his time for some of the debaters on the supernatural and for the evidential research scholars. Instead, Ji Yun's evidence consists of personal experience narratives. To show Ji Yun's use of such narratives for his arguments, we will analyse representative tales under three categories: encounter tales, accounts of supernatural causation, and anecdotes about the inexplicable.

Encounter Stories. The confrontation of the human with the supernatural generates some of the finest *zhiguai* stories. These can be classified according to the types of otherworldly creatures involved. The encounters with immortals in *Close Scrutiny* are few and appear mostly in spirit-writing séances, where immortals are summoned to diagnose illnesses or predict personal fortunes; in this *Close Scrutiny* reflects the popularity of spirit-writing divination among the elite at the time. Although there is a profusion of accounts of fox-spirits interacting with human beings and interfering with man's activities, few (if any) of them belong to the category of "encounters," and they are not meant to prove that fox-spirits indeed exist.[45] Rather, these are love stories

---

[45] In her study of the sources for *LZZI*, Wang Panling notes that, during the Qing period, the belief in fox-spirits was prevalent in North China and the worship of frog spirits and the Five-element Gods was common in the Jiangnan region. See Wang Panling, *Pu Songling yu minjian wenxue*, pp. 241–247. This partly accounts for the abundance of stories in *YWCTBJ* about fox-spirits, most of which originated in the provinces of Shandong and Hebei.

(some of which end with intermarriage between the two species) or seduction tales (in which the succubus has an affair with an aspiring scholar). Some of the encounters described by Ji Yun's friends also involve deities, demons, and emanations (*jing* 精).

But the majority involve the appearance of ghosts. A case of an encounter-tale told to affirm the reality of ghosts occurs early in *Close Scrutiny* (*LY* VI:6). The exact circumstances when the story was first told were given: a conversation that Ji Yun had with his friends in 1739. The complete entry is as follows:

> In the *jiwei* 己未 year of the Qianlong reign [1739], I was studying with Li Yunju 李雲舉 and Huo Yangzhong 霍養仲 , both from Dongguang 東光 [in present-day Hebei], in the Living Clouds Academy. One night it happened that we discussed ghosts and deities. Yunju believed that they existed; Yangzhong thought they did not. While they were thus debating, a servant of Yunju's said quite abruptly:
>
> "Strange events there indeed are in this world. If I had not personally experienced it, I would not have believed it. Once while passing by the bushy mounds outside the temple of the city god, I accidentally trampled on a coffin and broke it. That night I dreamt of being arrested and brought before the city god, and charged with having destroyed someone's home. I knew it was connected with the coffin-breaking, so I defended myself: 'Your home should not have lain right across the path. I was no intruder.' 'The path runs right over my home; my home was not meant to be in the way,' the ghost retorted.
>
> "Smiling, the city god looked at me, saying, 'Everybody takes this path, so you cannot be blamed for taking it. But how come nobody who walked on it broke it but you? It would not do to let you go scot-free. You are responsible for making a compensation by [burning] paper money for the dead.' After a while, he added: 'Ghosts themselves cannot repair coffins. You should cover the coffin with a wooden board, and pile earth on top of it.'
>
> "The next day I burnt some paper money as instructed by the deity, and a whirlwind swept the ashes along. On another night, returning to the same place, I was invited by a voice to sit down. Knowing that it was the same ghost, I hastened back home. The ghost chuckled, his chattering voice like that of an owlet's. Just to think back on it now makes my hair stand on end."
>
> Yangzhong said to Yunju: "With your servant on your side, making it two against one, I cannot win. Yet I can never take what others have seen as something that I have seen myself."

Yunju said: "Were you to adjudicate a legal case, would you have to witness everything to believe? Or would you consider others' testimonies? Unreasonable as it is to expect to see everything that occurs, would we not accept their testimonies and take what they have seen as what we have seen? What do you think of that?"

Laughing, the two left it at that.

In this case the *zhiguai* story was offered in the debate between Li Yunju and Huo Yangzhong as evidence for the existence of the supernatural. It is worth noting that Ji Yun's interest in plot development and characterization is minimal.[46] This example in fact helps to explain why the narratives in *Close Scrutiny* never come across as scary stories or Gothic tales. The raconteurs never consider the creation of suspense to be an uppermost concern, for such mood-setting would weaken the argument. Such stories are also comparable to the medieval exemplar in the West, which in large measure consist of reports about the dead and of spirits and were used by the church to inculcate religious beliefs (in matters like purgatory and the Day of Judgment).[47] The encounter tales, of course, also resemble modern journalistic reportage in their emphasis on presenting objective facts.

The encounter tale is a primary form of the story of the strange and merits careful study. Because its main purpose is to verify the existence of the spiritual world, often it is encapsulated in a few sentences and ends just as soon as the spirit is identified. This structural brevity is illustrated by two other tales from *Close Scrutiny*. In one, a boy sees innumerable hideous-looking ghosts propping up the pillars of a hall. He raises an uproar, upon which the ghosts immediately rush out and the roofs collapse (*LY* VI:51). In the other story, a field-hand sights a giant luminous spirit, several yards tall, holding a lantern. This story consists of only a couple of lines and is followed by a discussion in which different views are presented concerning the true nature of the spirit (*RS* II:55). (Some said that it was the earth bogey

---

[46] This was explicitly stated by Ji Yun. See preface to *YWCTBJ*, p. 1.

[47] Gillian Bennett analyses the changes in Western Christian doctrine after about 1100 and notes the growing interest in reports about spirits and the dead, which became incorporated into church sermons as exempla. She also explains how such stories helped to shape public opinion. See Bennett, *Traditions of Belief*, chap. 4.

[*wangliang*罔兩] and others that it was the God-of-the-Night [*zhuyeshen*
主夜神].[48]) Indeed, the non-narrative, expository portions of the
entry are longer than the story proper and no attempt is made to
exploit the imaginative potential of the *zhiguai* plot.

The encounter tales are characterized by an insistence on the credibility of the events reported. Because the tales spread widely through
oral transmission, narrators were only on rare occasions first-person
witnesses. But usually they will take pains to indicate exactly when and
where an "encounter" occurred and thereby confirm its authenticity.
These details were then noted down, in one story after another, by Ji
Yun himself. One instance involves Ji Yun's great-uncle, An Jieran 安
介然, who narrates how, thirty years earlier in 1763, when he was returning from the Geng 耿 family's residence in Yanshan 鹽山, Hebei,
he personally witnessed a vengeful ghost taking the life of an old man
(*RS* 3:21).

For other accounts, like those relating to Master Aitang, the narrator takes care to indicate the exact lines of transmission. What follows is the conclusion to an entry concerning the dream-descent
of Master Aitang into the netherworld, his subsequent return to the
human world — to have a book previously stolen from hell burnt by a
relative so he would not be incriminated — and his eventual death
(*LY* VI:28): "This series of events was recorded by Master Yao'an [i.e.,
Ji Rongshu] in the family register. He heard it from his great grandfather. His great grandfather in turn got the story from his own great
grandfather — the person who undertook to burn the book [for the
deceased]. How can you say that spirits do not exist?" These authentic
records therefore supply the most reliable evidence to be used in the
argument against the sceptics.

One variation of the encounter tale concerns men who doubt the
existence of ghosts. Although told with utter seriousness, these stories
occasionally border on the humorous. As early as the fourth century,
In Search of Spirits told of doubters who were brought to a sudden

---

[48] The *wangliang* is a legendary demon metamorphosed from trees and rocks and mentioned in the biography of Confucius in *Records of History*. According to Ji Yun, a chant used
to subjugate the *zhuyeshen* is referred to in *The Classic of Mountains and Seas* (*Shanhai jing* 山
海經).

revelation when confronted by ghosts. Like Ruan Zhan, the sceptic in stories of this type often learns that the person with whom he debated the existence of spirits is, in fact, a ghost. Such tales, by apparently conceding to the sceptics' viewpoint and then suddenly turning the situation around, gain force by giving an unexpected surprise.[49]

In another variation of the *zhiguai* encounter tale, men disguised as ghosts actually invite supernatural beings to present themselves. One story in *Close Scrutiny* admirably blends the plots of man-denouncing-ghost and man-disguised-as-ghost in a way that validates belief while ridiculing the sceptical position. The story tells of a family tutor who believed that ghosts and spirits were fabricated by Buddhists (*LY* I:15). One of his disciples, Licentiate Tang, plays a trick on him by throwing mud at his window at night and imitating the whining of ghosts. The tutor falls sick and recants from his earlier scepticism, only to discover that he has been deceived. However, it is then that the real revelation comes along, for the disturbance, the whining, does not stop! The story is persuasive because the revelation occurs precisely at the point where sceptics think that they have won.[50]

As can be expected, *Close Scrutiny* includes many stories of fearless men who defied ghosts. Unlike the family tutor discussed above, these undaunted characters do manage to intimidate the ghoulish beings they encounter.[51] A story narrated by one of Ji Yun's ancestors — about a rowdy peasant who vows to catch ghosts so that he can turn them into sheep (by spitting on them) — is told to illustrate that "ghosts bully men only because men fear them" (*RS* II:47). Although presenting ghosts as less powerful than they are commonly thought to be, this tale shows nonetheless that they do exist.

---

[49] Linda Dégh and Andrew Vazsonyi call stories of this type "negative legends." See Dégh and Vazsonyi, "Legend and Belief," in *Folklore Genres*, edited by Dan Ben-Amos (Austin: University of Texas Press, 1976), p. 112.

[50] A comparable story is told by one editor of the *Complete Library* project who believes the fires at his home to have been started by arsonists until he personally witnesses flames shooting out from the roof for no understandable reason (*RS* III:28).

[51] In 1962, several ghost stories of this type from *YWCTBJ* were anthologized by the Chinese National Academy of Sciences in *Bupa gui de gushi* 不怕鬼的故事 (Not Being Afraid of Ghosts) (Hong Kong: Joint Publishing, 1961), but contrary to what the compilers might have thought, the underlying assumption of these tales is that ghosts *do* exist.

Accounts of Supernatural Causation.   Moving beyond the mere documentation of the sightings of spirits, many of the raconteurs in *Close Scrutiny* make claims for an over-arching supernatural order, of which individual spirits are simply embodiments. It is perhaps easier to prove such concepts as karmic retribution (*baoying* 報應) and predeterminism (*qianding* 前定) than to offer empirical evidence of the existence of spirits. For, confronted with reports of sightings, disbelievers can always argue either that the witnesses are mistaken — they may have suffered from delusions — or that the accounts have been fabricated. By contrast, the proponents of beliefs in karmic retribution and predeterminism can invent supernatural explanations for events that might otherwise be dismissed as perfectly natural. In this way, grounding their interpretations on these two principles of supernatural operation, Ji Yun and the raconteurs became engaged in what can be termed "*zhiguai* hermeneutics," taking the "strange" events as signs to be decoded in accordance with beliefs about an unseen, second order of reality.

The raconteurs use the principles of karmic retribution and predeterminism in various ways, some simple and some sophisticated. The case of a filial son saved from a disaster, a recurrent plot in many miracle tales in medieval Europe, is a simple event that can be used to illustrate the workings of supernatural causes. Events that are less amenable to a reasonable explanation — as when a filial son is saved when everybody else dies in the disaster — becomes, then, doubly effective in demonstrating supernatural intervention. In the following account, an entire family is miraculously saved from a fire (*GW* IV:40):

> In Ji'nan in the *jiachen* 甲辰 year of the Qianlong reign [1784] instances of fire were frequent. At the end of the fourth month, a fire broke out on West Street inside the South Gate and spread westward. Because the wind was strong in the narrow alleys, the fire ravaged every pathway. A certain Mr. Zhang 張, whose three thatched huts were found north of the road, could have escaped with his wife and children before the fire hit their home. However, his mother's coffin was there, and although they had planned to move it to avoid the fire, circumstances made that impossible. So the couple, with their four sons and daughters, held onto the coffin, wailing and vowing to follow the dead.
>
> At that time the Assistant Regional Commander of the regiment was in charge of combating the fire. He heard a faint weeping sound. He

ordered some soldiers of the regiment to climb up a house in the back alley. Following the sound a soldier came to the Zhangs' house. A rope was lowered to enable those trapped to climb out.

The husband and wife cried in one voice: "Our mother's coffin is here. How can we leave it behind?" The sons and daughters also shouted: "If our father and mother choose to die with their parents, should we not also die with our own parents?" They too refused to climb up the rope.

In no time at all the fire spread to the house and the soldiers escaped narrowly by taking shelter next door. Assuming that the whole family would be engulfed by the flames, the Assistant Regional Commander could only watch from afar, sighing. When the fire was eventually extinguished, it was discovered on inspection that the Zhangs' house alone was standing firm as ever, unscathed. The turbulent winds had suddenly blown back. The fire had spread north and, taking a detour around the house, had burned up the pawnshop next door before again making its way west. How could it have been possible if it had not been for the protection of the ghosts and deities!

Stories of supernatural causation work on the simple logic of elimination. After all the natural alternatives have been explored and proven inadequate, the supernatural explanation is introduced not only as viable, but also as challenge-proof, so that the only possible ground for refutation is that what happened was a coincidence.

Many narrators were able to advance powerful arguments for supernatural causality by lining up several events to show the working of the otherworldly order. In this case, the advocate of supernatural beliefs has absolute authority in the selection of materials to be narrated, and the shaping of plot becomes crucial in conveying the message. One important organizational device in many of the stories recounted in casual conversations among the late eighteenth-century elite is the juxtaposition of two events that, for the raconteurs, cannot be explained except by reference to the workings of a supernatural order (or again, as coincidence). One may readily question the validity of a supernatural explanation when it is offered for one event — even a "strange" event — but not when the supernatural explanation is offered for two. Indeed, in *Close Scrutiny* a large number of tales are about apparently unconnected events that become significant when brought together. In one tale, a Buddhist monk tells of an incident at the end of the Ming in which the scion of a prestigious family is captured by bandits who were then ravaging the country (*HX* I:18). The leader of the gang humiliates the young man publicly by taking liberties with his wife and concubine. Since, as another captive recalls, the young man's grandfather had an illicit relationship with his servant's wife some years ago, this was interpreted as a case of karmic retribution. In another, an anecdote narrated by Dong Yuandu, a widow is raped by a burglar who four years later is struck dead, supposedly, by the thunder god (*RS* II:4).

More complicated adaptations of this mode of storytelling are brilliantly illustrated by other tales in *Close Scrutiny*. Since sceptics can argue that the conjunction of two events is accidental, some storytellers strengthened their point by telling stories juxtaposing five or six different events and then tagging onto their account a reference to supernatural intervention. One story, told by a Banner military officer stationed in Urumqi, contains five events leading to the capture of an escaped convict: (1) the soldiers shoot some crows, (2) the oxen, startled, run amok, (3) the soldiers chase after the oxen, (4) the oxen knock down a farmer, (5) the soldiers are invited to the farmer's home, where (6) they bump into the convict who previously disappeared (*RS* IV:7). By piling up this sequence of events, the narrator argues for the inexorable working of a supernatural system that achieves its goals through machinations both demonic and divine.[52]

Although the believers attempted to gain much leverage through telling such tales, they did not go unchallenged. As some stories in *Close Scrutiny* show, the sceptics offered alternative explanations that severely undermined the supernatural explanation. Since Ji Yun remained faithful in his recording of the conversational narratives circulated, some entries in *Close Scrutiny* yield more than one interpretation for the same narrative. The various interpretations, given by both the narrators and listeners, appear either in one conversational situation or on several occasions when the tale was being told or retold. The debate then centres on the question of which explanation was most sound.

---

[52] *Bao* 報 is the Chinese word for "reciprocity," "retribution," or "recompense," but the fundamental point to be made about *bao* is that it operates on the principles of both reward and punishment.

Typical of entries reporting a conflict of interpretations is the one on the famous female impersonator in the Qianlong period, Fang Junguan 方俊官 . Fang Junguan tells of a prophetic dream he had at about the age of fourteen: sexually transformed, dressed in silk, and wearing ornaments of jade, he was ushered into a man's bed-chambers.[53] Speaking in favour of a theory of predetermination, he believes that the dream foretold his subsequent corruption by rascals and his entry into "the arena of song and dance." At this point, the entry records two opposed viewpoints (*RS* III:6). First, Ni Chengkuan 倪承寬 (1712–1783) tells Fang Junguan: "Probably you had such a dream because you harboured those thoughts. With those thoughts and that dream, you degenerated. From cause comes effect; the initial cause originated in the heart. How can you ascribe it to predetermined fate?"[54] Ji Yun interprets the dream differently: "I think that actors like Fang Junguan are the scum of the earth. Their degeneration is attributable to what they did in their former lives; they are bearing the brunt of their past actions in this life. One can't say that there is no such thing as pre-determination." Ji Yun thus refutes Ni Chengkuan's argument for "subjective imagination"; he is convinced that what happened to Fang Junguan is understandable in terms of retribution.

A confrontation between two opposite perspectives also occurs in a notice about a county magistrate of Jiaohe 交河 , who was said to have sent his bondservant off with money he had embezzled while in office (*LY* VI:22). The bondservant secretly gives the money to his assistant and claims to have lost it when his boat capsized. At the same time, however, the assistant tries to get away with the money himself but is killed by bandits. In response to the story, Ji Yun's uncle laments that his death shows the work of deities and ghosts, who, "holding the Mirrors of Destiny in their left hand, and the Rosters of Death

---

[53] Fang Junguan was among the best known of eighteenth-century actors who had homosexual liaisons with members of the gentry at Beijing. On the relationships between actors and members of the Qing gentry, see Bret Hinsch, *Passions of the Cut Sleeve: The Male Homosexual Tradition in China* (Berkeley: University of California Press, 1990), pp. 152–156.

[54] Ni Chengkuan came second in the 1754 *jinshi* examination that Ji Yun also took. For Ni's biography, see Qian Yiji 錢儀吉 , comp., *Beizhuan ji* 碑傳集 (Collection of Biographical Inscriptions on Stone) (Jiangsu: Jiangsu shuju 江蘇書局 , 1893), 42:11b.

in their right," dispensed retributive justice to the culprits. However, another person who hears the tale on the same occasion disagrees, offering a different argument:

> Men did all this; the deities and ghosts didn't. If it were as you said, then the spirits sent the bondservant to take away the money because [the magistrate] was destined for retribution. They sent the assistant to take away the money because the bondservant was destined for retribution. They sent bandits to rob and kill the assistant because he, too, was destined for retribution. If the deities and ghosts were supposed to administer retribution, why should men duplicate the work? Doesn't that sound unreasonable?[55]

In this way, dissenting viewpoints found expression even in narratives that voiced a belief in the supernatural. The conflicting interpretations recorded by Ji Yun underscore the extent to which, in the eighteenth century, sceptics and believers shared a common discourse.

Anecdotes about the Inexplicable.   Many of the tales in *Close Scrutiny* simply present supernatural events that do not fall within any explanatory schemes. Such entries are mostly anecdotal.[56] Whereas all the narratives in the previous category are amenable to some readily available explanation, these anecdotes are beyond interpretation: they simply do not "make sense." The sceptic, faced with materials of this nature, can either abandon them as absurd or defer detailed investigation, in the hope that something along the lines of a naturalistic interpretation will eventually turn up. For the believer, however, all phenomena that cannot be rationally accounted for simply become additional evidence for the belief in spirits. Characteristically, individual stories in this category from *Close Scrutiny* constitute statements of faith by imperceptibly blending subjective belief with objective "facts."

The anecdotes about the inexplicable are different from those about karmic retribution or the workings of fate, in that the narration usually revolves around one event rather than several juxtaposed

---

[55] *YWCTBJ*, p. 112.

[56] An "anecdote" is here defined as a short account of an amusing or curious event which is concerned with making a single, definite point.

events. At the end of the anecdote, the narrator often expresses bewilderment or stupefaction and, presumably, expects to elicit the same emotional reaction from the listener or reader. Unlike the encounter tales, the anecdotes contain no discernible pattern or recurrence of motifs,[57] since each tale portrays something never witnessed before. Again, these tales of oddities serve as accumulated empirical evidence for the existence of the spiritual realm, and *Close Scrutiny* is filled with hundreds of them. When considered individually, they may not make much of an impact: their effect is cumulative.

It is not possible, or necessary, to cite here all the anecdotes about the inexplicable recorded in *Close Scrutiny*, but the enormous diversity of narratives in this category can be shown by the following list of randomly chosen examples:

(1) A jade belt buried with a dead person turns into a white snake (*LY* II:10);

(2) An ox in Xian 獻 county (Hebei) gives birth to a unicorn (*LY* II:15);

(3) A horse comes of its own accord to the Guandi 關帝 temple in Urumqi on the first and sixteenth day of each month (*LY* III:3);

(4) Two Buddhist monks and two Daoist priests disappear from a monastery, leaving behind their belongings. Their dead bodies are later found in a dry well miles away, but no wounds are found on their bodies (*LY* V:45);

(5) Words from a poem are found scribbled over the walls of a rocky cave in the home of Ji Yun's grand-uncle. Nobody admits to having done it (*RS* I:63);

(6) For two months a young bee lives inside the vermilion-coloured rattan pillow on which Ji Yun's cousin, Ji Zhao 紀昭 (d. 1770), sleeps (*HX* I:58);

---

[57] For a listing of motifs in supernatural fiction, see Everett F. Bleiler, *The Guide to Supernatural Fiction*, pp. 559–609; for Western folktale motifs, see Stith Thompson, *Motif-Index of Folk Literature* (Bloomington: Indiana University Press, 1955–1958); and for Chinese tale-motifs, see Ting Nai-tung, *A Type Index of Chinese Folktales in the Oral Tradition and Major Works of Non-religious Literature* (Helsinki: Suomolainen Tiedeakatemia, 1978).

(7) Ji Ruchuan's 紀汝傳 (fl. 1808) newly-bought concubine looks just like his first wife, who died earlier (*HX* III:70);

(8) A damsel struts forward at great speed in a whirlwind, covering miles in the twinkling of an eye (*HX* III:30);

(9) A dark brown animal, looking neither like a dog nor a cow, is spotted under a locust-tree (*HX* III:32);

(10) A herd of horses lost at Urumqi reappears in the Hami 哈密 mountains within seven or eight days, though getting there should have taken twenty days (*GW* I:44).

In almost every instance, the short account is followed by some speculation — again, by either the raconteurs or the listeners — about the nature of the event or occurrence. Because Ji Yun's views often blend imperceptibly with those of the storytellers, it is not always clear who is engaged in the speculations. For example, the series of questions raised at the end of the "bee-in-the-pillow" anecdote could be either the narrator's or Ji Yun's:

> Some talked of metamorphosis (*huasheng* 化生). Well, a bee breaks out of a cocoon; it is not metamorphosed from nothing. Even if it were metamorphosed from nothing, why was it not found anywhere else but in the pillow? Why not some other pillow than this one? Without food inside the pillow, why was it still alive after two months? ... The reason behind this is undecipherable.

The inability to arrive at an explanation for the bee contrasts with the certainty expressed in stories of supernatural causation, in which supernatural "reasons" are always adduced and appended to the tale. In anecdotes of the inexplicable both Ji Yun and the raconteurs seem content to allow the events to speak for themselves, and in this way the anecdotes become *intimations* of a supernatural realm. At the end of one entry Ji Yun puts it thus: "There are things that do not follow [rational] principles. But they do exist. That being the case, they must have certain principles of their own. People who hold to their own principles are simply too obstinate."[58]

However, even when the enigma remains unsolved, there is no lack of speculation. In some cases the speculation becomes wild in the

---

[58] *YWCTBJ*, p. 252.

immediate verbal exchange among those listening to the story. In others a continuing debate is recorded in which layers of conjecture are heaped onto story as it is retold on one occasion after another. Story Four, which is exceptional in that it appears as an expanded narrative rather than just as an anecdote, deserves to be quoted in its entirety:

In the Twin Tower Village east of Xian county, two old monks lived together in the same Buddhist monastery. One night, two old Daoist priests knocked at the door, requesting permission to stay overnight. The monks at first refused, whereupon the Daoist priests said: "Although they are two different religions, Buddhism and Daoism are the same in their practice of renunciation. How come you are so narrow-minded?"

Thus they were invited to stay by the monks. The doors remained shut until the next evening. However loudly one shouted, there was no response. The neighbours, climbing over walls, went inside, but the four men were nowhere to be seen. Not a thing had been stolen from the monks' chamber, for the dozens of pounds of gold were still in the priests' baggage. Alarmed, [the neighbours] reported the event to the government officials. The prefectural magistrate, Master Li Qianzhong 栗千鍾,[59] came to investigate, and at this point a shepherd boy claimed that there seemed to be a dead body in a dry well over three miles south of the village. The group went to the well on horseback; there the four corpses were piled up, one on top of another. There were no wounds at all on the bodies.

Li Qianzhong said, "This is not a case of theft, for nothing is missing. Given that they were so decrepit, it could not have been rape. A chance meeting and an overnight stay — there could be no hatred involved. Not a wound on the bodies — it's not murder. Why did all four men die together? That is beyond the limits of reason and credibility. I have judged cases involving men, not ghosts. When no men can be brought to trial, we can settle this case by labelling it 'unsolved.'" He went ahead and reported it to his superiors. Surprisingly enough, one of them, who found nothing disputable or questionable, adopted his report.

Ming Sheng 明晟 of Yingshan 應山 [in present-day Hubei 湖北], a competent magistrate, had this to say: "I heard of this case on arriving at Xian county. For years I turned it over in my mind but couldn't make any sense of it. As to matters of this type, one 'solves' them by refusing to offer a solution. If one presumes upon one's cleverness, one creates a

---

[59] Li Qianzhong, a native of Guangxi 廣西, obtained the *jinshi* degree in 1715.

thousand loopholes. It was said that Li Qianzhong was muddle-headed; I would in fact subscribe to his muddle-headedness."

Of course the solution offered by Ming Sheng (fl. 1723), a magistrate who was Ji Yun's personal friend, is no solution at all — as he himself recognizes. It is Li Qianzhong who makes the explanatory leap by recourse to the supernatural; after his explanation, is there any way to imagine the case without ghosts? Interestingly, Ming Sheng borrows a judicial expression and labels the anecdote an "unsolved case" (*yi'an* 疑案). This is precisely what all inexplicable events are.

Story Ten, about the quick reappearance of the lost horses, is equally mind-boggling. Some of those who hear the story suspect there is a short-cut; others suggest that the mountain gods have accepted the herdsmen's sacrifices and lent a hand. Yet one listener raises an objection: "If the gods could send the horses on, why didn't they send them back to Urumqi?"

The anecdotes about the inexplicable rarely involve ghosts and do not frequently feature the best-known deities and immortals. The supernatural beings that do appear in these anecdotes are the more marginal types, the extremely weird varieties hovering at the edges of human knowledge. In terms of their subject matter and brevity, such anecdotes can be said to belong to a sub-genre of the *zhiguai*: the mirabilia such as those collected in Han and Six Dynasties works like *The Classic of Mountains and Seas* (*Shanhai jing* 山海經) and *Records of Wide-ranging Matters* (*Bowu zhi* 博物志). This sub-genre can be easily differentiated from both the one-event encounter stories (the majority of them "ghost-stories") and the multiple-event narratives of supernatural causation. The multiple-event stories are often comparable to the full-fledged, more "artistically conscious" *chuanqi*, and hence more satisfying.[60] Yet the plotless anecdotes continued to make up the bulk of *zhiguai* compilations through the Qing.

---

[60] Hu Yinglin was the first critic to note that writers of the Tang dynasty used the *xiaoshuo* to display their literary talents. It was Lu Xun, however, who elaborated at length on the contrast between the reporting of facts in the Six Dynasties *zhiguai* and the "artistically conscious" use of narrative material found in the Tang *chuanqi*. See Lu Xun, *Zhongguo xiaoshuo shilue* 中國小説史略 (A Brief History of Chinese Fiction) (Hong Kong: Datong shuju 大通書局, 1959), p. 54; and his "Zhongguo xiaoshuo de lishi bianqian" 中國小説的歷史變遷 (The Historical Changes in Chinese Fiction) in *Zhongguo xiaoshuo shilue*, p. 280.

The three types of narratives in the foregoing discussion are different not just in terms of structure and genre, but also in terms of the strategies deployed in the debate over the existence of spirits. In all three types, the evidence consists of factual accounts — either of firsthand experience or of hearsay — but in each type the evidence makes markedly different demands on the storytellers. Those of encounter stories assert their truth-value; those of accounts of supernatural operations seek to "read" events as signs of another order of reality; and those of inexplicable marvels confront and challenge naturalistic explanations.

The storytelling might have been interpolated into elite conversations and thus used to continue the discussion of the argumentative essays. Viewed thus, the stories can be said to have spiced up the arguments. But it is interesting to contrast the two (the narrative and the essay) as different forms of discourse on the supernatural. For one thing, the stories bear similarities to essays by Yuan Mei and Luo Pin — in the first case to disprove, in the other to prove, supernatural beliefs. But the essays rely much more heavily than the stories on evidence culled from the Classics and Histories. In tune with the intellectual milieu of the eighteenth century, the essays accord the ancient texts more weight, even though the examples they quote often resemble the firsthand accounts of encounters with the supernatural.

Furthermore, if we see the narrative evidence as being manipulated by storytellers intent on making inferences and drawing conclusions, then the stories stand or fall by their ability or failure to vindicate belief. Certainly, in *Close Scrutiny*, the argument made in a story is occasionally eclipsed by satire, wit or humour. But it would be hard to say for sure that the *zhiguai* is less effective than the essay. For one thing, the evaluation of the narrative as argument is complicated by the fact that the tales in *Close Scrutiny*, as in other *zhiguai* collections of the time, were printed (and read) in huge compilations. The great number of stories must have reinforced the "message" and thus worked cumulatively to induce belief.

To sum up, the dialectical opposition between sceptical views and beliefs in the supernatural created the groundwork for the narratives of the strange recorded in *Close Scrutiny*, even though, in that collection, the believers appear to have gained the upperhand. All three types of stories considered here challenge sceptical rationalism and affirm the realm of spirits. That many (if not all) of the storytellers are intensely engaged in their tales is itself strong evidence of their belief. In fact, Ji Yun's collection, in revealing how powerful the belief in the supernatural was among the eighteenth-century elite, forces us to question the view still prevalent today that the traditional elite consisted of "Confucian rationalists" who deplored the supernatural.

In the last two chapters, we have looked in depth at the oral discourse on the supernatural in the late eighteenth century through examining the tales in *Close Scrutiny*. The motives behind the storytelling is shown to be complex and diverse, although we have as yet excluded the didactic motivation (which is, after all, built upon a fascination with the supernatural as well as a concomitant belief in it). Also excluded is attempt to fathom the realm of spirits. It is precisely to this that we shall now turn.

Chapter 4

Boxue: *Understanding the Supernatural*

> When insentient beings change into sentient beings such as birds or insects, or when foxes and badgers take on human form — are these not the strangest of all strange things? Thus, the universe and all things are without a single exception strange and wondrous when examined carefully.
>
> — *Motoori Norinaga*

Undeniably, an intrinsic fascination with the supernatural and a concern to vindicate its existence were both important motivations behind the storytelling in and the compilation of *Close Scrutiny*. They gave rise to the detailed descriptions of the character, functioning, and norms of the spiritual realm. The collection is replete not only with information about the world of ghosts, fox-spirits, demons and deities, but also with explanations for unwieldy phenomena. This explains why the activities of both Ji Yun (who compiled) and the narrators (who reported) need to be understood as more than plain storytelling. If one bears in mind one of the traditional arguments used to valorize the *zhiguai* — namely, that it allows one to exhibit one's broad learning — then one will see in *Close Scrutiny* a link between the telling of *zhiguai* stories and a conscious display of knowledge of the supernatural. The storytelling is carried out in the context of an attempt to widen the reader's "intellectual" horizons.

As with the didactic argument, the justification of *zhiguai* by the *boxue* argument is often viewed with scepticism, especially by twentieth-century readers. This makes necessary a close analysis of *Close Scrutiny*, which documents most clearly the attitudes of the raconteurs and of Ji Yun — especially the latter, since the manipulating hand of the compiler is everywhere in evidence. The attempt to apprehend the strange and to explain phenomena unexplainable at first sight is definitely a crucial aspect of the presentation of *zhiguai* stories in *Close Scrutiny*, and it had an impact on the particular shape which the collection took.

While earlier collections of *zhiguai* display similar orientations, in its approach to the supernatural *Close Scrutiny* is distinctly a product of its own time. To put it simply: *Close Scrutiny* is cast specifically in the dominant mode of intellectual discourse in the eighteenth century. It cannot be fully understood unless read against the prevailing scholarly trend of "searching for evidence." It is, in the first place, a collection of data for detailed investigation. However, while the search for proof is undertaken with full seriousness and interpretations are freely given, Ji Yun never seeks to offer one grand, systematic, over-arching scheme of explanation for diverse strange phenomena and incidents. The hallmark of the exploration of the strange in *Close Scrutiny* is that it is haphazard and piecemeal, and at most there are only intimations of a cosmology — and a partial one at that. In fact, the occasional consistency in Ji Yun's explanations is only the result of his adopting the neo-Confucian analytic systems, in particular one of them, that of *qi*. But this is perhaps as it should be: of all things, the "strange" is indeed the one that most fully stretched human understanding to its limits.

Previously we noted how strongly Ji Yun emphasized the authen-ticity of the materials he collected: any doubt cast on the existence of spirits could be detrimental to *zhiguai* didactics. This stress on verifi-ability is relevant to Ji Yun's purposes in another way. As a scholar, an intellectual, and very much a man of his own time, he may have found himself compelled to present his supernatural materials in a way acceptable to his readership, which consisted of people like himself. Indeed, we can surmise that few of the scholars of his time would have felt uncomfortable with *zhiguai* stories; rather, many would have been amused to read the vast assemblage of bizarre accounts couched in a form that they were familiar with. In casting his stories in terms of a study of empirical, factual (albeit unorthodox) evidence, Ji Yun obviously has his readers' interests at heart.

Hence *Close Scrutiny* must be related to the dominant mode of Qing intellectual discourse for it to be fully appreciated. It was affected by the evidential approach, which stressed a commitment to objective evidence and an inductive method. This was in contrast to neo-Confucian analysis, with its (often condemned) preference for abstract conceptual categories and its use of deductive norms. What the "evidential approach to the supernatural" means will be made clear in the present chapter. Throughout I shall mainly be referring to Ji Yun's opinions, most of which are directly appended to the stories, but it needs to be remembered that his views were also often expressed in the context of opinions voiced by others in his circle, with which he either agreed or disagreed. What this amounts to is that, as with the debate on belief and disbelief, the understanding of the supernatural in *Close Scrutiny* is as much characteristic of an entire social group in a particular historical moment as it is of Ji Yun's.

Intellectual Background

To set the stage for the following discussion, it will help to sketch briefly the sort of intellectual atmosphere in which Ji Yun found himself, especially the concern for "investigation of things." In an impressive series of scholarly articles, Yu Ying-shih 余英時 has analysed the "shift of emphasis in neo-Confucianism from the moral element to the intellectual element" in the early Qing period.[1] He explains the foundations on which eighteenth-century Confucian intellectualism was built with reference to leading figures like Dai Zhen. Put simply, the ascendancy of the philological movement was a natural consequence of the increased focus on what Zhu Xi called the "investigation of things" and "extension of knowledge," and it reflected a growing emphasis placed on the mind's ability to know myriad phenomena. While it may be a bit far-fetched to speak of the

---

[1] Yu Ying-shih, "Tai Chen and the Chu Hsi Tradition," in *Essays in Commemoration of the Golden Jubilee of the Fung Ping Shan Library (1923–82)*, edited by Chan Ping-leung, *et al.* (Hong Kong: Hong Kong University Press, 1982), p. 380. Yu's articles on the subject are numerous, but see especially "Towards an Interpretation of the Intellectual Transition in Seventeenth-century China," *Journal of the American Oriental Society*, vol. 100, no. 2 (1980), pp. 115–125, and "Some Preliminary Observations on the Rise of Ch'ing Confucian Intellectualism," *Qinghua xuebao* 清華學報, new series 11 (1975), pp. 1–20.

germination of a scientific spirit in China,[2] there is little doubt that there happened to prevail in the scholarly realm a commitment to knowledge for its own sake and an eagerness to delve into concrete causes.

That Ji Yun successfully accommodates his collection to readers with such dispositions can be demonstrated. *Close Scrutiny* distinguishes itself by being more than a mere sampling of *zhiguai* tales; it is a *zhiguai* collection couched very clearly in the evidential mode. Anomalous phenomena are presented not as facts to be marvelled at, as in earlier centuries; they are proven to be real, thus lending support to belief in the supernatural. Ji Yun's approach is exploratory and inductive, as seen in the explanations he offers whenever he can. In doing so, he resorts to a wide arsenal of interpretive tools.

That readers in Ji Yun's time were aware of the so-called *boxue* dimensions of *Close Scrutiny* is made clear by Sheng Shiyan, who prefaced the collection. He speaks of the reactions of probably the first readers of the collection:

> I have often noted that the collections by Ji Yun, though purportedly *xiaoshuo*, embody teachings; there is nothing said that is not of universal application. This is known to all under Heaven. In the clarification of names and principles, he is meticulous and penetrates to the smallest detail. In alluding to ancient meanings, he shows his solid foundations as well as his knowledgeability.[3]

Hence readers were said to be reading the collection as much for the insights into and knowledge of the world conveyed by the author as for the teachings embedded therein. To the modern reader trained to respond aesthetically to literature, praising an author of a short-story collection for his knowledgeability may seem unusual; however, this was certainly not the case here, as the preface shows.

---

[2] Evidential methods can be said to be "scientific" only in their respect for accuracy and inductive verification. Nowhere do they approach Western scientific methods. The scholarly aspect of *kaozheng*, specifically, differentiates it from Western notions of scientific procedure. Where one starts from scratch in the search for truth, the other seeks corroboration primarily in ancient texts — the contrast, in validation theory, cannot be more pronounced.

[3] *YWCYBJ*, p. 472.

A clearer understanding of Ji Yun's "evidential" approach to *zhiguai* material is possible by placing him against Dai Zhen, undoubtedly the leading thinker of the age. There is no suggestion here that there was any direct influence between the two, but a glance at Dai Zhen's ideas sheds light on facets of Ji Yun's thinking. The intellectual affinity shared by them also furnishes some proof that a commonality of interest was sustained by a particular elite group at the time. The attempt to detect links between Ji Yun and Dai Zhen is not unwarranted: they were related, in real life and in thought, in more ways than one. It is well-known that both were staunchly anti-Cheng-Zhu,[4] and Dai Zhen's attacks on the neo-Confucian insistence on the suppression of human desires as the guiding principle of moral behaviour are echoed in many of Ji Yun's comments recorded in *Close Scrutiny*. The extent of mutual influence has been discussed by Yu Ying-shih, who suggests that both attempted to undermine Song Confucianism, though Ji Yun did so "not only in high culture but in popular culture as well" in his *Close Scrutiny*.[5]

---

[4] See *Eminent Chinese of the Ch'ing Period* (1644–1912), pp. 122–123. Among the other Qianlong scholars who spoke against the Cheng-Zhu school were Qian Daxin and Zhu Yun. In general, during the halcyon days of Han learning in the eighteenth century, adherents of Song learning were few and defenceless in the face of repeated attacks. Practically the only person of note is Yao Nai who, it is sometimes argued, became an advocate for the Song-Ming neo-Confucians owing to his rejection by Dai Zhen. It was not until the early nineteenth century that there was a revival of Song learning with the emergence of scholars like Fang Dongshu, who severely criticized philological methods. The complicated scenario has been treated by He Yousen 何佑森, "Qingdai Han Song zhi zheng pingyi" 清代漢宋之爭平議 (An Evaluation of the Han-Song Dispute in the Qing Dynasty), *Wenshizhe xuebao* 文史哲學報, vol. 27 (1978), pp. 97–113; Yu Ying-shih, "Tai Chen's Choice between Philosophy and Philology," *Asia Major*, third series, pt. 1 (1989), pp. 79–108; and Hu Jiancai 胡健財, "Dai Zhen fan Cheng Zhu sixiang zhi yanjiu" 戴震反程朱思想之研究 (A Study of the Anti-neo-Confucian Thought of Dai Zhen) (M.A. thesis, National Chengchi University 政治大學, 1989). For descriptive surveys of important Song learning and Han learning scholars through the entire Qing period, see the sections on "Xingli lei" 性理類 (Category: Principles) and "Jingshu lei" 經書類 (Category: Classics) of Xu Ke, *Qingbai leichao*, vol. 7. For a discussion of the anti-Cheng-Zhu perspective of *YWCTBJ*, see Hu Yimin 胡益民, "*Yuewei caotang biji* fan lixue wenti xinlun" 閲微草堂筆記反理學問題新論 (A New Approach to the Question of Anti-Neo-Confucianism in the *Yuewei caotang biji*), *Wenxue yichan* 文學遺產, no. 2 (1990), pp. 120–125.

[5] Yu Ying-shih, "Tai Chen's Choice between Philosophy and Philology," p. 103.

Innumerable instances can be cited from *Close Scrutiny* to illustrate the new brand of morality that Ji Yun advocated,[6] as well as the repugnance he shared with Dai Zhen for the moral obtuseness of "talk-mongers" of the Cheng-Zhu persuasion.[7] In the main, he encouraged the exercise of personal judgments in each individual situation rather than adherence to the rigid ethical strictures of moralists. Such concern with the individual situation as a manifestation of understandable general principles is one of the central tenets of Dai Zhen's philosophy, and it colours Ji Yun's approach to supernatural occurrences too.

Besides this, the ideas expressed in Dai Zhen's seminal work, *Disquisition on the Meanings of Terms in the Mencius* (*Mengzi ziyi shuzheng* 孟子字義疏證), provide a fruitful point of departure in the comparison attempted here. A unique contribution of Dai Zhen is the redefinition of the concept of *li* 理 (principle) — in Cheng-Zhu neo-Confucianism, an abstraction opposed to human desires — as the "internal texture" (*tiaoli* 條理) of miscellaneous phenomena. His philosophy reflects the general movement, over a prolonged historical period that began with the demise of the Ming in the seventeenth century, from what was often called "empty speculation" about metaphysical realities towards focusing attention on uncovering the principles resident in things themselves. As recent scholars of Qing intellectual history have demonstrated, a belief is expressed by Dai Zhen and by others in intellectual circles of his time that philology and close textual study — evidential study, that is — could serve as useful tools in the objective discovery of such principles.[8]

---

[6] See, for instance, the story of the widow who abandoned her baby in order to save her mother-in-law and was reproved by the "talk-mongers" (*HX* II:34) as well as the story of the man who refused to awaken a mother when her child was falling into a well because "males and females should keep a respectable distance" (*GW* IV:45).

[7] For a study of the anti-Cheng-Zhu polemics in *YWCTBJ*, see Xu Zhenqian 徐鎮乾, "Shilun *Yuewei caotang biji* fan lixue de deshi" 試論閱微草堂筆記反理學的得失 (A Preliminary Study of the Merits and Drawbacks in the Attack on Neo-Confucianism by the *Yuewei caotang biji*), *Zhejiang shifan xueyuan xuebao sheke ban* 浙江師範學院學報社科版, no. 3 (1984), pp. 19–26. Such polemics, however, was only part of Ji Yun's moral vision and not an end in itself.

[8] For a concise introduction to the philosophical thought of Dai Zhen as well as a translation of his *Yuan shan* 原善, see Cheng Chung-ying, *Inquiry into Goodness: A Translation of the Yüan Shan, with an Introductory Essay* (Honolulu: East-West Center Press, 1971). Dai

The ascendancy of the evidential approach in the eighteenth century was founded on a belief that things are understandable and that human understanding is possible. While it would be stretching the point to argue that the eighteenth century in China is an "Age of Reason" or even her "Augustan period,"[9] the concern for giving proper explanations and for offering concrete proofs for one's assertions is nevertheless the hallmark of intellectual undertakings of this era. While such a mode of inquiry was popular among scholars at the time, Dai Zhen stresses more strongly than most the immense power of human reason. Using light as a metaphor for the ratiocinative faculties of the human mind, he has this to say in *Disquisition*:

> Reasoning is the ability exercised by the mind-heart ... The extent of discernment differs [from one creature to another]. It can be compared to light shining on things: when weak, it reveals things close by. What is revealed clearly will not be misinterpreted; otherwise doubt and misunderstanding arise. One arrives at the principle by entertaining no errors. A great light reveals things far off: one discovers more principles and loses few.[10]

In this way Dai Zhen, confident that man differs from animals in his capacity for using his intellect, voices a prevailing idea of Ji Yun's time.

Zhen's seminal work, the *Mengzi ziyi shuzheng*, is translated in Chin Ann-ping and Mansfield Freeman, *Tai Chen on Mencius: Explorations in Words and Meaning* (New Haven: Yale University Press, 1990).

[9] It is Hou Jian 侯健 who compares seventeenth- and eighteenth-century China to the Age of Reason in Europe and Helen Dunstan who talks of the eighteenth century as "China's Augustan Age." See Hou Jian, "*Yuewei caotang biji* de lixing zhuyi" 閱微草堂筆記的理性主義 (Rationalism in the *Yuewei caotang biji*), in *Zhongguo xiaoshuo bijiao yanjiu* 中國小説比較研究 (Comparative Studies on Chinese Fiction) (Taibei: Dongda chubanshe 東大出版社, 1985), p. 151; and Helen Dunstan, "Review (of R. Kent Guy's *The Emperor's Four Treasuries*)," *Harvard Journal of Asiatic Studies*, vol. 49, no. 2 (1989), p. 659. Even Western scholars like James Sambrook view such period designations as inadequate and misleading clichés; see Sambrook, *The Eighteenth Century: The Intellectual and Cultural Context of English Literature, 1700–1789* (London: Longman, 1986), pp. 206–211. Also, the stress in the term "Age of Reason" was on abstract reason, not empirical reason (for which Francis Bacon would be the *locus classicus* a century or more earlier).

[10] *Dai Zhen zhexue zhuzuo xuanzhu* 戴震哲學著作選注 (Selected Philosophical Works of Dai Zhen, with Annotations), edited by An Zhenghui 安正輝 (Beijing: Zhonghua shuju 中華書局, 1980), pp. 73–74.

The ensuing discussion indeed takes off from this point. Ji Yun in his collection of *zhiguai* tales in fact exemplifies this mood of intellectual enquiry by attempts to present his facts in such a way as to invite satisfactory explanations. The problem is that his task is, from one angle at least, most formidable. What, after all, is less accessible to logical understanding than the realm of spooks and bogeys? It is because he is dealing with the unseen, supernatural realm that his explanations are shifting, tentative, and in many places open to queries. Yet he had a host of predecessors in Chinese intellectual history who provided the ways and the means. It has been remarked that there are different types of rationalities, as well as different spheres of life which can be rationalized.[11] That is clearly revealed in what can be called the rational approach to supernaturalism, deployed by Zhu Xi as much as Ji Yun. It is interesting to see how, in *Close Scrutiny*, Ji Yun first looks at bits and pieces of evidence, interprets and explains the eerie landscape of the spirits, and finally presents full-scale explanations.

That the supernatural realm can be a viable object for the "investigation of things" undertaken by a Confucian should come as little surprise. As Irene Bloom remarked, "a distinction between the divine and the natural or between faith and reason has scarcely any analogue in the history of Chinese thought."[12] There is no reason for the Confucian to limit his sphere of inquiry to the observable world: no distinction is seen between nature and the supernatural; both are valid fields of study. The interconnectedness of what the West would conceive of as two realms enables Ji Yun, for instance, to move from one to the other with remarkable ease and facility. Similar laws can be seen to govern both. As *Close Scrutiny* shows, it is not at all difficult to amass evidence for an empirical study of supernatural events and phenomena.

The study of anomalies could very well constitute one of the newly-emerging disciplines. Eighteenth-century scholars attempted to

---

[11] Max Weber goes so far as to say, "What is rational from one point of view may be irrational from another." Weber, *The Protestant Ethic and the Spirit of Capitalism*, translated by Talcott Parsons (New York: Scribner's Sons, 1958), p. 26.

[12] Irene Bloom, *Knowledge Painfully Acquired: The K'un-chih chi by Lo Ch'in-shun* (New York: Columbia University Press, 1987), p. 41.

define and classify the fields of human knowledge in one bibliographic project after another. The compilation of the critical abstracts in *An Annotated Catalogue*, for which Ji Yun is largely responsible, could on the one hand be regarded as an attempt at generic definition; on the other hand, it is an effort to enhance research by delineating carefully the parameters of different disciplines. The emergence in the mid-Qing of new, specialized fields of scholarship like the study of rhymes and ancient pronunciations, epigraphy, and archaeology, has often been noted. Ji Yun's study of the supernatural, too, was a branch of knowledge that, having been pursued for centuries, was once again brought to the forefront.

Emulation of the Evidential Approach

Regarding Ji Yun's emulation of the evidential mode, we will look at three of the main characteristics of evidential research as they affect the writing of the stories of *Close Scrutiny*: the concern for comprehensive coverage, the pursuit of verifiability, and the attempt to generate plausible explanatory rules. However, we will not attempt to draw extensive parallels between Ji Yun's method and the methods of adherents of the evidential school. The very marked difference in concerns precludes such a possibility. Those carrying out research in the evidential mode in the Qing — for instance, Wang Mingsheng, Yan Ruoju 閻若據 (1636–1704), and Duan Yucai 段玉裁 (1735–1815), besides Dai Zhen — centred their work (on philology, ancient pronunciations, and so on) around clearer explication of the Classics. They were almost entirely preoccupied with documentary, not physical, evidence, and the generalizations they drew from a consideration of particulars were used mostly to facilitate reconstructions of old texts; they often strove to achieve an accurate picture of the origin and historical development of matters like customs and institutions. None of these is applicable to Ji Yun. What he shared with these researchers was a similarity in methodological *orientation* and above all an essentially sceptical attitude which stressed "looking at concrete things for what they are" (*shishi qiu shi* 實是求是).

Collecting Information. The eighteenth century in China saw the grand enterprises of "collecting, categorizing and clarifying," and attitudes fostered by these efforts were doubtless carried over not just to *Close Scrutiny* but also to other *zhiguai* collections of the period. A few examples can be cited from Yuan Mei's two collections of *What the Master Would Not Discuss*. He says, for instance, that cadavers move because a dead body, completely *yin* in its nature, becomes magnetically attracted to the *yang* essence emitted by a living person, and thus cadavers follow men about. One is also advised not to sleep with one's soles against those of a cadaver, for *yang* energy is easily discharged through the soles. In one entry, Yuan Mei notes the fact that the *hun*-soul is active while the *po* 魄-soul is dull. Hence a dead body can be revived when the *hun*-soul returns to attach itself to the body, but as soon as the *hun*-soul leaves again, the body falls limp and becomes lifeless.[13] Elsewhere there are entries on three kinds of drought-demons, the special behaviour of the ghost of a man eaten by a tiger, and ghosts' fears of strong wind, extreme cold, and hunger.[14] From this perspective, *What the Master Would Not Discuss*, much like *Close Scrutiny*, appears as an encyclopaedia of information on the supernatural.

The multitudinous accounts of the supernatural thus reveal a cosmos inhabited not only by human beings but also by demons, ghosts and ghoulish beings. With occasional glimpses of the other realm only accorded to the chosen few, everybody else has to rely on the "tales" in *zhiguai* collections for the knowledge that would enable him or her to relate to the spiritual world in a meaningful way. Such knowledge would presumably help in the eventuality of a real-life encounter. From innumerable anecdotes in *zhiguai* collections one also knows about the disasters that befall those who, ignorant of the proper codes of behaviour, offend the inhabitants of the supernatural realm.

To say the least, one could even be punished for ignorance of the proprieties to be observed in interacting with supernatural beings. Countless stories in eighteenth-century *zhiguai* collections describe how men were faulted for this, but one kind of misconduct involved, interestingly enough, urinating in "inappropriate" places. In *Close*

---

[13] See "Shi ben" 屍奔 (Running Cadavers), *ZBY*, pp. 512–513, and "Nanchang shiren" 南昌士人 (The Scholar of Nanchang), *ZBY*, p. 3.

[14] See "Hanba you sanzhong" 旱魃有三種 (Three Types of Drought-demons), *ZBY*, p. 490; and "Liehu shuo hu" 獵戶說虎 (Hunters Talking about Tigers), *ZBY*, pp. 560–563.

Scrutiny there is a story of a farmer who falls sick after he urinates into the mouth of a female ancestor's skull (in the process he exposed his genitals to the ancestor). *What the Master Would Not Discuss* contains a tale of a woman who loses her undergarments when she relieves herself in a sorghum field. She is still wondering about it when an offended ghost comes to her house that night to claim her husband's head. Exactly the same account is given in Yue Jun's *Hearsay Accounts*, which also includes a commentator cautioning women against urinating in the open. Finally, again in *Hearsay Accounts*, a drunkard is possessed by a spirit after he urinates right into the mouth of a skull.[15] Such tales are indubitably of some "educational" value to the reader, and they also show the importance of observing rules of propriety. After all, ghosts are a part of the human world and deserve to be treated on an equal footing.

Such a model for presenting *zhiguai* tales was adhered to quite consistently in *Close Scrutiny*. In particular, information about fox-spirits is abundant. It is a fact which is understandable, given the intimacy between human beings and fox-spirits, who often become friends, intermarry, or live under the same roof.[16] The details given about the fox-spirit in a conversation between Liu Shitui 劉師退 , a pedantic scholar, and a fox-spirit can be read as a guide to the various kinds of fox-spirits one is likely to meet (*RS* IV:36). The fox-spirit explains two paths of spiritual cultivation:

> Those [fox-spirits] who seek alchemical transformations and try to gather spiritual essences are like scholars who attain fame by studying diligently. Those who entice men and deplete them of their sexual energies for their own benefit are taking short-cuts in order to achieve their goal

---

[15] See *YWCTBJ*, p. 71; *LYWB*, 8:14a–14b; *Ershi lu*, pp. 138–139 and p. 141.

[16] Important studies of the fox-spirit as well as foxlore include: J. J. M. de Groot, *The Religion of the Chinese* (Westport, Conn.: Hyperion Press, 1980), vols. 4 and 5; Nishioka Haruhiko 西岡晴彦 , "Hōjō kō" 狐妖考 (On Fox-spirits), *Tōkyō Shinagaku hō* 東京支那學報 , vol. 14 (1968), pp. 59–73; Uchida Michio 内田道夫, "Hōjō" 狐妖 (The Fox Demon), *Tōyōgaku* 東洋學, vol. 6 (1961), pp. 12–22; Fatima Wu, "Foxes in Chinese Supernatural Tales," Parts I and II, *Tamkang Review*, vol. 17, no. 2 (1986), pp. 121–153 and vol. 17, no. 3 (1986), pp. 263–294. On the fox-spirit as succubus, see N. H. van Straten, *Concepts of Health, Disease and Vitality in Traditional Chinese Society: A Psychological Interpretation* (Wiesbaden: Steiner, 1983), pp. 77–89.

quickly. But only [the former] can roam the islands of the immortals and ascend to the celestial realms; [the latter], by bringing harm to too many lives, often violate the code of Heaven.[17]

He then proceeds to note that the behaviour of fox-spirits is overseen by subterranean judges who mete out punishments to those who have erred; that according to supernatural law, fox-spirits give birth to human babies but not vice versa; that licentiousness among fox-spirits is excusable; and that fox-spirits on a low level of spiritual cultivation live in the wilderness while others who have attained the Way mix freely with mankind.[18] All in all, there is no mistaking that *Close Scrutiny* responds to the general reader's thirst for information about the fox-spirit and about the supernatural realm.

Verifying Reports. *Close Scrutiny* records in detail the conditions of transmission of individual tales, as well as the specifics of time and place for recorded events. This is comparable to the evidential approach to assembled data, in which a premium is put on "truthful" facts that are either textual or observable in the world of everyday life. Of all the means of verification, the use of antecedents was a particularly noticeable strategy, and although citations alone did not constitute research on evidence, references to previous records provided a foundation for further investigation. In the case of the unlikely events recorded in Ji Yun's collection, previous occurrences functioned to prove the authenticity of more recent events. The previous instances may have been reported elsewhere, or they could simply be other entries in *Close Scrutiny*. The latter case demonstrates how the entire collection can be said to work by a principle of corroboration, whereby the events gathered mutually "prove" each other's validity: a super-

---

[17] Ji Yun's display of scholarship in *YWCTBJ* is discussed by Goto Kuniko 五嶋久彌子, "*Etsubi sōdō hikki* ni miru Ki In no gakumonron" 閲微草堂筆記に見る紀昀の學問論 (Ji Yun's View of Learning as Seen in the *Yuewei caotang biji*), *Ochanomizu Joshi Daigaku bungaku kaihō*, vol. 6 (1987), pp. 69–88. The quotation is found in *YWCTBJ*, pp. 216–217.

[18] For some time it was widely known that foxes who did not achieve immortality status remained fox-demons (*huyao* 狐妖), and those that did became fox-immortals (*huxian* 狐仙) or celestial fox-spirits (*tianhu* 天狐). This was mentioned, for instance, in Guo Pu's 郭璞 (276–324) *Records from within the Recondite* (*Xuanzhong ji* 玄中記) and Ge Hong's *The Master Who Embraces Simplicity* (*Baopu zi* 抱朴子).

natural incident reported earlier proves the reliability of a later report.

Ji Yun's antecedents from outside of *Close Scrutiny* are cited primarily from earlier *zhiguai* and secondarily from the histories. His methods can be illustrated with a handful of examples. The first concerns the sighting of a girl who charges forward at great speed in a whirlwind and is able to cover miles almost instantaneously (*HX* III:30, noted earlier). With regard to this narrative, Ji Yun explains to his uncle that she is in fact a malignant spirit, whose appearance has previously been recorded in *Chronicles of Diverse Anomalies* (*Boyi zhuan* 博異傳).[19] Also, the exotic beast that looks partly like a dog and partly like a cow, is, according to Ji Yun, the tree-demon alluded to in *Records of History*, in Cao Pi's 曹丕 (187–226) *An Array of Anomalies* (*Lieyi zhuan* 列異傳), and in the writings of Yu Xin 庾信 (513–581) and Liu Zongyuan 柳宗元 (773–819).[20]

Close Scrutiny includes numerous accounts of ghosts who die unnatural deaths (often by hanging themselves) seeking human substitutes, as well as the "returning goblin" that emerges from a coffin in the form of a bird a few days after somebody dies.[21] The nature of the returning goblin is explained by Ji Yun with reference to two earlier records: in Zhang Du's 張讀 (?–ca. 853) *Records from the Chamber of Expositions* (*Xuanshi zhi* 宣室志) and Xu Xuan's *Records Examining Spirits*. A final example involves the various types of ghosts, and in the entry in question antecedents are cited for phenomena Ji Yun himself witnessed. Ji Yun's speculations are tagged onto the end (*LX* I:4):

> Both Hu Taichu 胡太初 , the Vice Censor-in-Chief, and the recluse Luo Liangfeng 羅兩峰 [Luo Pin] can see ghosts. So too can Heng Lantai 恆蘭台 , the Academician of the Grand Secretariat, though not all the time.

---

[19] The flying *yaksha* was seen by a monk as being pursued by the heavenly deities; see Li Fang, ed., *Taiping guangji*, chap. 357 (1753, reprint; Taibei: Xinxing shuju 新興書局, 1962). Neither the author nor the date of *Chronicles of Diverse Anomalies*, however, can be identified.

[20] *YWCTBJ*, p. 304.

[21] See also *LY* III:4, *HX* II:41, *HX* II:42, *HX* II:63, and *GW* III:21. According to Ji Yun, sublunary law had it that people taking their lives too lightly would not be promptly sent on to the wheel of rebirth. *YWCTBJ*, p. 281.

In the fifth month of the *wuwu* 戊午 year [1798], while at my summer mountain retreat, this became the subject of a casual conversation.

According to Lantai, ghosts are shaped like men, but they stare straight ahead. The clothes they wear hang on their bodies in strips which, tied together, fall loosely about them. In these ways they are slightly different from human beings. They are of the substance of smoke and fog, vaguely like human shadows when you look closely at them. From a side view, they appear in their entirety; but from the front only half of their bodies is visible, the other half as though concealed in a wall. They are either black or grey. They stand aloof, always keeping a distance from men. On occasions when they fail to stay away, they may huddle together in a corner or disappear into a well, coming out stealthily when men have passed by. One should not be startled if one comes across them under a dim light on a dark night, or on an evening with gloomy clouds.

Lantai's account resembles roughly what Hu Taichu and Luo Liangfeng have said, though it has greater descriptive detail. Such are the principles in the realms of the living and the dead. The ghosts are black or grey because they are the vestigial elements of men, whose ether is dispersed gradually until it becomes non-existent. Hence according to *Zuo's Commentary*, new ghosts are big and old ones small. Could that be attributed to the fact that ether can be thick or thin, and colours are weak or strong?

By citing from *Zuo's Commentary* Ji Yun closes the discussion on the sizes of various types of ghosts neatly. In this case textual evidence is made to lend support to experiential evidence.[22]

Illustrating Principles. Having accumulated verifiable data from diverse sources, Ji Yun works on them analytically, with the aim of drawing conclusions of general applicability. It is possible to see connections between the efforts of Ji Yun to develop explanations for the supernatural and the contemporary emphasis on uncovering principles through the objective study of pertinent facts. Such efforts set Ji Yun apart from *zhiguai* compilers who did not go beyond mere reportage.

---

[22] See "Wengong ernian" 文公二年 (The Second Year of the Duke of Wen), in *Chunqiu Zuozhuan baihua xinjie* 春秋左傳白話新解 (The *Chunqiu Zuozhuan*, Newly Annotated) (Taibei: Wenhua tushu gongsi 文化圖書公司, 1969), p. 107.

A decisive shift in strategy had thus occurred in the course of centuries of *zhiguai* recording: while earlier instances of this genre emphasized the "strangeness," the alien quality of the accounts, Ji Yun took pains to show the way in which such events followed rules and principles of their own that were within the reaches of human understanding. If the Six Dynasties interpreted bizarre phenomena as deviant, Ji Yun approached them from an assumption that the supernatural can be understood and is even susceptible to quasi-rational analysis.

An initial sign of Ji Yun's steadfast adherence to such an exploratory method is his matter-of-fact acknowledgement that certain phenomena simply prove to be inexplicable. He does not force his arguments when confronted with such phenomena, and yet he does not abandon them as absurd. Characteristically, in every instance listed below, Ji Yun simply remarks that "the [underlying] principle is beyond the reach of reason" (*li buke jie* 理不可解):

(1) Zhang Xuan'er 張鉉耳 composes a quatrain in his dream that someone unknown to him has already written (*LY* II:18).

(2) A friend of Ji Yun's resembles exactly the poet Tao Qian as portrayed in a scroll (*LY* II:18).

(3) A special type of lotus is found north of the Great Wall that disappears immediately into the snow when men come to look for it (could the Mountain-gods have hidden it?) (*LY* III:27).

(4) Visitors to the netherworld never meet ghosts from any part of the world but China (*RS* I:7).

(5) The immortals of early times like those noted by Liu Xiang 劉向 (ca. 76–ca. 6 B.C.) in *Biographies of Various Immortals* (*Liexian zhuan* 列仙傳) have all but disappeared (*RS* I:7).

(6) The weather turns unseasonably cold when the Dragon-god controlling snowfalls is roused (*RS* II:53).

(7) A phrase from Su Shi's "Rhapsody on the Red Cliff" ("Chibi fu" 赤壁賦) is revealed in the texture of a rock (*HX* I:6).

(8) Eggs emit light at night (*HX* I:65).

(9) The question whether there is one Stove-god or one to each household (Who discharged the Stove-god? Would there be too many of them? What happens to Stove-gods assigned to families that have moved?) (*HX* III:5).

(10) The gold ingot of the Tang, when swallowed in its powdered form, is efficacious in healing bone fractures (*HX* III:78).[23]

By thus frankly admitting the limits of his own ability to discover principles, Ji Yun secures the reader's confidence in the objective standards he uses. On the other hand, by withholding comment, he implies that the possibility of interpretation is not ruled out, although he is not prepared to offer an interpretation of his own.

Such being the case, when it came to phenomena that *were* explicable in his terms, Ji Yun pressed his arguments unrelentingly. It must be noted, however, that Ji Yun sought to adhere to the facts of a case; he allowed what might be considered proper evidential methods to constrain him. I cite here a few cases of his evidential analysis where he stresses his adamant adherence to the principle of being "reasonable" (*you li* 有理). (In the next section we will look at the underlying groundwork on which most of his explanations are in fact predicated.)

The typical method in which Ji Yun carries out his "investigation of principles" can be illustrated by the debate concerning why several people have taken their own lives at a mountain cliff at Jehol (*HX* III:25). Most chose to explain the deaths by saying that the ghost of one who stumbled over the cliff had returned to seek human substitutes. Ji Yun, however, contests the logic of such an explanation by contending that only suicides come back for other human lives, not someone who died of an accident. He would rather interpret the deaths as having been caused by either vengeful ghosts seeking retribution or mountain-spirits haunting the area.

Similar explanations of the supernatural appear elsewhere in *Close Scrutiny*. As a whole, Ji Yun is implicitly making the point that inductive thinking can reveal many facts about the spiritual world,

---

[23] There are many other cases where Ji Yun simply admitted his own inability to account for anomalous events. He would say that "the principle is beyond comprehension" (*qili moming* 其理莫明), or "[the wherefore] cannot be logically inferred" (*wucong tuijiu* 無從推究), or "how [can one] find out why?" (*wuhu zhizhi* 烏乎知之). See *LY* II:24, *LY* V:41, and *RS* I:5. A sceptical attitude, as well as a willingness to attempt original theories, is one fundamental element in Qing *kaozheng* methodology. See Yang Guorong 楊國榮, "Qingdai puxue fangfa fawei" 清代樸學方法發微 (An Explication of the *Kaozheng* Methodology of the Qing Dynasty), *Huadong shifan daxue xuebao* 華東師範大學學報, no. 4 (1985), pp. 79–84.

although some phenomena may not be explicable in this way. In one entry, he narrates the misfortunes that befall those who lived in a house he himself had occupied at one time (*RS* III:19). He first reports the argument advanced by his mentor Chen Baiya 陳白崖 on the question of inauspicious abodes. He then registers his own concurrence:

In the summer of the *xinmao* 辛卯 year [1771], I returned from my military excursion to Urumqi and rented a house in the eastern section of Pearl-Nest Street, right next to the home of Long Chengzu 龍承祖 of the Provincial Surveillance Commission. In the southernmost one of the five rooms in the second house in the compound, the cloth screens always hovered about a foot from the ground, as if carried by the wind. That did not occur with the cloth screens in the other four rooms. One simply could not account for it.

The children screamed in fear whenever they entered the room, saying that a fat monk was sitting on the bed grinning at them. Why the heinous ghost of a monk should thus occupy a human abode is beyond explanation. Often, after the third watch was sounded at night, one could hear some woman weeping in the house of the Longs. That was heard by the Longs too, who claimed that the weeping originated from our house. Sceptical as I was, I could not understand it at all, and since it could hardly be something benevolent, I moved to the Twin-tree Studio of Master Zhenan 柘南 .[24]

Those who lived in the two houses later encountered evil fortune. Bai Huanjiu 白環九 , the Minister of Justice, died suddenly, without having an illness, in the house that the Longs had previously occupied. Now I believe that the doctrine of inauspicious abodes is not a fabrication. My mentor Chen Baiya said, "Those who live in propitious houses do not necessarily have good fortune, while without exception calamities befall those staying in inauspicious houses. For a comparison: mild conditions and the sun's warmth do not necessarily ward off diseases, but once one comes in touch with freezing cold and severe dampness, one inevitably falls sick. Good medicine and proper nourishment do not necessarily make one healthy right away, but once one takes very strong medicine meant to combat illnesses, one inevitably vomits and has loose bowels."

This certainly makes sense, and one cannot dispute it with reference to ideas of predeterminism. Thus has Mencius said, "Those who know their fate do not stand under a wall about to collapse." (emphasis mine)

---

[24] Master Zhenan is Qian Chenqun 錢陳羣 (1686–1774), one of Ji Yun's mentors.

In much the same vein, Ji Yun also adduces reasons for believing in the predictive nature of some poems (*LX* I:20) and the existence of immortals (*LX* I:18).

The pursuit of patterns of explanation for accumulated evidence engaged Ji Yun as he compiled *Close Scrutiny*. The extent to which he was determined to go would not have surprised even Dai Zhen, for whom:

> Heaven and earth, human beings and physical matter, occurrences and events — of these there are no principles that cannot be spoken of ... [For the myriad phenomena,] seek what is fixed and unalterable, and then the principle emerges crystal clear. Further, instead of talking about "the principle resident in things," we would say that "principles are everywhere to be seen."[25]

Ji Yun can be said to to have exemplified the use of human ratiocinative powers by bringing his own understanding to bear on the discernment of principles in the realm of the unseen. Hence, the enterprise of recording the tales of the supernatural becomes legitimized and Ji Yun is suggesting, in effect, that his tales merit consideration as a worthwhile field of investigation. In one entry he notes most succinctly: "There are things which do not follow [rational] principles. But they do exist. That being the case, they must embody certain principles of their own. People who hold to their own principles are simply too obstinate."[26] Such a statement is nothing less than Ji Yun's affirmation of the validity of his own enterprise.

There is one interesting aspect of Ji Yun's explanatory approach. When pursued to its logical conclusion, it can bring about a drastic subversion of "strangeness," that psychological or emotional response of man to the manifestations of the non-human order. Four naratives from *Close Scrutiny* suffice as examples. In the first, on hearing about the awesome death, by accident, of a man who forced his sister-in-law to remarry and sold his nieces into the *quartiers-libre*, one of Ji Yun's great grandfathers commends the fairness of divine retribution: "This is far from strange. It would be strange if it were not so" (*HX* I:35).

---

[25] *Dai Zhen zhexue zhuzuo xuanzhu*, pp. 92–93.
[26] *YWCTBJ*, p. 148.

Then, Ji Yun himself shows no surprise after witnessing the antics of a practitioner of magical arts. He offers a quick explanation: since fox-demons and one-legged mountain elfs (*shanxiao* 山魈) can be ordered about by the magicians and made to perform various tasks, their feats should hardly be considered bizarre or strange (*LY* I:24). Third, when commenting on a tale of a fire in Jinan in 1784 which left the home of a filial son unscorched while all other houses in the village were burnt to the ground, Ji Yun remarks that it should not be considered a "bizarre" event (*GW* IV:40). Finally, an entry in Zhang Jingyun's *zhiguai* compilation *New Words on Autumnal Plains* tells of a widow's portrait of her dead son which shows a remarkable likeness in every detail. Ji Yun explains this anecdote with reference to ideas of ether and spirit (of which more will be said in the next section).[27] Once again, to Ji Yun, the phenomenon is nothing outlandish or unusual. In this way a demystification, or dismantling, of strangeness by recourse to eviden-tial methods of analysis is achieved. When the strange is unfathom-able no more, but coherent, understandable, and explicable in accordance with schemes both imagined and real, it becomes part of commonplace, everyday reality. As He Bang'e says in his preface to *Occasional Accounts of Conversations at Night* (quoted in Chapter One), "There are principles behind everything that happens. If principles exist, how can anything be strange?"

The attempt to "make sense" of supernatural occurrences is sig-nificant for two reasons: in the first place, it provided justification for the activity of *zhiguai* recording. Rather than wild, fantastic narrations, the stories of Ji Yun were a storehouse of information, no different from other facts of life, worth studying for underlying principles that were of practical use. Secondly, this exploration of the world of the strange must be seen to be supportive of the supernatural arguments discussed in our last chapter. By showing the supernatural realm to be amenable to understanding and its principles to be analysable, Ji Yun was at the same time validating its reality. And by couching his compi-lation in the evidential mode, Ji Yun is making his supernatural world "real" to an eighteenth-century audience.

---

[27] *YWCTBJ*, p. 481.

The "World" of the Supernatural

As mentioned above, Ji Yun's concern was to discover principles from a close study of concrete particulars; in general, he demonstrates little interest in offering an internally coherent, all-encompassing framework for understanding the supernatural. There is no discernible cosmology, in other words, in *Close Scrutiny*. Nevertheless, it is possible to speak of certain systems of explanation that Ji Yun resorts to with some consistency. There were, in fact, ways of interpreting the functioning of spirits and of delineating the relationship between humans and spirits that Ji Yun (and the storytellers, and the listeners as well) returns to repeatedly. When these are studied closely, it is possible for us to reconstruct the world of the supernatural in *Close Scrutiny*.

Few readers of *Close Scrutiny* fail to notice the fantastic array of spiritual beings that figure in the profusion of recorded narratives. Virtually every conceivable category of spiritual being appears. Within the broader divisions of ghosts, demons, and deities, one discerns revenants, *poltergeists*, incubuses, *doppelgangers*, spooks, bogeys — the list goes on.[28] What has gone almost unnoticed is that there is a makeshift hierarchical order. The relationships among diverse types of creatures are roughly defined, and there is always an explanation for categories that do not appear to fit neatly into the hierarchy at first. Comprising over one thousand entries, the compilation is most remarkable in presenting several schemes (unsystematic though they may be) to explain the nature of supernatural beings, the activities they are engaged in, and their destinies.

The extent of Ji Yun's contribution as author (as against some kind of "folk" contribution) cannot be determined with any degree of precision. On the one hand, it is obvious that in many cases Ji Yun is voicing opinions and interpretations current in his time. While one may identify many of these views as elitist, one does well to remember that distinctions between elite and folk were not only arbitrary but also rather fluid in late imperial times. On the other hand, the

---

[28] The *YWCTBJ* encompasses many of the motifs found in supernatural tales. See the "motif index" to Everett F. Bleiler, *The Guide to Supernatural Fiction*, especially the subcategories of demons (p. 565), ghosts (scolding, perturbed, amorous, humorous, protective, revelatory, tempting, punitive, nasty, and premonitory) (pp. 573–575), and gods (p. 576).

systems of explanation that Ji Yun used reveal the influence of diverse strands of thinking, including those most clearly attributable to earlier neo-Confucians like Zhang Zai and Zhu Xi. Thus we can see the interplay of all sorts of ideas in the interpretations that Ji Yun gives to the phenomena and activities of the spirits. Nonetheless, it is certain that he attempted to explain as much as he could, and it would be fair to say that he contributed interpretations of his own as well.

Ji Yun's approximation of the idea of the operations of *qi* (material force) is everywhere in evidence. In the Song neo-Confucians' dualistic scheme of the universe, said to consist of *li* (principle) and *qi*, supernatural beings belong to the latter. Neo-Confucians like Zhu Xi thus made room for the deities and spirits, and even abnormal events are explained by Zhu Xi and Cheng Yi 程頤 (1033–1107) in one way or another. For instance, the ascent of the *hun*-soul and the descent of the *po*-soul at a person's death are interpreted as part of the "natural principle." Theories of *qi* are also often called upon by these thinkers to explicate controversial issues concerning the functioning of portents and the existence of immortals.

As any careful reader of *Close Scrutiny* can see, ideas similar to these were imported into the collection. For the sake of convenience, we will first look at the philosophy of *qi* before moving on to consider two other systems of explanation that Ji Yun uses — the transformations (*bian* 變) of *qi* through the *yin-yang* modes of interaction. Together these allowed Ji Yun (as well as some of the raconteurs and commentators) to distinguish ontologically between the various categories of supernatural beings and, further, to present them as a hierarchical continuum which permits both upward and downward movements. A niche is found in this scheme for men too, with whom those beings were engaged in both friendly interaction and hostile combat.

The Concept of Qi. The primary scheme used to explain the world of spiritual beings in *Close Scrutiny* is built around the concept of *qi*. Mentioned by the earliest Confucians and Daoists,[29] it was developed by

---

[29] Feng Yu-lan, *The Spirit of Chinese Philosophy*, translated by E. R. Hughes (Westport, Conn.: Greenwood Press, 1970), pp. 112–129. A general survey of the concept of *qi* is provided by Onozawa Seiichi 小野沢清一, Fukunaga Mitzuji 福永光司, and Yamanoi Yū 山井湧, eds., *Ki no shisō* 氣の思想 (The Philosophy of *Qi*) (Tokyo: Tokyo Daigaku 東京大學, 1978).

Zhang Zai of the Northern Song into a doctrine whereby all natural processes can be explained, since *qi* is the fundamental substance of the universe. The elevation of *qi* to a position of equal importance with *li* is seen in the work of the fifteenth-century neo-Confucian Luo Qinshun 羅欽順 (1465–1547), who through his philosophy of *qi* encouraged a focus on actual things in the real world of human experience.[30] By the early Qing, after the late Ming tendency to indulge in wild metaphysical speculation had subsided, the philosophy of *qi* returned once again to the forefront, with Wang Fuzhi's 王夫之 (1619–1692) exposition of the dynamic structure of *qi* and, later, Dai Zhen's stress on the centrality of *qi*.[31] Dai Zhen, in particular, refuted vehemently the neo-Confucian bifurcation of *li* and *qi* and built his monistic philosophy on the basis of *qi*. The growing importance of *qi* in philosophical discourse was in fact one of the distinguishing features of Qing thought. It exemplifies the "materialistic" bent of the time.

A cosmology centring on *qi* thus fitted in perfectly with the prevalent philosophic trend of the eighteenth century. To be sure, a system of explanation that uses *qi* to lend support to belief in the supernatural, though rare, was not unprecedented. Nevertheless, *Close Scrutiny* must be considered one of the more exciting attempts in traditional literature to document so many of the possibilities inherent in that system, showing the scheme to be flexible enough to accommodate the myriad bizarre occurrences in daily life. Ghosts and deities were

---

[30] For a descriptive account of Zhang Zai's philosophy of *qi* and its significance, see Huang Siu-chi, "Chang Tsai's Concept of Ch'i," *Philosophy East and West*, vol. 18 (1968), pp. 247–260; and Ira E. Kasoff, *The Thought of Chang Tsai (1020–1077)* (New York: Cambridge University Press, 1984), chap. 2. For studies of Luo Qinshun, see Irene Bloom, *Knowledge Painfully Acquired*; and "On the 'Abstraction' of Ming Thought: Some Concrete Evidence from the Philosophy of Lo Ch'in-shun," in *Principle and Practicality: Essays in Neo-Confucianism and Practical Learning*, edited by Wm Theodore de Bary and Irene Bloom (New York: Columbia University Press, 1979), pp. 69–126.

[31] On Wang Fuzhi's concept of *qi*, see, among the innumerable critical studies, Alison Harley Black, *Man and Nature in the Philosophical Thought of Wang Fu-chih* (Seattle: University of Washington Press, 1990), especially chap. 2; and Luo Guang 羅光, *Zhongguo zhexue sixiangshi: Qingdai pian* 中國哲學思想史清代篇 (A History of Chinese Philosophy: The Qing) (Taibei: Xuesheng shuju 學生書局, 1981), pp. 146–210.

seldom Dai Zhen's concern,[32] and the eighteenth century did not prove particularly conducive to theorizing about the supernatural — quite a few people, in fact, chose to denounce such attempts.[33] In fact, only two figures advocated views that showed some affinity with Ji Yun's: Cheng Tingzuo 程廷祚 (1697–1767) who, according to Hu Shi 胡適 (1891–1962), brought the philosophy of Yan Yuan 顏元 (1635–1704) and Li Gong 李塨 (1659–1733) to the attention of Dai Zhen,[34] and Yao Ying, whose ideas were discussed in the last chapter.

One of the raconteurs in *Close Scrutiny*, Jiang Bingzhang, narrates a story about a mountain-spirit through whom he propounds a theory of the origin of spirits. Ji Yun, in his comments, indicates that he endorses the theory (*RS* I:44). According to the spirit:

---

[32] Dai Zhen mentioned deities and ghosts three times in his *Yuan shan*, and three times again in his *Mengzi ziyi shuzheng*. See *Dai Zhen zhexue zhuzuo xuanzhu*, pp. 8, 10, 23, and pp. 93, 118 and 167. Quoting from *The Book of Changes* in the first instance and twice from *Doctrine of the Mean* (*Zhongyong* 中庸) (in the fourth and fifth instances), he subscribed to the idea that spirits existed as manifestations of *qi*, and were products of the transformation of Heaven and Earth (p. 23). To him ghosts and deities were constitutive elements of the universal order, as much as men and things were, and a system of correspondences existed among all of them. For "the activity of the natures [of men and things] are commensurate with the five elements and *yin-yang*; the capability of [such] natures commensurate with ghosts and deities; and the virtue of [such] natures commensurate with that of Heaven and Earth" (p. 10).

[33] Note must also be made of the publication in 1794 of Xiong Bolong's 熊伯龍 (ca. 1617–1669) masterpiece, *Without Anything* (*Wuhe ji* 無何集), which represents an apex in the historical development of traditional agnostic thought.

[34] Hu Shi was the first to suggest that Cheng Tingzuo was the link between the pragmatic Yan-Li philosophy of the seventeenth century and the philosophy of Dai Zhen, although Cheng Tingzuo himself would not admit to it. Hu Shi, "Yan Li xuepai de Cheng Tingzuo" 顏李學派的程廷祚 (Cheng Zingzuo of the Yan-Li School), in his *Hu Shi xuanji: renwu* 胡適選集：人物 (Selected Works of Hu Shi: Personalities) (Taibei: Wenxing shudian 文星書店 , 1966), pp. 111–158. Studies of Cheng Tingzuo's philosophy are scarce. Rarely is he discussed at any length in the historical surveys of Chinese philosophy. See, however, Yamanoi Yū 山井湧 , "Cheng Tingzuo de qi de zhexue," 程廷祚的氣的哲學 (The *Qi* Philosophy of Cheng Tingzuo), translated by Hu Fagui 胡發貴, *Zhongguo zhexueshi yanjiu* 中國哲學史研究 , vol. 30, no. 1 (1988), pp. 71–78; Zhou Zhaomao 周兆茂 , "Lun Cheng Tingzuo de zhexue sixiang" 論程廷祚的哲學思想 (On the Philosophical Thought of Cheng Tingzuo), *Anhui shifan xuebao: zhexue ban* 安徽師範學報：哲學版 , no. 1 (1988), pp. 44–51; and Paul S. Ropp, *Dissent in Early Modern China: Ju-lin wai-shih and Ch'ing Social Criticism* (Ann Arbor: University of Michigan Press, 1981), pp. 164–166.

> When Heaven and Earth were created, the myriad forms crystallized into being. Primal energies were gathered in these forms, and vital essences were in turn bred within the primal energies. Such essences gave birth to concrete substances, which embodied a spiritual nature.[35]

In this same process the deities, too, were created. Evidence of their existence in the ancient past is seen in the rituals and sacrifices recorded in the Six Classics. Misunderstanding of the Way of the deities was created later by, among others, the petty officials of Zhou times who endorsed erroneous popular beliefs (like those connected with the River God).[36] In concluding his account, the mountain-spirit cites two examples of supernatural beings that came into existence through a similar process: the demonic creature of the mountains (called *kuiwang* 夔罔) born of the distilled essences of woods and rocks, as well as the androgynous sheep (called *fenyang* 羵羊) born of the essences of wet earth.

Ji Yun offers his own explanation of the functioning of *qi*. In his native place he occasionally has glimpses of a tower rising from the mist, as though in a mirage (*LY* VI:29). Noting that others who encountered this phenomenon were unable to give an adequate explanation for it, he observes that "all things with physical form are imbued with the vital essences" and such essences accumulate where the earth is particularly thick. Although the original tower had been pulled down, its essence collected over the course of centuries at the place where it had been built. Thus it appeared as a real structure in the eyes of beholders. As for the question of why it was visible only to some and only rarely, once again Ji Yun draws an analogy from the world of the dead — one simply does not see the ghosts of all who have died.

The use of *qi* theory to explicate the world of ghosts occurs in *Close Scrutiny* with some degree of consistency. On one occasion it is cast in the form of a debate (*HX* IV:12). Ji Yun counters the popular

---

[35] *YWCTBJ*, p. 140.

[36] The origins of the River-god, also known as Master Lu, as well as the legend concerning his marriage, is discussed by Gu Yanwu 顧炎武 (1613–1682) in his *Rizhi lu* 日知錄 (Record of Daily Learning) (Shanghai: Shanghai guji chubanshe 上海古籍出版社 , 1985), 25:4a–5a.

view that Zhu Xi was an advocate of the "no-ghost theory" by citing opinions compiled in the *Classified Sayings of Zhu Xi*. The extracts he cited show Zhu Xi applying *qi* to an interpretation of ghosts much as Ji himself would. The basic tenet of Zhu Xi's theory recounted by Ji Yun is that *qi* is generally dispersed — returned to Heaven and Earth — when a man dies, but that it does not in the case of three types of people: those who were wronged, Buddhist monks and Daoist priests who practised spiritual cultivation, and those who died unnatural deaths.[37] For those in the last group, *qi* is not exhausted, so they can return to haunt the living, as exemplified by Boyou's 伯有 story in *Zuo's Commentary*.[38] In one extract from the collected sayings of Zhu Xi, the *qi* of a man — in spectral form — is said to be following the tiger by which he was devoured. In another, Zhu Xi mentions how undissipated *qi* attaches itself to "living *qi*" in order to be reborn.

---

[37] *YWCTBJ*, p. 332.

[38] The narrative has it that Boyou, a wronged soul returning again and again to do violence, was pacified only when Zichan 子產 (d. 496 B.C.) adopted someone as his heir. As one of the earliest instances where the activities of ghosts were explained, Zichan's view of how Boyou became a ghost is worth quoting at length:

> At a man's birth the *po*-soul appears. With this the *hun*-soul also comes into extence. By the use of things the essences are increased, thus strengthening both the *hun* and the *po*. They acquire etherealness and brilliance, becoming spiritual and intelligent. After ordinary men or women meet violent deaths their *hun* and *po* still hang about men, causing much violence.

See "Zhaogong qinian" 趙公七年 (The Seventh Year of the Duke of Zhao) in *Chunqiu Zuozhuan baihua xinjie*, p. 292. The *Zuo's Commentary* also records the descent of a deity in a place called Shen 莘 in "Zhuanggong sanshiernian" 莊公三十二年 (The Thirty-second Year of the Duke of Zhuang). The incident later becomes a popular allusion. The historiographer interpreted the reason for that deity's appearance thus:

> When a state is about to prosper, the intelligent deities will descend on it, to survey its virtue. They also descend on a state about to perish, to witness its wickedness.

He advises that the proper rituals to them be performed. See *Chunqiu Zuozhuan baihua xinjie*, p. 39. Some of the other earliest accounts of ghosts are found in the *Records of History*. See Alvin P. Cohen, "Avenging Ghosts and Moral Judgment in Ancient Chinese Historiography: Three Examples from *Shih-chi*," in *Legend, Lore and Religion in China: Essays in Honor of Wolfram Eberhard on His Seventieth Birthday*, edited by Sarah Allan and Alvin P. Cohen (San Francisco: Chinese Materials Center, 1979), pp. 97–108.

The convolutions of *qi* were held accountable for phenomena other than those related to ghosts. Instances for which similar explanations were offered by Ji Yun include:

(1) *Twin births*   Ji Yu endorses a fox-spirit's pseudo-scientific explanation of human procreation (*LX* III:6). The foetus, according to the fox-spirit, is born of the compounding of the *yin* and *yang* essences. When the *yang* essence penetrates the *yin* essence and becomes enveloped by the latter, the foetus is male; conversely, it is female. Twins result from the collision of two equally potent essences: two foetuses are produced from the force of the clash. Furthermore, because the essences, like seeds, find perfect nourishment in new blood (compared to the "earth" element), sexual intercourse after the discharge of the menses each month proves most likely to lead to childbirth.

(2) *Painting-demons*   Ji Yun notes that painting-demons cannot simply have been transformed from the pictures themselves. Instead, he argues that, according to *Records of Wide-ranging Matters*: "The painting is the material form, and it is drawn to resemble what is real. By capturing the real it becomes imbued with spirit. This is not to mention the fact that whatever is drawn on the painting becomes the object that can be possessed by demons."[39] In this case, interestingly, the cosmological explanation is textually based: the reference to another source or authority gives support to his analysis.

(3) *Omens*   A friend and a relative's misfortunes coincide with the appearance of the numinous mushroom. To Ji Yun this is a case of external phenomena responding to the reverberations of *qi* set off by auspicious or inauspicious events about to occur (*LY* VI:15). Much the same was said of the wriggling of Ge Dongchang's 戈東長 (Ge Dai 戈岱, *jinshi*, 1742) pigtail, supposedly signalling his imminent dismissal from office (*LY* VI:38), and the bouncing of the swine's head on the floor (*RS* I:35).

(4) *Incantations*   With regard to a chant recorded in the Tang *zhiguai* collection by Duan Chengshi 段成式 (fl. 843), *Sundry Anecdotes at the Youyang Caves* (*Youyang zazu* 酉陽雜俎), and the efficacy of a word recited to cure diseases, Ji Yun notes that *qi* can be evoked when the mind is sufficiently concentrated (*HX* II:27).

---

[39] *YWCTBJ*, p. 291.

(5) *Geomantic practices* An earlier generation of the Ji family decides to seal its south-facing door and instead opens the one facing north because several miles to the south is a place called "Wolf's Mouth" (*HX* I:52). To Ji Yun, the good luck that ensued was caused by the relocation of the pneumatic *qi* of the earth brought about by the opening of the door. He affirms the belief that "fate" is determined by the circulation of *qi* in Heaven, Earth, and Man, the three interlocking spheres of existence.[40]

(6) *Thunder* There are, according to Ji Yun, three kinds of thunder (*HX* IV:4). Those sent down from Heaven are designed to take human lives, and those moving horizontally are in pursuit of demons. The most common type of thunder, however, is supposed to erupt from the ground. But because "when men are gathered, *qi* can circulate freely between Heaven and Earth," it never really accumulates enough strength to burst forth as thunder.

(7) *Roosters' eggs* Ji Yun verifies an account in *What the Master Would Not Discuss* about eggs laid by stout roosters locked up in cages and segregated, but not far removed, from hens (*GW* II:3). Such eggs, said to be of utmost medicinal value, are crystallizations of *qi* activated in the roosters.

(8) *Animal "intelligence"* A peasant woman is reputedly saved when her pack of hens, by attracting her attention, makes her leave her house moments before it collapses (*GW* III:29). This Ji Yun compares to a similar tale in Zhang Du's *Records from the Chamber of Expositions* about rats repaying a kindness to men.[41] To Ji Yun, animals and birds have intimations of future occurrences because of their responsiveness to the forces of *qi* in the universe — as witnessed, for instance, in the cock's alertness to the onset of dawn.

(9) *Reincarnation* Using as evidence, first, the story of a man who claimed to have been a monk in his previous life, and then, the case of

---

[40] Gary Seaman calls this "environmentalist thinking, which sees the earth as the conduit of forces whose analogues are found in other parts of the cosmos." Gary Seaman, "Only Half-way to Godhead: The Chinese Geomancer as Alchemist and Cosmic Pivot," *Asian Folklore Studies*, vol. 45, no. 1 (1986), p. 1.

[41] The tale referred to concerns rats that, in an attempt to repay the kindness of the Li family, induced the Lis to leave their house before it collapsed. Recorded in Zhang Du, *Xuanshi zhi* 宣室志 (Records from the Chamber of Expositions), in *Congshu jicheng chubian*, 3:26.

the rebirth of a baby boy in a neighbouring family, Ji Yun affirms Zhu Xi's theory of a dead person's *qi* attaching itself randomly to *qi* that is floating freely in the world and thus initiating the reincarnation process (*LX* III:1).[42] Two more tales illustrating the same point are included in the same chapter (*LX* III:20), but there Ji Yun queries whether this phenomenon is the same as what the Buddhists called "reincarnation."

(10) *Dreams* Ji Yun resorts to several schemes for interpreting dream-stories. Referring to a dream-encounter that his student claimed to have had with him before their first encounter in 1796, Ji Yun suggests that dreams are either a product of the human consciousness or a premonition of impending events (*LX* III:21). He cites Confucius' dream of the Duke of Zhou as an instance of the former. As for the latter, he observes that dreams are like all other ominous manifestations in that they are aroused by the forever vibrant *qi*. An example is Confucius' dream of sacrificial rituals performed in front of two pillars. Nevertheless, the explanation of dreams as auguries of future happenings does not seem to Ji Yun to be altogether satisfactory.[43] He raises a series of questions:

> Of all who live — and they are as numerous as sand by the river — why do the *ghosts and deities reveal the dream* to just this person? Of all

---

[42] Hence Zhu Xi seemed on the whole to object to the Buddhist doctrine of transmigration, but he was not against some kind of *qi* interpretation of the processes of rebirth. See also Wing-tsit Chan, *Chu Hsi: New Studies* (Honolulu: University of Hawaii Press, 1989), p. 117.

[43] Ji Yun enlarged on his personal views on the premonitory nature of dreams by discussing the origins of "dream-reading" on the one hand and by citing instances where this mode of interpretation was turned to good use. Passages from *The Rites of Zhou* and the *The Classic of Poetry* were quoted to prove the connection between dream-divination and ancient shamanistic practices, while *zhiguai* anecdotes and *chuanqi* stories from Duan Chengshi's *Sundry Anecdotes at the Youyang Caves* and Zhang Zhuo's *Comprehensive Records of Affairs within and outside of the Court* (*Chaoye qianzai* 朝野僉載), as well as Bai Xingjian's "The Chronicle of Xie Xiao'e" ("Xie Xiao'e zhuan" 謝小娥傳) were used as evidence of the absurdities involved in dream explication, which at times did become exceedingly far-fetched and bewildering. This lengthy entry provides an aperture into the kind of "discourse" linked to the narration of a strange event — it became the occasion for an evidential dialogue — and it shows the way in which classical tales of different collections could be made to mutually illuminate each other in an argument.

the buffetings of good and evil fortune to which a person is subject in his life, why is this particular one made manifest [in a dream]? ... Premonitions as the dreams are, why should they be so puzzling and elusive to human understanding?[44] (italics mine)

What is of interest here, besides the fact that Ji Yun is shown to be confronted with the limits of his rationalizations, is that Ji Yun also believes in the role that spirits can play in the unfolding of dreams. Yet another interpretation of dreams is made transparent in another entry, one concerning the salacious dreams of a licentious man (*HX* IV:16). The lustful thoughts set off a chain of *qi* reverberations which activated the lascivious ghosts who came to the man in his dreams.

All in all, the elasticity of the concept of *qi*, which is the building block of Ji Yun's supernatural "system," makes it one of the most convenient interpretive tools in *Close Scrutiny*. Not only can it be applied to a diversity of unusual or supernatural phenomena, but it can also subsume a host of other plausible explanations (psychological, magical, religious) without detracting from their individual validity — as is evidenced by examples in categories (9) and (10). Applied with some consistency in *Close Scrutiny*, the concept of *qi* becomes for Ji Yun the basis of some coherent explanations for the multiplicity of anomalous phenomena and occurrences.

Yin-Yang *Polarities*.　The *yin* and *yang* forces, traditionally associated with the opposed principles of female and male, dark and light, and weak and strong, are marvellously adaptable for use in explaining natural phenomena and human affairs. But such explanations are also extended to the non-human realm as well. Zhang Zai, for one, interprets ghosts and deities as embodying the dual nature of *qi* which, when gathered, gives rise to the myriad things but returns to the Great Void when dispersed. Using homophones, he glosses the character for "deity" as "to extend" (*shen* 伸), and that for "ghost" as "to return" (*gui* 歸).[45] In this way he turns ghosts and deities into products of two different sorts of *qi* activity — *yin* and *yang*.

---

[44] *YWCTBJ*, p. 517.

[45] The idea is that spirits come forth from *qi* and then return to it eventually. *Zhang Zai ji* 張載集 (Collected Works of Zhang Zai) (Beijing: Zhonghua shuju 中華書局, 1978), p. 19.

The statement, "the paths of darkness and light never converge" (*youming yilu* 幽冥異路), expresses another binary opposition, that between ghosts and men, who belong to the realms of *yin* and *yang* respectively. A ghost appears in one of the stories of *Close Scrutiny* to expound upon the resulting differences: human beings are active in the daytime, ghosts at night; man takes up his abode where no ghosts any present, and vice versa (*GW* I:19). At the end of the brief conversational exchange narrated here, the ghost as well as the narrator of the tale go their "separate" ways. In another story, a female ghost enters the dream of one man whose generosity she wishes to repay; she engages in sexual intercourse with him every night (*RS* II:57). As to why it was possible, the explanation was:

> ... human beings partake of the *yang* element, and ghosts the *yin* element. Harm is done to man when the *yin* invades the *yang*. In sleep, however, the *yang* is restrained and one enters the *yin* mode. This enables one to remain unharmed when interacting with ghosts. Only their spirits meet; the physical forms do not.[46]

Rather than simply equating human beings with *yang* and denizens of the netherworld with *yin*, however, Ji Yun points out that while ghosts are predominantly bearers of the *yin* element, they also partake of the *yang*. After all, ghosts are begotten of what is left of a man's *yang* after his death (*RS* III:35). On the other hand, living humans are not entirely devoid of the *yin* element, since they are made up of the *hun* and *po* components. Ji Yun discusses, in this connection, the phenomenon of the walking cadavers: they are reinvigorated by the temporary return of the *hun*-soul that is active, alert, and *yang* in orientation (*RS* IV:53). Ji Yun is also able to explain the phenomenon of the *hun*-soul (that is, as the genuine *yang* element) leaving a human body when the latter is in a dream-like state (*GW* I:54).[47]

---

[46] *YWCTBJ*, p. 172.

[47] Stories of the *hun*-soul leaving the body, a kind of dream-like experience, must be counted yet another subgenre of the *zhiguai*. Ji Yun theorized on this phenomenon in *HX* IV:43. For a discussion of classical tales of this type, see Dell R. Hales, "Dreams and the Daemonic in Traditional Chinese Short Stories," in *Critical Essays on Chinese Literature*, edited by William H. Nienhauser, Jr. (Hong Kong: The Chinese University Press, 1976), pp. 71–88.

Ultimately, *yin-yang* theory helps account for all phenomena, not just supernatural ones. Ji Yun uses it in his pseudo-scientific explication of three bewildering cases: (1) the discovery of water underneath a mound of earth in the Gobi desert, (2) the severe burning of a coffin buried deep underground, and (3) the shifting of the bones inside another coffin (*RS* II:16). To him, the first was caused by the mutual attraction of water and earth, both of the *yin* element. The second and third cases were the result of burying the *yang* ether under the earth, which caused fire and wind to appear. By an extension of the second argument, Ji Yun says, even the underground presence of minerals like sulphur and cinnabar can be satisfactorily accounted for.[48]

Bian-*Transformation.* As befits their dynamic, rather than fixed, character, the *yin* and *yang* are engaged in constant activity and perpetual interaction. Given this situation, the possibility exists for the myriad things of the cosmos, all fragments of *qi*, to transform themselves or to be metamorphosed. Innumerable anecdotes in *Close Scrutiny* document the possibility for inanimate objects to become animate, for humans to turn into spirits and demons, and for different categories of supernatural beings to be transmogrified. Besides the account of the demon that emerged from a painting, Ji Yun also records a servant's tale of some naked spirits engaging in lecherous acts in a dilapidated house (*RS* II:36). It is discovered later that a private secretary who previously occupied the house often played with a set of figurines that matches the servant's description of the lustful spirits. Ji Yun interprets the incident this way: the transmutation of the figurines into spirits occurred due to their contact with the *qi* of a human being.

Quoting from Gan Bao's *In Search of Spirits*, Ji Yun notes that tortoises, snakes, fish, sea-turtles, grass and plants can all be transformed

---

[48] Ji Yun also attempted to explain the will-o'-the-wisp as the "fire of ghosts" (and not, according to *Records of Wide-ranging Matters*, as the blood of men killed in battle) by reference to *yin-yang* theory. Ghosts, while created of the left-over *yang* ether of man, was essentially *yin* in nature. For him, when the *yang* element became oppressed by an abundance of *yin*, it would gather strength and emit light. Following this line of reasoning, Ji Yun identified the seasons and geographical locations where the will o'-the-wisp was most easily observable. See *RS* III:35.

into demons if they are old enough.[49] Ji Yun considers such mutant prodigies to be part of the natural world, in which change is part of order.[50] A snake, once turned into a demon, can sneak in through the window sill (*LY* II:37). An apricot-spirit explains why he is having sexual intercourse with a human being—to gather essences so that he can assume human shape (*RS* II:48). Yet another explanation for the phenomena of transformation is given in one story, with regard to bogies and sprites of the mountains (*GW* I:43). The *qi* of the mountains and rivers, it is said, resembles dew at first; then, getting increasingly saturated, the *qi* condenses into shape, though it has as yet no substance. Only after hundreds of years have elapsed, when concrete form is finally assumed, does the *qi* turn into bogies and sprites.

If *qi*, *yin-yang* and *bian* are the three governing forces in the "world" of the supernatural in *Close Scrutiny*, what sort of hierarchy of beings does Ji Yun present? What paradigmatic structure of relationships exists among these beings? In the supernatural system depicted in *Close Scrutiny*, the most astonishing fact is the meticulousness with which subtle differentiations are effected. There is an elaborateness of detail and a complexity of organization. Subgroups, minor divisions, and transitional categories are established underneath the broad quadripartite division into men, deities, ghosts, and demons.[51]

An illustrative example of the minute distinctions made is seen in the apricot-spirit's discussion, referred to above, of the difference between an emanation (*jing* 精) and an evil demon (*mei* 魅) (*RS* II:48). For him, an emanation comes into existence through the distillation of essences within living things — like trees — for prolonged periods of time, a process likened to Daoist self-cultivation. By contrast, when a ghost, by attaching itself to a tree or plant, begins to haunt others, it is a case of an evil demon. In the same manner, a malignant *yaksha*

---

[49] The idea that all sorts of creatures can turn into demons when they are old enough is ascribed to Confucius, who advocated the theory of the "five old things" (*wuyou* 五酉). See Gan Bao, *Soushen ji*, p. 148.

[50] *YWCTBJ*, p. 196.

[51] The immortals do not seem to justify the setting up of a separate category, belonging as they do to the order of deities. Some of the marginal categories of fox-spirits will be discussed below. Note that there are ghosts of fox-spirits, mentioned in *RS* III:8.

demon of the sea is said by Ji Yun to be comparable to the mountain elf but sharply differentiated from the evil demon, ontologically "an entity between man and objects" (*RS* II:20).[52]

Fox-spirits are contrasted with ghosts in a variety of ways. The most notable difference, Ji Yun observes in one entry, is that ghosts thrive on the remnants of man's *qi* (*GW* I:30). But why ghosts are as adept as fox-spirits at transformations of all sorts (metamorphosing themselves into beauties, for instance) is something Ji cannot explain, though he contends that the sages must have understood. Another insightful comment is appended to the tale of a young man and his fox-spirit lover, both of them killed in a fire (*HX* IV:42). The tale can be quoted here at length:

> It is rumoured that during mid-Kangxi times, a fire broke out at a shop selling melon seeds. (It was located south of the Main South Gate, and slightly to the east of it.) A sick youth could not escape from the house and was burnt along with it. When the fire was put out, people dug up the charred body, together with a fox who had joined him in death. It became clear then that the youth had fallen sick due to the fox's seduction. However, why the fox also died was not understandable.
>
> Some said, "The fox was strongly attached to him and, unable to save him, chose to stand by him." Others said, "The deities have struck the fox dead for seducing — and thus killing — a man."
>
> Neither is correct. Both foxes and ghosts can transform themselves, and ghosts can depart by penetrating the walls of houses. (That is what Luo Liangfeng said.) Ghosts have shape but no substance — they are pure *qi*. As *qi* can go anywhere, nothing can block them. Like dragons, foxes can become bigger or smaller, but with both substance and shape, they can shrink, but cannot disappear altogether. A fox can escape even through a crevice, but without a crevice there is no possibility of excaping. The most ingenious of foxes come and go by way of doors and windows. Before the youth died the fox had come to seduce him. All of a sudden the fire started, burning up the doors and windows, so the fox could not but be reduced to ashes as well.

The contrasts between the ghost and the fox-spirit drawn by Ji Yun are most elaborate and "convincing." By the same token, the world of man is clearly demarcated from that of ghosts. Quoting Luo Pin, Ji

---

[52] *YWCTBJ*, p. 154.

Yun indicates that it is in man's best interest to avoid vengeful ghosts who died unnatural deaths (*LY* II:23). Before midday, when the *yang* element is predominant, ghosts choose to stay under the shades of walls. They only roam about after midday, when *yin* sets in. In general, these inhabitants of the world of the dead keep a certain distance from human beings, for the latter exude the *yang* essence. Men are bedeviled by ghosts only when there is a diminution of the *yang* in them.

It is, however, in Ji Yun's explanations of the fox-spirit's ontological and taxonomic status that we find the most interesting examples of his approach to understanding the supernatural in *Close Scrutiny*. Due to the transformational ability of the fox-spirit as well as its mercurial character, considerable fuzziness had accrued around the question of its real nature. Stated simply, the question was where the fox-spirit stand in relation to (1) man, (2) other categories of supernatural beings, and (3) the various types of fox-spirits themselves. Ji Yun tackles the first two parts of this question at the same time. To him:

> Human beings and physical objects belong to two different categories; fox-spirits stand somewhere between the two. The paths of light and darkness never converge: fox-spirits stand somewhere between the two. Immortals and demons go different ways; fox-spirits stand somewhere between the two.[53]

In another entry, the additional point is made that fox-spirits stand between men and ghosts as well (*LY* VI:16). All this makes fox-spirits a special category, definable, in the last analysis, only in relation to contrasting groups. As for the taxonomy of fox-spirits, two similar systems were offered in *Close Scrutiny*, both taking into account their mutability. Fox-spirits who discarded their original forms were distinguished from those who had not in one story (*GW* I:43). In another, fox-spirits who achieved immortality were called "celestial fox-spirits" (*tianhu* 天狐), in contrast to those who had not — the "fox-demons" (*huyao* 狐妖) (*HX* II:68, *RS* IV:36).

---

[53] *YWCTBJ*, p. 216.

The impression conveyed by Ji Yun's attempts to explain spiritual phenomena is that virtually all aspects of the interaction among the miscellaneous groups of human and non-human beings could be explained, categorized, and analysed. Knowledge of the nature of each supernatural category is supplemented by knowledge of the intricate patterns of relationships between men, demons, fox-spirits, ghosts and deities. The possession of such knowledge means, further, that methods could be devised to subjugate spirits. A tree-demon, Ji Yun remarks, was easily subdued by two carpenters because of the *qi* they had accumulated in cutting down trees (*LY* V:49). It is for the same reason that fox-spirits fear hunters most. Then, *yin-yang* theory is invoked to account for several experiences that Ji Yun himself had combating malicious spirits (*HX* III:26). Fire was effective in chasing off some mountain elfs in Fujian and in killing a spirit in Urumqi, because ghosts and demons, both *yin* in nature, are powerless in the face of the fire's *yang*.[54]

Despite human ingenuity in devising strategies to control supernatural beings, the ironic fact remains that they did not come to haunt men unless they were "called upon" to do so. This is a point reiterated time and again in *Close Scrutiny*. The principle that "demons are invoked by man" (*yao you ren xing* 妖由人興) governed the relationship of men to these otherworldly beings.[55] Specifically, disturbances arose, and the "strange" appeared, when there was dislocation caused by man's *immoral* actions. That being the case, the operation of the entire supernatural realm became controllable through human behaviour. In this way Ji Yun's explanations of the supernatural realm were relatable to his moral-didactic goal.

---

[54] Demons are also subjugated by Daoist priests (see, for instance, *HX* II:24) and higher authorities in the cosmic hierarchy (see *LY* I:20). By comparison, however, there seems to be less interest in *YWCTBJ* than in Yuan Mei's *ZBY* in the very dramatic cosmic warfare among the rank and file of celestial and terrestrial beings as well as in the means by which malefic spirits can be extirpated. See Leo Tak-hung Chan, "Subjugating Spirits: Yuan Mei's *What the Master Would Not Speak of* [*Zi bu yu*]," *Asian Culture Quarterly*, vol. 19, no. 4 (1992), pp. 40–47.

[55] *YWCTBJ*, p. 111. The *yao* here refers to all spiritual beings, not just demons. The same expression, suggesting the arousal of spirits by *qi* association, appears in a number of other places; see pp. 7, 84, 169, 243. A point to be stressed is that it cannot be literally taken to imply a psychological or mental origin for spiritual phenomena.

There are countless stories in *Close Scrutiny* about evil spirits avoiding morally upright men and haunting degenerate or ignoble characters, but more germane to our present analysis are four anecdotes concerning the "supernatural" consequences of immoral actions or thoughts. In the first, a courier from Taiwan is able to repel a female fox-spirit in the daytime, but as soon as he harbours one lustful thought in his sleep, the fox-spirit returns to hound him (*LY* I:18). The reason is that "the ghosts and deities are sensitive to the tremors of the human heart."[56] Another tale is circulated concerning a dead husband's ghost coming to rebuke his licentious wife (*LY* V:4). Appended to it is Ji Yun's comment: "Demons do not arise of themselves; they are invoked by men. The *qi* of an aggrieved soul in hell sets off hidden vibrations, and the mischievous demons avail themselves of the opportunity to appear."[57] In the third account, a fox-spirit prevented from exacting revenge on a woman when she was chaste succeeds when she turns licentious (*HX* III:20). Finally, Ji Yun's father, who harboured no fear of ghosts, is said to have dared to sleep in a room rumoured to be haunted (*RS* III:16). Working from the idea that ghostly assailants only come to those lacking the *yang* element, Ji Rongshu argues that one should not be afraid because those who are benevolent, honest and steadfast have the *yang*, while those who are ferocious, cunning and partial have the *yin* by nature. Human behaviour, therefore, is related to the extent of the control that can be exercised over the forces of the supernatural.

There is no knowing to what extent Ji Yun's system of explanations was acceptable to Ji Yun's contemporaries, but for sure Ji Yun has attempted to dissect an unseen realm and construct knowledge about it. His explanations may seem bizarre to the modern mind, but there is undeniably an inner logic to his explanations, and no reason why an eighteenth-century reader should not have found them palatable. As Francis L. K. Hsu has said:

> Magic and real knowledge are not only intertwined, but may not even be distinguished, so that, for reaching one and the same end, the individual

---

[56] *YWCTBJ*, p. 8
[57] *YWCTBJ*, p. 84.

oscillates between one and the other, or resorts to both simultaneously, with the greatest facility and ease of mind.[58]

This being the case, many of Ji Yun's explanations must have found a congenial audience in friends of his own circle, and these explanations must have been debated by them, just as Ji Yun questions, endorses, or disagrees with the explanations of others in *Close Scrutiny*. The interpretive apparatus is not entirely of Ji Yun's making; rather, it is traceable back to classics of ancient times and to the Confucians of the Cheng-Zhu school. But in pulling together the diverse strands of thinking on the subject, Ji Yun demonstrated how much the supernatural was accessible to human understanding. And in presenting the supernatural in *Close Scrutiny* in this way, the collection shows how very much it is a product of the intellectual climate of the late eighteenth century.

---

[58] Francis L. K. Hsu, *Religion, Science and Human Crisis: A Study of China in Transition and Its Implications for the West* (Westport, Conn.: Greenwood Press, 1973), p. 8.

Chapter 5

Didacticism and the Zhiguai Genre

Confucians of superior quality must have their *dao*. For there
to be *dao* there must be *wen*. If *dao* does not link up with *wen*
then the moral intent will be over-powering; if *wen* does
not acquaint itself with *dao* then the impetus is weak.

— *Liu Mian (fl. 779–797)*
tr. David Pollard

The exploration of the supernatural realm in *Close Scrutiny* is closely
connected to Ji Yun's didactic goal: exhortations to moral behaviour
gain force from a belief in the existence of deities and demons.
Supernatural beings in the *zhiguai* are agents of punishment and reward which they mete out in proportion to an individual's deeds. As
shown in our last chapter, the supernatural system also implies that
humans do have some control over what the spirits do, and consequently over their own human fate, by practising virtue. Hence the
didactic moves in the *zhiguai* stories of Ji Yun and his raconteurs are
justified by recourse to a metaphysical reality which, though challenged
from time to time, still managed to hold its own in the late eighteenth
century. That was not to be the case even just a few decades later,
when the outbreak of the Taiping rebellion and the war with Britain
led to a serious re-evaluation of the traditional Chinese order.

Ji Yun's use of the *zhiguai* as a didactic vehicle is inseparable from
his understanding of the *zhiguai* as a genre. The prominent contribution of Ji Yun to the scholarship on the generic nature of the *zhiguai*
is beyond dispute; he is equal in stature to theoreticians like Liu
Zhiji and Hu Yinglin. Interestingly enough, these three critics have
different emphases in their normative generic descriptions. While Liu

Zhiji considers the *zhiguai* essentially to have value as pseudo-historical material and Hu Yinglin defines its distinctness with reference to its supernatural content, Ji Yun stresses the didactic function.[1] To clarify Ji Yun's views it is necessary first to review the meaning of the term "didacticism," especially in reference to its cultural and literary contexts. This will then allow one to characterize Ji Yun's formulation of a theory of the didactic *zhiguai*.

Didacticism in the Chinese cultural context can first be defined with reference to two characters: *quan* 勸 and *jie* 戒 . *Quan* refers to acts of advising, giving counsel, guiding and encouraging: it can be said to express the positive, "hortatory" aspects of didacticism. *Jie*, on the other hand, connotes acts of admonishing, forbidding, and warning. It presupposes limits to our actions, hinting that punishment will be inflicted should the injunctions go unheeded. It can be said to express the "cautionary" dimension of didacticism. In the modern binomes that contain these characters, one finds *guiquan* 規勸 , "offering cautionary advice," and *chengjie* 懲戒 , "administering disciplinary action." The cluster of ideas linked to didacticism therefore moves in two directions, the preventive and the punitive, and underscores the phrase *shi quanjie* 示勸戒 (serving to exhort and caution), which is so often encountered in *zhiguai* critical discourse.

These specific "directional" aspects of didacticism are further highlighted in three other characters: (1) *Jian* 諫 is used with reference to a person pleading or remonstrating with someone superior in status — the *jianguan* 諫官 of the past was in fact the censor. (2) *Yu* 喻 refers to injunctions or orders issued by a superior. Certain forms of writing, including the remonstrance, are denoted by these two characters or the compounds they form. This shows that didacticism is present not just in imaginative literature, but in other literary forms as well.[2] (3)

---

[1] Liu Zhiji moved the *xiaoshuo* from the "Philosophers" (*zi* 子) to the "Histories" (*shi* 史) section. For Hu Yinglin, generically the *xiaoshuo* straddles the three sections of "Philosophers," "Classics" (*jing* 經) and "Collected Writings" (*ji* 集).

[2] The biography of Yang Xiong 揚雄 (53 B.C.–A.D. 18) in chap. 87 of *History of the Han Dynasty* refers to *zhen* 箴 (admonition) as a genre of writing that was concerned with giving advice and warning to the reader. Xiao Tong 蕭統 (501–531) in his preface to *Anthology of Literature* (*Wen xuan* 文選) also mentioned *jie* as one kind of cautionary literature. The association of didactic expression with various forms of writing has thus had a long history.

Feng 諷, a Chinese character of special interest, refers in present times to satirizing and ridiculing, but it originally meant "admonishing by indirection," a technique fully exploited by Qu Yuan 屈原 (340?–278 B.C.) in his "Encountering Sorrow" ("Li sao" 離騷).[3] Didacticism, in sum, has many facets, and imaginative literature is no more than one area in which the didactic imperative is made manifest.

The difficulty of talking about didacticism in Chinese literature is created by its pervasive presence. It can probably be argued that much that appears in print is didactic. In imperial times, the standard histories provided one readily available example, and religious literature another. Witness, for instance, the proliferation of morality books, designed to exhort the unsophisticated masses. The turn of the present century witnessed the lingering influence of the didactic theories of the Tongcheng school (founded at a time roughly contemporaneous with Ji Yun's), whose prestige was still high even as the Qing was nearing its demise. In more recent times, in Communist China, a marriage has been effected between literature and propaganda: the former was used to facilitate the spread of doctrinaire ideas. Given such a situation, it seems appropriate, therefore, to define didacticism more narrowly in relation to the corpus of materials at hand before proceeding to consider Ji Yun and his *Close Scrutiny* in the didactic context.

There is a broader sense in which the term "didacticism" can be used to denote the mode of literary expression in which a text is made to illustrate some truths outside of itself in ways distinct from allegory or analogy. Scholes and Kellogg distinguish between two kinds of fiction, designated "representational" and "illustrative," and proceed to point out that the latter seeks not to reproduce actuality but to present selected aspects of the actual, in order to reveal deeper truths.[4] While this is valid as a general definition of the way didacticism works,

---

[3] For the didactic approach to Qu Yuan's poetry, see Geoffrey R. Waters, *Three Elegies of Ch'u: An Introduction to the Traditional Interpretation of the Ch'u Tz'u* (Madison: University of Wisconsin Press, 1985).

[4] To Robert Scholes and Robert Kellogg, illustrative (read: didactic) fiction "presents selected aspects of the actual, essences referable for their meaning not to historical, psychological, or sociological truth, but to ethical and metaphysical truth." Scholes and Kellogg, *The Nature of Narrative* (Oxford: Oxford University Press, 1966), p. 88.

this definition's emphasis on technique and style renders it virtually inapplicable to the Chinese context. Chinese theories of didacticism are more content-oriented, and obviously it is moral didacticism that is at issue in the case of Ji Yun's collection.

On the part of the didactic writer, it is the moral message that engages his attention as he allows the events in the story to unfold. Readers' attention is directed through a variety of devices, not the least of which is direct commentary (which is the central didactic technique deployed in *Close Scrutiny*), stating the moral statement or truth implicit in the narrative. Rather than asking, "How are events going to turn out?" the readers probably ask, "What is the point of this story?" Regarding the literary text itself, it can appropriately be described as having an educational, as opposed to an entertainment, value.[5] It may be that the best way of pinpointing the nature of the didactic narrative is to see it in contrast to the aesthetic narrative, in which events are allowed to unfold on their own with no authorial interference.

The focus of the present chapter is on the tradition of literary didacticism as it relates to Ji Yun's approach to the *zhiguai*. The tradition is analysed in the wider context of discussions about didacticism as a literary mode in traditional China and in the more immediate context of a growing interest, in the late eighteenth century, in the didactic role of the *zhiguai*. This interest was stimulated by a series of publication events in the mid-eighteenth century, not the least important of which is the appearance of Pu Songling's *Studio of Leisure*. In this context Ji Yun figures neither as the compiler who listens to and puts down in writing the oral narratives circulated among a circle of friends and relatives, nor — as in the next chapter — as the moralizing author of *Close Scrutiny*, deftly manipulating the materials at his disposal to illustrate distinct didactic points. He is here the literary theorist who established the rationale for writing didactic *zhiguai*.

---

[5] The point is made by Northrop Frye in his *Anatomy of Criticism: Four Essays* (Princeton: Princeton University Press, 1957), pp. 52–53. It must also be noted that no attempt is made here to exhaust all the possible implications of didacticism in literature. Western notions of the "sugar-coated pill" theory of literature, which one traces from Horace and his *utile et dulce* to Sir Philip Sidney with his notion of moral profit, to Samuel Johnson's requirement that poetry "instruct by pleasing," constitute a tradition that would be completely beyond the scope of this study. Only the essential Chinese formulations will be detailed in this chapter.

Especially important in what follows is the question of the *zhiguai* as a genre. Ji Yun's didacticism was not solely a matter of arbitrary personal choice. It was a solution to the problem of where to fit the *zhiguai* among the manifold types of literary writing. For Ji Yun, of course, this issue also happened to have personal relevance under rather special circumstances. As Chief Editor of the *Complete Library of Four Treasuries*, engaged in classifying and categorizing an astronomical number of texts from ancient times to the eighteenth century, he had to decide where to situate the *zhiguai* works. But, essentially, it appears that a crucial point was arrived at in the late eighteenth century, for precisely at this time perceptions of genre and the didactic imperative came together in a unique way in connection with the *zhiguai*. It was Ji Yun who articulated the nature of this new configuration.

The Didactic Approach to Literature

The belief in the didactic value of literature can be said to have emerged as early as the time of Confucius, whose interpretation of *The Classic of Poetry* as a book embodying a moral function furnishes one of the earliest instances of the Chinese emphasis on using literature as a means of elucidating the Dao 道.[6] As Chow Tse-tsung 周策縱 has shown, the principle of using "literature as a vehicle for conveying the Dao" (*wen yi zai dao* 文以載道) is one of the two basic doctrines regarding the role of literature. (The other role is that of "poetry expressing intentions in words" [*shi yan zhi* 詩言志].[7]) The strong hold that the didactic imperative had on Chinese men of letters in ancient

---

[6] A discussion of the didactic use of *The Classic of Poetry* by Confucius is found in Donald Holzman, "Confucius and Ancient Chinese Literary Criticism," in *Chinese Approaches to Literature from Confucius to Liang Ch'i-ch'ao*, edited by Adele A. Rickett (Princeton: Princeton University Press, 1978), pp. 21–41.

[7] See Chow Tse-tsung, "Ancient Chinese Views on Literature, the *Tao*, and their Relationship," *Chinese Literature: Essays, Articles, Reviews*, vol. 1, no. 2 (1979), pp. 3–29; and "The Early History of the Chinese Word *Shih* (Poetry)," in *Wen-lin: Studies in the Chinese Humanities*, edited by Chow Tse-tsung (Madison: University of Wisconsin Press, 1968), pp. 151–209. It should be noted that the phrase *wen yi zai dao* was first coined by Zhou Dunyi 周敦頤 (1017–1073) and not Han Yu (as is commonly assumed).

times is seen in the fact that it governed not only the writing of literature, but also that of history. The interpretive goal of the earliest commentators on *The Spring and Autumn Annals* (*Chunqiu* 春秋)was to bring
to light the methods whereby Confucius, the imputed editor, meted
out, through careful editing, "praise and blame" to the historical
figures of the early Eastern Zhou period.

It could be said that, in the realm of poetry, the didactic doctrine
was enshrined by Mao Chang 毛萇 (2 A.D.), whose approach to *The
Classic of Poetry* is outlined in his Great Preface. A tract familiar to all
students sitting for the imperial examinations, it had an indelible
influence on posterity. According to the Great Preface's didactic view,
The Classic of Poetry was composed to "make permanent the tie between husband and wife, to perfect filial reverence, to deepen human
relationships, to beautify moral instruction, and to improve the
customs of the people."[8]

In the genre of the essay, it was Han Yu, acclaimed theorist of the
didactic approach, whose contribution was best known. Reacting
against the Six Dynasties emphasis on form at the expense of content,
as evidenced by the popularity of the transformation texts, Han Yu
sought to salvage literature from the depths of decadence and irre-
sponsibility to which he felt it had descended by reasserting its didactic utility. Noting that literature serves to reveal the Dao, he made
moral instruction the sole criterion for judging the worth of any literary work. Such an approach had two important ramifications. First,
the focus of literary criticism is shifted onto a new plane. Instead of
concentrating on the intrinsic merits in the work, the critic focuses on
matters of extra-literary significance. Second, in terms of the creative
process, the personal satisfaction the author is supposed to derive from
his act of creation is considered less important than the influence he
potentially exerts on the reader.

This theoretical basis provided Han Yu with the rationale for the
ancient prose movement. One point to be noted, however, especially
when Han Yu's theory is pitted against Ji Yun's formulation of a

---

[8] James J. Y. Liu, *The Art of Chinese Poetry* (Chicago: The University of Chicago Press,
1962), p. 66.

didactic type of *zhiguai*, is that Han Yu spoke more broadly about the nature of didacticism. For him, didacticism is roughly equivalent to an "utilitarian" function that all literature should fulfil. Thus, for instance, poems making comments of a political nature are also supposed to be "didactic." On the other hand, Han Yu also stipulated a different kind of didactic technique. Didacticism for him works by means of "allegorical lodging" (*xingji* 興寄),[9] whereby the moral point is hidden, or "lodged," in the work itself. The direction of Ji Yun's didacticism was clearly moral, and it was achieved through more explicit, expository techniques.

Other proponents of the didactic approach to literature came in the wake of Han Yu. In the Song, leading literary figures like Ouyang Xiu 歐陽修 (1007–1072) and Su Shi continued the tradition of Confucian didacticism and perpetuated the ancient-prose writing style. The neo-Confucians of the era also added a philosophical dimension to this theory of literature. First equating the Dao with principle, Zhu Xi proceeded to reject the duality of literature and the Dao and concluded that all literature is but part of the Dao, so that constant study of, as well as investigation into, the Dao is conducive to the production of good literature.[10] It would appear that in the Song, the theory that literature should be a didactic vehicle had largely gained ascendancy over the view of it as a means of artistic expression.

As a whole, the idea that literature is a vehicle for embodying the Dao served to crystallize thinking among the elite in imperial times on the role that literature ought to play in a Confucian society. A sign of the dominance of the didactic imperative is seen in the fact that its influence was felt in every literary genre, not the least in the narrative genres.

The vernacular novel, which flourished in the late imperial period and was considered to contain heterodox material that presented a threat to orthodox ethical values, often clothed itself in

---

[9] See Charles Hartman, *Han Yü and the T'ang Search for Unity* (Princeton: Princeton University Press, 1986), p. 225.

[10] A brief discussion of Zhu Xi's literary ideas is given by David E. Pollard, *A Chinese Look at Literature: The Literary Values of Chou Tso-jen in Relation to the Tradition* (Berkeley: University of California Press, 1973), pp. 19–21.

didactic garb to avoid censure.[11] Much of the didacticism in the
novels was no more than a shield: their authors were paying only lip
service to conventional morality. But the fact that they felt constrained
to do so shows the hold that the tradition of morality-in-literature had
on men of letters. Further, a cacophony of voices was raised in protest
against the vernacular novel for its explicit immorality. The scholar
and classicist of the Ming, Jiao Xun 焦循 (1763–1830), for one, is known
to have recommended the proscription of all novels that did not have
a didactic purpose.

It may not be too wide of the mark to characterize the first century of the Qing dynasty as an age of didacticism. The late seventeenth
century saw a revival of the concern for moral effort and proper ethical values, objectives that had been eclipsed by the "excesses" of the
late Ming. The eighteenth century continued this trend, and the rise
of the "evidential research" school, with its stress on the use of historical and philological methods to uncover the fundamental teachings
of Confucianism, must be understood, at least in part, as reflecting
the urge among intellectuals to re-establish a definitive, workable set
of social ethics through the proper study of the ancient classics. This
commitment on the part of the elite to maintaining Confucian norms
of social behaviour was the root cause of the social conservatism that
informed the era. The didacticism encouraged in literature was but
one of its facets.[12]

The intensification of the didactic strain is observed not only in
the classical tale in mid-Qing times, but also in other kinds of narrative. Some critics have maintained that didacticism sapped the
colloquial story of its strength and thus brought about its eventual

---

[11] The issue relates in particular to the didacticism discernible in many of the erotic
novels written before the early Qing, as for instance, *Plum in the Golden Vase* and *Prayer Mat
of Flesh* (*Rouputuan* 肉蒲團).

[12] To Chow Kai-wing, the moral conservatism of this era is evidenced by the classical
studies and the researches into lineages undertaken by scholars at the time. The commitment on the part of the elite to uphold norms of behaviour reflected what he calls a trend
of ritual fundamentalism or "purism." Chow, *The Rise of Confucian Ritualism in Late Imperial
China: Ethics, Classics, and Lineage Discourse*, p. 8.

demise.[13] Didacticism was also the bane of the vernacular novel, and among the more outstanding examples of the boring, preachy novel is Li Lüyuan's 李綠園 (1707–1790) *Lamp at the Crossroads* (*Qilu deng* 歧路燈).

Yet while novels were being produced that are admittedly over-burdened with didacticism, some people insisted that there was not enough of it. The fact is that there was a general fear of *xiaoshuo* running rampant. An abhorrence for *xiaoshuo* that propagated immorality was voiced by Qian Daxin, the famed Qing historian who was also one of the raconteurs in *Close Scrutiny*. To him:

> Even Buddhists and Daoists exhort people to do good, but *xiaoshuo* guides them into paths of evil. Confucians, Buddhists and Daoists all refrain from mentioning affairs of an adulterous, wayward, licentious, or treacherous nature. Writers of the *xiaoshuo*, however, would relish talking about them, and describe [such things] at length, down to the very last detail.[14]

The following remark from *Occasional Notes from the Studio of Living Nowhere* (*Wusuozhuzhai suibi* 無所住齋隨筆) strikes a similar note:

> Present-day writers of the *xiaoshuo* either indulge in licentious and amorous descriptions, or display frivolous and thoughtless attitudes.... [They] undermine what is proper and righteous, entering the labyrinths of extreme waywardness. Could words do justice to the evil [they propagate]?[15]

That didacticism once again struggled to assert its hold on literature in the mid-Qing period is demonstrated by the emergence on the scene of new theorists, this time those of the afore-mentioned Tongcheng school. Fang Bao 方苞 (1668–1749) and Yao Nai, chief

---

[13] Could the same be said of the demise of the classical tale? Did didacticism really "kill" fiction-writing? See Dong Guoyan 董國炎, "Jiaohua zhishang yu xiaoshuo" 教化至上與小說 (Fiction and the Supremacy of Didacticism), *Wenxue yichan* 文學遺產, no. 1 (1988), pp. 93–101. As noted in chap. 1, Keith McMahon made a strong case for a revived didacticism in early Qing fiction.

[14] Qian Daxin, "Zhengsu" 正俗 (Rectifying Folkways), in *Qianyantang wenji*, 17:14b.

[15] For the hundreds of comments of a similar kind indicting the *xiaoshuo*, see Wang Liqi 王利器, *Yuan Ming Qing sandai jinhui xiaoshuo xiqu shiliao* 元明清三代禁毀小說戲曲史料 (Historical Documents on the Censorship of Fiction and Drama in the Yuan, Ming, and Qing Periods) (Shanghai: Guji chubanshe 古籍出版社, 1981), especially pp. 204–367.

members of the school, worked hard to re-invigorate the ancient prose styles of the Eight Tang-Song Masters and to reiterate the necessity for literature to uphold social morality. Yao Nai's argument for an integration of rightness (*yi* 義) and method (*fa* 法) came very close to a reaffirmation of the neo-Confucian statement of the basic unity of literature and the Way, and he also remarks: "To explain ethical principles, to uphold public morals, to be a guide to society, this is the calling of the civilized men. And the form of words that adequately expresses his calling is the literature of the civilized man."[16] It can be said that the Tongcheng school did not add much that was new to the theorizing of didacticism in China, but without a doubt it affirmed didacticism as the orthodox literary doctrine and restored it to a position of importance.

Such is the background of didactic thinking through the centuries as well as in the mid-Qing. Didacticism is a way of thinking remarkable for its tenacity and pervasiveness. The *zhiguai* was not immune to its influence. Recent studies have identified two strands of *zhiguai* writing in the Six Dynasties, the period which witnessed the first flowering of the genre. Collections like those by Gan Bao and Zhang Hua 張華 (232–300), which documented awe and wonder at freakish phenomena (and hence were non-didactic), are now differentiated from the Buddhist miracle tales collected in, say, Wang Yan's *Records of Miraculous Omens* and Liu Yiqing's *Records of Revealed Marvels* (*Xuanyan ji* 宣驗記).[17] The Buddhist miracle tale collections, also known as marvel books and mostly appearing in the Southern dynasties (420–589), were in essence pietistic-cum-didactic texts. In these texts, promoting Buddhist norms of moral behaviour was as central a goal as demonstrating the reality and efficacy of Buddhist deities. The didacticism that Ji Yun considered to be a central element to the *zhiguai*

---

[16] David E. Pollard delineates at length the theory and practice of the Tongcheng school. See Pollard, *A Chinese Look at Literature*, pp. 22 and 140–157. The reader is also referred to James J. Y. Liu, *Chinese Theories of Literature* (Chicago: The University of Chicago Press, 1975), pp. 45–46 and 95–97; and Theodore Huters, "From Writing to Literature: The Development of Late Qing Theories of Prose," *Harvard Journal of Asiatic Studies*, vol. 47, no. 1 (1987), pp. 51–96.

[17] The miracle tale was placed at the service of competing religious faiths, and instances connected with the propagation of the Guanyin cult were particularly numerous.

is by nature different from that in the didactic Southern dynasties *zhiguai*, and Ji Yun's formulation of a theory of the didactic *zhiguai* is also the product of a unique set of circumstances in the late eighteenth century.

Rejection of the Aesthetic Mode

Ji Yun's view of the *zhiguai* as a genre must be studied in relation to three publication events in the middle of the eighteenth century. *Studio of Leisure* had, of course, been circulated in manuscript form for nearly a century, and it was well-known to some readers. However, only in 1776 was it printed in full for the first time and made widely available to men of letters. Whether they liked it or not, subsequent writers of the classical tale could not remain unaffected by this masterpiece. Of equally profound impact were two other publication events: the reprinting in a portable form (the *jinxiang ben* 巾箱本) of the massive Song compendium, *Extensive Gleanings from the Taiping Reign*, in which most early *zhiguai* were collected — a project undertaken by Huang Sheng 黃晟 (fl. 1752) in 1753 — and the printing of *The Second Collection of the Records of Yijian* (*Yijian zhizhi* 夷堅支志) by Zhou Qi 周棨 in 1778, which added considerably to the number of tales from *Records of Yijian* already in circulation in Hong Bian's 洪楩 (fl. 1545) 51-chapter Ming edition.

The popularization of *zhiguai* literature in the late Qianlong era must be understood as more than mere historical accident. The keen enthusiasm for the genre was stimulated by the availability of the three most popular *zhiguai* collections of all time. The publication of these three works must also have fostered some sense among *zhiguai* writers of an independent literary tradition, marked by identifiable generic properties which were modelled on specific canonical works. Evident in many prefaces to *zhiguai* collections at the time is an awareness of a line of literary descent stretching from the earliest collections by legendary compilers of strange tales like Qi Xie 齊諧 and Yu Chu 虞初,[18]

---

[18] Qi Xie is arguably the first *zhiguai* writer in Chinese history, mentioned by Zhuangzi in his "Free and Easy Wandering" ("Xiaoyao you" 逍遙遊) chapter. There is, however, the possibility that "Qi Xie" was the name of a book rather than of a person. Modern

through the Six Dynasties masterpieces (especially *In Search of Spirits*),
to the two voluminous Song compilations. That Yuan Mei chose to
abandon the title *What the Master Would Not Discuss* for his collection
and to rename it *A New Collection by Qi Xie* (*Xin Qi Xie* 新齊諧) after
discovering a work called *What the Master Would Not Discuss* by a Yuan
author, is a sign of this consciousness of a full-fledged *zhiguai* tradition, within which each individual work occupies a unique place.[19]

Though *Extensive Gleanings* and *Records of Yijian* won unanimous
acclaim, the responses by *zhiguai* writers and critics of the time to
Studio of Leisure were at best ambivalent. In contrast to the praise
that it received from some readers, dissatisfaction was expressed by
many, and some even rejected the collection. Such negative attitudes
contrasts sharply with the decidedly positive reception given the collection in the present century.[20] Late eighteenth-century imitators of
Studio of Leisure were legion; innumerable critics, in surveying the tradition of random jottings literature in the late Qing, have come up
with lists of collections on which Pu Songling's characteristic stylistic

---

scholarship generally considers "qi xie" as a fictional device. Yu Chu was a minor official at
the time of Emperor Wu 武帝 of the Former Han responsible for collecting "street talk." In
both "Prose-poem on the Western Capital" ("Xijing fu" 西京賦) by Zhang Heng 張衡 (78–
139) and the Bibliographies section of *History of the Han Dynasty*, his *Zhou Dynasty Tales by Yu
Chu* (*Yu Chu Zhou shuo* 虞初周說) was noted. In later times Yu Chu was generally acknowledged as the father of the genre.

[19] Yuan Mei explained the change in his preface to the collection in *ZBY*, p. 2. The
Yuan work entitled *Zi bu yu*, however, is no longer extant. Another sign of the awareness of
a tradition is seen in the practice among compilers of highlighting certain previous *zhiguai*
works in their prefaces; see in particular those written by Ji Yun, Yuan Mei and, much later,
Xu Shuping 許叔平 (preface to *The Four-horse Chariot in the Neighbourhood* [*Li cheng* 里乘]).

[20] O. L. Fishman has succinctly described the negative reactions of Ji Yun and Yuan Mei
to the innovations of Pu Songling: while Ji Yun rejected them, Yuan Mei ignored them.
Both preferred to "adhere to the canonical tradition of *biji*." Fishman, *Tri kitaïskikh novellista
XVII–XVIII vv: Pu Songling, Ji Yun, Yuan Mei* (Three Chinese Novelists of the Seventeenth
and Eighteenth Centuries: Pu Songling, Ji Yun, Yuan Mei) (Moscow, 1980), p. 428. That the
modern reader prefers *LZZI* is seen in Wang Tongshu 王同書, "Cong *Liaozhai zhiyi* yu *Yuewei
caotang biji* de bijiao kan wenyan xiaoshuo chuangzuo de deshi" 從聊齋誌異與閱微草堂筆記的
比較看文言小説創作的得失 (A Look at the Successes and Failures of Innovations in Classical
Tales from a Comparison of the *Liaozhai zhiyi* and the *Yuewei caotang biji*), *Fudan xuebao* 復旦
學報, no. 2 (1990), pp. 66–71.

manoeuvres left an indelible imprint. Yet the leading writers of tales of the strange at the time were also the most vehement of critics of *Studio of Leisure*. In the original preface to *What the Master Would Not Discuss*, while admitting his desire to continue in the vein of *Records of Yijian*, Yuan Mei denounces Pu Songling's collection as "superficial."[21] It still remains unclear why Yuan Mei had such a low opinion of *Studio of Leisure* and why he decided to write a collection which evidently was a departure from Pu Songling's model. Even more puzzling is the fact that he eventually deleted this negative judgment from the preface that appears with the collection as we have it today. Ji Yun too, as is well known, took Pu Songling to task and rejected *Studio of Leisure* outright. He preferred to adopt the Six Dynasties *zhiguai* as models for his *Close Scrutiny*.

Both Ji Yun's advocacy of Six Dynasties specimens of *zhiguai* literature and his rejection of *Studio of Leisure* are two sides of the same coin and closely related to questions of canonicity. *Zhiguai* works had always been viewed as non-canonical and not favourably compared to the dominant, "respectable" literature. But by the eighteenth century, in the minds of some, an independent canon of *zhiguai* had emerged, and judgments on *zhiguai* works were passed with reference to an implicitly acknowledged group of works. This was the attitude not only of Ji Yun but also of Yuan Mei and other writers and critics of the genre. Such a situation also explains the repeated allusions by *zhiguai* writers to *Extensive Gleanings*, *Records of Yijian*, and Six Dynasties works like those by Gan Bao and Liu Yiqing. As outstanding works in the tradition, those collections were also the exemplars of what kind of *zhiguai* should be written. The importance of Ji Yun is to be seen

---

[21] There are two versions of the *ZBY* preface. The earlier version, in which the criticism of *LZZI* appears, is now retained in Yuan's collected literary writings. Among the deletions is the following: "*Extensive Gleanings from the Taiping Reign* is admirable; *Accounts of a Cartload of Ghosts* (*Kuiche zhi* 睽車志) and *Records of Yijian* survive only in parts. *Tales of Anomalies from the Studio of Leisure* is outstanding but too superficial." See Yuan Mei, *Xiaocang shanfang shiwenji* 小倉山房詩文集 (Collected Poetry and Prose from the Retreat at Xiaocang Mountain), in *Jindai Zhongguo shiliao congkan xubian* 近代中國史料叢刊續編 (Collectanea of Historical Documents on Early Modern China, Second Collection) (Taibei: Wenhai shuju 文海書局, 1981), chap. 28.

precisely in his attempt to systematically shape vaguely articulated ideas about *zhiguai* writing into a general theory.

The issue of systematic theorizing acquired special urgency because *zhiguai* writers wished to establish the *zhiguai* as a viable genre of writing, one that befitted even the Confucian gentleman. For centuries, eminent scholars, historians, and men of letters had been compiling collections of tales of the supernatural, but this enterprise had been consistently denigrated. In the Bibliography sections of the standard histories, *zhiguai* had often been classified under the *xiaoshuo*, purportedly the last and least noteworthy among the ten schools of learning.[22] Thus the *zhiguai* shared the low repute traditionally accorded the *xiaoshuo*, of which Confucius was supposed to have said: "Far-fetched and lacking in seriousness, it is something that the civilized man would not dabble in." In tackling the question of genre, then, Ji Yun became involved with the issue of how to elevate the *zhiguai* from its ignominious position as a genre of little value.

Before detailing Ji Yun's indictment of the mode of *zhiguai* writing exemplified by *Studio of Leisure*, it seems appropriate to note, very briefly, Ji Yun's attitude towards genre in general. *Close Scrutiny* itself contains a few hints of Ji Yun's full seriousness towards the issue of genre. What was proper or what was improper from a generic angle is often stated unequivocally, and time and again Ji Yun notes that there should be no mixing of genres. As Chief Editor of the *Complete Library*, of course, it was natural that Ji Yun should have developed a heightened sensitivity to generic issues, and this sensitivity spilled over from the imperial compilation project to his own compilation. In one entry from *Close Scrutiny* (*LX* IV:16), he stresses the need to distinguish among the miscellaneous records of the minor officials of Zhou times, epigraphs, historical chronicles, and poetic writings, for they belonged to different generic compartments.[23] In another, he notes how upset

---

[22] To Ban Gu, "Only nine of the ten philosophical schools are worth reading." Liu Xiang in *Garden of Talk* (*Shuoyuan* 說苑) claimed that *xiaoshuo* was "shallow and unrelated to principles." The editors of *New History of the Tang Dynasty* were the first to classify *zhiguai* materials as *xiaoshuo*, since they were unworthy of consideration even as "miscellaneous history."

[23] *YWCTBJ*, p. 529. To talk of generic purity in regard to the *xiaoshuo* is, however, most paradoxical, for it is the most hybrid of genres, as Ji Yun observed in the last entry to *Miscellaneous Accounts West of the Locust Tree*. See *YWCTBJ*, p. 358.

he is about the failure of *xiaoshuo* writers to observe generic conventions. For him most of them freely cram their collections with entirely irrelevant mishmashes of anecdotes (*RS* I:62). In this context he commends the *xiaoshuo* collection of his friend Ge Tao 戈濤 (fl. 1751), gazetteer for Xian county in Hebei. Ji Yun remarks on how tightly it is organized, how generically "proper" it is, and how it rivals the standard histories.[24]

The colophon that Sheng Shiyan penned for the 1793 edition of the first four volumes of *Close Scrutiny* is the only document which reflects Ji Yun's attitude towards *Studio of Leisure*. It discloses much of Ji Yun's thinking on *zhiguai* writing, which is largely concealed in the prefaces to the five collections of *Close Scrutiny*. Evident in it is Ji Yun's concern for observing proper generic parameters (*tili* 體例) for the *xiaoshuo* in general and the *zhiguai* in particular; this is a point that he does not make in his prefaces. Sheng Shiyan begins by noting the "universally acknowledged fact" that the first three collections of *Close Scrutiny* successfully served their author's didactic purpose. For readers who might suspect Ji Yun of having taken a rather careless approach to his compilation, Sheng counters by stating that, as one keenly aware of the principles of authorship, Ji Yun adheres faithfully to generic requirements even when compiling something as hybrid and amorphous as a *xiaoshuo* collection.

At this point Sheng Shiyan quotes Ji Yun, who indicts Pu Songling's breach of generic boundaries by indiscriminately blending different modes of writing in his *Studio of Leisure*:

> The Master [Ji Yun] once said, "*Studio of Leisure* enjoyed great popularity, but it came under the brush of a genius, not just that of a writer. Most ancient books from Yu Chu on, up to Gan Bao, are no longer extant. As for those that still exist in their entirety, Liu Jingshu's *Garden of Anomalies* (*Yiyuan* 異苑) and Tao Qian's *A Sequel to In Search of Spirits* (*Xu Soushen ji* 續搜神記) belong to the category of *xiaoshuo*, while 'An Unofficial Chronicle of Zhao Feiyan' ('Feiyan waizhuan' 飛燕外傳) and 'Rendezvous with an Immortal' ('Hui zhen ji' 會真記) are of the category of biographies. *Extensive Gleanings from the Taiping Reign* comprises works of

---

[24] To Ji Yun, Ge Tao could be faulted for the inclusion of two *zhiguai* items in the local gazetteer, but he nevertheless commended these for their hortatory value.

both groups because it collects matters under diverse classifications. Now
for one book to blend two genres is incomprehensible to me ..."[25]

When he refers to the "writer" (in the first sentence above), Ji Yun
obviously has in mind the "transmitter," a role that he himself played
in *Close Scrutiny*. The entire quotation, in fact, echoes the invectives
against generic meshing in some of the entries in Ji Yun's collection.
In distinguishing between the two groups of works in the above quotation, Ji Yun is in fact underscoring the generic differences between
the *zhiguai* (as a kind of "small talk") and the biography. It is most
revealing to compare Ji Yun's theoretical formulations and our post-
modern Western understanding of genres, especially with regard to
the use of categories. What is today loosely called the classical tale was
analysed by Ji Yun into two genres, and he related all written tales
either to formal history through the biography or to informal history
through the *zhiguai*. There were, consequently, two points of contact
between history and narrative, and this gives rise to two generic categories that are not to be mixed, except in the case of an anthology
like *Extensive Gleanings*.

    Ji Yun then explains why mixing them as Pu Songling did is plainly
misguided. Perhaps the word "genius" as he uses it in reference to
Studio of Leisure may not even carry a positive connotation after all:

> Since the *xiaoshuo* is a record of matters observed or heard, it rightfully
> belongs in the realm of narrative, and is unlike dramatic plots that can
> be altered or embellished at will. The biography of Ling Xuan 伶玄
> (fl. 1) [author of "An Unofficial Chronicle of Zhao Feiyan"] originated
> with Fan Ni 范嬺 — hence the promiscuous details. Yuan Zhen's [author
> of "Rendezvous with an Immortal"] chronicle was an account of firsthand
> experience — thus he was able to elaborate on its finer points. Even in
> writing *Miscellaneous Secrets Revealed* (*Zashi mixin* 雜事秘辛), Yang Shen 楊
> 慎 (1488–1559) was cognizant of this principle, for Yang had read a lot
> of ancient books.[26]

The apparent reason for the indictment is that the *Studio of Leisure*
mode was not established practice: the ancients did not work in this

---

[25] *YWCTBJ*, p. 472.
[26] Ibid.

way, nor did those who followed their example. But a more fundamental reason is that works like *Studio of Leisure* were judged to be
inadequate when they failed to meet the criterion of plausibility —
when they were not created on the basis of an adherence to facts.
From the examples given, however, it is clear that Ji Yun was trying to
apply this criticism not only to the *zhiguai* but also to works commonly
understood to belong to the *chuanqi* genre like Yuan Zhen's tale. The
chuanqi might include more details than the *zhiguai,* but still nothing
should be fabricated. It was in this sense that the works of Ling Xuan
and Yuan Zhen were instances of good *chuanqi.*

It is argued by critics that Ji Yun was wrong to critique *Studio of
Leisure* by viewing it as generically belonging to the *zhiguai*; he is said
to have given Pu Songling's collection the wrong test. But what seems
clear from Sheng Shiyan's colophon is that *Studio of Leisure* would not
have received a better treatment had it been regarded as an example
of the *chuanqi.* In the last part of Sheng Shiyan's quotation, Ji Yun
inveighs against the "excesses" of *Studio of Leisure*:

> Now amorous conversations and indecent behaviour, disclosed in intri-
> cate detail, are delineated as though they were real. It seems unreason-
> able to expect these words to have come direct from the mouths of the
> characters themselves. If these were words that the author has said on
> their behalf, how could he have heard them in the first place? That is
> virtually impossible to understand. In full earnestness, I would not con-
> sider myself as having the tiniest portion of Pu Liuxian's 蒲留仙 [Pu
> Songling's] talent, but with regard to these two points, I am like the in-
> sect of summer doubting the existence of ice.[27]

Ji Yun here attacks the elaborate depictions of promiscuous affairs in
Studio of Leisure, which at times went so far as to report actual dia-
logues between licentious lovers. To Ji Yun this was objectionable on
the grounds that the informants would not have gone into such details and that the author, himself no more than a transmitter, could
not possibly have known so thoroughly about the actual conversations
narrated. If one reads these lines closely enough, one realizes that Ji
Yun was dissatisfied with Pu Songling less because of the explicit immorality of the narratives than because of their implausibility.

---

[27] Ibid.

From a broader perspective, Ji Yun's rejection of *Studio of Leisure* amounts to a rejection of what could be called the "aesthetic mode" to *zhiguai* writing.[28] Ji Yun repeatedly lashes out at Pu's fondness for artistic invention, yet, ironically, this is what endears *Studio of Leisure* to the modern literary critic. The very verisimilitude of Pu's narrations, in which incidents whose factual basis was ambiguous or debatable were presented as real, was especially discomforting to Ji Yun. His primary criterion of acceptability was facticity, not imaginative recreation. His criticism of Pu Songling is understandable only if one remembers that few *zhiguai* writers before Pu undertook the drastic move of virtually abandoning the link between *zhiguai* narratives and circumstantial, objective reality.

One should note, in passing, how different Ji Yun's understanding of the *chuanqi* (which most likely reflects the judgement of the eighteenth century) is from the modern evaluation of the genre. Since Lu Xun, we have been accustomed to consider the *chuanqi*, especially those of the Tang, as prime examples of "consciously created fiction," in which aesthetic considerations are paramount.[29] But Ji Yun saw the situation differently: the *chuanqi* had to pass tests similar to those the *zhiguai* did. Moreover, Ji Yun did not valourize *chuanqi* above the *zhiguai*. The uncertain (low) position which the *chuanqi* held for Ji Yun (or for people at the time) is demonstrated by its total exclusion as a category from the lists in *An Annotated Catalogue*. By contrast,

---

[28] For critical discussions of Ji Yun's views in this regard, see Judith Zeitlin, *Historian of the Strange: Pu Songling and the Chinese Classical Tale*, pp. 39–40; and Coy L. Harmon, "Ch'ü Yu's *Chien-teng hsin-hua*: The Literary Tale in Transition" (Ph.D. dissertation, University of Arizona, 1985), pp. 69–71. Juxtaposing an aesthetic mode against a didactic one may be unacceptable to some, and there is little question that some classical tales obscure the boundaries between the two. There is also the possibility that something didactic could be aesthetic and vice versa. Also, if we consider didacticism as a content factor, and aestheticism as a stylistic or formal factor, then there are works (like *Dream of the Red Chamber*) which belong to both categories equally well.

[29] To distinguish the *chuanqi* from the *zhiguai* solely on the basis of this criterion of "literariness" is obviously inadequate when one considers post-Tang classical tales. Nevertheless it is a useful way of differentiating the Six Dynasties *zhiguai* from the Tang *chuanqi*, as seen in the "Introduction" to Karl S. Y. Kao, ed., *Classical Chinese Tales of the Supernatural and the Fantastic*, pp. 1–51.

disparaged as it was, the *zhiguai* nonetheless made its way into the catalogue and was one of the three categories of *xiaoshuo* in the "Philosophers" section.[30]

The Didactic Standard of *An Annotated Catalogue*

Ji Yun's rebuttal of Pu Songling's "brush of the genius" (*caizi zhi bi* 才子之筆) states by implication what, generically speaking, the *zhiguai* is *not* supposed to be; for what it should be one needs to turn to *An Annotated Catalogue*. Published along with the Imperial Library, the catalogue contains editorial comments (in review form) on over ten thousand titles. It includes titles copied into the Imperial Library because they were commendable, as well as the less praiseworthy ones, which received no more than their due evaluation in the catalogue and were not made part of the Library.[31]

For some time a heated debate has focused on the the authorship of the catalogue. Ji Yun's contemporaries were unanimous in attributing the work to him. Both Zhu Yun (in his epitaph for Ji Yun) and Ruan Yuan 阮元 (1764–1849) (in his preface to Ji's posthumous collection of writings) considered the writing of the reviews one of Ji Yun's prime achievements.[32] In *Record of Lineages in the Transmission of Han Learning* (*Hanxue shicheng ji* 漢學師承記), Jiang Fan 江藩 (1761–1831) further claimed that all the "annotations" — from the general discussions in the four main divisions to individual comments on such subjects as medicine, divination, and poetry — were attributable to

---

[30] *SKQSZM*, chaps. 140–144. Note that the words *tiyao* 提要 (abstracts) are added to some editions of *SKQSZM*. A useful introduction to *SKQSZM* is provided by William Hung, "Preface to an Index to *Ssu-ku ch'üan-shu tsung-mu* and *Wei-shou shu-mu*," *Harvard Journal of Asiatic Studies*, vol. 4, no. 1 (1939), pp. 47–58.

[31] For the organization of the catalogue as well as the nature of the material allotted to the four main divisions and the forty-three subdivisions, see the "Explanatory Notes" at the beginning of the catalogue.

[32] See the epitaph Zhu Gui penned for Ji Yun, collected in his *Zhizuzhai wenji*, chap. 5; for Ruan Yuan's preface to the posthumous collection of Ji Yun's works, see Ji Shuxin 紀樹馨 (b. 1771), ed., *Ji Wendagong yiji* 紀文達公遺集 (Posthumous Collection of the Writings of Ji Yun) (Beijing, 1812). While Zhu Yun noted that Ji Yun was singlehandedly responsible for *SKQSZM*, Ruan Yuan praised him for his balanced judgments there.

Ji Yun himself.[33] Even in his random notes, Ji Yun claims, quite explicitly, that he was solely responsible for the 200-chapter catalogue.[34]

The celebrated nineteenth-century scholar and poet, Li Ciming 李慈銘 (1830–1894), however, attributes the compiling of the reviews of the first three divisions — namely, Classics, Histories, and Philosophers — to Dai Zhen, Zhou Yongnian and Shao Jinhan, respectively.[35] Draft reviews written by Shao Jinhan and Yao Nai have also been discovered, and some of these were recently analysed in great depth by R. Kent Guy as documents upon which the final versions were based.[36] Guy was of the opinion that the collection was a collective effort to which Ji Yun obviously contributed. Also, according to a prefatory note to the Wensu Pavilion 文溯閣 version of *An Annotated Catalogue*, Weng Fanggang drafted many book reviews, though his versions differ significantly from those which eventually appeared in the catalogue.[37]

It may seem unlikely that, voluminous as the catalogue is, it could be the work of a single author. But that by no means annuls the possibility that an editorial hand was at work in each of the four main divisions of the catalogue, shaping and pruning the submitted draft reviews. It is certainly in that sense that Ji Yun claimed his "responsibility" for *An Annotated Catalogue*. Clearly, the reviews of the catalogue passed through his hands for final shaping, and thus they were not inconsistent with his views. Perhaps, then, it is a moot point whether Ji Yun was the sole compiler or the ultimate editor.

In any case, it is on similar grounds that the twentieth-century scholar Wang Chongmin 王重民 (1903–1975), having gathered evidence on the organization of the Bureau for the *Complete Library* project and studied the distribution of work among its staff members, challenges propositions like those advanced by Li Ciming. A few other scholars are also ready to take certain reviews in the catalogue as

---

[33] Jiang Fan, *Hanxue shicheng ji* (Shanghai: The Commercial Press, 1934), pp. 94–97.

[34] See *YWCTBJ*, p. 459.

[35] Li Ciming's view is found in his *Yuemantang riji* 越縵堂日記 (Daily Notes at the Hall of Zhejiang Curtains) (Beijing: Zhejiang gonghui 浙江工會 , 1920), p. 1119.

[36] R. Kent Guy, *The Emperor's Four Treasuries*, chap. 5.

[37] See Lu Jintang, "Ji Yun shengping jiqi *Yuewei caotang biji*," p. 75a.

reflections of Ji Yun's intellectual standpoint.[38] As far as the present analysis is concerned, one remarkable feature of the reviews in the *xiaoshuo* section of the annotated catalogue is the coherence of the arguments presented: a guiding vision unmistakably lies behind the 319 reviews on books, which range from the earliest *zhiguai* collections to early Qing compendia of miscellaneous anecdotes.[39] Another striking fact that supports the view that Ji Yun penned at least the reviews on the *xiaoshuo* section is the resemblance between the ideas in those notes and his standpoint as quoted in Sheng Shiyan's colophon and as mentioned in Ji Yun's own prefaces to *Close Scrutiny* as well as in several entries of the collection. In the following discussion, however, adopting established practice I will continue to refer to "the editors."

---

[38] See Zhang Hongsheng 張宏生, "Ji Yun zai *Shijing* yanjiushi shang de gongxian" 紀昀在詩經研究史上的貢獻 (Ji Yun's Contribution to the History of *Shijing* studies), *Nankai daxue xuebao* 南開大學學報, no. 5 (1989), pp. 18–23; Huang Yunmei 黃雲眉, "Cong xuezhe zuoyong shang guji *Siku quanshu* zhi jiaji" 從學者作用上估計四庫全書之價值 (Evaluating the *Siku quanshu* in Terms of Its Use for Scholars), *Guoli Beiping tushuguan guankan* 國立北平圖書館館刊, vol. 7, no. 5 (1933), pp. 51–62; and Wang Chongmin 王重民, "Lun *Siku quanshu zongmu*" 論四庫全書總目 (On the *Siku quanshu zongmu*), *Beijing daxue xuebao* 北京大學學報, no. 2 (1964). The strongest arguments yet presented in favour of Ji Yun's "authorship" of the reviews in *SKQSZM* are found in: Wang Zhenyuan 王振源, "Ji Yun wenxue sixiang chutan" 紀昀文學思想初探 (A Preliminary Study of the Literary Thought of Ji Yun), *Gudai wenxue lilun yanjiu* 古代文學理論研究, vol. 11 (1986), pp. 256–285; and Zhou Jiming, *Ji Yun pingzhuan*, pp. 68–80. The view propunded by Wang Zhenyuan is similar to mine, and he treats the question of the draft reviews by Yao Nai, Shao Jinhan, and Weng Fanggang (which Guy relies on to make his point) in great detail, arguing convincingly for extensive revisions undertaken by Ji Yun.

[39] *Extensive Gleanings from the Taiping Reign* and *Retiring from Farming* (*Chuogeng lu* 輟耕錄) were often referred to as paradigms, respectively, of excellence and mediocrity in the *zhiguai*. The latter, criticized in the review for its prurient elements, was also mentioned elsewhere at least seven other times; see *SKQSZM*, pp. 2772, 2781 (twice), 2782, 2814, 2832, and 2843. It provides a persistent comparison with other works discussed: *New to the Ears* (*Erxin* 耳新) was derogatively characterized as "belonging to the order of *Retiring from Farming*"; *The Chicken Ribs Collection* (*Jilei bian* 雞肋編) was superior to it; *Miscellaneous Records at Suichang* (*Suichang zalu* 遂昌雜錄) contained hard facts and not "the carelessly gathered materials of books like *Retiring from Farming*." Such consistency would be unlikely if the book reviews were to have come from more than one person.

The *xiaoshuo* section of the annotated catalogue consists of five chapters (only the first three of these discuss books chosen for inclusion in the Imperial Library). It is organized around the tripartite classificatory system of:

(1) miscellania (*zashi* 雜事),
(2) reports of anomalies (*yiwen* 異聞), and
(3) idle chatter (*suoyu* 瑣語).

The second category (or "school") is primarily devoted to reviews of *zhiguai* works. Some *zhiguai* narratives also figure amongst the "miscellania," though this category includes primarily quasi-historical materials that are, for one reason or another, not included in the section on standard histories.[40] *Zhiguai* works are almost totally absent from the "idle chatter" subdivision. Dominating this category are collections of folk sayings, conversations by noted historical figures like Su Shi, fables and humorous vignettes, accounts of local customs, offhand remarks, and popular tales in particular regions of the country.[41] The three-fold division does at times appear arbitrary, for included in it are compilations of a polymorphous nature that can be placed in more than one category. The common element that holds these materials together, making them all *xiaoshuo*, is not their "fictionality" as such but is rather the fact that they are all related to various forms of oral discourse, denoted by the word *shuo* 説 (to speak) (see Chapter Two).

The catalogue evaluates each individual *zhiguai* work cited in the light of criteria expounded in the introductory remarks to the *xiaoshuo* section. In most modern editions, these remarks are inserted at the beginning of Chapter 140, and they deserve to be looked at more closely. Here "the editors" begin by tracing the origins of the genre to

---

[40] The reason why these were not admitted into the section on miscellaneous history is explained in *SKQSZM*, p. 2784: "Courtly affairs and military matters are in the section on miscellaneous history; leisurely talk of bypaths and back alleys … counts as miscellanea."

[41] There are exceptions, though, for included in this third category are works often simply classified as *zhiguai* like Zhang Hua's *Records of Wide-ranging Matters* and *Narrating the Anomalous* (*Shuyi ji* 述異記), attributed to Ren Fang 任昉 (460–508). See Liu Yeqiu, *Lidai biji gaishu*, pp. 11–17; and Li Jianguo, *Tangqian zhiguai xiaoshuoshi*, pp. 260–268 and pp. 396–404.

works in existence even before the 943 pieces by Yu Chu, the Western Han writer who was reputedly the originator of the entire *xiaoshuo* tradition.[42] These earliest examples include those found in Qu Yuan's "Asking Questions of Heaven" ("Tian wen" 天問) and in *The Master of Qingshi (Qingshizi* 青史子).[43] Thus, the editors conclude that *Zhou Dynasty Tales by Yu Chu (Yu Chu Zhou shuo* 虞初周説) is no more than a high point in early *xiaoshuo* writing.[44] After a rather cursory overview of the tradition and some brief mention of the proliferation of such works after the Tang and Song periods, the editors note that:

> Specious and obfuscating hearsay is plenteous, yet scattered within [these reports] are those that instruct as well as admonish, broaden our horizons, and provide materials for the search for evidence. Selected for inclusion now is that which is refined and edifying.... Nothing that is salacious, vulgar, absurd, or distracting for readers will be mentioned here.[45]

The first standard by which "praise-and-blame" was to be adjudicated, here candidly stated, is a didactic one, and it clearly supersedes the consideration discussed in the last chapter — the contribution to knowledge. Repeatedly these two principles are emphasized in the critical reviews on the individual books to follow, but the didactic argument predominates. In addition, there is an insistence on the authenticity of the records, an interesting emphasis when set against the didactic imperative. Naturally, the emphasis on authenticity is understandable if such oral records were viewed as materials for

---

[42] *SKQSZM*, p. 2733.

[43] *The Master of Qingshi* is one of the fifteen earliest *xiaoshuo* works listed in the Bibliographies section of *History of the Han Dynasty*. It was no longer extant even by the Sui dynasty.

[44] Some perspectives on these ideas may be gained by consulting: Lu Xun, *A Brief History of Chinese Fiction*, chap. 1; and Li Changji 李昌集, "Zhongguo zaoqi xiaoshuoguan de lishi yanbian" 中國早期小説觀的歷史演變 (The Historical Development of the Early Views of Chinese *Xiaoshuo*), *Wenxue yichan* 文學遺産, no. 3 (1988), pp. 1–9. Each discusses the early history of the *xiaoshuo* from a modern point of view.

[45] For a discussion of the introductory remarks to the *xiaoshuo* section, see Maeno Naoaki, "Lun Ming Qing liangzhong duili de xiaoshuo lilun — Jin Shengtan yu Ji Yun" 論明清兩種對立的小説理論 — 金聖嘆與紀昀 (On Two Opposed Theories of Fiction in the Ming and Qing — Jin Shengtan and Ji Yun), translated by Wu Biyong 吳璧雍, *Zhongwai wenxue* 中外文學, vol. 14, no. 3 (1985), pp. 77–97.

historical studies or investigations of a sociological or scientific character. But as we shall see, the verifiability of the tales also lent force to the didacticism.

The editorial comments pertaining to individual *zhiguai* collections which allow us a glimpse into Ji Yun's generic formulations can be studied in terms of two sets of value judgments. There is first an explicit condemnation of falsehood and of licentiousness; correspondingly, veracity and moral value are praised unreservedly. Not all of the works referred to below were *zhiguai* collections "pure and simple": a few were miscellanea with varying proportions of tales of the supernatural, and some were not even of the *zhiguai* category. But taken together, what might appear to be scattered and superficial remarks cohere into a consistent and comprehensive theory of the *zhiguai* and of the potentials of this genre.

Against Falsehoods.   The tendency for *xiaoshuo* to contain inaccuracies in reporting was explained as something inherent, in part, in the genre itself. In the review of *Record of Conversations* by Kang Pian, it is said, "Having been partly derived from hearsay, [the *xiaoshuo*] narrates both truths and falsehoods.... Hence it is neither totally reliable nor totally unfounded."[46] This focus on authenticity and verifiability was the reason why many *xiaoshuo* collections are denounced in the catalogue. And as the least plausible type of *xiaoshuo*, devoted completely to a record of the bizarre and inexplicable, the *zhiguai* naturally came under the severest of attacks.

The review of Li Kang's 李伉 (or 李亢) *Accounts of the Exceptional and Anomalous (Duyi zhi* 獨異志) offers a typical example of a *zhiquai* collection being castigated for being "perverse and absurd." Its account of the marriage between Nüwa 女媧 and her brother, and the tales from *Liezi* that it included, like the one about the boy from the sea who was on intimate terms with a seagull, were dismissed as ridiculous.[47] The eminent Daoist theorist and writer of the late Tang, Du Guangting 杜光庭 (850–933) was also said to be notorious for spreading absurdities in his accounts of immortals and prodigious events in

[46] *SKQSZM*, p. 2796.
[47] For the Nüwa story, see Li Kang, *Duyi zhi* , in *Congshu jicheng chubian*, vol. 134, p. 51.

Recording Anomalies (*Luyi ji* 錄異記).[48] The failure to pass the authenticity test, in fact, caused some works to be relegated to the *xiaoshuo* category when they should have been classified otherwise — perhaps as miscellaneous histories. Despite Huang Fu's 黃輔 frequent assertions, in the preface to his *Records of Spirits and Anomalies at Mount Xia* (*Xiashan shenyi ji* 峽山神異記), that the bizarre events he records are backed by renowned statesmen and supposedly trustworthy personalities like Su Shi, his work was not classified in *An Annotated Catalogue* as a geographical treatise; it was simply assigned to the section on *xiaoshuo*.[49]

Perhaps it was typical of the high Qing, when the empiricist trend held full sway in the intellectual sphere, that criteria of authenticity were adhered to so adamantly. The editorial comments on two Ming *zhiguai* collections elaborate further on this standard. Chen Liangmo's *Admonitory Records of What Was Heard and Seen* was said to contain "too much wild talk,"[50] while an extreme example of the unwieldy fabrication to which *xiaoshuo* writers were prone was Yang Yi's 楊儀 (fl. 1541) *Anomalies Collected at the [Residence of] High Slopes* (*Gaopo yizuan* 高坡異纂). Yang compiled the collection after his conversion to supernaturalism, which occurred when he heard the story of his close friend's encounter with an immortal on a crane. The collection's account of the God of Literature spying upon a lascivious rendezvous between the Weaving Maid and the Boy Cowherd, who was later punished by the Supreme God, was said to be "an insult to Heaven."[51] The dissatisfaction with the perpetuation of falsehoods in some *zhiguai* was, however, tempered by a reiteration of the view that it is a genre of little appreciable value: "Books recording anomalous events have

---

[48] All of Du Guangting's hagiographies of immortals as well as his anomalous records were condemned as "sheer nonsense." *SKQSZM*, p. 2836.

[49] According to the review of Huang Fu's collection: "Since [the informants] are trustworthy personalities, the events should be worth believing." *SKQSZM*, p. 2838. Note must also be made of the fact that for the first time in its bibliographical history, *The Classics of Mountains and Seas* was re-classified as *xiaoshuo* rather than a geographical treatise.

[50] *SKQSZM*, p. 2840.

[51] The story is found in Yang Yi, *Gaopo yizuan*, in *Shuo ku* 説庫 (Storehouse of Talk) (Shanghai: Wenming shuju 文明書局 , 1925), vol. 33, 2:4a.

nothing to do with knowledge and learning. There is no need to probe deeply into questions of completeness [in the reporting].["52]

Against Licentiousness.   A second charge brought against the *xiaoshuo* in the "introductory remarks" was that of "obscenity and vulgarity." Such criticisms, interestingly enough, were almost never targeted at pre-Song *zhiguai,* just as the Six Dynasties collections generally emerged unscathed by condemnations of untruthful reporting.[53] This information suggests an awareness, on the part of the editors of the *Complete Library* project, that a qualitative change occurred in the *zhiguai* over the course of its evolution through the ages. One collection that allegedly promoted impropriety was said to be the Song compilation, *Comprehensive Records at the Cloud Studio* (*Yunzhai guanglu* 雲齋廣錄). It divided the anecdotes it records into nine categories; three of these ("Spirits," "Anomalous Occurrences," and "Immortals"[54]) include materials on supposedly supernatural occurrences and phenomena. In comparison with *Cloud Studio,* Liu Fu's 劉斧 (eleventh century) *Remarkable Opinions under the Green Latticed Window* (*Qingsuo gaoyi* 青鎖 高議) was described in another review as superior by virtue of the fact that it serves a commendable hortatory function despite an occasional vulgarism.[55]

---

[52] *SKQSZM,* p. 2844.

[53] The one noted exception is *Tale of Han Emperor Wu* (*Hanwu gushi* 漢武故事) purportedly written by Ban Gu. It was said to have diverged significantly from accounts in *Records of History* and *History of the Han Dynasty.* Also, Ji Yun's preference for the Six Dynasties *zhiguai* must have left its mark here.

[54] *SKQSZM,* pp. 2837–2838.

[55] The amount of argumentation found in *Remarkable Opinions under the Green Latticed Window* makes it an early example of the didactic use of commentaries in the classical tale. Appended to some of the entries is a commentarial section headed by the words: "Thus it is argued," and precisely it is the idea of "arguing" that gives this collection of both *zhiguai* and *chuanqi* stories its name ("opinions"). Lu Xun contrasted the discursiveness of Song tales with the lack of it in their counterparts at other times, ascribing the difference to the rise of neo-Confucianism and the consequent fondness for moralizing. See Lu Xun, *A Brief History of Chinese Fiction,* chap. 11. No doubt *Remarkable Opinions under the Green Latticed Window* could be adduced to prove his point. More interesting in the context of the present analysis is the similarity this collection bears to the late eighteenth-century *zhiguai* works in question.

The criticism levelled against Lu Cai's 陸采 (ca. 1495–1540) *Discourses by Guests at Yecheng* (*Yecheng kelun* 冶城客論) deserves special attention because the critique is strongly reminiscent of Ji Yun's remarks on *Studio of Leisure.* This collection originated in the anecdotes circulated in the conversations of some of the most prominent elite members of the mid-Ming like Shen Zhou 沈周 (1427–1509) and Zhu Yunming, who were both eminent poet-painters of the time. Its last tale was said to have rendered the illicit love scenes of Madam Shi 施 and her paramour as though "[the raconteur] had personally witnessed them."[56] The criticism was double-edged: lasciviousness was compounded with infidelity in the recounting. The review in the catalogue summarily dismisses the collection and notes that it had "run counter to the orthodox teachings."

Apparent in the catalogue is a persistent antipathy towards not only the *zhiguai* but also the *xiaoshuo* as a whole for allegedly promulgating promiscuous attitudes. In the "miscellania" section, *Retiring from Farming* (*Chuogeng lu* 輟耕錄) by the Yuan polymath Tao Zongyi is derided for including sexual obscenities, trivial and vulgar talk among the commonfolk, and tales in very poor taste.[57] The review of another Yuan compilation also classified as a miscellany, *Records of Events Heard in the Southeast,* drives home the argument even more forcefully. One of the stories in it, "Madame Southern Mountain" ("Nanshan furen" 南山夫人) is singled out as grossly salacious: "[It] has fallen into the old rut of the *xiaoshuo* genre, and hence becomes defiled."[58]

The Value of Veracity.   What suggests that the reviews in the *xiaoshuo* section of *An Annotated Catalogue* were put together by one hand is that implicit comparisons are made over and over again between the works discussed, and some kind of ranking is occasionally proposed. The collections of Wang Mingqing were said to be among the very best of those written in the Song. Zhuang Chuo's 莊綽 (fl. 1133) *The Chicken Ribs Collection* (*Jilei bian* 雞肋編) was praised as superior to Tao Zongyi's *Retiring from Farming* and on a par with the *Words of the Retired*

---

[56] *SKQSZM*, p. 2841.

[57] Ibid., p. 2782.

[58] Ibid., p. 2778.

Scholar from Eastern Qi (*Qidong yeyu* 齊東野語) by Zhou Mi 周密 (1232–1308) of the Southern Song.[59] One criterion of judgment was the degree to which the author could be relied upon to recount actual events. The review of Wang Mingqing's four *Waving a Chowry* collections concludes with the observation that Wang's reportage, based on actual contacts he had with prestigious old clans in North China, is more reliable than the chit-chat of back alleys and bypaths. Zhuang Chuo's *The Chicken Ribs Collection* was also credited as having value for research with empirical evidence. Zhuang Chuo himself was characterized as someone with broad learning and a willingness to "keep his ears open" for new information.[60]

To the editors, the value of the recording of hearsay was that the events narrated, if verifiable, helped advance knowledge and learning, or else more harm was done than good. Needless to say, this standard was especially difficult to uphold in the case of *zhiguai* material. Be that as it may, *zhiguai* information was never thoroughly rejected. The editors suggested that what is required to confront the mix of truths and falsehoods perpetuated by the *zhiguai* is discernment and the ability to sift valuable facts from fiction. Of *The Chronicle of Prince Mu* (*Mutianzi zhuan* 穆天子傳), therefore, the review says that its account of Prince Mu's adventures seems "closer to the truth" than those in *The Classic of Mountains and Seas* and *Huainan zi* 淮南子, although the editors do not say why that is the case.[61]

The *zhiguai* compilers had, of course, responded to the challenge. The practice of documenting meticulously the specifics of time and locale was utilized to lend greater credibility to a fantastic event. As we noted earlier, the practice originated with Su E's *Collection of Miscellania at Duyang*, in which the informants are consistently noted. This

---

[59] Ibid., p. 2772. In the review of the *Tingshi* 桯史 (Bedside Footstool), it was said that, among Song *xiaoshuo*, this collection must be regarded as inferior to those of Wang Mingqing; see p. 2774.

[60] *SKQSZM*, p. 2771.

[61] At the end of the review on *The Chronicle of Prince Mu*, the editors noted that because of the unverifiable nature of the work, the decision had been made to relegate it to the "reports of anomalies" section rather than "daily records" (*qijuzhu* 起居注). *SKQSZM*, p. 2786.

eventually became standard for many *zhiguai* collections.[62] Ji Yun, too, seems to have practised what he taught: the majority of the tales of the supernatural in his *Close Scrutiny* are preceded by indications of who the informant is, as well as when and where the story actually took place. In his collection Ji Yun also criticizes certain *zhiguai* reports as unfounded and not amenable to careful investigation. Stories about exotic plants discovered in the ancient kingdoms outside of China like Dayuan 大宛 , Wusun 烏孫 , and Yutian 于闐 were denounced as fabrications (*HX* I:73). Commenting on a story of a woman's soul leaving her body (*HX* IV:43), Ji Yun also scoffs at the implausibility of a minor plot detail, and believes such absurdities to be characteristic of those *xiaoshuo* writers whose sole concern was to garnish their tales and curry favour with readers. In the very last entry of *Close Scrutiny* (*LX* VI:18), Ji Yun discusses two anecdotes in another *zhiguai* collection circulated at the time, *New Words on Autumnal Plains* by Zhang Jingyun. While the first is simply said to be deficient in specifics, the second he flatly denounces as a scandal. Ji Yun thus laments the difficulty of being accurate in reporting such accounts: "If [inaccuracy] is the case even with the annals of the State of Lu, how much more so with the collected anecdotes of the minor official of Zhou times."[63]

The Value of Didacticism.   The premium placed on accurate reporting, supposed to further the goal of broadening one's knowledge and enhancing "research," may actually lead to the denunciation of much of *zhiguai* literature as worthless. What saves it, as *An Annotated Catalogue* makes clear, is its cautionary and hortatory functions. In fact, didacticism was more highly valued at times in the catalogue than verifiability, and the presence of the didactic in particular items often justified their inclusion in the catalogue. An example is Liu Fu's *Remarkable Opinions under the Green Latticed Window*. The catalogue points out that this collection contains an erroneous account — that of Sun Mian 孫勉 chasing the sea turtle and Weigong 魏公 becoming the Immortal of the Purple Court (Yama) on his death — but the collection

---

[62] According to the review of *Ertan* 耳談 (Ear-talk), in *SKQSZM*, p. 2844.

[63] *YWCTBJ*, p. 552.

was nevertheless commendable, since it promoted moral behaviour.[64] Guo Tuan's 郭彖 (fl. 1165) *Accounts of a Cartload of Ghosts* (*Kuiche zhi* 睽 車志), a *zhiguai* collection of the Southern Song, is criticized for per-petuating absurdities like the belief that the Song calligrapher Mi Fei 米芾 (1051–1107) was a python-demon. Yet the collection's redeem-ing element is its moral scrupulousness:

> At the end of each entry there is an indication of who the informant is. In so doing it is following the example of the *Collection of Miscellanea at Duyang*. The primary aim is the explication of cause and effect, which serves to warn and admonish [those who read it]. In particular, because the selections are wide-ranging, there are often embellishments and con-trivances that run counter to actuality.... [However], such has been the way of the *xiaoshuo* since time immemorial. It cannot be measured by the standards of the historical biographies. One should judge it by the general goal of encouraging people to do good.[65]

There is a recognition here that, of the two criteria of facticity and didactic utility, pre-eminence should be given to the latter, in as much as the former is virtually unattainable.

The Sui 隋 dynasty *zhiguai* compilation, Yan Zhitui's 顏之推 (530–590?) *Accounts of Grievances Requited* (*Huanyuan zhi* 還冤志), also entitled *Accounts of Aggrieved Souls* (*Yuanhun zhi* 冤魂志), is aptly characterized by the editors as Buddhist in orientation. It is devoted essentially to the exposition of doctrines of karmic retribution.[66] In the review of this work there is a brief digression on the likelihood that men turn into spirits upon death because of *qi*'s permutations.[67] It does not appear that the editors entirely approved of the work. Several instances of supernatural events in it, also found in the official histories, were accepted as what might conceivably have occurred, but

---

[64] See "Zifu zhenren ji" 紫府真人記 (Record of the Immortal at the Purple Court), in Liu Fu, *Qingsuo gaoyi* (Shanghai: Shanghai guji chubanshe 上海古籍出版社, 1983), pp. 14–15.

[65] *SKQSZM*, p. 2803.

[66] For studies of *Accounts of Grievances Requited*, see Albert E. Dien, "The *Yüan-hun chi* (Accounts of Ghosts with Grievances): A Sixth-century Collection of Stories," in *Wen-lin: Studies in the Chinese Humanities*, edited by Chow Tse-tsung, pp. 211–278; and his disserta-tion on the same topic.

[67] *SKQSZM*, p. 2794.

such tolerance was not extended to Buddhist concepts of the afterlife expressed in the collection. To justify the inclusion of *Accounts of Grievances Requited* in the Imperial Library, the didactic argument is once again brought up:

> This book is entirely about Buddhist ideas of retribution. [In the Spring and Autumn period] there was Mr. Peng 彭 in the state of Qi 齊 , Mr. Shen 申 in the Jin 晉 state, Poyou in Zheng 鄭 , and Hunliang 渾良 in the state of Wei 衛 . Their stories are documented in the commentaries to *The Spring and Autumn Annals*.... Strong and unswerving souls undergo transmutations, with *qi* as a catalyst. This is in accordance with principles. Such matters are not as airy and as unamenable to investigation as paradise and hell. [However,] the language of the book is rather refined, and it is different in that it does not partake of the superficiality of *xiaoshuo*. It will be preserved for instruction and admonition.[68]

The lack of respect for Buddhist ideas is clearly reflected in this review. Also reflected here is emphasis on the moral function of the collection as a criterion of acceptability.

It is worth noting that most of the better known *zhiguai* compilations of the Six Dynasties period, the Tang, and the Song, made their way into the Imperial library — that is to say, were copied and preserved — while others from those same periods, as well as those of the Ming and Qing, were simply listed in the "Not Copied" lists. There existed then, among the elite, a core of *zhiguai* works, distinguished in one way or another, which demanded recognition. These works constituted an identifiable canon. Nowhere did the editors argue for their value as the modern critic would, in terms of their significance as "the first instances of Chinese narrative" or "the earliest examples of fictional writing in China." It was through rather different rationalizations that the works could be found acceptable. The most powerful of those relates to moral teaching.

Frequently, both major and minor *zhiguai* works were measured by the same yardstick of didacticism. Probably due to its ready availability, only the second collection of the immensely influential *zhiguai*, *Records of Yijian*, receives mention in *An Annotated Catalogue*. Written by Hong Mai in his old age and steeped in the superstitious beliefs

---

[68] Ibid.

prevalent in the Southern Song, the collection was praised precisely for its attempt to encourage moral behaviour.[69] The Tang collection, Zheng Huangu's 鄭還古 *Accounts of Diverse Anomalies* (*Boyi zhi* 博異志), was said to "give advice and injunctions, although in a rough manner, as well as words that fall flat on ears of the rebellious."[70] Other works with *zhiguai* materials that were praised for their didacticism include:

(1) *Records of Predeterminism* (*Qianding lu* 前定錄), by Zhong Lu 鍾輅 (early ninth century);

(2) *Guest-talk at the Thatched Pavilion*, by Huang Xiufu;

(3) *Ancient and Recent Affairs Classified* (*Fenmen gujin leishi* 分門古今類事), by an anonymous compiler;

(4) *Poor Imitations* (*Xiaopin ji* 效顰集), by Zhao Bi 趙弼 (ca. 1399– 1450);

(5) *Admonitory Records of What Was Heard and Seen*, by Chen Liangmo;

(6) *Records of Recompense in the Next Life*, by Lu Qi; and

(7) *Roster of Retribution by Thunder* (*Lei pu* 雷譜), by Jin Kan 金侃 (?–1703).

The catalogue's positive evaluation of this type of *zhiguai* literature underlines an attempt to legitimize the *zhiguai* in a "canonical" or "orthodox" tradition. A rough idea of what the editors think the *zhiguai* should be can be gleaned from the comments on individual *yiwen* collections in Chapters 142 (the "Copied" list) and 143 (the "Not Copied" list) in *An Annotated Catalogue* (see pages 182–183). The arguments may not be at all times convincing, nor were they applied universally to all the works discussed in the reviews, but they were clearly there. Needless to say, there were works that had come to be regarded as somehow "canonical" partly by virtue of their popularity but which did not fulfil the criteria informing the evaluative judgments of *An Annotated Catalogue*. This is not to belittle or denigrate Ji

---

[69] The other portions of *Records of Yijian* were reviewed later in Ruan Yuan, *Siku weishou shumu tiyao* 四庫未收書目提要 (Bibliographies Unlisted in the *Four Treasuries*) (Taibei: Shijie shuju 世界書局 , 1967), pp. 41–42.

[70] *SKQSZM*, p. 2795.

Yun's critical efforts. The prime aim of the cataloguing, classification, exclusion, and ranking that one sees enacted in the project of the *Complete Library*, of which the writing of reviews is but one part, is to impose homogeneity and orthodoxy on what is considered heterogeneous or heterodox material.[71] In light of the vast terrain of *zhiguai* literature that had to be covered, what was achieved in the catalogue is indeed remarkable.

On the other hand, by banning some *zhiguai* works as lascivious, accepting others that were didactic despite their lasciviousness, and praising a significant group of *zhiguai* for their exhortatory value, Ji Yun was doing more than establishing standards of analysis and criticism. He was in fact pointing to the kind of *zhiguai* that should be written. In terms of what was discussed earlier, we can even say that he was defining a special mode of *zhiguai* writing that was to replace the aesthetic mode of *Studio of Leisure*, which he found decidedly inadequate and which he criticized time and again in the editorial reviews. He indeed adopted this mode some twenty years later, in the compilation of *Close Scrutiny*.

The Immediate Predecessors

Maeno Naoaki considers Ji Yun's critical formulations as outlined in *An Annotated Catalogue* to occupy one extreme of a spectrum of literary theories on Chinese narrative and the ideas of Jin Shengtan 金聖 嘆 (1610–1661) to occupy the other end.[72] He argues further that Ji Yun's views eventually gained both acceptance as well as prominence, in the course of the Qing period up to the early twentieth century and triumphed over those of Jin Shengtan. While Naoaki's views certainly need to be further qualified, there is little doubt that the didactic imperative dominated much literary production in the nineteenth century. In the field of the *zhiguai*, didacticism had become a serious topic for discussion as early as the mid-seventeenth century. As

---

[71] On the same point, see Sheldon Lu Hsiao-peng, *From Historicity to Fictionality: The Chinese Poetics of Narrative* (Stanford: Stanford University Press, 1994), pp. 37–52.

[72] See Maeno Naoaki, "Lun Ming Qing liangzhong duili de xiaoshuo lilun — Jin Shengtan yu Ji Yun," p. 77.

COMMENTS ON *ZHIGUAI* COLLECTIONS IN
AN ANNOTATED CATALOGUE

Title of Collection	Category	Comments
Caigui ji 才鬼記	Not copied	"Tales of the strange by *xiaoshuo* writers are plentiful. Mei Dingzuo 梅鼎祚 [1549–1615] compiled this book by gathering fragmented, left-over material. It is already not meant to have much significance. And with this confusion in applying conventions, the compilation can be considered worthless!"
Gusheng 觚賸	Not copied	"Niu Xiu is much given to an ornamented style of writing. This collection contains [a great deal of] poignant and moving narration, and is reminiscent of *xiaoshuo* from the Tang. But often there is considerable embellishment and patching that spice up the stories, and thus [one] cannot attempt any thorough verification of their truthfulness."
Huanyuan zhi 還冤志	Copied	"It uses a refined, classical prose, differing noticeably from the low taste of *xiaoshuo*. It should be kept for purposes of admonition [for posterity]; it will do no harm to morals."
Jutan lu 劇談錄	Copied	"The accounts of minor officials [in ancient times] were derived from hearsay, where truths and falsehoods were mixed. Such a situation has persisted up to the present. So the accounts are neither totally reliable, nor completely fabricated. Readers have to verify their merits and drawbacks. It is not [for us] to abolish the category [of *xiaoshuo*] altogether."
Kuaiyuan 獪園	Not copied	"In the two chapters the reported names and incidents contradict each other. If it is like this with events witnessed, one can imagine what it is like with events heard!"
Mutianzi zhuan 穆天子傳	Copied	"To classify this collection as veritable history … is to violate the conventions governing historicial genres. We have relegated it to the category of *xiaoshuo*."
Shanhai jing 山海經	Copied	"Not one of a hundred items [reported in this collection] is veritable. Various authorities have placed it first among geographical treatises. That is inappropriate."

(CONT'D)

Title of Collection	Category	Comments
Yiyuan 異苑	Copied	"Its style is simple and unadorned. It does not smack of the vulgarity of *xiaoshuo*. Hence it certainly could not have been written after the Six Dynasties."
Zanyunlou zaji 簪雲樓雜記	Not copied	"The miscellaneous accounts and assorted hearsay [in this collection] often involve strange-talk. The only incident recorded that is worth verifying is that of the adopted daughter of Wei Zhongxian 魏忠賢 [1568–1627] going under the name of Ms. Zhang 張, queen of Emperor Xizong 熹宗 of the Ming dynasty [r. 1621–1627]."

mentioned earlier, it is often hard to draw the line between those *zhiguai* works that were seriously didactic and those that only pretended to be so, but a brief look at what some *zhiguai* writers of the late seventeenth and early eighteenth centuries say about their own compilations will be relevant in the present context.[73] These *zhiguai* collections are, after all, the immediate predecessors to *Close Scrutiny*.

Didacticism has, of course, always been one of the functions carried by the *zhiguai*. The compiler of the Tang collection, *Accounts of Diverse Anomalies*, notes in his preface that he aimed "not just to induce laughter, but also to counsel and restrain in a small way."[74] By the late seventeenth century, didacticism became a line of defense elaborated with more and more rigour, and at the same time *zhiguai* compilers were increasingly conscious of the instructive role their work was supposed to play. A striking reversal had occurred in Li Zhao's formulation of the relative importance of the three aims of anecdote-collecting discussed in Chapter One.[75] The didactic function now took precedence over "exploring principles" and "clarifying doubts."

---

[73] Thus Wang Xianpei 王先霈 speaks of a didactic tradition of the *zhiguai*. Wang Xianpei, "Fengjian lijiao sixiang tong xiaoshuo yishu de diduixing" 封建禮教思想同小説藝術的敵對性 (The Opposition between Feudal Ethical Beliefs and the Art of Fiction), *Wenxue pinglun* 文學評論, no. 2 (1987), pp. 132–137.

[74] See the preface to *Boyi zhi* (Beijing: Zhonghua shuju 中華書局, 1980), p. 1.

[75] See p. 30.

The prevalence of the argument for didacticism in early Qing *zhiguai* compilations is demonstrated by those anthologized in the collectanea *Bell-talk* by Wu Zhenfang. Almost all of these collections seem to have eventually fallen into oblivion and are by now virtually unread.[76] According to Lu Qi, one of the compilers, in his *Records of Recompense in the Next Life,* he only narrated incidents that depict the felicities attendant on virtuous acts and the calamities overtaking the evil-minded.[77] Another compiler, Xu Qing 徐慶, asked learned members of the elite not to scoff at his *Record of Testimonies to the Faith* (*Xinzheng lu* 信徵錄) for being less worthy than the classics and histories, for it served to promote virtue and discourage vice.[78] Yet another, Dong Han 董含 (1626–?), while defending the factuality of his records in *Additional Notes at Chun Village* (*Chunxiang zhuibi* 蓴鄉贅筆) by saying that some of them could be verified by accounts published in the government gazetteers, was of the opinion that his compilation would play a positive didactic role.[79]

Many of these collections anthologized in *Bell-talk* differ from *Close Scrutiny* in both style and format. The most noticeable difference is a thematic focus that Ji Yun discards. *Records of Recompense in the Next Life* expressly documents the operations of the retributive order in a specific location — hell. As its title suggests, *Roster of Retribution by Thunder* assembles cases of punishment exacted by the thunder-god,

---

[76] *Bell-talk,* consisting of two separate volumes, is a compendium of fifty-three collections of *biji, chuanqi* and *zhiguai* writings of the late seventeenth century. Over half a dozen *zhiguai* works can be found in vol. 2, *Bell-talk, Second Collection.* Little is known about its compiler Wu Zhenfang, except that he was the elder brother of Wu Chenyan 吳陳琰, author of *Miscellaneous Records from a Spacious Garden* (*Kuangyuan zazhi* 曠園雜志), a *zhiguai* collection to which he contributed a preface.

[77] According to its preface, *Records of Recompense in the Next Life* was written, despite the Confucian inhibitions against talking of ghosts and spirits, to "inculcate in the populace the right beliefs, just as one puts warning signposts on the roads." Wu Zhenfang, *Shuoling houji,* 14:1a.

[78] Wu Zhenfang, *Shuoling houji,* 13:1a–b.

[79] Wu Zhenfang, *Shuoling houji,* 19:1b. A brief discussion of the background to the compilation of *Additional Notes at the Village of the Chun Plant* is given by Lai Xinxia 來新夏, "Qingren biji suilu: guanyu *Sangang shilue* he *Chunxiang zhuibi*" 清人筆記隨錄：關於三岡事略和蓴鄉贅筆 (Random Records of Qing *Biji*: Concerning the *Sangang shilue* and the *Chunxiang zhuibi*), *Xuelin manlu* 學林漫錄, vol. 1, no. 2 (1981), pp. 171–175.

a deity commonly believed to mete out punishment to the wicked. *Occasional Records of Retribution during the Present Life* (*Xianguo suilu* 現果隨錄), in contrast to *Records of Recompense,* contains only narratives of "rewards and penalties actually witnessed (by the compiler) as occurring within a person's lifetime."[80] These contrast clearly with the broad range of freakish phenomena included in most *zhiguai* compilations, including *Close Scrutiny.*

To conclude: in one sense Ji Yun must be regarded as the foremost *zhiguai* theorist of his own age. Taken together, his five prefaces, scattered remarks in *Close Scrutiny,* personal comments to his disciple Sheng Shiyan, and undeniable contributions to the *xiaoshuo* reviews of *An Annotated Catalogue* provide a coherent, well-formulated statement on the meaning and significance of *zhiguai* writing. His significant contribution is seen in the fact that he ventures to defend the *zhiguai* against the charge of triviality and frivolity. In other words, he attempts to rid the *zhiguai* of the stigma which had long been attached to it. For Ji Yun, the moral purpose in *zhiguai* literature is its saving grace, and a whole literary tradition is justified by reference to the didactic function. *Close Scrutiny* is, in this light, a concrete example of how "small talk" can edify even while it entertains.

---

[80] In the Buddhist scheme there are three different kinds of retribution, administered during one's lifetime, in one's next life, and in future lives. *Occasional Records of Retribution during the Present Life* contains evidence of the first type.

Chapter 6

The Didacticism of Close Scrutiny

> Traditional hermeneutics actively constructs a cultural tradition in
> the guise of a unified realm of meanings and values separated
> from social relations of domination and power.
>
> — *John Brenkman*

It should be clear by now what determined Ji Yun's choice of the didactic mode as a means to present his collection of *zhiguai* narratives. What then does *Close Scrutiny* itself show us of how he uses individual tales for moral edification of the masses? Since Ji Yun's main goal was to "teach and instruct" — the root meaning of the Greek word *didaktikos*, from which we derived the word "didacticism" — one aspect of our undertaking is that of unravelling the methods and strategies used to direct attention to the moral messages behind the tales. This task is made complicated by the fact that in *Close Scrutiny* it is not only Ji Yun who engages in didacticism, but also his group, for the collection documents the active participation of a huge number of raconteurs and commentators in the didactic effort. To focus the discussion, we shall first concentrate on how Ji Yun, as a member of the eighteenth-century elite, saw the issue of didacticism.

Didacticism is more than a matter of technique. As attested by Ji Yun's collection, dispensing moral injunctions was seen as a responsibility of the traditional elite. In encouraging others to do good, members of the elite were not just assisting in social control; they were also fulfilling their role as guardians of public morality. In grounding moral exhortations on their own interpretation of the order of the universe, they indirectly asserted the extent to which they could control the available forms of discourse. This is perhaps as it should be. Habermas, for one, has analysed didacticism as one of the many cultural practices through which the elite as a collectivity secures its identity. It is through the use of didacticism that the elite differentiates itself from other collectivites with which it has relations of competition or cooperation.

While few would entertain doubts about the presence of Ji Yun's didacticism in *Close Scrutiny*, no one has determined to any degree of specificity the extent of that didacticism, with perhaps one exception. By carrying out an extensive statistical analysis of the compilation and by contrasting it with similar sets of figures obtained for *Studio of Leisure* and *What the Master Would Not Discuss*, O. L. Fishman, the Russian folklore scholar, seeks to give quantitative evidence to the impression that most readers have long had of Ji Yun's moral-didacticism.[1] For instance, she discovers that there is a higher percentage of didactic tales in Ji Yun's collection (42.8%) than in Pu Songling's (39.2%) and that very few of Yuan Mei's tales (21.2%) make any pretence of moralizing. Her findings, as adapted, appear in the table below.

Division of Stories by Group	PU	JI	YUAN
Didactic stories of the supernatural	145	413	254
Didactic stories about nature	49	85	25
Didactic notes on the supernatural	—	1	—
Didactic notes on nature	—	12	1
Non-didactic stories on the supernatural	263	518	626
Non-didactic stories on nature	25	23	48
Non-didactic notes on the supernatural	9	30	41
Non-didactic notes on nature	3	106	28
Others	—	5	—
Total	494	1,193	1,023

---

[1] O. L. Fishman's statistical findings are listed in the appendices to her work. See Fishman, *Tri kitaĭskikh novellista XVII–XVIII vv: Pu Songling, Ji Yun, Yuan Mei*, pp. 379–421.

According to her study, Ji Yun also wrote more stories than the others in which the negative reactions of supernatural forces towards human beings are depicted. While *What the Master Would Not Discuss* outnumbers the other two collections in tales of the supernatural, by a careful count, stories of sinners being punished are found to be most abundant in *Close Scrutiny*. Thus, in the terms that we used earlier, Ji Yun's didactics partakes more of a cautionary than a hortatory nature. (Fishman's statistical comparison of didactic stories of the supernatural in *Studio of Leisure, Close Scrutiny*, and *What The Master Would Not Discuss* appears on the next two pages.)

Fishman's work also represents an advance over other *zhiguai* studies in that she does not analyse *zhiguai* collections by categorizing their stories simply by the types of spiritual beings or supernatural phenomena represented in each. Such an approach has been applied almost universally in *zhiguai* criticism from Mainland China and Taiwan and has turned much of this criticism into a descriptive cataloguing of motifs. The two comprehensive studies of the Six Dynasties *zhiguai* by Wang Guoliang 王國良 and Zhou Ciji 周次吉 typify such an approach. Each begins with its own typology of supernatural beings. Among more recent studies deploying a similar sort of analysis are Wu Yuhui's 吳玉惠 thesis on *What the Master Would Not Discuss*, in which she identifies nine categories (demons, souls departing the body, beliefs in fatalism, prophecies, deities, resurrections, ghosts, immortals, talismans); Lin Yaling's 林雅玲 thesis on Xuan Ding's 宣鼎 (1832–1880?) two collections of *Records on Rainy Nights and under the Autumn Lamp* (*Yeyu qiudeng lu* 夜雨秋燈錄), in which she lists five (immortals, ghosts and demons, Daoist and Buddhist figures, immortals and fox-spirits, strange people, things and events); and Zheng Huijing's 鄭惠璟 thesis on the Tang *zhiguai*, with four (deities, ghosts, demons, men).[2]

Such studies, typically, begin with an account of the *zhiguai* author's life and the social and historical background to the compilation. But

---

[2] See Wu Yuhui, "Yuan Mei *Zi bu yu* yanjiu," pp. 57–61 and appendix II; Lin Yaling, "Xuan Ding *Yeyu qiudeng lu* ji *Yeyu qiudeng xulu* yanjiu" 宣鼎夜雨秋燈錄及夜雨秋燈續錄研究 (A Study of Xuan Ding's *Yeyu qiudeng lu* and *Yeyu qiudeng xulu*) (M.A. thesis, Tunghai University 東海大學, 1989), pp. 62–72; and Zheng Huijing, "Tangdai zhiguai xiaoshuo yanjiu," pp. 90–132.

DIDACTIC STORIES OF THE SUPERNATURAL IN
PU SONGLING (PU), JI YUN (JI), AND YUAN MEI (YUAN)

Types of Plot	PU	JI	YUAN
People and Heaven			
1. Heaven rewards a person	8	8	1
2. Heaven helps	0	27	2
3. Heaven saves from danger	1	0	0
4. Heaven instructs	0	2	0
5. Heaven punishes	21	69	23
6. Heaven reveals	1	6	0
7. Heaven cautions	1	3	0
8. Heaven forgives	0	2	1
Gods and Spirits			
1. Gods and spirits reward	8	0	5
2. Gods and spirits help	13	5	22
3. Gods and spirits show respect	1	0	4
4. Gods and spirits save from unclean spirits	2	0	8
5. Gods and spirits save from danger	6	0	13
6. Gods and spirits punish	11	1	20
7. Gods and spirits take revenge	1	0	8
8. Gods and spirits reveal	1	0	0
9. Gods and spirits judge	0	6	1
10. Gods and spirits laugh at	0	1	1
11. Gods and spirits warn	1	1	2
12. Gods and spirits reveal qualities	0	0	1
In the Underworld			
1. In the underworld they reward	3	5	4
2. In the underworld they help	2	0	0
3. In the underworld they punish	6	14	7
4. In the underworld they warn	1	2	3
5. In the underworld they forgive	2	1	1
People and Unclean Spirits			
1. Unclean spirits help	16	23	9
2. Unclean spirits show respect for	0	4	0
3. Unclean spirits punish	7	28	7
4. Unclean spirits reveal	0	6	0
5. Unclean spirits judge	1	14	0
6. Unclean spirits joke at	4	23	4
7. Unclean spirits warn	0	3	1
8. Unclean spirits do not touch	0	16	0
9. Unclean spirits behave righteously	2	10	1

(CONT'D)

Types of Plot	PU	JI	YUAM
People and Unclean Spirits (cont'd)			
10. Unclean spirits more righteous than men	0	4	0
11. People act worse than unclean spirits	1	3	1
12. People triumph over unclean spirits	12	45	37
Spirits of the Dead			
1. Spirits of the dead help	5	5	1
2. Spirits of the dead save from unclean spirits	0	0	1
3. Spirits of the dead save from danger	0	0	6
4. Spirits of the dead punish	0	5	4
5. Spirits of the dead avenge	1	0	21
6. Spirits of the dead judge	0	8	0
7. Spirits of the dead laugh at	0	3	0
8. Spirits of the dead warn	1	4	1
9. Spirits of the dead fear	0	1	1
10. Spirits of the dead act honourably	4	26	8
Reincarnation			
1. The reincarnated person is rewarded for past life	5	4	19
2. Living/supernatural beings are rewarded in a new life	2	0	4
3. The reincarnated person is punished for past life	2	9	3

here the shortcomings of this "folkloristic" approach become blatant: the *zhiguai* is written as well as oral in nature. Unlike all other forms of literature, the *zhiguai* involves authors, compilers, and narrators on the one hand, and a host of oral storytellers, listeners, and readers of the published text on the other. These create a complicated set of factors governing the origination, gathering, and dissemination of the stories. These factors can be found even in a single *zhiguai* collection. In her book-length study of the three *zhiguai* writers, Fishman can be said to redress the imbalance in *zhiguai* criticism by distinguishing the stories on a functional basis — they are identified as either didactic or non-didactic — before she proceeds to discuss types and taxonomies, which, though of interest as elements of folklife, often have very little bearing on the significance of the narratives.

In the case of *Close Scrutiny*, a typology of supernatural events and phenomena would not help one understand the author's design and purposes. It would be even less useful in allowing one to apprehend the meaning of the text. It is thus necessary to dispense with any effort at classification and instead focus on function. With Ji Yun's didactic intentions established beyond doubt, we will begin with an analysis of his didactic strategies, as seen in representative tales. Structurally, a great majority of Ji Yun's entries in *Close Scrutiny* are split into two parts: the story proper and the commentary portion. The relation between the two is the basis of our study of the poetics of didacticism in *Close Scrutiny*. As the use of the commentary is particularly crucial in the didactic *zhiguai*, we will also broaden the field of our investigation and examine examples from other collections in the period. Only then will we return to a more theoretical discussion of the meaning of didacticism for Ji Yun and for a social group that participates in the discourse on the strange.

Between the Story and the Message

At the outset, one can say with regard to the tales of the strange collected in *Close Scrutiny* that each of them generates meaning by moving in any one of three directions. On what can be called a primary level, events are depicted for what they are and the story is to be taken literally. Tales of this type are, quintessentially, narrations of "facts" untainted by opinions. On a secondary level, the events narrated create an opportunity for moralizing, which Ji Yun or the raconteur, or one or more commentators may freely indulge in. On a tertiary level, the tale is an allegorical vehicle for discourse on any likely subject, and the supernatural serves a symbolic, "signifying" function. It is a vehicle for conveying latent meanings.

The second or didactic mode is the focus of our attention here, but stories of the first type are not devoid of a didactic function. For Ji Yun, only when events are "true" can one draw moral lessons from them. His "didactics of the strange" is of a different order than, say, the didactics of Bunyan's *Pilgrim's Progress*, in which moral exhortations are voiced in the context of a fictionalized narrative.

As for the allegorical mode, the lines dividing it from the didactic mode are not hard and fast, but in the strict sense in which the allegory is defined here, allegories are quite rare in *Close Scrutiny*. None of them are told by Ji Yun himself, but they will serve as an illuminating foil for the other two types of narratives.

Literalist Tales. Since, from one perspective, the intention of compiling narratives of strange events and phenomena was to provide a pool of broad-based information on all aspects of the supernatural, Ji Yun recorded some tales very much as Yuan Mei had done with his. He does not seem to have bothered to preach through them. Critics of the collection often point out the way in which the depictions of hell and of the activities of the dead are meant to throw into relief, by comparison or contrast, the world of the living.[3] Taking this to the extreme, Zhang Shengkang 張聖康 ventures to suggest that tales containing such descriptions are "about men, not ghosts."[4] However, quite a number of tales in *Close Scrutiny* should be read quite literally for what they are, though it needs to be stressed that they, too, serve to build up the significance conveyed by the collection as a whole.

Several tales featuring fox-spirits and ghosts can be discussed as factual accounts of this type, and the element of human involvement in the lives of supernatural beings portrayed in these stories renders attempts to extract "deeper" levels of meaning superfluous. Two narratives recount in a matter-of-fact manner strategies for dealing with fox-spirits that disrupt humans lives and reveal the extent to which fox-spirits were ready to accept reasoned arguments and well-worded persuasions. Rather than reading hidden meanings into these stories, one should note that the ostensibly human characteristics that the fox-spirits displayed were understood to be traits commonly found in their species. What stories of the strange had always been telling their readers was that the supernatural creatures were simply like human beings in many ways, though unlike them in others. An allegorical reading should in these cases give way to a literalist reading.

These two stories concern the tensions created, in the first case, when human beings and fox-spirits live together in close proximity

---

[3] Anthony C. Yu says of ghostlore that "though its focus concentrates on the dead and dying, the values and concerns of the living predominate." Anthony C. Yu, "Rest, Rest, Perturbed Spirit: Ghosts in Traditional Chinese Prose Fiction," p. 434. Gao Qihua also notes the large number of critics who read the stories in *YWCTBJ* for the oblique comments on the human world. Gao Qihua, "*Yuewei caotang biji* yanjiu zongshu."

[4] Zhang Shengkang, "Shuo *Yuewei caotang biji*" 説閲微草堂筆記 (On the *Yuewei caotang biji*), *Nankai xuebao* 南開學報, no. 6 (1981), p. 78.

and, in the second, when they co-habit in the same house.[5] In the first story (*LY* V:12), a priggish pedant curses fox-spirits residing in a Buddhist temple for throwing stones at people, and he himself is humiliated when the fox-spirits place a pornographic picture in his sleeve. The second concerns the seduction of young men and women by fox-spirits who absorb their vital essences through sexual intercourse (*HX* III:18):

> According to Liu Youhan 劉友韓 the Attendant Censor, he once lived in a friend's house in Shandong, and heard that the girl next door was seduced by a fox. The girl's father followed the fox and discovered its cave. Using every method conceivable he caught a baby-fox, and proposed a deal with the fox, saying, "I will release your son so long as you release my daughter."
>
> The fox agreed. However, after the baby-fox was released, the fox returned. When he was scolded for not keeping his word, he retorted, saying:
>
> "Frequent is the deceit that men practise on each other. Why do you only condemn creatures of my type?"
>
> Extremely bitter and rancorous, the father forced his daughter to make a pretense of entreating the fox to drink, while he secretly put arsenic in the fox's drink. Thus poisoned, the fox became transformed and fled in panic. The following night bricks and shingles were thrown at the house. Windows and doors were shaken. A horde of foxes, raising a hue and cry, had come to demand human lives as compensation.
>
> The father, in a stern voice, recounted the incident [to Liu] from beginning to end. He reported what an old fox seemed to have said [to the horde of foxes]:
>
> "Sad indeed it is that you folks only see men deceiving each other, and choose to follow their example. You do not know of the way of Heaven and the inevitability of retribution. Those skilled at deception will eventually be deceived themselves. The master speaks boldly, and to harm him would bring evil fortune. Let the whole gang come back with me."
>
> When this was said, all was quiet again. This old fox was far superior in his insight.

---

[5] More often than not an entire clan of fox-spirits would be found living in the upstairs of a house. Chap. 1 of *YTSL* contains an extended narrative about the continual friction between the fox-spirits above and the human inhabitants below, ending in an intermarriage between members of the two species.

The series of strategies and counter-strategies designed by each party to outwit the other is the focus of this story. It was presumably told as much for fun as for the knowledge to be gained of the fox-spirits: their cunning, their vengeful nature, and their unruly character. There is, admittedly, a slight hint at the end of the tale of a moral lesson to be taught, but Ji Yun manages to end the story abruptly, as soon as the conflict between the gang of fox-spirits and the embittered father is resolved.

Stories about ghosts and about the specific nature of their inter-action with human beings are also plentiful in Ji Yun's collection. Some of the most interesting involve a battle of wits. The archetypal example of the man-against-ghost story is the tale of Zong Dingbo 宗 定伯 in Cao Pi's *An Array of Anomalies*. This story refers specifically to ghosts' fear of human spit,[6] and this knowledge enables Zong Dingbo to exercise control over a ghost. Read in comparison with this tale, many of the stories in *Close Scrutiny*, as in other *zhiguai*, can be seen as offering instructions for handling ghosts, in the event that one should come across them. Parenthetically, it can also be noted that such tales, by showing that ghosts do not need to be feared, fulfil what might be termed the "exorcizing" function of ghostlore.

Tales in this category should not be understood in any sense other than the literal one. One story can be cited as an appropriate example (*RS* II:47). It concerns a rowdy character who vows to catch one ghost each night, for he has discovered that a ghost will turn into a sheep when spat on. It will become, then, his daily meal. When the ghosts learn about this, they skilfully avoid him, and he is eventually frustrated in his scheme. According to Ji Yun, this tale reveals the fact that "ghosts bully men only when men fear them"; the fearlessness and violent temper of this man is enough to frighten off all the ghosts that might cause trouble.[7] Ji Yun's factual account becomes good-intentioned advice to those at a loss about what to do about ghosts.

In one particularly revealing entry, further advice is offered to help men in their perennial battle with ghosts (*HX* I:39). A ghost-seer

---

[6] Cao Pi, *Lieyi zhuan*, collected in Li Fang, ed., *Taiping guangji*, pp. 2366–2367.
[7] *YWCTBJ*, p. 168.

elaborates on the rules governing the behaviour of ghosts, for the benefit of his listeners. He explains, for instance, how ghosts manage to evict human beings from places they themselves want to occupy:

> A feeble *yin* is powerless against a burgeoning *yang*, so ghosts fear human beings. Those that don't are either feeling uncomfortable about men taking up their abodes, and so transform themselves [into fearful shapes] to chase men away, or they haunt men in order to obtain sacrificial offerings.[8]

Additionally, the ghost-seer discusses the different types of ghosts men encounter: lascivious ghosts impelled by sexual desires, ferocious ghosts driven by murderous intent, and recriminating ghosts aroused by excessive resentment.

One might suggest (as Zhang Shengkang does in his allegorical reading) that, for many stories in *Close Scrutiny*, correspondences should be drawn from the world of supernatural beings to that of men. But one can just as easily argue the reverse: rules of human interaction and observable patterns of human behaviour were used as parallels to the rules and patterns of the world beyond. In other words, by this other argument, in order to understand the realm of the strange, one needs to apply one's understanding of how things work in the human world. A tale concerning an incident that occurred in 1747 (*HX* IV:37) furnishes a most illuminating example of the use of human parallels to understand the world of spirits. In response to Licentiate Han's queries, a ghost expounds on three different categories of ghosts, each found in a different locale: ghost-underlings living in the underworld, city-dwelling ghosts, and ghosts in the wilderness. Only the first two types can tell who will fail and who will succeed in the public examinations at various levels. They accomplish this by either eavesdropping on the higher officials who have access to the Roster of Successful Candidates kept in hell and by listening to rumours spread only in the cities. The ghost then draws an analogy from the human world: scholars studying at home would naturally not be expected to be cognizant of events outside the magistrate's

---

[8] Ibid., p. 245.

quarters, nor would they know of the stratagems and intrigues at the imperial court. For him, each group operates in its own (human or spiritual) sphere of activity.

One must guard against reading unintended meanings into tales of the supernatural transmitted in *zhiguai* collections and be especially wary when discussing the parallels discernible between the suprahuman and the human realms. After all, to eighteenth-century writers and readers, both realms were equally real. Many *zhiguai* storytellers seem, in fact, to be more concerned with presenting the supernatural realm than with illustrating truths in the human world through their stories. There is yet one other consideration. Scholarly studies of Chinese concepts of hell and the afterlife have long revealed the extent to which the bureaucratic structure of the underworld was modelled on that of the human world.[9] From one age to another, it is clear that the Chinese continued to enrich their conceptions of hell by drawing on the human model, and thus they created exceedingly complex portraits of the otherworldly realm by late imperial times.[10] The subterranean government, just like the celestial government, became more and more elaborate. The forms of punishment of offenses multiplied, and the activities of ghosts became more varied. But all this ran parallel to what could be observed in the human realm. What the modern reader sees as allegorical parallels in the *zhiguai* is nothing more than the presentation of hard facts.

---

[9] See, for instance, Yu Ying-shih, "'O Soul, Come Back!': A Study in the Changing Conceptions of the Soul and Afterlife in Pre-Buddhist China." *Harvard Journal of Asiatic Studies*, vol. 47, no. 2 (1987), pp. 384–395.

[10] It cannot be doubted that the *zhiguai* stories of late imperial times were considerably enriched by popular conceptions of hell. After the Song, popularly circulated tracts which contained "transformation drawings" of hell, Buddhist miracle tales (mostly culled from *zhiguai* collections), and short admonitory essays became the basic source of information about hell and the afterlife for the populace. In the Ming and Qing periods, ideas of hell were also spread by the *baojuan* 寶卷 (precious scroll), long prosimetric narratives that promulgated popular Buddhism and various folk religions. The link between the *zhiguai* and popular religious literature is a subject discussed in Liang Zhai 量齋, "Diyu guannian zai Zhongguo xiaoshuo zhong de yunyong he gaibian" 地獄觀念在中國小說中的運用和改變 (The Concept of Hell as Used and Transformed in Chinese Fiction), *Chun wenxue* 純文學, vol. 8, no. 6 (1971), pp. 34–51.

Allegories.   That having been said, some tales of the supernatural in *Close Scrutiny* are, indeed, allegorical in import. To begin with, however, one needs to distinguish the allegory from the didactic story with great precision. Both involve a bifurcation of the text into "content" and "meaning." Unfortunately, both are often translated as *yuyan* 寓言 .[11] Yet, despite the wide field of reference connoted by *yuyan*, its individual components *yu* 寓 (to lodge) and *yan* 言 (words) are basically equivalents of "vehicle" and "tenor." The broader, looser senses in which the English term "allegory" is currently used do not help clarify the confusion in the critical discourse.

For the purposes of the present analysis, allegory will be defined more narrowly as a narrative operating on two levels in which an analogy is consistently drawn between the story and its meaning. Hence the reader's feeling that the story is "saying one thing and meaning another."[12] In the didactic story, the reader or listener is not continuously aware of a parallel signification, although he understands that an underlying lesson will eventually be made plain. To the didactic story category also belong the fable (which involves animal characters), the parable (which involves human characters and situations), and the exemplum (which concerns an event that has occurred).[13] While some prefer to distinguish the allegory from the didactic story in terms of length, this criterion does not appear to work in the case of most *zhiguai*.

The reason for the scant use of the allegorical mode in Ji Yun's collection should by now be obvious. Carried to its extreme, this mode often amounts to a denial of the facticity of the events reported, becoming practically synonymous with "fictionalizing." Ji Yun refers to

---

[11] The expression originated in the *Zhuangzi*, where it appears three times. For the multiplicity of meanings conveyed by the word *yu* 寓, see Jin Jiaxi 金嘉錫, *Zhuangzi "yu" zi zhi yanjiu* 莊子「寓」字之研究 (The Word "*Yu*" as Used in *Zhuangzi*) (Taibei: Huazheng shuju 華正書局 , 1986), chap. 1.

[12] Karl Beckson and Arthur Ganz, *Literary Terms: A Dictionary* (New York: Farrar, Straus and Giroux, 1975), p. 9.

[13] Stories in *YWCTBJ* often find their way into anthologies of Chinese fables and parables, as do those in *LZZI*. See Chen Puqing 陳蒲清, *Zhongguo gudai yuyanshi* 中國古代寓言史 (A History of Fables in Traditional China) (Changsha: Hunan jiaoyu chubanshe 湖南教育出版社 , 1983); and Wolfram Eberhard, *Chinese Fables and Parables: A Catalogue* (Taibei: Orient Cultural Service, 1971).

several stories, which he was unwilling to take literally, as "unfounded"
or "unreal"[14] — and these are stories in which the literal sense was
subsumed under a figurative meaning. His idea of "lodging meaning"
was similar to what was expounded by one spirit-writing deity:

> The cauldron, tripod, lead, and mercury mentioned in *The Kinship of the
> Three* (*Can tongqi* 參同契) are all names in which meanings are lodged
> [*yu*]; they do not refer to alchemical processes *per se*. Necromancers drew
> strained interpretations and came to mistaken conclusions, thus causing
> endless harm.[15]

Ji Yun's mistrust of allegorical interpretations must have been similar
to the deity's mistrust of necromancers.

To talk figuratively (allegorically, that is), however, appears to
have been accepted as a mode of oral discourse in Ji Yun's favourite
conversational circles all the same. Tian Baiyan, for instance, was well
known as a humorous and fun-loving person who liked to convey (*ji*
寄) meanings through his stories.[16]

Several stories in *Close Scrutiny* can be cited here as clear-cut allegories. The first (*LY* I:21), narrated by Zhu Ziying, needs to be read
in the context of the intellectual debate between adherents of Han
learning and Song learning in the late eighteenth century. The story
concerns a scholar's discovery of a magnificent collection of the
ancient classics preserved by supernatural beings in the Pavilion of
Fragrance of the Classics at Mount Tai. Ji Yun suspected, with good
reason, that the story was a veiled diatribe against the scholars of Song
learning who had ignored the canonical Confucian works and turned
instead to empty speculation — while the spirit and deities had not.

An anecdote told by Shen Cangling 申蒼嶺 (Shen Dan 申丹) about
the refusal of a "ghost of refinement" to appear in its true form before
a scholar (*HX* I:49) reveals one motive behind the telling of allegorical stories of the supernatural: to display the narrator's ingenuity. The
narrative, it must be noted, was discredited by Ji Yun for being unfounded and no more than a "playful" allegory. This also happens to

---

[14] *YWCTBJ*, pp. 104, 149, and 447.

[15] Ibid., p. 190.

[16] The two tales that he narrated (*LY* I:17, *RS* II:5) were said to be allegories and hence
not to be taken literally.

be one of the few instances in which the usually credulous Ji Yun dis-
trusts the authenticity of an encounter-tale. But being a veiled satire
of pedantic scholars, the tale bears witness to the liveliness of social
conversations and the conviviality of intellectual gatherings at the time.

Dai Zhen's account of the ghost-recluse displays a comparable
ingenuity in its manipulation of analogues (*LY* VI:10). In his former
life, a ghost had been a Ming dynasty official who resigned from the
post of district magistrate during the Wanli 萬曆 reign (1573–1619)
to lead an eremitic existence. He finds to his dismay that in the
netherworld, corruption and pettiness are just as entrenched as they
are in the world of the living, so he avoids other ghosts by retiring to
the mountains in Anhui 安徽. At the end of the tale this ghost-
recluse, like the traveller in Tao Qian's "Peach Blossom Spring," re-
quests that the words for "recluse" be inscribed at the entrance to his
cave. As an allegory of the difficulty of extricating oneself from politics once one gets involved, Dai Zhen's story must have amused its
listeners by its display of wry but sardonic humour just as it entertained them by its skilful allegorizing.[17]

Didactic Stories.   Whether told to defend certain ideological stances,
to satirize human weaknesses, or to implicitly criticize various facets
of experience, narratives with an allegorical bent are in the minority
in *Close Scrutiny*. They tend to undermine the factual basis of events,
whereas by contrast it is precisely upon facticity that didactic tales are
founded. The didactic tale also differs from the allegory in that its
message, rather than implicit, is almost always explicitly stated in a
separate part when the story proper ends. In comparison with the
literalist tales, in which the supernatural is no more than simply itself,
in the didactic or illustrative mode the supernatural is an element at

---

[17] Dai Zhen's narrative takes the form of a dialogue with a ghost, which David L. Keenan
links to Zhuangzi's encounter with a skull by the roadside. Keenan, "The Forms and Uses of
the Ghost Story in Late Eighteenth-century China as Recorded in the *Yüeh-wei Ts'ao-T'ang
Pi-chi* of Chi Yun" (Ph.D. dissertation, Harvard University, 1987), pp. 144–145. Spirits, however, did more than just narrate their own experiences. They described the supernatural
realm (see *RS* IV:36) and debated fiercely with men (see *LY* IV:40, *GW* II:13).

the service of an idea.[18] But, in any given tale, the didactic mode does not militate against a literalist reading: the didacticism is merely a dimension added to a literalist tale. The veritable records of events are made to suggest a wider scheme of moral significance, and the didactic writer makes this clear. Each tale provides, that is, a point of departure from which the narrator can draw inferences and illustrate moral truths that may at times bear only a tangential relationship to the tale itself.

Some of the most exemplary didactic tales in *Close Scrutiny* do not come from Ji Yun himself, but from his father, Ji Rongshu. The story of the old scholar in Huaizhen, Hebei demonstrates the use of parallels to illustrate a didactic point (*LY* III:4). The Ma 馬 family, bedevilled for over a year by ghosts who whined at night and by demons who hurled bricks and stones, decides to sell its house when all attempts at appeasement prove futile. They are approached by an old scholar who believes his virtue sufficient to shield him from malicious spirits. Indeed, the spirits are silenced after he has taken over the place, but then the truth leaks out: the ghosts and demons are actually rascals in disguise, who were sent by the scholar to hound the Mas.

The narrative is unpretentious enough and can be understood literally as just another variation on the "men-as-ghosts" motif. It can also be utilized by sceptics as proof that spirits are "man-made."[19] It is, however, Ji Rongshu's comment, tagged on to the tale, that reveals the moral lesson based on an analogue between men and demons: "Demons are in essence no more than transmuted beings. Adept as he is at the art of transmutation, the old scholar must be considered a real demon."[20]

---

[18] Tzvetan Todorov would have placed the literalist tales in the category of "semantic" stories. Besides this, according to Todorov, there are two other functions of the supernatural in literature: a "pragmatic" one, in creating suspense; and a "syntactic" one, in providing or enhancing narrative development. Todorov, *The Fantastic: A Structural Approach to a Literary Genre*, translated by Richard Howard (Cleveland: The Press of Case Western Reserve, 1973), p. 170.

[19] Hong Liangji had in fact used such an argument. See his "Tiandi pian" 天地篇 (Heaven and Earth), in *Juanshige wenji*, collected in *Hong Beijiang shiwenji*, 1:14a.

[20] Ibid., p. 41.

The justification for drawing moral truths from parallels is provided, albeit inadvertently, by Ji Yun in one notice. To him, "ghosts were originally men, and fox-spirits are akin to men."[21] Like the allegories, of course, the didactic stories often derived meaning from comparisons drawn between the human and the supernatural. But a difference between them is that the two realms in a didactic tale could sometimes be played off *against* one another. Though some didactic stories portrayed the evil of supernatural beings as a reflection of similar phenomena in the mundane world, in others the wickedness of man was contrasted with the virtue of non-human creatures. Whether a reader ought to compare or contrast would, in all cases, be made clear by the didactic narrator or the author himself.

No consistent picture of supernatural beings emerges from the stories in *Close Scrutiny*: their behaviour is as variable as that of men. Thus the lessons to be drawn vary from one case to another. Several tales, for instance, depict fox-spirits with commendable qualities, focusing in particular on the tact and cool-headedness with which they settle disputes and conflicts with men. In one case at least the narrator is prompted to reflect on the wisdom of remaining calm and self-composed in the face of adversity (*RS* IV:52).[22] Other accounts present the female fox-spirit as a virtuous wife and daughter-in-law, though elsewhere she figures as a seductress, a prostitute, and a shrew.[23] In one story a fox-spirit is wounded by her husband upon his discovering that she is not human. She leaves, but remains faithful to the end, and she returns to take care of her parents-in-law after her husband's death. She becomes, for the narrator, a paragon of feminine virtue in traditional Chinese society so that "those who have fallen short can be shamed."[24] Positive portrayals of ghosts were not lacking either. One female ghost, buried naked for a hundred years,

---

[21] *YWCTBJ*, p. 149.

[22] In the same entry, He Li'an 何勵庵 (He Xiu 何琇 , *jinshi*, 1733) also praised the fox-spirit for his willingness to listen to reason, while Ji Qinghu 紀晴湖 (Ji Zhuo 紀暉, b. 1706) noted how difficult it is to subscribe to the superiority of a fox-spirit.

[23] In *LX* II:9, by an interesting reversal of logic, a prostitute is likened to a fox-spirit by Ji Zhuo.

[24] *YWCTBJ*, p. 283.

searches for clothes to put on before she enters the gates of hell (*RS* I:28). Consequently, stories of ghosts and fox-spirits could be used to present not only messages regarding sycophants, tricksters, marauders, hypocrites, and pedants, but also messages on filial sons, virtuous wives, benevolent ancestors, and loyal servants.

What this means is that Ji Yun's didactic stories rely *only to a certain degree* on universally shared perceptions of the character and nature of ghosts, foxes, and demons of various types. Those perceptions constituted, of course, a readily available arsenal of tropes that could be deployed by the didactic narrator. (This has occured in many fables, which differ from the didactic *zhiguai* only in that they contains animal instead of supernatural characters.[25]) However, in the stories in *Close Scrutiny*, the didacticism might arise in unpredictable ways from an elaboration of the demon-like, ghost-like, or fox-like nature of some men. In other words, the complex analysis of individual spirits is more useful for understanding the didacticism in *Close Scrutiny* than a simple study of stereotypes would be.

It can actually be said that this didacticism applies to practically any situation in which men confront supernatural beings. Consider the two stories narrated by Wu Lintang 吳林塘 in *Miscellaneous Accounts West of the Locust-tree*, whose targets of attack are avarice and opportunism. These stories exemplify very well the dynamics of the didactic techniques that concern us here. In the first, two men who eagerly consented to a marriage proposal from the same fox-spirit soon discover that she has been depriving both of them of their male spiritual energy (*HX* I:31). To the hunter who hears their story, it is a case of "good bargains that may not be really worth it,"[26] and he proceeds to note how fish were baited and orangutans lured by wine. In the second, the moral lesson is conveyed through the fox-spirit (*HX* I:32):

> Wu Lintang also told of a young man who was seduced by a fox, and though he was gradually wasting away, the fox kept coming. His energies became so depleted that finally he was not able to satisfy her when the

---

[25] The demarcation of difference between the fable, the parable, and the allegory is a thorny problem. See H. J. Blackman, *The Fable as Literature* (London: The Athlone Press, 1985), pp. xi–xix.

[26] *YWCTBJ*, p. 241.

two were in bed together. Putting on her clothes the fox made ready
to depart. Much as the young man, weeping, implored her to stay, she
adamantly refused.

When reprimanded for her lack of feelings, the fox retorted in anger, "There are no marital obligations between us; I came for the specific
purpose of getting spiritual nourishment. The cream and essence of your
being has been exhausted. With nothing more to gain, why should I not
go? *This is like liaisons built on power and influence that are broken when there
is no more power or influence. Liaisons built on wealth, too, are severed when
there is no more wealth. Humans curry favour with those whose wealth and power
have aroused their attention, not out of any genuine feelings.* Previously didn't
you ingratiate yourself with so-and-so, whom you now no longer care
about? And I am being reproached!" (italics mine)

These two stories also reveal that the moralizing does not have to
come from Ji Yun himself. Moralizing pervades *Close Scrutiny*, whether
originating from a character, a narrator, a listener, a storyteller or the
compiler. While nodding approval to some of the views expressed, Ji
Yun contradicts others. At times he synthesizes divergent views, but
elsewhere he accepts the opinions of others without reservation (as in
the case of stories emanating from his father). Yet, in the cacophony
of moralizing voices, his own voice rises loud and clear.

Despite the huge number of didactic tales in *Close Scrutiny*, we can
cite only a few entries to demonstrate Ji Yun's *own* moralizing. In the
following entry, the moral message focuses on the misbehaviour of a
pedantic scholar in his dealings with fox-spirits (*LY* V:12):

Dong Qiuyuan 董秋原 of Pingyuan 平原 [Dezhou 德州 in present-day
Shandong] told of a Buddhist temple in Haifeng 海豐 [in present-day
Shandong] which had for long been haunted by foxes who pestered men
by throwing stones and bricks at them from time to time. A pedantic
scholar requested the use of three sections of the eastern wing to teach
his pupils. On hearing about the foxes, he went to the temple hall
to reproach them. There was peace and quiet for a few nights, so the
pedantic scholar was openly complacent.

One day, the landlord came over for a chat. While the two were
bowing and saluting one another, a scroll fell from the pedant's sleeve
onto the floor. Picking it up, the landlord saw that it was an erotic picture, and without a word he left. The next day none of the students
reappeared [for class].

Men harass foxes without themselves being harassed in the first place, and unexpectedly are hit by the latter right on the mark. *The gentleman is vigilant against small-minded men; to touch their sharp edges without cause is to court certain defeat.* (italics mine)

Here, Ji Yun's moral message is not related to the character of the fox-spirits, but to that of the scholar himself.

In the majority of Ji Yun's didactic tales, attention is focused not on a specific moral point, but simply on the general necessity of behaving morally. Such a message is tagged conveniently onto stories showing the disastrous consequences of immoral actions and examples are everywhere. In fact, among *zhiguai* collections from the Song dynasty and later, there is a preponderance of tales of this type ("vice punished") over and above stories of propitious fortune emanating from virtuous behaviour ("virtue rewarded"). It has been emphatically noted, for example, that there are "more cases of evildoing punished than moral behaviour rewarded" in *Records of Yijian*.[27] With regard to *Close Scrutiny*, it has been noted earlier that Fishman's findings reveal that there are more stories delineating the negative reactions of the supernatural forces towards the actions of "bad" men than there are tales of the benevolence shown by supernatural powers to "good" people.[28]

The basis of Ji Yun's moralizing was religious. For the very foundation of his didactic admonitions was a belief in the efficacy of the spirits and in the unerring working of the retributive system. His indictment against sexual licentiousness is made explicit through the story of a gang-rape and its disastrous consequences (*HX* II:19):

Fa Nanye mentioned another incident. In a local community there were several young rakes. On learning that, at the deserted gravesite belonging to a certain clan, there were vixens who could assume form and seduce men, they took traps with them at night and, laying them at the mouths of holes and crannies, caught two. Lest the vixens should change

---

[27] Such is the conclusion drawn by Liu Jingzhen 劉靜貞 , "Songren de mingbaoguan: Hong Mai *Yijian zhi* shitan" 宋人的冥報觀：洪邁夷堅志試探 (Song Concepts of Hell: A Preliminary Study of Hong Mai's *Yijian zhi*), *Shihuo yuekan* 食貨月刊 , vol. 9, no. 11 (1980), pp. 34–40.

[28] Fishman, *Tri kitaĭskikh novellista*, p. 277.

their forms, the rakes quickly stabbed them in their thighs with daggers and tied them up with ropes. Brandishing their knives they threatened the vixens:

"If you can assume human form and serve us wine, we'll release you. Or else we'll have you butchered."

The two vixens yelped and leapt about, as though they did not understand. The rakes, much angered, stabbed one of them to death. The other then spoke in a human voice:

"I have neither clothes or shoes. How could I face you when transformed into a human being?"

The rakes held their knives under her chin. By a series of twists and turns she metamorphosed into a beautiful woman, but stark naked. The group was ecstatic with pleasure, and one after another made indecent advances at her. With their arms around her, they forced her to present them with wine, all the time holding fast to the rope with which the woman was tied. She spoke softly and enticingly, pleading with them to loosen the rope. Once it left their hands, however, she disappeared in a twinkling.

As they approached home, the rakes could see flames at a distance. All their houses were burnt to the ground, and a daughter of the man who killed the vixen was burned to death.

From this one knows of the revenge of the fox. Though these foxes did not give men trouble, the men chose to disturb them. Appropriate enough are the consequences for those who do evil frequently! (italics mine)

Another, a tale of virtue rewarded already discussed in Chapter Three, includes a comment on the power of filial piety (*GW* IV:40):

In Jinan in the *jiachen* year of the Qianlong reign [1784], instances of fire were frequent. At the end of the fourth month, a fire broke out on Western Street inside the South Gate ...

This event was recorded in the seventh month of the *guichou* 癸丑 year [1797] by Mr. Zhang Qingyuan 張慶源 , the Educational Commissioner of Dezhou, and sent to me. It is comparable to the incident of the widow, recorded in my *Record of Spending the Summer at Luanyang*. Yet for the husband, wife and children to be of one heart is most difficult of all. Given that "two who are united in their hearts have a sharpness that can break gold," how much more so when six people are thus united! If thunder strikes when a lowly woman cries out,[29] what could not happen

---

[29] The reference is to an incident in the *Huainan zi.*

when six people were bound by pure filial piety! *When wholehearted dedica-
tion and deep grief touch the spirits, even fate cannot but be reversed. This is
another example of how men can surely triumph over Heaven.* While this is an
anomalous event transmitted by hearsay, we can call it an instance of the
working of ordinary principles. (italics mine)

The didacticism of *Close Scrutiny* is usually carried in the commentaries inserted in the entries, like a refrain threading its way in and
out of, as well as between, the individual tales in the collection. It is
precisely this that creates the "preachy" tone of the entire work. To
quantify the point: Ji Yun appended (roughly) a total of 184 comments to the entries. Besides Ji Yun's comments, Ji Rongshu's
comments are found in thirty-eight places, friends' and relatives' comments in eighty entries, and more than one viewpoint is included in
the commentary portion in at least fifteen cases. Although not all
the commentaries are necessarily didactic in nature — nor is the
didactic message in all cases conveyed in the commentarial portion —
this gives a rough idea of the extent to which the *zhiguai* stories are
couched in discursive "talk," a great part of which is decidedly didactic in implication.

The *Zhiguai* Commentarial Tradition

The inclusion of didactic injunctions in the *zhiguai* commentaries is a
feature worth studying in a wider literary context. Given the predilection for moralizing among *zhiguai* writers, it is hardly surprising that
the use of didactic commentaries as seen in *Close Scrutiny* should be
found in some other collections of the period. To begin with, this
didactic strategy needs to be understood in terms of the oral elite
discourse which provided the occasion for the narratives of the strange.
In conversational situations where the stories of the strange were
narrated, it was inevitable that remarks would be expressed by the
listeners in response, and Ji Yun had simply jotted these down along
with the stories themselves. In this way a special commentary portion
is created.

But the didactic commentaries also need to be understood by looking *outside of* the *zhiguai* compilations. From this perspective, the way
the written story (in contrast to the oral story from which it was derived) was circulated is of the utmost importance, and the remarks of

readers of *zhiguai* collections like *Studio of Leisure* enable us to construct a scenario of the life of a written *zhiguai*. Initially, an author would, as Ji Yun did, write down a story in his own words and from his own point of view. But as the story was then circulated in manuscript or printed form among a circle of friends and acquaintances, the latter would append their views to it when they read it or talked about it. More often than not, the written remarks appeared first as "eyebrow" commentary on the top of a folio page, in the blank space in the margin, or between two chapters, and eventually they were incorporated into the text itself when it was copied, re-copied, printed, or reprinted. This entire process will merit our attention for what it can tell us not only about the possible reception of a collection like *Close Scrutiny* but also about how the collection became what it is. This process will also reveal how some of the didactic commentaries came into existence.

The two *zhiguai* collections that will be used to substantiate our argument were roughly contemporaneous with *Close Scrutiny*: He Bang'e's *Occasional Accounts of Conversations at Night* and Xu Kun's *Unauthorized Compilations of Willow Cliff*. The didactic strain, pervasive as it was, operates in surprisingly similar ways in the commentary portions of the three compilations. However, the extensive deployment of a commentator's voice, or several commentators' voices, so integral to the didactic *zhiguai*, ought to be regarded as being at least partly inspired by the inclusion in *Studio of Leisure* of the Fantastorian's (Yishishi 異史氏) commentaries.[30] Of course, at the time the commentarial tradition in historiography already reached back several centuries, traceable to the *Records of History* of Sima Qian in which the "Grand Historian" (Taishigong 太史公) proffers comments at the end of individual sections. In many standard histories, too, as well as in Sima Guang's 司馬光 (1019–1086) *Comprehensive Mirror for Aid in*

---

[30] The "Fantastorian" is a widely used translation for "Yishishi". For discussions on the use of commentaries in *LZZI*, see Luo Jingzhi 羅敬之, *Pu Songling jiqi Liaozhai zhiyi* 蒲松齡及其聊齋志異 (Pu Songling and His *Liaozhai zhiyi*) (Taibei: Guoli fanyiguan 國立翻譯館, 1986), pp. 370–374. I have also relied for my analysis of *LZZI* on Marlon K. Hom, "The Continuation of Tradition: A Study of the *Liao-chai chih-i* by P'u Sung-ling (1640–1715)" (Ph.D. dissertation, University of Washington, 1979); and James V. Muhleman, "The *Liao-chai chih-i*: Themes and Art of the Literary Tale" (Ph.D. dissertation, Indiana University, 1978).

Governance (*Zizhi tongjian* 資治通鑑), commentaries — mostly of a "praise and blame" nature — were appended to the main texts. But the possibility that the immediate inspiration for Ji Yun's commentaries might have come from the example of *Studio of Leisure* could not be discounted.

To highlight the didactic mode in *Close Scrutiny*, we cannot do better than juxtapose its "commentaries" against those of Pu Songling's collection. One view regarding the use of commentaries in the latter was expressed by Zhao Qigao 趙起杲 (d. 1766), its first publisher: the commentaries in *Studio of Leisure* was said to have encouraged a reading of the *zhiguai* narratives similar to one's reading of the "histories."[31] In this sense, Pu Songling was passing an evaluation on the events recounted or, in other words, controlling interpretations through the Fantastorian, his altered persona. This too was a characteristic feature of eighteenth-century *zhiguai* collections: the didactic interpretation of the standard histories became transposed into a didactic interpretation of anomalous events and phenomena. The analogy with traditional historiography is singularly appropriate. Like the historian who was supposed to "praise virtues and condemn vices," Ji Yun himself was clarifying the moral significance behind the hodgepodge of events involving the supernatural and deriving ethical lessons for the edification of readers.[32]

Some other critics are of the opinion that the commentaries in *Studio of Leisure* are essentially a framing device that enhances the impression that what is narrated was "real" by engaging the reader in a suspension of disbelief. To Judith Zeitlin, for instance, the commentaries "enhance the authority of the primary text by *increasing the illusion* that the tale is real."[33] By this reading, the commentaries in *Studio*

---

[31] See Zhao Qigao's explanatory notes for the first printing, in *LZZI*, pp. 27–28.

[32] A recent study of the didacticism of *LZZI* that compares it to the standard histories is Bi Shuchun 畢庶春, "Shilun *Liaozhai zhiyi* yu wu shi zhi guanxi" 試論聊齋志異與巫史之關係 (An Attempt to Explain the Relationship of the *Liaozhai zhiyi* to Shamanism and History), *Wenxue yichan* 文學遺產, no. 3 (1988), pp. 95–102. The idea that, by being didactic, even the *xiaoshuo* could serve the proper function of history seemed to be deeply ingrained and is a clue to understanding the parallels constantly drawn between the two genres.

[33] Zeitlin, "Pu Songling's (1640–1715) *Liaozhai zhiyi* and the Chinese Discourse on the Strange" (Ph.D. dissertation, Harvard University, 1988), p. 43.

of Leisure function as a highly successful fictional technique for a piece of imaginative literature. Apparently analogous commentaries in other eighteenth-century *zhiguai*, like *Close Scrutiny*, however, work differently. By separating the story proper from the author's comments or from remarks by other persons, Ji Yun asserts the independence of the tale from the people who talk about it. He stresses not so much the illusion of reality as the facticity of the narration itself. The elaborate deliberations on the moral meanings of purportedly actual occurrences also urge the reader to take these *zhiguai* tales first and last literally.

Yet one more difference is observable between the end-of-entry remarks in the aesthetic and didactic modes of presentation of tales of the strange. It has been argued that the Fantastorian of each tale presented in actuality the opinions of one implied reader rather than those of the author Pu Songling himself.[34] Theoretically, this contradicts the first point discussed above, according to which Pu Songling was the Fantastorian. Yet the truth seems to be that the appended remarks in *Studio of Leisure* do at times point in one direction, and at times in another, so that the Fantastorian represents something like a conglomerate readership. With *Close Scrutiny* and some other eighteenth-century *zhiguai*, however, the commentator and the author are clearly identified individuals, and their viewpoints belong to disparate portions of a *zhiguai* entry. (Occasionally, slight confusion arises when Ji Yun fails to identify himself, but this lack of clarity is unintentional.) This understanding goes a long way towards vindicating the special character of these later *zhiguai* writings, for it marks them out as more than poor imitations of *Studio of Leisure*.

Finally, the commentaries in *Close Scrutiny* differ from those in *Studio of Leisure* in that they are intimately related to the actual oral storytelling activity. One should remember that, while at times only one person's remarks are recorded, in other tales there is evidence of the different responses of several people. Often present is the sense of a group participating in the analysis of a particular story. Ji Yun's compilation and the other collections in the same mode (these have been said to carry on the "*Close Scrutiny* mode" in *zhiguai* writing) in

---

[34] Ibid.

fact duplicate in their entries the conversational give-and-take of real life, in which a number of listeners proffer, individually, their personal reactions to a story narrated in front of a group. These reactions become the "comments" attached to the story concerned. Alternatively, what happened can be understood as a continuous transmission process in which reactions by different individuals were added each time the story was told or retold.

The remarkable thing is that, despite the presence of more than one viewpoint, the majority of comments are unified in their didactic bent. That is to say, they are fuelled, almost unanimously, by the same impulse towards moral instruction. Such being the case, we will not be much amiss if we say that *zhiguai* collections of the *Close Scrutiny* category document a late eighteenth-century didactic discourse carried on by the elite, in which the events of the strange serve as a springboard for didacticism. It is a polyphonous discourse with a unidirectional orientation which occurred on an oral level, on a written level, between the oral and written levels, and among a gallimaufry of texts.[35] It took place at a specific moment and involved a distinct group whose members, nevertheless, held individual opinions and had personal preferences.

This partly explains why the presence of a multiplicity of opinions in *Close Scrutiny* does not necessarily detract from Ji Yun's instructive purpose. More often than not, the different remarks reinforce one another. When they do not, as when two "commentators" disagree over the moral point conveyed by a narrative, it is usually the precise significance that is being debated rather than whether the story had a moral orientation. By admitting into an entry more than one didactic frame, Ji Yun thus enriches, almost paradoxically, the story's potential for extensive moralizing.

Of course, *Close Scrutiny* differs from many *zhiguai* collections in that it does not have a separate commentarial section headed by the words "According to...." Furthermore, Ji Yun does not speak through

---

[35] There was abundant intertextual reference among *zhiguai* collections of the Qing period. A network of references informed *YWCTBJ*, *ZBY*, and *YTSL* — to the extent that some critics talk of "plagiarism" on the part of the compilers. A similar problem is found in *LZZI* and the *Chibei outan*.

an altered ego or persona; his own remarks are simply inserted into the narratives.[36] Deftly integrated into the didactic discourse, his voice resonates in perfect harmony with the other voices in the collection's brilliant orchestration of a chorus of opinions.

As already noted, next in importance to Ji Yun's own comments were those of his father which, in situations where more than one response is noted, invariably constitute the definitive, conclusive opinion regarding the tale in question.[37] The well-known anecdote involving the woman who chooses to save her mother-in-law rather than her son in the flooding river is a representative example (*HX* II:34). Ji Rongshu flatly rules out the criticisms of the much ridiculed "talk-mongers" (*jiangxuejia* 講學家):

> Circumstances being what they were, abandoning the child and saving the mother-in-law would be in keeping with the just operations of Heavenly principles; it would put one's heart at ease. Were the woman to save her child and allow the mother-in-law to die, would she not feel guilty the rest of her life? Would there not then be people scolding her for abandoning her mother-in-law out of love for her son?[38]

Other instances show Ji Rongshu resolving a conflict of opinions (*RS* II:33), adjudicating a legal dispute (*HX* II:59), and refuting the views of carrot-and-stick moralists who attempt to dictate to a filial son what he must do at his father's funeral (*HX* IV:30). All this establishes Ji Rongshu as a perfectly reliable "commentator" in *Close Scrutiny*.

Specific instances can be cited at this point to illustrate both the interplay of multiple commentaries accompanying one entry and the didactic stance each commentary embodies, keeping in mind that Ji Yun was often present as one of the "commentators." Frequently,

---

[36] For a discussion of the function of authorial discourse in narratives in general, see Susan S. Lanser, *The Narrative Act: Point of View in Prose Fiction* (Princeton: Princeton University Press, 1981), especially pp. 19–20.

[37] For Ji Rongshu's comments, see: *LY* II:4, *LY* III:4, *LY* III:5, *LY* III:23, *LY* III:30, *LY* IV:1, *LY* IV:11, *LY* IV:26, *LY* IV:45, *LY* V:23, *LY* V:30, *LY* V:41, *LY* VI:47, *RS* I:12, *RS* I:36, *RS* I:61, *RS* II:33, *RS* III:17, *RS* III:56, *RS* IV:41, *HX* I:10, *HX* I:21, *HX* II:31, *HX* II:59, *HX* III:37, *HX* IV:17, *HX* IV:29, *HX* IV:30, and *LX* IV:21.

[38] *YWCTBJ*, p. 276.

contradictory opinions are voiced, but by leaving these largely un-reconciled, Ji Yun substantially broadens the scope for moralizing with respect to the same narrative.

One tale concerns a man married to a fox-spirit who reveals that, owing to a debt incurred in a previous existence, she is obligated to be his wife for a stipulated length of time, but not a day more, and not a day less (*LY* I:8). However, as the time draws near, she departs early and thus cheats him of three days. Years later she returns to spend three more days with her lover. Characteristic of the response to fox-spirit lore that drew analogues between the behaviour of such creatures and that of human beings were these two comments:

(1) This fox-spirit has done well by stocking up what is left. In the same way one should cherish one's good fortune (according to Chen Deyin 陳德音).[39]

(2) Why leave three days behind when one will eventually be separated? Though this fox-spirit has had four hundred years of cultivation, it has not reached a state of readiness to let everything go when circumstances so demand. This is not how one should handle one's problems (according to Liu Jizhen 劉季箴).[40]

The views of the two "commentators" on the supernatural protagonist of the tale are diametrically opposed: there is concurrently both praise and blame. For Ji Yun, however, "both were right, each in his own way," and whether the reader concurs with Chen Deyin or Liu Jizhen, there is no mistaking that the two moral points they are making — cherishing one's good fortune and being ready to let everything go should the need arise — are equally valid.

A comparable situation obtains in the story of the woman instructed to remarry by her husband at his deathbed (*LY* II:13). When she does so, she finds not only that, contrary to her expectations, her love for her former husband does not die, but also that she is continually plagued by him in her dreams. Eventually his ghost even suggests that she be reunited with him in death. A real-life episode that Ji Yun

---

[39] Chen Deyin was one of Ji Yun's grand-uncles on his father's side.
[40] *YWCTBJ*, p. 4.

heard at around the age of eleven, it stimulated the following comments from two of the listeners:

(1) To die out of longing for the husband is hardly comparable to killing herself upon his death. (according to He Zishan 何子山).

(2) *The Spring and Autumn Annals* admonishes virtuous men, but one should not restrain women with the principles of the educated. We should mourn the tragic experiences of this woman, and pity her for her choice (according to He Li'an 何勵庵 [He Xiu 何琇 , *jinshi*, 1733]).[41]

The issue of a widow's chastity was a problematic one in late imperial times, and the conflicting opinions surrounding a narrative like this one are a sign of its virtual irresolvability. Particularly noticeable in this entry is the ease with which the narrative flows into the didactic discourse, and the scope of moralizing allowed in *Close Scrutiny* is seen in the fact that Ji Yun accepts both the view of the more stringent moralist (He Zishan) and the call for greater flexibility in moral judgments voiced by someone more lenient (He Li'an). By choosing to present both sides of the argument and thus to break loose from the rigid, even frozen, moral standards of the mid-Qing "talk-mongers," Ji Yun is able to avoid some of the less appealing didactic strategies typically associated with works in this vein. In his comments, he does not take any sides but says: "To remarry is to betray one's former husband; to marry and then have one's heart set on somebody else is to betray the second husband. This woman is caught in a dilemma."

This pursuit of greater elasticity in moral judgments, paradoxically, serves to augment rather than undermine Ji Yun's didacticism. It also gives his didacticism a refreshing quality. Readers of *Close Scrutiny* do not feel as though Ji Yun's views are forced upon them. As Hou Jian 侯健 has perceptively remarked,[42] his didacticism works in the style of mild persuasions — readers are inclined to place their trust in Ji Yun by the good sense, gentle humour, and sympathetic understanding that he unmistakably displays. Readers are, in effect, almost

---

[41] Ibid., p. 26.

[42] Hou Jian, "*Yuewei caotang biji* de lixing zhuyi," p. 155. To Hou Jian, it is Ji Yun's "candour" and "sincerity" that invite the reader to agree with his opinions.

"coaxed" into agreeing with the author's views because of the moral latitude displayed. The multiple commentaries play a significant role in making possible the creation of a mood of authorial congeniality.

Yet another instance worth looking at is the account of the woman who committed suicide as a result of her mother-in-law's mistreatment (*LY* IV:28). Her ghost appears to Shen Cangling, demands restitution, and will not be appeased even when told that a coroner's inspection of her body will bring disgrace to both families. Shen Cangling comments in this way:

> Government officials and emperors do not sue each other at court; nor do sons and fathers. Others will sympathize with you for being wrongfully killed, and reprimand your mother-in-law for her maliciousness. But for you, the daughter-in-law, to even think of suing her in court is to violate what is proper and correct.[43]

Shen Qianju 申謙居, his brother, while not disagreeing with these views, nevertheless qualifies this moral stance: "What Cangling said could be made known to all the daughters-in-law of the world. To tell this to the mothers-in-law would not do" — showing clearly not only where his sympathies lay, but also his concern for mothers-in-laws behaving properly. The need for judiciousness when offering moral imperatives is echoed at the end of this entry by Ji Yun, for whom one should talk of filiality to sons, but of benevolence (towards one's children) to fathers.

To see the didactic mode — or the commentarial mode — of *Close Scrutiny* in its wider literary context, we need to pause briefly to look at several *zhiguai* works exemplifying a similar approach. The following is a list of some late eighteenth- and early nineteenth-century *zhiguai* collections which capitalize on the commentaries and conclude their tales with one or more "voices":

(1) Yin Qinglan's 尹慶蘭 (ca. 1735–1788) *Exotic Grass at the Glow-worm Window* (*Yingchuang yicao* 螢窗異草). The majority of comments are penned by the Unofficial Historian (Waishishi 外史氏), with occasional remarks by "the Old Man of the Garden of Contentment." However, even though the author's father, the eminent Manchu

---

[43] *YWCTBJ*, p. 73.

administrator and Grand Secretary Yin Jishan 尹繼善 (1696–1771),
was Yuan Mei's long-time patron, it is doubtful that Yuan Mei did in
fact insert these remarks.[44] The compilation appeared in mid- to late
Qianlong times.

(2) He Bang'e's *Occasional Accounts of Conversations at Night*. Most
of the entries in this collection are accompanied by the author's own
remarks under his other name Nizhai 閑齋 and remarks by somebody
called Lanyan 蘭岩 . There are, additionally, scattered comments by
three other readers. The earliest edition, presently housed in the
Shanghai Library, is dated 1778.[45]

(3) Shen Qifeng's *Words of Humour from an Ancient Bell*, with commentaries by the "Ancient Bell." Yin Jie's 殷杰 preface to it is dated
1791.

(4) Xu Kun's *Unauthorized Compilations of Willow Cliff*. Commentaries by the author's persona, "the Master of Willow Cliff " (Liuyazi 柳
崖子), are tagged onto almost every entry. Li Jinzhi's 李金枝 preface is
dated 1791, but there is evidence that the work was in circulation for
years before it was published.[46]

(5) Yue Jun's first and second collections of *Hearsay Accounts*.
Approximately half of the entries conclude with comments by Master
No-no (Feifeizi 非非子). The two prefaces were written by Yue Jun
himself in 1792 and 1794.[47]

---

[44] A descriptive account of the relationship between Yuan Mei and Yin Jishan is found
in Yuzi 餘子, *Zhanggu mantan* 掌故漫談 (Casual Talk of Past Anecdotes) (Hong Kong: Dahua
chubanshe 大華出版社 , 1974), pp. 454–462. See also Yang Honglie 楊鴻烈 , *Yuan Mei
pingzhuan* 袁枚評傳 (A Critical Biography of Yuan Mei) (Shanghai: The Commercial Press,
1927); and Fu Yuheng 傅毓衡, *Yuan Mei nianpu* 袁枚年譜 (A Chronology of Yuan Mei) (Hefei:
Anhui jiaoyu chubanshe 安徽教育出版社 , 1986).

[45] For the controversy on the actual name of the author of *YTSL*, see Mai Ruopeng 麥
若鵬, "Chu jie 'Xianzhai' zhi mi" 初揭閑齋之謎 (Unravelling for the First Time the Puzzle of
"Xianzhai"), *Guangming ribao* 光明日報, 2 July 1986; Xue Hong 薛洪, "'Xianzhai' yu 'Nizhai'"
閑齋與閑齋 ("Xianzhai" and "Nizhai"), *Guangming ribao* 光明日報, 10 September 1986; Jiang
Dongfu 姜東賦, "Ye shuo He Bang'e" 也說和邦額 (Also on He Bang'e), *Guangming ribao* 光明
日報, 10 September 1986; and Meng Xingren 孟醒仁, "Ye jie 'Xianzhai laoren' zhi mi" 也揭
閑齋老人之謎 (Again Unravelling the Puzzle of "Xianzhai laoren"), *Guangming ribao* 光明日
報 , 17 December 1986. For a discussion of the various editions, see Fang Zhengyao, "He
Bang'e *Yetan suilu* kaoxi."

[46] See Maeno Naoaki, *Chūgoku shōsetsushi kō*, p. 323.

[47] *Ershi Lu*, pp. 1 and 167.

(6) The Retired Scholar of Indolence and Reticence's *Records of Events Heard in the Vicinity*, with a preface dated 1843. There are sparse comments by a certain Informal Historian (Yeshishi 野史氏).

(7) Xu Qiuzhai's 徐秋坨 *Accounts of Anomalies Heard and Seen* (*Wenjian yici* 聞見異辭), with a 1847 preface. A special feature of the compilation is that the commentary portion of each entry is written as a quatrain.

(8) Tang Yongzhong's 湯用中 *Miscellany of the Winged Chariot Drawn by Four Horses* (*Yisi baibian* 翼駟稗編). Comments are written by a friend. The two prefaces date the work with some accuracy to 1849.

Naturally, not all of the remarks contained in the above collections, most of which are *zhiguai* works, are morally didactic. Authors, readers, and listeners might choose to respond to a story of the strange by querying the events described or by reacting emotionally to what was narrated;[48] another story or incident might be told to corroborate the first;[49] further information might be given with respect to, say, a folk belief;[50] some background to the narration might be provided.[51] Even philosophical ruminations on the nature of the anomalies might be occasioned by a *zhiguai* item.[52] (Comments of these types are, of course, also present in *Close Scrutiny*.) The significant fact about most of the remarks is that they evince a concern with the supernatural as a real and concrete entity, something to be reckoned with. In a few instances, doubt is cast on the accuracy of the reports, but instances in which the existence of supernatural beings is refuted are also extremely rare. Obviously the prevalence of supernatural belief at the time lent support to the moral message being presented.

---

[48] See "Lu Gui" 陸珪 (Lu Gui), *YTSL*, 3:15a–16a; and "Sha Bai" 傻白 (Foolish Bai), *YTSL*, 4:11b–12a.

[49] See "Gui Huang" 詭黃 (Wizard Huang), *YTSL*, 1:29b–39b; and "Li Wu" 李五 (Li the Fifth), *LYWB*, 3:19a–20b.

[50] See "Tiannan sanguai" 滇南三怪 (The Three Demons in Southern Yunnan), *LYWB*, 4:12b–16a.

[51] See "Luotai shan" 羅台山 (Mount Luotai), *Ershi lu*, pp. 181–183; and "Wu xiansheng" 吳先生 (Mr. Wu), *LYWB*, 7:17a–18a.

[52] See "Xieguai" 血怪 (The Blood-demon), *LYWB*, 2:25a–27a, where the commentator discussed the nature of the demon with reference to *yin-yang* theory; and "Huang Lao" 黃老 (Old Huang), *LYWB*, 8:1a–2b, with its comments on the transformations of *qi* as the basis of causality.

Of particular interest are *Unauthorized Compilations of Willow Cliff* and *Occasional Accounts of Conversations at Night*. Both are built on the same principles of didactic discourse as *Close Scrutiny*; both contain strata of commentary that attach themselves to the stories. Not much is presently known about the reading habits of the Qing elite in connection with *zhiguai* materials.[53] As noted earlier, however, there are hints that the collections were as much the source materials for the elite conversations — the collections were referred to for information on the supernatural rather than just read silently — as they were products of such verbal exchanges. If the number of compilations in the period is any indication at all, *zhiguai* collections must have been eagerly sought after by elite circles, among whom the collections enjoyed wide circulation. Looked at from this angle, the two works by Xu Kun and He Bang'e reveal further and hidden dimensions of the didacticism inherent in Ji Yun's collection.

Unauthorized Compilations of Willow Cliff.   The Guangwen 廣文 reprint of *Unauthorized Compilations*, edited by Ren Meiyou 任郿佑 and Ren Lanyou 任蘭佑 of Liushe 聊攝 (in Shandong), provides valuable

---

[53] David Johnson has noted: "Adequate assessment of the social and historical significance of any text requires that we know how widely it is circulated, how many people it influenced, and who they were." David Johnson, "Communication, Class, and Consciousness in Late Imperial China," in *Popular Culture in Late Imperial China*, edited by David Johnson, Andrew J. Nathan and Evelyn J. Rawski, p. 34. The many printings that *YWCTBJ* went through show that it found favour with a great number of readers. This was remarked upon by Liu Shengmu 劉聲木, who was particularly fond of the collection, in his *Changchuzhai suibi* 萇楚齋隨筆 (Random Jottings at the Studio of Carambolas), in *Jindai Zhongguo shiliao congkan*, 4:7b–8a. *ZBY* was also widely read, as noted earlier, though that can be ascribed to its being circulated with others of Yuan Mei's immensely popular writings. The popularity of *LZZI* is beyond dispute. But almost nothing is known about the circulation of the lesser *zhiguai* works of the period. On the other hand, research into the *Records of Yijian* has shown that this second largest *zhiguai* collection of all was reportedly the "number-one bestselling work of the Southern Song." See Guo Licheng 郭立誠, "*Yijian zhi* yanjiu — jiantan Songdai de minsu shiliao" 夷堅志研究 — 兼談宋代的民俗史料 (A Study of the *Yijian zhi*, with Additional Remarks on the Historical Documents Related to Song Folk Customs), *Zhonghua wenhua fuxing yuekan* 中華文化復興月刊, vol. 10, no. 2 (1977), p. 42. In any case, the *zhiguai* has had a much wider audience than it would at first appear.

clues as to what might have happened during the written (as against the oral) transmission of the narratives and sheds some light on the nature of the multiple commentaries. Evidence is found of the presence of didactic voices other than Xu Kun's which are scribbled on the upper margins of over a dozen pages, at the end of Chapter One, and on the very last page of the collection. These commentators were obviously among the first readers of the compilation. The different calligraphic styles suggest that more than one commentator had the opportunity to read it, though only one clearly identified himself as "the Recluse in Possession of Bamboos."[54]

Let's look closely at a few instances of this inscribed commentary. There is, first, the entry on Feng Qiushui 馮秋水, an official who intercedes on behalf of thousands of rebels captured in Xining 西寧 and is about to be executed. After the general in charge accedes to Feng Qiushui's suggestion that only the rebel-leaders be killed, Feng dreams of Guanyin 觀音 descending on him amidst wondrous clouds and informing him of the impending birth of a son to him.[55] Right above Feng Qiushui's words to the general is scribbled: "Just because of these words, future generations will prosper."

Next are the "eyebrow" remarks jotted down in connection with the entry "Two Filial Sons" (see fig. 6). They point in the same moral direction as those in the first example, signalling an attempt to instigate the practice of filiality. The pet saying, "of a hundred virtues, filial piety comes first" (*baixing xiao wei xian* 百行孝為先), is written down, and the commentator continues to say how piqued he is at people's reluctance to practice this simple virtue.[56]

As for the vices most often censured, voluptuousness and greed, the attack comes in the form of a couplet inserted at the end of Chapter One (see fig. 7):

The knife in [the character for] "voluptuousness" (*se* 色) is on its head;
The knife in [the character for] "gain" (*li* 利) is on its side.

---

[54] *LYWB*, 6:20b.

[55] Ibid., 4:23a–24b. There is another story in which Feng Qiushui figures — see 4:24b–26a.

[56] Ibid., 6:3b.

Below these lines there is a song entitled "Warning Against Sexual Licentiousness" written over the entire page.[57] At the end of the collection, finally, is a remark stating that while certain parts of *Unauthorized Compilations* may not be authentic, one should "select what is virtuous and abide by it."[58]

These didactic injunctions interspersed by readers in *Unauthorized Compilations* must be understood to reflect a pattern of elite response to the transmitted tales of the supernatural which is determined by the inner dynamics of *zhiguai* discourse. The marginal commentaries, unlike those in vernacular novels of the same era like *Dream of the Red Chamber*, were not written out of an interest in plot, character, or structure.[59] They either raised points about the verifiability of the event, advanced an explanation of the supernatural, or extracted a certain moral significance from the tale. The comment might at times be only remotely related to the story to which it attached itself, but it seldom moved beyond the parameters just outlined. The reader of the *zhiguai* who jotted down comments brought with him, therefore, a different set of expectations than when he was reading a full-length novel. Put simply, he approached a *zhiguai* collection differently. It seems, also, that the dominant concern for *zhiguai* reader-commentators (as for authors) was that the story should impart a moral message. The incorporation of comments into the circulated collection, rather than distracting from this concern, generally served to reinforce it. The comments, taken collectively, function to prompt further interpretations of the text from an ethical perspective, and the end result is a reinforcement of the didactic message.[60]

Occasional Accounts of Conversations at Night.   The publication history of He Bang'e's *Occasional Accounts*, from its earliest version until

---

[57] Ibid., 1:33b.

[58] Ibid., 8:25b.

[59] The various types of comments written for the vernacular novel are discussed in David Rolston, ed., *How to Read the Chinese Novel* (Princeton: Princeton University Press, 1990), pp. 42–74.

[60] This is an aspect of the "collaboration between author and audience" as discussed in Eugene Eoyang, "A Taste for Apricots: Approaches to Chinese Fiction," in *Chinese Narrative: Critical and Theoretical Essays,* edited by Andrew H. Plaks, pp. 53–69.

its late Qing editions, is an apt illustration of the complicated process of eighteenth-century *zhiguai* compilation-circulation-publication. Previously, scholars like Maeno Naoaki maintained that *Occasional Accounts* was first published in 1791, because the more widely known edition carries a preface by He Bang'e dated that year.[61] The recent discovery by Fang Zhengyao 方正耀 of a 1778 edition makes possible new views of the early history of the work. It seems almost indisputable now that the collection arose out of conversations that the young He Bang'e had with his friends at the imperial academy at Beijing as early as the 1760s.[62] Since He Bang'e's preface also indicates that the work went into print when he was forty-four, the commentaries by various friends must have been added to the collection over an extended period of time. According to Fang Zhengyao, the Jinbu shuju 進步書局 deleted "eyebrow" comments by an anonymous person from their 1913 edition, which left a 141-entry version with commentaries by five people — He Bang'e himself, Lanyan, Fu Jitang 福霽堂, Ji Zhaiyu 季齋魚 and En Maoxian 恩茂先. What this means is that originally there must have been at least six layers of discursive remarks in *Occasional Accounts*.

The bulk of the commentaries in *Occasional Accounts* was contributed by someone named Lanyan, also known as "Master of the Sunflower Garden" (Kuiyuan zhuren 葵園主人), whose exact identity is still an open question. The subtitles to each of the chapters indicate that his remarks were included in the very first printing, unlike those of the other commentators. Quite a few of the moral lessons he drew from He Bang'e's narrations were based on comparisons between the behaviour of human beings and that of supernatural beings, most notably the fox-spirits. An exemplary instance is found at the end of "Miss Red" ("Hong guniang" 紅姑娘), a tale of a beautiful fox-spirit who fights off some promiscuous rakes and repays the debt she owes to a field officer by instructing him in Daoist magical techniques for prolonging life. Here Lanyan quips, cynically:

---

[61] See Maeno Naoaki, *Chūgoku shōsetsushi kō*, p. 312. The *Biji xiaoshuo daguan* version even has a preface by He Bang'e dated 1913.

[62] Fang Zhengyao, "He Bang'e *Yetan suilu* kaoxi," pp. 104–105.

Even weird creatures like the fox would reciprocate kindnesses bestowed on them as well as guard their true inner tranquillity. Further, they would abstain from seducing others with their charm. How come the whole world would not think it weird that even stately-built men fawn on those from whom they seek favours? Instead it sees the upright and unbending as foolish.[63]

Similar moral lessons are given in the comment on the first story of the collection, "Scholar Cui" ("Cui xiucai" 崔秀才). The story portrays a fox-spirit who returns to help his patron when the latter falls on hard times, though all the other protégés have fled. This leads Lanyan to scoff at the superficiality of human friendships: "[We are in] the common habit of gathering around the rich and prestigious, and staying away from the poor and lowly. Men should be ashamed of themselves, for they are hardly comparable to fox-spirits."[64]

As in *Close Scrutiny*, in a majority of cases parallel commentaries serve to complement one another in *Occasional Conversations*. At times the nature of this complementarity may be more oblique than in *Close Scrutiny*. One of the five narratives in a section (entitled "Miscellaneous Records") on events related to a variety of fox-spirits reveals the interplay between two sets of commentaries. Before telling his stories, He Bang'e begins with a theoretical discussion of the nature of the fox-spirit as a category of spirits and gives a brief taxonomy of its diverse types. This provides a context against which the five narratives to follow are to be read.[65] At the end of each narrative are attached first He Bang'e's remarks, then Lanyan's.

The first story in the series is especially relevant to the present discussion. It concerns a fox-spirit who takes revenge on a maid by castrating the maid's father when he is with a prostitute. Two contradictory views are then presented. For He Bang'e, the form that the revenge took was singularly ironic because fox-spirits were known to

---

[63] *YTSL*, 1:19a.

[64] Ibid., 1:3b. Lanyan consistently made comparisons between the behaviour of fox-spirits and men, in a way reminiscent of the "commentators" in *YWCTBJ*. The comments he made about "Scholar Cui" ("men should be ashamed of themselves, for they are hardly comparable to fox-spirits") are typical in this regard. See *LYWB*, 1:3b.

[65] According to He Bang'e, there were seven types of foxes which metamorphosed into demons when they were old enough. See *YTSL*, 2:5a–5b.

dabble in licentious activities themselves, but for Lanyan the fox-spirit's ruthlessness was a sign of its evil character. Apparently the two commentators are engaged with different aspects of the fox-spirit's character, but they are in fact united in their censure of two kinds of immoral behaviour — sexual laxity and vindictiveness.

As with some of the examples from *Close Scrutiny*, the presence of more than one didactic frame clearly does not blur the intended interpretation but actually reinforces it. The entry "Records of Anomalies in the Examination Halls" ("Jiwei zhiyi" 棘圍志異) begins with a prefatory note by He Bang'e, in which he stresses the theme of karmic retribution in the eight tales to be narrated. Deities and ghosts, it is said in the note, are invited into the examination halls by a ritual performed the night before candidates are admitted, and they will "oversee the settling of all accounts."[66] The individual stories that follow are all accompanied by Lanyan's comments. In the sixth story, which received a comment from Fu Jitang, a spirit enters into one candidate's dream and blinds him — presumably because he had been peeping through a hole in the wall at a woman in her toilet — at the same time as another candidate, who previously reproached the voyeur, receives news that he has won first place in the same examination. Both commentators take the opportunity to moralize on the need to behave morally even when one is alone. While Lanyan highlights the lesson to be learnt from the contrasting fortunes of the two candidates, Fu Jitang comments metaphorically: "He who is blinded in the eyes is first blind at his heart."

One last example from *Occasional Accounts* can be cited to illustrate the nature of multiple commentaries in the *zhiguai* of late imperial China. In "Brigade-general Jin" ("Jin Zongbing" 靳總兵), an anecdote is recounted of a fish-demon which even Daoist priests are unable to subdue. It is captured only when Brigade-general Jin drains the entire stream in which it lives. This leads He Bang'e, in his commentary, to talk about a kind of ice-rat in the northern regions that he believes should belong to the same species of weird creatures. It may seem at this point rather unlikely that the story could be turned to any good didactic use. But then a close friend of He Bang'e's, En Maoxian,

---

[66] *YTSL*, 2:30b–31a.

proceeds in his commentary to narrate two further incidents. The first concerns how He's father prevented some hailstorms and the second, how he succeeded in obtaining rain from a local deity. Both incidents, perhaps only remotely related to He Bang'e's story, are said to have taken place in Wuwei 武威 prefecture in present-day Gansu 甘肅, so that even a geographical link is out of the question. But the entry then concludes with Lanyan's comment: "The deities are touched by extreme sincerity: that is clear and without exception. The same principle was at work behind the chasing away of the alligator by Han Yu."[67] Sincerity, then, becomes the common element that links all these incidents. Through leaps and bounds, what begins as a disinterested description of a "supernatural" event turns out, therefore, to be once again a vehicle for didactic observations on what is correct human behaviour.

To sum up: the most important feature revealed in the use of multiple commentaries in *Close Scrutiny, Unauthorized Compilations,* and *Occasional Accounts* is the unanimity of the didactic outlook. Didacticism is then not only a literary, but also a socio-historical, phenomenon. Why the scholarly elite chose to manipulate narratives of the supernatural for didactic purposes is a question to be studied further in the next section. How Ji Yun formulated his theory of *zhiguai* didacticism with regard to the social functions that such literature could serve will be the subject of discussion. It seems sufficient here simply to point the way by characterizing the didacticism of the eighteenth-century *zhiguai* collections as a manner of response to supernatural affairs on the part of the educated elite. And in its efforts to compile the *zhiguai,* this elite was preserving its own interpretation of what was morally significant.

In spite of what is said above, there is no denying that the eighteenth century also saw *zhiguai* literature representing the opposite pole. In his *What the Master Would Not Discuss,* Yuan Mei, the major proponent of expressionist theories of poetry in the eighteenth century,[68] does away with all the basic props of Ji Yun's didactic method,

---

[67] Ibid., 4:36a–37b.

[68] Studies of *ZBY* are scarce. Besides Wu Yuhui's M.A. thesis mentioned above, see also: Hoshino Akihiko 星野明彦, "En Mei to *Ko fugo* — shōsetsuka toshite no ishiki o chushin ni"

though he does not follow the "*Studio of Leisure* model" either. He seldom incorporates a commentarial portion; his emphasis is primarily on the unfolding of the narratives themselves, which, as he said, are meant to be read for pure enjoyment. He is also more successful in the creation of atmosphere — Arthur Waley calls the stories "tales of psychic horror," and N. H. Van Straten interprets them as a means of expressing "the subconscious aspects of a situation."[69] Yuan Mei did not merely reject Ji Yun's didactic approach; he also included plenty of salacious depictions. No wonder Ji Yun and Qian Daxin regarded the collection as inducing and encouraging promiscuous attitudes.[70] Time and again, too, Yuan Mei exhibits a rather ambiguous stand on the issue of the existence of spirits, reflecting a sceptical view noted earlier in Chapter Three.[71]

袁枚と子不語 ― 小説家として意識を中心に (Yuan Mei and the *Zi bu yu*: Concerning the Consciousness of Fiction-writers), *Geibun kenkyō* 芸文研究, vol. 51 (1987), pp. 69–89; Funazu Tomihiko 船津富彦, "En Mei no shōsetsuron ― tatemae to honne ni tsuite" 袁枚の小説論 ― 定前と本音について (Yuan Mei's Theory of Fiction: On His Principles and Intentions), *Tōyōgaku rōnsō* 東洋學論叢, vol. 35, no. 7 (1982), pp. 63–76; Yu Lei 余雷, "*Xin Qi Xie* yu Yuan Mei de zunzhong gexing sixiang" 新齊諧與袁枚的尊重個性思想 (*Xin Qi Xie* and Yuan Mei's Respect for Personal Character), *Zhejiang xuekan* 浙江學刊, no. 1 (1984); Li Mengsheng 李夢生, "Yuan Mei *Zi bu yu* qiantan" 袁枚子不語淺探 (An Overview of Yuan Mei's *Zi bu yu*), *Zhongguo gudian wenxue luncong* 中國古典文學論叢, no. 4 (1986), pp. 256–271; and the chapter "*Zi bu yu (Xin Qi Xie)*" 子不語 (新齊諧) in Huang Jinhong 黃錦鋐, et al., *Zhongguo wenxue jianghua shi (10): Qingdai wenxue* 中國文學講話史 (10)：清代文學 (Discussions on Chinese Literature (10): Qing Literature) (Taibei: Juliu shuju 巨流書局, 1987). Very brief mention is made of *ZBY* in Jian Youyi 簡有儀, *Yuan Mei yanjiu* 袁枚研究 (A Study of Yuan Mei) (Taibei: Wenshizhe chubanshe 文史哲出版社, 1988), pp. 306–307.

[69] Arthur Waley, *Yuan Mei: Eighteenth-Century Chinese Poet*, p. 122; and N. H. Van Straten, *Concepts of Health, Disease and Vitality in Traditional Chinese Society: A Psychological Interpretation*, p. 7.

[70] *ZBY* indeed had to face charges of inaccuracy and lewdness, both repeatedly condemned in the book reviews of *SKQSZM*. See Yuan Mei, *Xiaocang shanfang chidu*, 7:122–123. The element of promiscuity in the *zhiguai* can also be seen, for example, in *LZZI* and — very conspicuously — in *YTSL*. Whether the emphasis on didacticism, in an age of severe censorship, was merely a cover for writing erotica is a question that merits further investigation.

[71] Yuan Mei's scepticism, discussed in chap. 3, can also be seen in *ZBY*. See, for instance, "Tiantaixian gang" 天台縣缸 (The Cauldron in Tiantai Subprefecture), *ZBY*, pp. 287–288, where he attacked superstitions related to a jar.

What the Master Would Not Discuss generated great interest, but Yuan Mei never attracted a following and was virtually the only compiler of non-didactic *zhiguai* in his time.[72] By contrast, as Lu Xun and several other critics have remarked, Ji Yun's didactic mode persisted into the nineteenth century (so much so that there was a school of imitators of *Close Scrutiny*).[73] There were vestiges of its influence even in late Qing times. One example is particularly striking. In the 1874 preface and explanatory notes to his *The Four-horse Chariot in the Neighbourhood* (*Li cheng* 里乘), Xu Shuping 許叔平 elucidates the principles behind his compilation, and three of these are strongly reminiscent of those that Ji Yun articulates in *An Annotated Catalogue*.[74] According to Xu Shuping, (1) his work is intended to prove that the doctrine of retribution is not fabricated; (2) the lascivious descriptions so prevalent in the *zhiguai* have been strictly avoided; and (3) unlike *Studio of Leisure*, all the accounts narrated are verifiable, having been heard or seen by him in the previous thirty years. In addition, he also notes that didactic works often do not find much favour with readers. For that reason, he collected narratives both shocking and enlightening, so that readers would be alerted to the message conveyed — a view with which Ji Yun, presumably, would have agreed.

A Theory of Didacticism

Turning from a consideration of *how* Ji Yun moralized to *why* he moralized, one needs to address the question whether he was a believer in

---

[72] In addition to all the differences from *YWCTBJ* already mentioned, *ZBY* had also been found to be less reliable in its reporting. There is the famous case of "Li Xiangjun jianjuan" 李香君薦卷 (Li Xiangjun Recommending a Script) (*ZBY*, p. 55). Yuan Mei was openly upbraided by the eminent dramatist Yang Chaoguan 楊潮觀 (1712–1791) for playing havoc with the facts of the tale he had first narrated.

[73] Among the critics who have spoken of a "Ji Yun style in *zhiguai* writing" are: Lu Xun, *A Brief History of Chinese Fiction*, pp. 269–271; Liu Yeqiu, *Lidai biji gaishu*, pp. 173–174; Lai Fangling 賴芳伶 , *Yuewei caotang biji yanjiu* 閱微草堂筆記研究 (A Study of the *Yuewei caotang biji*) (Taibei: Taiwan University Publications, 1982), pp. 115–117; and Fang Nansheng's "introduction" to Yu Jiao, *Meng'an zazhu*, p. 1–3. Their listing of works supposedly influenced by *YWCTBJ* is, however, debatable.

[74] See the introductory notes to Xu Shuping, *Li cheng*.

the supernatural.[75] This question is complicated by the possibility that Ji Yun might not have genuinely believed in the existence of the spiritual realm but merely feigned belief. Lu Xun suggests that Ji was not a believer and simply wrote stories of fox-spirits and ghosts in order to criticize his society.[76] Lu Xun's view is affected by his own concern for using literature for social reform. His characterization is most apt for those tales from the collection whose satiric force is aimed at corrupt officials, scholars of the eight-legged essay, and unbending neo-Confucian moralists. However, considering that most of Ji Yun's stories are not satiric, Lu Xun's "reading" of Ji Yun's motives is certainly open to doubt. Lu Xun's view is further flawed because he fails to distinguish the attitudes of the individual narrators from that of the compiler. The inability of critics to appreciate the multiple levels at which *zhiguai* collections work is not uncommon.

More recently, in his collection of essays comparing Chinese and Western works of fiction, Hou Jian notes that Ji Yun was actually more concerned with the "principles" revealed in the narratives than with the narratives *per se*, and he has raised doubts about Ji Yun's belief.[77] Hou Jian argues that Ji Yun's attempt to provide rational explanations for supernatural occurrences distinguishes the collection and makes it a unique product of the eighteenth-century Chinese "Enlightenment." According to Hou Jian, *Close Scrutiny*, by upholding reason (over and above belief) as the guiding principle for human understanding, is comparable to roughly contemporaneous European works like Samuel Johnson's *Rasselas* and Voltaire's *Candide*. Hou Jian is obviously too quick to laud what he sees as the use of deductive reasoning in Ji Yun's compilation. He fails to look closely at Ji Yun's specific goal of proving the existence of the supernatural by ruling out naturalistic explanations. Hou Jian might very well have characterized Ji Yun as a sceptic, though he never uses this term.

---

[75] For reasons of space, only the views of twentieth-century critics are discussed here. For the critical reception of *YWCTBJ* in the nineteenth century, see Lu Xun, *Xiaoshuo jiuwen chao* 小説舊聞鈔 (Collection of Past Writings on Fiction) (Hong Kong: Datong shuju 大通書局 , 1959), pp. 117–120; and Jiang Ruizao 蔣瑞藻 , ed., *Xiaoshuo kaozheng* 小説考證 (Evidential Research on the *Xiaoshuo*) (Shanghai: The Commercial Press, 1935), p. 176.

[76] Lu Xun, *Zhongguo xiaoshuo shilue*, p. 176.

[77] Hou Jian, *Zhongguo xiaoshuo bijiao yanjiu*, p. 162.

In her monograph on *Close Scrutiny,* Lai Fangling 賴芳伶 contends that Ji Yun neither believed nor completely disbelieved.[78] She bases her view on what Ji Yun once said about leaving the issue of the real existence of spirits alone, since it "may or may not be understood."[79] In support of Lai Fangling's position one can also cite Ji Yun's occasional expressions of doubt about immortality and the reality of hell. Lai Fangling argues that since Ji Yun's main aim was moral edification of the masses, he deliberately advocates belief, for this was common practice among writers of the late *zhiguai* tradition. She indeed belongs to the camp of critics who argue that, for moral-didactic purposes, Ji Yun feigned belief.

A similar — though more extreme — view, which focuses on Ji Yun's manipulation of readers' credulity, is advanced by Zhu Shiying 朱世英. Insisting that Ji Yun did not believe in the supernatural at all, Zhu Shiying explains that Ji Yun's attacks on the no-ghost theory were a matter of expedience, for sceptical theories undermine efforts to promote virtue and indict reprehensible behaviour.[80] Both Lai Fangling and Zhu Shiying appear, in effect, to ascribe to Ji Yun a motive that Hong Liangji, almost two centuries ago, condemned many of his contemporaries for — lying about the spiritual realm in order to exhort moral behaviour among the masses. Indeed, critics who characterize Ji Yun as an ardent moralist tend to favour the view that he did not believe in ghosts and deities, as though moral earnestness and supernatural beliefs are incompatible. Following Zhu Shiying's line of reasoning, Yao Mang 姚莽 and Li Jinquan 李錦全 propose reading the tales in *Close Scrutiny* as "fables" or "allegories."[81]

Lu Jintang is among the few who maintain that Ji Yun is a believer of the supernatural. The strength of his argument derives from his

---

[78] Lai Fangling, *Yuewei caotang biji yanjiu,* p. 10.

[79] *YWCTBJ,* p. 155.

[80] Zhu Shiying, "Lun *Yuewei caotang biji* zhi 'chang'" 論閱微草堂筆記之長 (On the Strengths of the *Yuewei caotang biji*), *Wenxue yican* 文學遺產, no. 1 (1983), pp. 94–102.

[81] Yao Mang, "*Yuewei caotang biji* yishu chengjiu chutan" 閱微草堂筆記藝術成就初探 (A First Study of the Artistic Achievements of the *Yuewei caotang biji*), *Beifang luncong: Harbin shida xuebao* 北方論叢：哈爾濱師大學報, no. 4 (1985), pp. 60–65; and Li Jinquan, "Zai yinguo baoying shuo de beihou" 在因果報應說的背後 (Behind the Theory of Retribution), *Beifang luncong: Harbin shida xuebao,* no. 5 (1984), pp. 65–70.

determined effort to go beyond a mere analysis of the text and to contextualize it in terms of the elite life centring around Ji Yun. In his dissertation, he traces what amounts to a history of family superstitions in the Ji household and concludes that Ji Yun was "earnest in his belief in deities and ghosts."[82] *Close Scrutiny* itself abounds in evidence that Ji Yun dabbled in spirit-writing, geomancy, and other means of divination. In one recorded instance he clearly states that he believes in fortune-telling because his banishment to Urumqi was foretold accurately in a poem.

Lu Jintang's point is substantiated by a quatrain Ji Yun composed after completing the first volume of his collection:

Karmic causes and effects are proved beyond doubt,
A wagon full of ghosts gathered in desultory jottings.
Let the word be passed to Cheng-Zhu disciples,
The collector of anecdotes does not belong to the company of Confucians.[83]

As seen in this poem,[84] Ji Yun knew not only that he had abrogated the Confucian injunction "not to talk of ghosts and deities," but also that he had insulted the neo-Confucians of his time, who disparaged the writing of *zhiguai*. His denunciation of the neo-Confucians in *Close Scrutiny* is often noted by critics. What has gone unnoticed is that the compiling of *zhiguai* stories itself can be connected to his "quarrel" with the neo-Confucians, who refuted supernatural beliefs. In this regard, Ji Yun may be likened to Hong Mai who, it might be suggested, compiled his *Records of Yijian* specifically to refute the sceptical position of Zhu Xi and others.

If Ji Yun did believe in the supernatural, why does he sometimes indicate that he has doubts? To be sure, it can be argued that Ji Yun conveyed his moral messages without taking the tales seriously — without even believing in the supernatural. But if, as in traditional

---

[82] Lu Jintang, "Ji Yun shengping jiqi *Yuewei caotang biji*," p. 2b.

[83] Ji Yun, *Ji Xiaolan quanji* 紀曉嵐全集 (Complete Writings of Ji Yun) (Beijing: Dongfang Wenxueshe 東方文學社, 1935), p. 114.

[84] The allusion to a "wagon full of ghosts" is taken from *The Book of Changes*. The topmost line of the *kui* 睽 hexagram shows a pig bearing a load of mud on its back, as well as a carriage of ghosts. Wang Hansheng 王寒生, ed., *Yijing qianzhu* 易經淺注 (*The Book of Changes, Briefly Annotated*) (Taibei: Xinshiming zazhishe 新使命雜誌社, 1970) p. 132.

times, moral injunctions were to be grounded on the vindicability of a
supernatural order (of which the spirits were concrete embodiments),
the moralist could not teach at all unless spirits were presumed to
exist. This was a point agreed upon by supernaturalists and sceptics
alike. Ji Yun was duplicating precisely what many raconteurs did —
grounding their didactic messages on supernaturalist belief. His task
was facilitated considerably when the authenticity of the tales was accepted in the first place, for the retributive order could manifest itself
through supernatural events that were reportedly real. In the event
he simultaneously persuaded his readers of the reality of the realm of
spirits and achieved his moral-didactic goals.

Ji Yun both believed in the veracity of the supernatural accounts
and imposed on them a didactic meaning. Truthfulness and didactic
utility were the twin principles that buttressed his compilation. This
is, as we have said, the reason why the majority of Ji Yun's stories are
decidedly un-allegorical. Rather than beginning with a message which
he seeks to embody through his narratives, Ji Yun worked only with
supernatural happenings in real life that were replete with moral implications. Ji Yun's didacticism is thus of a special order, and it is the
didacticism of the *zhiguai* genre. Whether the events involving the
supernatural did occur and whether the accounts were authentic
were of crucial significance.

It would also be inconceivable for one who disbelieved to choose
to confront the profusion of bizarre and untoward events and conclude, as Ji Yun does in many cases, that the supernatural is real.[85]
Misgivings do figure in his ruminations, and their inclusion in the
text is a means of winning acceptance among readers. Ji Yun's sincerity is proven by his willingness to voice doubts where evidence is
wanting or not persuasive enough. By the eighteenth century, the possibility of a naive trust in the supernatural was all but nullified, and Ji
Yun was in all likelihood creating a firmer foundation for supernatural belief by subjecting the narratives and incidents he had recorded to reasonable explanations. The occasional doubts therefore

---

[85] There were quite a few cases where Ji Yun stated quite unequivocally that "the Way of
the deities is no deception" (*shenli buwu* 神理不誣) or used words to that effect. See *LY* IV:7,
RS III:5, *RS* III:53, *LX* IV:3.

do no more than reinforce the veracity of those incidents that were verifiable.

But what kind of moralist was Ji Yun? Arthur Waley remarked that "the men of the early eighteenth century were on the whole stern and puritanical, those of the mid-century pleasure-loving and tolerant, those of its closing years and the early nineteenth century, once more straightlaced and censorious."[86] His description of the final years of the eighteenth century certainly is borne out by the spate of didactic *zhiguai* works that constitute the subject of this study, especially *Close Scrutiny* itself. The collection is filled with all sorts of moral injunctions, and indeed it is remarkable how, through a deft manipulation of multiple viewpoints, Ji Yun succeeded in quelling possible charges of moral obtuseness and presenting a well-reasoned call for proper moral behaviour.

Yet, as borne out by *Close Scrutiny*, Ji Yun's moral values are in no way fresh or innovative. Though at times he shows a readiness to adapt to individual circumstances, on the whole he upholds a conservative standpoint and adheres to orthodox Confucian core values like chastity, loyalty, and filial piety. Specific instances which can serve as illustrations of such conservativeness include, first, the entry in which Ji Yun comments on the principles of filiality and brotherliness as "cornerstones of our humanity" (*LY* III:30). On other occasions he berates familial intrigues and squabbling, lauds widows who take good care of their mothers-in-law, and stresses the importance of harmonious conjugal relationships (*GW* III:53). The rules of family conduct pertaining to a wife are summed up in one entry in which he exhorts her to (*HX* III:32)

(1) suppress personal pride and avoid arguing,
(2) perform wifely duties conscientiously,
(3) act in a filial manner towards parents-in-law,
(4) keep peace with sisters-in-law, and
(5) bestow kindness on lesser wives and maids.[87]

---

[86] Arthur Waley, *Yuan Mei: Eighteenth-Century Chinese Poet*, p. 131.
[87] *YWCTBJ*, p. 305.

Elsewhere, Ji Yun also extolls behaviour of a similar sort in fox-spirits (*LX* V:24).

The "cautionary" aspects of Ji Yun's didacticism are equally conspicuous in his collection. The character-type pilloried most fiercely by Ji Yun is that which is sexually indulgent or lascivious. Accounts abound in *Close Scrutiny* of persons of this type seduced by fox-spirits who eventually destroy them, though the form of punishment meted out varies from tale to tale. In one, a rascal who incites his friends to gang-rape a young woman discovers later, to his dismay, that the victim is his own wife (*LY* I:7). Sexual immortality, regarded as having a corrosive impact on personal and public ethics, came under the severest of attacks, seen in the condemnation of prostitution by both females and males.[88] Implicit analogies are repeatedly made between prostitutes on the one hand and malicious fox-spirits and demons on the other.[89] The judge of the netherworld reportedly said that shameless pansies and whores cheated others of their money "as tigers and leopards devour man, and whales and [huge] salamanders swallow boats."[90]

Historical circumstances lie behind Ji Yun's didactic and preachy attitude, and *Close Scrutiny* contains clues to the moralistic temper of the late eighteenth century. Ji Yun often laments the degeneracy of the times and makes references to the cunning and dishonesty (*qiao* 巧) that was rife.[91] It appears that both he and many of the raconteurs were reacting against the trickery they saw around them. Naturally, the traditional association of the fox (and hence the fox-spirit) with

---

[88] *YWCTBJ* included several narratives of deviant or aberrant sexual behaviour, an instance involving bestiality being that of *HX* II:6.

[89] *HX* IV:39 contains a story of a fox-spirit tricked by a prostitute, and in *RS* I:46 a woman with bewitching charm was thought of, by some, as a demon and, by others, as a prostitute.

[90] *YWCTBJ*, p. 145.

[91] *Qiao* was, however, not always used in a derogatory sense, and sometimes could even be ambiguous in its connotations. Surprised to find that one fox-spirit was reportedly hounded by another, Ji Yun remarked on the unusual laws in operation in the natural world as well as the wonderful ingenuity (*qiao*) apparent everywhere in the universe of living things (*HX* II:68). Cf. *RS* IV:23, *HX* I:6, *HX* III:13, *HX* III:59, *HX* III:66, *HX* IV:19, *HX* IV:22, *GW* I:3, *GW* I:32, *GW* III:4, *GW* III:39, *GW* IV:32.

deviousness makes it an excellent vehicle for moralizing on deceitfulness. But since even the ghost could be deceitful — with the classic example provided by the ghost of Liqiu 黎丘, who, according to *Mr. Lü's Spring and Autumn Annals* (*Lüshi chunqiu* 呂氏春秋) plays tricks on a dead man's son by appearing as his father[92] — ghost stories were also put to good use in this context.

That Ji Yun was especially disconcerted by human contrivance (*jixie* 機械) is seen in the anecdotes about thieves disguised as demons (*HX* IV:22), swindlers who claimed to be experts in spirit-writing divination, and so on.[93] The trickery of Buddhist monks is the subject of the following entry (*HX* IV:22):

> The schemes of the unvirtuous are varied. Their intricacies are revealed when adapted in response to changes in circumstances.
>
> I heard of the following when I was young. A villager heard some footsteps at night and, carrying torches to search for what were presumably thieves, found no sign of men. Believing that there were phantoms, he did not inquire any further. When this became known to some burglars, they went to his house at night. As the entire family assumed that they were phantoms, they slept soundly and did not get up to check. The burglars were thus able to have their own way. This is a case of profiting by a good opportunity.
>
> A certain county magistrate was fond of preaching to others, but he abhorred monks as if they were his personal enemies. One day, a monk reported a case of theft. In the main hall the magistrate scolded him: "If your Buddha is not efficacious, why do you offer sacrifices to him in the temple? If he were, could he not have brought the thief to retribution? Would he have passed on the trouble to the government officials?"
>
> After dismissing the monk, he told others: "If all the local magistrates in this world adopted the same method, there would be no need to eliminate monks. They would disperse of their own accord."
>
> The monk happened to be extremely cunning. He proceeded to carry out confessionals and rituals for the Buddha publicly with his

---

[92] According to this ancient legend, recorded in the *Lüshi chunqiu*, one man killed his own son, mistaking him for the Liqiu ghost. See *Lüshi chunqiu*, in *Sibu beiyao*, vols. 1398–1401 (Shanghai: Zhonghua shuju 中華書局, 1927–1936), 22:6a–6b.

[93] *Jixie* is a recurrent phrase in *YWCTBJ*, and is closely connected with the *qiao* theme mentioned above. See, for instance, pp. 246, 310, 348, 440.

disciples, while secretly bribing beggars to come with clothes and other articles, and kneel in front of the temple as though in a trance. Everyone said that the Buddha was efficacious, and people gave more alms to the temple than before. This is a case of twisting around an opportunity and using it, so that the persecutor comes to the aid of the victim. Such is the nature of human affairs. What advantage can one gain if one holds adamantly to principle and lashes out directly at one's adversary?

In a lengthy entry in *Listen in a Rough Way*, Ji Yun lists five vignettes as proof that "treachery and deception is nowhere as bad as in the capital [Beijing]" (*GW* III:50).[94] In most cases money is involved: goods of poor quality are sold at an exorbitant price; a tenant pulls down the pillars and windows of his rented house and sells them. These stories reflect a society in which traditional moral values were increasingly threatened by the growth of a wealth-oriented, highly commercialized, urban culture. The seriousness of the situation is touched on by Qian Weicheng, one of Ji Yun's mentors, who says in this entry that one should consider oneself lucky if not cheated in dealings with the Beijing urbanite.[95]

It is, then, against this background that Ji Yun voiced his moral imperatives. It was obvious to him how a divine scheme of rewarding the good and punishing the bad could inspire moral acts and discourage wrongdoing. For he notes that the path of virtue is wide and easily accessible, and he counters the widespread belief that good and evil cancel each other out in the retributive scheme of things. To him, such belief "prevents the wicked from taking the path of virtue," for "acts of harm are not offset by acts of kindness ... and great good does not compensate for great evil."[96] Furthermore, he asserts that the operation of supernatural logic is universal, well-regulated, and unerring. Ruminating on a case that supposedly was tried for over fifty

---

[94] *YWCTBJ*, p. 440.

[95] It seems hard to document the corrosive impact that the increasing use of money had on traditional morality in late imperial China, but Judith Berling has dealt with this issue with reference to one vernacular novel. See Berling, "Religion and Popular Culture: The Management of Moral Capital in *The Romance of the Three Teachings*," in *Popular Culture in Late Imperial China*, edited by David Johnson, Andrew J. Nathan and Evelyn J. Rawski (Berkeley: University of California Press, 1985), pp. 188–218.

[96] *YWCTBJ*, p. 313.

years in the netherworld court, Ji Yun concludes that no one can escape the consequences of his own actions. Some are apprehended earlier and some later, but "the Way of the deities is no deception" (*shenli buwu* 神理不誣) (*RS* III:53).[97]

In this way a moral scheme was buttressed by a retributive system. But what role was assigned to the ghosts, deities, and fox-spirits? Ji Yun clarifies the relationships among the moral scheme, the system of reward and punishment, and the spiritual beings that roamed the world by first making a comparison with Buddhist and Daoist beliefs:

> The moral vision of the sages is coterminous with Heaven and Earth. How can this be likened to the Buddhist and Daoist religions, where belief is founded on miracles and prodigies, and which rely on the strength of guardian-spirits of the *dharma*? Yet, it seems reasonable enough for this moral vision to be revealed by deities and ghosts.[98]

Two meanings inhere in this statement. The ghosts and deities are concrete embodiments of the way of Heaven and Earth, and through them people have glimpses of the order beyond. Ghosts and deities are also the agents through which divine retribution is carried out, as "even the slightest tremors of the human heart do not escape their notice."[99] To put it in another way, spiritual beings are the only visible actors in a drama of spiritual forces; they are concretizations of the supernatural order. That is why they play such a pivotal role in *Close Scrutiny.*

The final question concerns both the role of didacticism in this conception of the human and supernatural orders and the significance of didacticism for the *zhiguai* writer, the *zhiguai* raconteurs, and the *zhiguai* commentators. Ji Yun's argument begins with the "sages." In *Close Scrutiny* Ji Yun refers repeatedly to the ancient past, when the sages, living in perfect harmony with the Dao, were much closer to the truth than were people of later periods. Ji Yun was of the opinion that the sages never denied the existence of the spirits. Rather, it was the later Confucians who, fearing that the commonfolk would over-indulge themselves in worship of the spirits, prevaricated on the issue

---

[97] Ibid., p. 193.
[98] Ibid., p. 369.
[99] Ibid., p. 5.

(*GW* IV:12). What seemed most despicable to him about the later Confucians was that they chose to advocate disbelief despite their knowledge that spirits existed.

A second point pertaining to the sages is that they were intimately aware of the Way of the deities (*shendao* 神道). Ji Yun observes that the wise sages showed their knowledge of the supernatural realm by creating funerary objects as early as Xia and Shang 商 times (*GW* II:36). Jiang Bingzhang also makes a similar point in a tale that he was supposed to have fabricated (*RS* I:44): only the sages were initiated into the mysteries of creation, when deities (or spirits) were born alongside heaven and earth. This is why the sages instituted the ceremonial rites in the Six Classics, including the burning of firewood in heaven-worship (*fanchai* 燔柴) and the burial of jade in mountain-worship (*yiyu* 瘞玉).

Thirdly, the sages were reputed to have put their knowledge to good use in their composition of *The Book of Changes*. Chapter Ten of Great Appendix I of this classic says: "As a text *The Book of Changes* is of broad scope. It contains within itself the Way of Heaven, the Way of Man, and the Way of Earth."[100] This book was, too, a bridge between the Way of Heaven and that of Man. The sages' aim, according to a ghost-interlocutor in one entry in *Close Scrutiny*, was to address the multitude who, "blind to the way things work, are undecided in the face of alternatives" (*LY* VI:8).[101] While the sages themselves had no need for divination, they helped ordinary people along, so that they knew when to advance and when to retreat, with *The Book of Changes*. And the sages imparted to the masses the knowledge of ghosts and deities so that the latter could perceive that "matter is derived from ether, and changes with the wandering away of the soul; [in this way] they can understand the character of ghosts and deities."[102]

The recourse to the ancients can be interpreted as a strategic move, characteristic not just of Ji Yun but of men of letters generally in the eighteenth century. (An extension of this strategy was the use of solid precedents in the classics as the basis for one's arguments). The

---

[100] Wang Hansheng, ed., *Yijing qianzhu*, p. 253.

[101] *YWCTBJ*, p. 106.

[102] Wang Hansheng, ed., *Yijing qianzhu*, p. 221.

unassailability of the sages is utilized in *Close Scrutiny* to support the argument for the existence of the supernatural realm. After all, it was the sages who knew about it. The sages also upheld the supreme, cardinal principles, by which all other standards are to be measured. The neo-Confucians' emphasis on the elimination of human desires, for instance, was disparaged because the sages would rather choose the path of the Golden Mean (*GW* II:13); the sages preferred temperance though the commonfolk was prone to excesses (*RS* IV:45). The advocacy of the sages was characteristic of eighteenth-century anti-Cheng-Zhu polemics, but for Ji Yun, restoring authority to the sages — whose vision was congruent with his — allowed him to rationalize his whole enterprise.

It is, too, in terms of the *role* of the sages that Ji Yun formulated his theory of didacticism. Ji Yun, who for years had been an administrator, was (like members of his class entrusted with administrative duties) aware of the importance of moral instruction for the maintenance of social order. This is partly reflected in *Close Scrutiny* in his attempts to tackle the tensions within the family (between masters and servants and men and women) by remonstrating with those who do not observe their proper roles. Overseeing moral standards in traditional Chinese society went hand in hand with enforcing the legal code, since both were geared to the same end. Morality worked by way of injunctions, and law, by way of commands. Both were fundamentally means of mass control. Observance of ethical rules was as essential as observance of the laws of human society, since moral failings were judged by the world beyond just as aberrations were punishable in the world of here and now.

The educated elite in traditional Chinese society, as guardians of morality, had the responsibility for propagating correct behaviour among the masses, who were easily led astray. While conceding the effectiveness of the penal code in encouraging proper behaviour, Ji Yun, like others in his class, was cognizant of the usefulness of efforts at ethical exhortation, though there are different ways of admonishing the masses. It is in this context that one can understand why Ji Yun time and again lashed out at the neo-Confucians, the so-called "talk-mongers." For not only were their methods irrelevant and superficial, but also their moral norms were stilted and inflexible. Paradoxical as it may seem, the neo-Confucians were often held accountable for the moral laxity then widespread.[103] In particular, their "no-ghost theory" had had a most detrimental impact. A ghost blamed his teacher — a "talk-monger" — for telling him that the belief in spirits and divine retribution was unfounded. The wrong teaching caused him to indulge in all sorts of evil, for he believed that nothing would happen at his death except that his *qi* would be reintegrated into the Great Void (*HX* IV:60). Subsequently the ghost found that he had been cheated, since Yama did exist, and so did hell. This much can be said of Ji Yun's view of the neo-Confucians as teachers: they were, simply, pedagogically unsound.

More incisive criticisms were levelled directly at the neo-Confucians by another ghostly apparition (*LY* II:44). He first states the neo-Confucians' position: they believe that the good works of the Buddhists are motivated by selfish desires for salvation or reward, whereas true Confucians deem such impure motives beneath them. The ghost, however, contests such logic. For him, high-sounding arguments like this are of no use to the commonfolk. The neo-Confucian policy is flawed because, while the cultivated neo-Confucian could develop his inborn inclination to do good and avoid evil, not everybody else could be expected to do the same.

To Ji Yun, the methods of the Buddhists to induce moral behaviour in the masses were far superior. He believed that although the three religions in China differ, they share the same goal: to induce people to act morally. He compares the religions in terms of the substance-function dichotomy in one entry in *Close Scrutiny*:

> Confucianism has self-cultivation as its substance (*ti* 體) and governance of others as its function (*yong* 用). Daoism has tranquillity as its substance and yielding as its function. Buddhism has devotion as its substance and the exercise of benevolence as its function.[104]

---

[103] The extent of the impact of neo-Confucian ethics on Ming-Qing society is examined in one area — the cult of female marital fidelity — by T'ien Ju-k'ang. See T'ien Ju-k'ang, *Male Anxiety and Female Chastity: A Comparative Study of Chinese Ethical Values in Ming-Ch'ing Times* (Leiden: E. J. Brill, 1988). While much of the blame, for instance, for widow suicides was laid on neo-Confucians, the extent to which they were truly responsible is debatable.

[104] *YWCTBJ*, p. 80.

For him, Buddhism was particularly effective in encouraging ethical behaviour among the populace by promoting the idea of retribution. In a second entry, yet another ghost compares Buddhism (and Daoism as well) to medicine that is to be taken at crucial moments and Confucianism to staple food eaten daily (*LY* IV:44). According to him, Buddhism is more efficacious in treating the sorrows and grief encountered in everyday life; its theory of reward for good deeds and punishment for evil doing is more effective in encouraging commonfolk to abide by moral norms. Yet, the ghost adds, an overdose of Buddhism is more likely to do harm than good, and it is Confucianism that one cannot survive without.

The Buddhist use of karmic beliefs to entice ordinary people to do good and avoid evil can be understood within the broader framework of the Buddhist doctrine of *upaya* ("skill in means," or *fangbian* 方便 in Chinese), which is essentially the Buddhist theory of didacticism.[105] According to this doctrine, much of Mahayana Buddhist teaching consists of a series of skilfully devised expedients to induce belief in the *dharma*. The expedients are no more than the means to effect an end. To a certain extent, the same pedagogical principle is embedded in Ji Yun's attitude towards the use of the belief in deities, ghosts, and a retributive order. They were stratagems, involving perhaps an element of deception, that were justified by the purpose for which they were intended — to admonish the masses to do good. As was the case with unenlightened beings, the mediocre and the lowly could only be moved by concrete doctrines of cause and effect. They could not be expected to follow the path of those who possessed higher wisdom.

Nevertheless, the paradigm for Ji Yun's didactics in *Close Scrutiny* is not to be sought in the Buddhist preacher, but in the Confucian sage. Subscribing in general terms to the usefulness of the three religions, he was very much a man of his own time: nowhere does he

---

[105] *Upaya* is a Sanskrit and Pali term meaning "device," "stratagem," or "means." Often used in Mahayana Buddhism in the compound *upayakausalya* ("skill in means"), it denotes methods of teaching that are used to draw ordinary, unenlightened people into the Buddhist path. As its justification lies in the aim to be achieved, it can be considered a provisional expedient with an element of deception.

doubt the superiority of Confucianism. Comparing the various strategies for inculcating ethical behaviour, he points out one essential difference in the (Confucian) sages' methods. While the rulers had recourse to the penal code and the Buddhists to karmic retribution, the sages, with their insights into the principles of heaven and earth, proceeded by setting the moral standards to be followed.[106] Thus the Confucian gentleman set great store by self-cultivation — just as the Buddhist adherent would stress repentance, and the Daoist practitioner, reverence — because he held himself accountable to the sages for every word or deed.

With the masses, however, things were different, for they could not be expected to do good without encouragement from without. According to *The Book of Changes*, the sages observed the natural rhythms of the four seasons and saw in them the Way of the deities. Subsequently they used this knowledge to establish teaching for all under Heaven.[107] This is what is known as "establishing teaching through the Way of the deities" (*shendao shejiao* 神道設教), a concept which Ji Yun reiterates in *Close Scrutiny*. He strongly endorses a ghost-seer's story of a ghost who persistently follows his living wife and children about, for he feels helpless in the face of his wife's remarriage and neglect of his children (*LY* IV:12). To Ji Yun, tales like this one reveal the weakness of the neo-Confucian's no-ghost theory, which had a negative effect on the multitude by placing no restraints at all on human actions. (The wife in the story would not have remarried if she had known how her dead husband would suffer.)

The sages' teaching worked in two ways: by encouraging virtuous acts (as denoted by the word *quan*) and inhibiting those inclined to act maliciously (denoted by *jie*). The reason why the sages talked so much about deities and spirits was neatly summarized at one point by Ji Yun in *Close Scrutiny* (*LY* II:44):

---

[106] *YWCTBJ*, p. 199.

[107] In the section on the *guan* 觀 hexagram in *The Book of Changes*, it is said that "[The sages] contemplate the sacred activities of heaven and note how the seasons unfold, each in its proper time. It is because the holy sage makes these matters the subject of his teaching that all the world accepts his dominion." John Blofeld, tr., *The Book of Change* (New York: E. P. Dutton, 1966), p. 127; Wang Hansheng, ed., *Yijing qianzhu*, p. 72.

The sages established their teachings in order that men behave morally. Those who will not [behave morally] are induced to do so by tricks. Those who refuse [to behave morally] are compelled to do so by admonitions. Hence rewards and punishments arose.[108]

Rewards and punishments were, in this view, just the means. The sages would not reprimand one for performing a good act for the sole aim of being rewarded or for refraining from misdeeds because punishment was feared, so long as one acted morally. Exactly the same intention can be seen to underlie Ji Yun's effort to compile the narratives in his *Close Scrutiny*. Putting himself in the position of the sages, he inserts his moral "teachings" in his stories, and encourages belief in a supernatural retributive order. And exactly the same intention must have informed those raconteurs and commentators who, consciously or unconsciously, turned the stories they narrated or heard into didactic vehicles.

Of course the idea of "establishing teaching by the Way of the deities" can be interpreted differently by agnostics and by proponents of supernaturalism.[109] While it can be said that the existence of spiritual beings is vindicated by the sages whose honesty is beyond doubt, it can just as well be argued that this otherworldly realm has been fabricated for purposes of moral edification by the sages and hence does not really exist.[110] The possibility of alternative explanations also

---

[108] *YWCTBJ*, p. 33.

[109] While *shendao* literally refers to the "Way of the deities," it actually connotes the way of all spirits.

[110] Both sceptics and believers can show their support for the idea of *shendao shejiao*. In the case of one like Confucius, there is no telling where he stood on the question of belief in spirits. Confucius advocated the promotion of morals through worship and rituals of various kinds, and Mou Zhongjian 牟鍾鑒 argues on this basis for Confucius as a believer. On the other hand, Ya Hanzhang 牙含章 uses almost exactly the same facts to advance his view that Confucius was an agnostic. See Mou Zhongjian, "Zhongguo lishi shang guanyu xingshen wenti de zhenglun" 中國歷史上關於形神問題的爭論 (The Debate between "Substance" and "Spirit" in Chinese History), in *Zhongguo wushenlun sixiang lunwenji* 中國無神論思想論文集 (Collected Essays on Chinese Agnosticism) (Jiangsu: Jiangsu renmin chubanshe 江蘇人民出版社, 1980), p. 130; and Ya Hanzhang, "Kongzi xueshuo yu Zhongguo wushenlun sixiang de guanxi" 孔子學説與中國無神論思想的關係 (The Relationship between Confucius' Thought and Chinese Agnostic Thought), in *Zhongguo wushenlun wenji*, pp. 123–141. Ai

accounts for the division of opinion among critics concerning the issue of whether the didactic writer Ji Yun is a supernaturalist or a sceptic. However, as we have seen, biographical data in the case of Ji Yun make clear that he would not have begun from the standpoint of disbelief. The same cannot be said of the other writers in late imperial times who chose to use the *zhiguai* as a means of moral instruction. For all of them, however, the usefulness of supernatural beliefs in ethical indoctrination was beyond dispute. Even by the mid-nineteenth century, when the Qing dynasty began to show signs of decay and the traditional order was in a process of disintegration, Wei Yuan 魏源 (1774–1853), the eminent scholar and philosopher, said:

> The talk of deities and ghosts has positive value for the general public, and supplements the official teachings in a tremendous way. What lies beyond the reach of the legal arms of the state can be brought under control by such secret teachings.[111]

The fact stressed by Wei Yuan is a central theme in the present study of the late eighteenth-century *zhiguai* narratives as they were told (and retold), written down (and rewritten), read, and re-edited for publication. The narratives document the prevalence of moral didacticism in various aspects of the life of the traditional elite; didacticism was not present only in their literature. Viewed in the context of relations of domination and subordination between different social collectivities, the discourse on ghosts, fox-spirits and demons, for which stories of the strange furnish the material, reveals the intricate dynamics at work as a social group sought to assert, legitimize, and perpetuate

---

Linong 艾力農 stresses that Confucius (as well as subsequent Confucians) utilized beliefs in the supernatural as a means of moral indoctrination, but does not broach the issue of whether Confucius believed in spirits. See Ai Linong, "Tantan 'shendao shejiao'" 談談神道設教 (On Establishing Teaching through the Way of the Gods), in *Zhongguo wushenlun sixiang lunwenji*, p. 160.

[111] Wei Yuan argued forcefully for the existence of spirits himself. See *Wei Yuan ji* 魏源集 (Collected Writings of Wei Yuan) (Beijing: Zhonghua shuju 中華書局 , 1976), pp. 2–3. For an analysis of traditional scholar-officials' perception of their role as teachers and behavioral models, see Robert C. Neville, "The Scholar-official as a Model for Ethics," *Journal of Chinese Philosophy*, vol. 13, no. 2 (1986), pp. 185–201.

its dominance. Holding the keys to the interpretation of the super-natural and dispensing instructions for what needed to be done for one to be "saved," the eighteenth-century members of the elite had successfully appropriated the role of the ancient sages.

Conclusion

Zhiguai *as Discourse*

> To understand a narrative is not only to follow the unfolding of
> the story but also to recognize in it a number of strata, to
> project the horizontal concatenations of the narrative
> onto an implicitly vertical axis.
>
> — *Roland Barthes*

Questions pertaining to the didactic story in particular, and to the
zhiguai genre in general, are raised in the foregoing discussion of *Close
Scrutiny*. The bifurcation between the narrative and discursive portions, which occurs because the stories of the supernatural originally
appeared embedded in social conversations, presents itself as the most
crucial interpretive problem. If it is indeed true, as Jerome Bruner
has noted, that narrative and argument are "two modes of cognitive
functioning, two modes of thought, each providing distinctive ways of
ordering experience, of constructing reality,"[1] then the didactic *zhiguai*
must be viewed as a special order of discourse by virtue of its fusion of
story and persuasion.

It is precisely this admixture of modes that has exacerbated the
problem of generic definition for the *zhiguai*. When used to prove a
point, to instruct, and to edify, a *zhiguai* collection like *Close Scrutiny*
falls squarely within the traditional Chinese "Philosophers" category.
Ji Yun himself might well have placed his collection there. At the same

---

[1] Jerome S. Bruner, *Actual Minds, Possible Worlds* (Cambridge, Mass.: Harvard University Press, 1986), p. 11.

time, the evident interest in the reported tales themselves, the way in which some stories gravitate towards the fictive, and the conditions of *zhiguai* circulation and reception make an equally strong case for calling compilations of this type "literature" (as we do today), albeit literature of a didactic bent.

Not even by analysing the motives of the *zhiguai* compilers can one be certain of an easy answer to this question of classification. Naturally the purposes of compiling *zhiguai*, as evidenced by the eighteenth-century examples considered above, were multifold and, at times, complicated. It may be difficult for some to decide whether Ji Yun, the Confucian pedagogue, put together his *Close Scrutiny* primarily for moralizing reasons or whether it reflects no more than his exuberant delight in telling tales of strange occurrences. The most one can say is that both elements must have been involved in the work, and at times one figures more prominently than the other. The plethora of stated and hidden motives enunciated by compilers like Yuan Mei and Yue Jun, among others, makes the question of intentions even more complicated. It is not unreasonable to say that the multiple impulses that cause human beings to communicate are present in the *zhiguai*, and one does little justice to the *zhiguai* by relegating it arbitrarily to any one of the conventionally accepted conceptual categories.

"Didactic literature" is itself a contradiction in terms; the post-Romantic notion that literature is aesthetic expression almost automatically excludes from the realm of literature the goals of persuading and instructing. However, these are precisely what one finds in didactic texts and they bring didactic literature within the corpus of Chinese "Philosophers" writings. The best way out, perhaps, is to explain the didactic *zhiguai* as an offshoot of conversational discourse in which storytelling and discursive remarks flow easily into and mingle almost imperceptibly with one another. The boundaries between narrative and argument in this way become blurred. In conversational contexts, stories can be narrated whenever and wherever they make a point relevant to the speaker, the audience, or the world in which the stories are enveloped.

The "points" made by the eighteenth-century raconteurs are primarily ethical in orientation. Having a validity beyond the confines of the narratives, these "points" constitute the moral message being conveyed. The tales can also serve a multiplicity of other functions — a great number vindicate the existence of spirits and others show a concern for finding out about the operations of the spiritual world. These are factors that make the narratives "tell-able" in the first place, but the fact that they were told orally has important repercussions. *Zhiguai* narratives are special texts that are not only written but also oral, linked inextricably to circumstantial background. This being the case, *zhiguai* narratives are indispensable as a key to the socio-religious realities of their time.

The model of interpretation adopted in this book is grounded in current research, both theoretical and practical, on conversational narratives. The relative neglect that the *zhiguai* has suffered can partly be explained by the failure of critics to apply to it the proper interpretive tools. Obviously, when considered as "literary narrative," the *zhiguai* pales beside the *chuanqi*. It is, by comparison, deficient in plot and character development, and stylistically it is decidedly inferior. The Six Dynasties *zhiguai* are only of interest as "the first instances of Chinese narrative." Neither do these tales of the strange appear in light any more favourable when placed alongside the complex full-length novels of the late imperial period. What seems to have been under-emphasized is that the *zhiguai* is in a category all its own — the category of naturally occurring, unaestheticized narrative.

The folklorists have not done any better with *zhiguai* literature. It is reasonable to expect that it would yield itself most readily to the kind of formal analysis first utilized by folklore scholars like Vladimir Propp to explore the folktale. Indeed, a number of critics have resorted to the cataloguing of *zhiguai* motifs, and a more comprehensive picture of the functions of the *zhiguai* in society may emerge through analytical methods comparable to those that folklorists have applied to "belief legends" (or "belief stories," or "true stories") in the West.[2] Unfortunately, as our study of *Close Scrutiny* has shown,

---

[2] Vladimir Propp's formalist approach is exemplified in his study of Russian folktales in *The Morphology of the Folktale* (Austin: University of Texas Press, 1968). The possibility of understanding the *zhiguai* as belief legends, one of three main subdivisions of folk narratives (the other two being the myth and the fairytale), has yet to be explored. Among the most important scholarly studies of the genre are undertaken by Linda Dégh. See, in particular, her *Folktales and Society: Storytelling in a Hungarian Community*, translated by Emily M. Schossberger; and "The 'Belief Legend' in Modern Society: Form, Function, and Relation

the majority of *zhiguai*, having been compiled and edited by members of the elite, do not really convey the viewpoint of the commonfolk. Instead they resemble literary folktale collections of the West. It is for this reason, precisely, that *zhiguai* materials do not appear to certain folklorists to be worthy of investigation. One could argue, however, that what is needed is a broader outlook on the *zhiguai*, in particular an acceptance of a more elastic concept of what constitutes the "folk." The functional analyses of *zhiguai* tales will become fruitful when these analyses are undertaken on a socio-cultural basis and related to traditional Chinese society.

The above discussion shows, by indirection, the almost insuperable difficulties encountered in interpreting a work like Ji Yun's *Close Scrutiny*. It is surely less of a literary accomplishment than *Studio of Leisure*, with which it naturally invites comparison. It hardly matches *What the Master Would Not Discuss* as a repository of folk beliefs and practices. It does not appear even remotely comparable to the philosophical essays of the period, some of which (like those by Hong Liangji) have already figured in our discussion. *Studio of Leisure* is more aesthetically satisfying; *What the Master Would Not Discuss* is more encyclopaedic; the essays of Hong Liangji are more intellectually appealing. It is ironic that, while Ji Yun regarded his collection as generically pure — he considered *Studio of Leisure* extra-categorical, not fitting within existing classifications — present-day scholars of diverse disciplines should consider *Close Scrutiny* an anomaly.

This study has attempted to propose a new point of departure for *zhiguai* interpretation by viewing the *zhiguai* as a special type of dynamic, interactive discourse whose basis is oral narratives which are surrounded by (or interpolated with) elaborations, comments, evaluations, and general discussions. Without losing sight of the fact that the discourse takes place simultaneously on the oral and written levels, we have tried to relate the eighteenth-century *zhiguai* stories to

---

to Other Genres," in *American Folk Legend: A Symposium*, edited by Edward Hand (Berkeley: University of California Press, 1971), pp. 55–68. In folklore studies in the West, the belief legend is frequently contrasted with the fairytale (the *märchen*). Could the *zhiguai* be distinguished from the *chuanqi* on a similar basis? For a brief account of the differences between the two folklore genres, see Alan Dundes, "The Psychology of Legend," in *American Folk Legend: A Symposium*, pp. 21–36.

the particular discourse community to which the conversations belong. Such a community consists, in this case, of a circle of renowned poets and painters, eminent statesmen, and intellectual luminaries centred around Ji Yun — this is the "folk" whose life *Close Scrutiny* reflects. With the methods of several disciplines, it is possible to holistically assess the character of the shared culture of this social group — the literati — at a particular moment in history.

Our analysis of the structures and conventions of *zhiguai* discourse may be reminiscent of those of contemporary discourse analysts like William Labov and Katharine Young, but the materials studied are as different as can be imagined.[3] Labov's materials are narratives from New York Black English vernacular culture, and Young works with stories she records from peasant families in Dartmoor, England. But in both cases folk, oral sources are used. Labov constructs a theoretical model according to which conversational narratives are analysable into six parts: the abstract, orientation, complicating action, evaluation, resolution, and coda. The evaluation, consisting of all that is said to establish the "point" of a story and permeating all the other sections, is regarded by Labov as the central component of the discourse. Young, on the other hand, resorts to "frame analysis." Among other things, she focuses on the frames that direct movement from the realm of conversation to the "storyrealm" and from the "storyrealm" to the "taleworld." More than just transitional devices moving conversationalists from realm to realm and breaking the boundaries between the fictive and the real, these frames, for Young, control the interpretation of the embedded narratives.

Labov talks of evaluation and Young of framing. In the present study of *Close Scrutiny* the commentarial remarks are shown to be the distinctive hallmark of the *zhiguai* of late imperial China. Such an approach to eighteenth-century elite discourse on the supernatural

---

[3] See William Labov, "The Transformation of Experience in Narrative Syntax," in *Language in the Inner City: Studies in the Black English Vernacular* (Philadelphia: University of Pennsylvania Press, 1972), pp. 354–396; and Katharine G. Young, *Taleworlds and Storyrealms: The Phenomenology of Narrative* (Dordrecht: Martinus Nijhoff Publishers, 1987), especially chap. 2. The idea of using "frames" in the analysis of narratives is indebted to Erving Goffman. See Goffman, *Frame Analysis: An Essay on the Organization of Experience* (London: Harper Colophon Books, 1974).

signals a new departure in three respects. In the first place, the microscopic analysis undertaken by Labov and Young of individual narratives is dispensed with, for compiled *zhiguai* narratives are considerably shorter in length than the oral stories from New York and Dartmoor. For this reason, nowhere does one find any trace of an Aristotelian plot structure, which is implied in the models propounded by Labov and Young. Second, the socio-dynamics of storytelling are not presented as involving independent acts of communication isolated in particular times and places. Eighteenth-century Chinese *zhiguai* discourse is studied against a vast backdrop. It is analysed with reference not only to Ji Yun's compilation, but also to a dozen other *zhiguai* collections written within a fifteen-year period and thematically related non-*zhiguai* material like the philosophical essays of the period. Third — and this marks the greatest difference of the *zhiguai* from the folk oral narratives Labor and Young have collected — *zhiguai* discourse as embodied in *Close Scrutiny* is seen to have both oral and written dimensions. It is in fact multi-levelled, if we take into consideration the complex network of relationships charted between the two modes.

If understanding of the world of the *zhiguai* has been so inadequate, what of the world of Chinese *xiaoshuo* and *biji* narratives in traditional China? It is common knowledge that these consist in the main of hearsay accounts, orally transmitted vignettes, jokes and humorous tales, and simply gossip and rumour. For a long time these forms have been regarded as writings of an amorphous and fragmentary nature which lack seriousness and do not properly belong anywhere. At different historical periods, too, they have been viewed, alternatively, as history, literature, folklore, and "philosophy." Would a rigorous application of such analysis as has been applied to *Close Scrutiny* breathe new life into this farrago of material, voluminous in quantity and long considered unclassifiable?[4]

---

[4] The emergence of discourse analysis as an independent discipline, beginning in the seventies, its multi-disciplinary nature, as well as its relation to the other academic fields (like sociolinguistics and literature), are discussed in articles collected in Teun A. van Dijk, ed., *Handbook of Discourse Analysis* (London: Academic Press, 1985), vols. 1–4.

APPENDICES

The stories that follow relate to the four themes discussed in earlier chapters: the issue of orality, the conflict between belief and disbelief, the investigation of supernatural phenomena, and the didactic uses of storytelling. They have all been referred to in the foregoing discussion.

Appendix 1

The "Oral" Tales

1. LY IV:29

When Dong Qujiang was staying temporarily at the capital he lived with a friend, who was not his travelling companion, in order (so he said) to save money on food and accommodation. In order to mix with the wealthy and famous, the friend often stayed out the whole night, while Qujiang slept in the study alone. Sometimes in the night he would hear someone turning the pages of books or fondling the antiques. Aware that foxes often were sighted in the capital, he did not find it strange.

One night he left the manuscripts of an unfinished poem on the desk, and then heard somebody reciting it. He asked who it was but there was no response. When he looked at the poem the next morning, he found that some sentences had been punctuated and circled. He repeatedly called out to the intruder, but there was no answer.

When the friend came back to stay in the house, however, there would be no disturbance all through the night. The friend was astonished to find that evil forces dared not meddle with him, presumably because he was destined to attain great wealth and honour.

It happened that Li Qingzi of Rizhao [in present-day Shandong] had to be put up at their house one night. After all the wine had been drunk, Qujiang and his friend went to bed. Li took a stroll in the garden, as it was a moonlit night. He saw an old man holding a child by the hand and standing under a tree. Knowing that they were foxes, Li concealed himself and watched the two from his hiding-place.

The child said, "It's very cold. Let's go back into the room."

The old man shook his head and said, "I wouldn't mind sharing the room with Master Dong, but the other fellow is vulgar and ill-bred. How can we stay in the same place with him? I'd rather sit out here in the wind and the chill."

Li later leaked out the story to some friends, and somehow it eventually became known to Dong's friend too. He was consumed with hatred for Li. Eventually, ousted from his circle of acquaintances and feeling awkward, Li packed his books and returned home.

2. HX II:20

Tian Baiyan narrated another anecdote. The young, charming second wife of a man was seduced by a fox, and all attempts to subdue the fox proved ineffective. Later a Daoist priest who was highly proficient in the magical arts came along. He called to his aid a deity, who tied up the fox and brought him to his altar. He forced the fox to make a confession.

All those who were present heard the fox say, "I'm originally from Henan province. Once, for some reason I beat up my wife, and she stole away, coming here and then becoming intimate with this man. I've always felt bitter about this, and am now seeking revenge on him."

The man confirmed that what he said indeed happened when he was younger, but that was already over ten years ago.

The Daoist priest asked the fox, "If there had been such great grievance, you should have retaliated right away. Why wait till now? Have you found out about this and made an excuse of it?"

"His first wife was a chaste woman. I was afraid I would be punished by Heaven, so I dared not come close. But his second wife was loose and so I managed to seduce her. Deities and ghosts will not penalize one for bringing into operation the principles of cause and effect, so why should you call me to account?"

The Daoist priest pondered on the case for a while and inquired of the fox, "How long was this man sexually involved with your wife?"

"Over a year."

"And how long have you been intimate with his second wife?"

"Over three years."

The Daoist priest shouted in anger, "You have more than avenged yourself, and justice is not on your side. If you don't leave her, I'll have you punished by the Thunder-god!"

The fox concurred with the judgement, and departed.

Mr. Song Qingyuan, the father of Song Mengquan, remarked, "From this we can see that all demons have concepts of right and wrong. Even ghosts and deities cannot annul principles of retribution."

3. *HX* II:21

Mr. Song Qingyuan then told us about a maid of a certain Mr. Zhu. She was at first rather plain, but she grew to be quite clever and artful. She was, moreover, getting prettier by the day. So Zhu took her as his concubine. Her shrewdness showed in her capable management of even minor household affairs relating to rice and salt. Nobody in the house dared to deceive her, and those who did inevitably found themselves caught. She was expert at hoarding goods, and whatever she hoarded would rise in price the next year. Zhu, turning wealthier this way, doted on her.

One day she asked him all of a sudden, "Do you know what I am?"

Zhu smiled. "Are you in your right mind?" He teased her by mentioning her childhood name.

"No. That girl ran away a long time ago, got married, and is the mother of a seven- or eight-year-old. I was originally a vixen, and nine lives previously you were a rich merchant, while I worked as an accountant for you. You were most generous to me, but I embezzled over three thousand taels of silver. I was punished by being turned into a vixen. After hundreds of years of striving, I was fortunate enough to have attained physical form. Yet with this burden of sin behind me, I did not achieve immortality status. Hence I took advantage of your maid's departure, assumed her form and served you. What I've done in the past ten years or so is enough to compensate for what I owed you. Now I'm leaving this body of mine to become an immortal. Once

I'm gone you will see my body. Ask a servant to bury it. I know he'll skin the body, but don't punish him. Four lives previously he was starved to death and I, not having yet acquired the powers of transformation, had eaten him up. Let him dismember me, for that way we'll get even."

Thereupon she turned into a vixen and fell to the ground. A beautiful woman of just a few inches in height emerged from the head of the animal and slowly vanished; this woman looked completely different from the maid, though. Zhu could not bear to leave the vixen with the servant, and buried her himself, but the servant secretly dug her up, got the skin, and sold it. Knowing it was predetermined, Zhu could only heave a deep sigh.

4. LY V:34

In the year *kuisi* [1773] or *jiawu* [1774], a planchette-diviner came from Zhengding [in present-day Hebei]. He would not talk about karmic retribution, but painted and did some calligraphy. Some suspected him of practising deceit.

Yet a scroll of landscape painting that he did in colours, as well as his portrait of the drunk Zhong Kui, queller of demons (both drawn at Cao Wutang's request), showed that he was indeed skilful with the paintbrush. He also wrote a couplet for Dong Qujiang:

Making friends through his generosity,
  he has great warmth of heart.
Returning home with silvery hair,
  he lives a carefree life in his dreams.

This gave a very accurate description of the kind of man Dong was.

5. GW IV:2

Dai Dongyuan said: a fox lived in the vacant house that belonged to a certain family. He conversed with the head of the household and sent him gifts. The two even shared household items, living happily together as neighbours.

One day the fox said, "The empty house in the adjacent compound has been haunted for years by ghosts of men who hanged themselves.

Recently you demolished it and the ghosts, having nowhere to stay, have come to fight with us for living space. Often they reveal their hideous forms to scare my little daughter. That's bad enough, but what's even more intolerable is that they also plague us, causing us to catch either a cold or a fever. There's a certain Daoist priest who can subjugate ghosts. Please ask him to help rid us of these evil ones."

To be sure, the man did obtain a talisman, which he burnt in the backyard. As he did so, a storm arose, and thunderclaps were heard. Everybody was frightened as they heard the roof tiles cracking. It was as though several dozen people were scuttling off, trampling on each other as they went. A voice came from the top of a roof: "My scheme has fallen through, and it's too late to regret it! In a second the deities will descend to exterminate us. The ghosts will be tied up while we will be chased away. I have to leave you now."

The truth is that, if a person is unable to contain his anger and wants only revenge on his adversary, both sides inevitably suffer. The example of what happened to the fox serves as a warning for us.

Also, a cousin surnamed Liu, who is the eldest son of my late aunt and whose first name I have forgotten, had this story to tell: A certain man was pestered by a fox and he solicited an incantation from somebody skilled in the magical arts. The fox left but the magician continued to extort money from him, often sending wooden figurines, paper tigers, and the like to his home to wreck havoc. The man paid some money but obtained only a temporary reprieve. After ten days or so, the magician returned and repeated what he had done, thus causing greater trouble than the fox. Eventually, only by moving his entire family to the capital was the man able to avoid further disturbance.

Those who seek help from vile characters, just so they can win a fight, will find themselves bitten by those vile characters instead. This story is just another example.

6. LX V:1

Dai Dongyuan said that an elderly member of his clan once rented a vacant house on a secluded alley. It had long been unoccupied, and rumour had it that it was haunted. But the old man loudly declared, "I'm not afraid."

One night, to be sure, he saw a shadow moving under the lamp, and it sent a piercing chill.

A well-built ghost taunted him: "You're really not scared?"

"No," he said.

The ghost then appeared in various hideous forms. He asked after a while, "You're still not scared?" Again the answer was "no."

The ghost assumed a more gentle countenance and said, "It's not as if I must drive you out. I'm just offended at your proud words. Once you say you're scared, I'll leave."

The grandfather spoke angrily, "I'm certainly not scared of you, so why should I lie. You can do what you want with me!"

The ghost went on nagging him for a while, but he did not respond at all. The ghost sighed and said, "I've lived here for over thirty years and never seen anyone so stubborn. How can I live with an idiot like you?" He then disappeared.

Someone once chided the old man this way: "To be afraid of ghosts is only natural; it's not humiliating. If you were to lie to him and say you're scared, you would at least have stopped a dispute and remained on good terms with him. Why provoke him?"

The old man replied, "Those who have cultivated great spiritual powers can exorcize demons with calm and assurance. I'm not of that type. When I intimidated him with my strength, I emitted an abundance of *qi* and the ghost would not dare come close. Even if I were to give in a little, then my *qi* would be weak and he'd seize the opportunity to get at me. He tried baiting me by various means, but luckily I wasn't trapped."

Those who expressed opinions on the incident agreed.

7. *HX* II:32

According to Zhu Daojiang, a scholar from Xintai [in present-day Shandong] had to go to the provincial capital [Ji'nan] to take his examinations. One half day before he was to arrive, in order to take advantage of the cool weather, he set off early with a couple of friends.

In the dark two donkeys were chasing after one another, and at different times it was a different one leading. There seemed nothing unusual about it. When it was bright enough to see clearly, the travellers found out that they were two women. Looking more closely, they saw a fat and dark old woman in her fifties, and a young, good-looking woman about twenty years of age. The scholar eyed the latter from time to time.

Suddenly the young woman turned around and shouted, "Aren't you my elder cousin?"

The scholar was nonplussed, and did not know what to say.

The young woman then said, "I'm your cousin. Since, according to our family rules, male and female cousins are not supposed to meet, you haven't seen me before. But I've once peeped at you from behind the curtains, and so I know you."

Remembering that there was indeed a female cousin who married someone from Jinan, he exchanged a few words of greeting with the young woman.

"Where are you going this early?" he asked.

"Yesterday I went to visit my sick aunt with my husband," she said. "At first we expected to return the same day. But my aunt was involved in a lawsuit and she asked my husband to accompany her to the capital. So today he's not returning home; I'm going back to pack his things for him." She glanced affectionately at him as she spoke, and she appeared most alluring. She even gave hints of how infatuated she had been with him when she saw him for the first time, in her teens.

The scholar's heart fluttered. Where the road forked, the woman invited him home for a meal. He gladly agreed, and arranged for his travelling companions to meet him somewhere later.

He did not show up at the appointed time. Nor did the friends hear anything about him the next day. Going back to where they parted, and then trying to track him down on the road they had not taken, the friends came across his donkey in the fields, its saddle still untied. They searched all over the village there, but nobody had ever heard of the two women. Inquiring still further, they found the home of the female cousin, and discovered that she had died half a year ago. No one could tell whether the scholar had been seduced by ghosts, eaten up by demons, or abducted by robbers. Nothing more was ever heard of this scholar.

This would be good enough as a moral lesson for flippant young men.

Fang Kecun happened to be there when the story was narrated, and he said he heard of a similar incident while in Gansu and Shaanxi:

"There was an attempt to bury a deceased man with his wife, who had died earlier. When the grave was opened, however, a male corpse was found lying by the side of the wife. One wonders how the wife could confront her husband in hell. According to Jiao Yanshou's *Forest of Changes*, 'The woman shared by two husbands would not know who to follow.' The divinatory message fits this situation very well."

Dai Dongyuan also happened to be among those present, and he said, "*History of the Latter Han Dynasty* even mentions a case of a wife having three husbands. You certainly are not knowledgeable enough!"

I said jokingly, "Let's not quarrel over this. Have you forgotten Princess Shanyin of the Liu-Song dynasty who married thirty husbands? Such women, however, are not afraid of their husbands. This ghost keeps the young man for herself and does not even think about getting buried together later. She is obviously succumbing to her carnal desires and not worrying about the consequences."

Dongyuan sighed and said, "Is it only this ghost that succumbs to carnal desires and does not worry about the consequences?"

8. LY V:27

Zhu Qinglei said that once he took a stroll with Gao Xiyuan on the riverbank. At the time the spring ice had just melted, and the water was clear and green.

Gao said, "I'm reminded of the lines from the late Tang poem:
The fish scales are a sad purple,
The duck feathers a natural green.

Not a word is used there to describe the spring water, yet the rippling water appears vividly before one's eyes. It's a pity I don't recall the poet's name."

Zhu, deep in thought, did not reply. Then he heard somebody saying behind an old willow, "This is a poem by Liu Xiyi of the early Tang, not from the late Tang."

They hurried over to look, but there was not a soul.

Zhu said, terrified, "We've met a ghost in broad daylight."

Gao said, smiling, "It's nice to meet a ghost like this, though it refuses to come forward." They bowed three times to the willow and left. Back home they checked Liu's poetry and, to be sure, the two lines were there.

I happened to tell this to Dai Dongyuan. In response, he told me an anecdote. Two scholars were discussing *The Spring and Autumn Annals* under the candlelight, arguing whether it followed the Zhou dynasty's calendrical calculations or the Xia dynasty's. The argument was becoming quite heated, when somebody outside the window sighed and said, "Zuo Qiuming [the author of *Zuo's Commentary*] lived in Zhou times. How can he not know the Zhou calculations? Why waste time arguing?"

They looked out of the window and saw only a boy-servant sleeping.

On the basis of these two stories, we see Confucian scholars talk every day about evidential research, about "examining ancient truths," and turn out scholarly essays that are one hundred and forty thousand characters long. They don't know there are ghosts standing right beside them and laughing at them for their follies.

9. *LY* VI:10

Dai Dongyuan said: a man surnamed Song at the end of the Ming dynasty came to some secluded mountains in Xi county [in present-day Anhui] when he was searching for a burial place. It was early evening and a storm was brewing. Seeing that there was a cave below the cliffs, he went inside for temporary shelter.

From deep inside he heard a man's voice: "There's a ghost inside the cave. Don't you come in."

"Why then are you here?" Song asked.

"I am the ghost."

When Song asked him to show himself, he replied, "If I were to appear before you, *yin* and *yang* elements would be brought into conflict, and you'd feel hot and cold, and rather uncomfortable. I'd rather you light a fire to protect yourself; we can also converse at a distance."

Song inquired, "Obviously you have a grave of your own. Why do you live here?"

"During the reign of Ming Emperor Shenzong, I was a county magistrate. I was weary of the government officials fighting with each other over personal advantages, so I resigned and returned to the fields. After I died I pleaded with Yama so I would not be reincarnated as a human being. Thus the merits already accumulated for my next life were transferred, and I was made an official in hell. Quite un-expectedly, in hell there was the same sort of bickering and competi-tion. So I quit my job and returned to my grave. Yet even to live amidst the hustle and bustle of ghosts in the graves was a cause of great an-noyance. I had no choice but avoid them by moving here. To be sure, there are bitter winds and chilly rains here, and I can hardly put up with the barren surroundings. But compared with the turbulent offi-cial life and the dishonest world of man, this place is heaven. Living a solitary life in these deserted mountains, I don't know how many years have passed. Neither do I know how many years have elapsed since I left the ghosts, or how many years since I left the company of men. I'm happy that I'm relieved of all pre-determined constraints, and I work hard cultivating my spiritual life. I didn't expect to meet a man again, so tomorrow morning I've got to move. You fisherman of Wuling, please do not come to the Peach Blossom Spring again!"

After saying this the ghost stayed silent. He would not tell Song his name even when he was asked. Song had with him a brush and an inkstone, so he dipped his brush in ink and wrote the words "Ghost Hermit" on the entrance to the cave, then returned.

10. LY I:17

Tian Baiyan from Dezhou [in present-day Shandong] told of a Commander-in-Chief of an Eight Banners army surnamed Er, who was crossing the mountains of Yunnan and Guizhou when, suddenly, he saw a beautiful woman being pressed down on a rock by a Daoist priest. The priest was going to slit open her heart, and the woman screamed for help. Er rode up to them at great speed and quickly held the priest by his hand. The woman gave off a loud cry, turned into a ray of light, and disappeared.

The Daoist priest stamped his feet and said, "You've ruined it all! This demon has seduced and killed over a hundred people. That's why I caught her. I was going to kill her to eliminate this cause of trouble. Yet, because she has absorbed much human essence and gradually acquired spiritual powers over a period of time, her soul will escape if I simply cut off her head. So in order to kill her I have to slit open her heart. Now that you've released her, there will be endless trouble. This is to pity the life of a tiger and let it return to the deep mountains, not knowing how many deer in the swamps and forests will be devoured by it!"

He put the dagger back in its sheath, crossed the stream despondently, and left.

This seems to be Tian Baiyan's fable, illustrating the principle [adumbrated by Fan Zhongyan] that "one family's suffering is nothing comparable to the sufferings of people in an entire administrative region." Some think that they can accumulate merit by practising leniency toward corrupt officials, and others will regard them as kind and forgiving. They never pause to consider how the poor will have to sell their wives and children just to survive. What do we need officials like these for?

Appendix 2

The Belief Tales

1. LY VI:22

When I was eight or nine, I heard the following story by the elderly Su Donggao in my maternal uncle Mr. An Shizhai's home: A county magistrate of Jiaohe [in present-day Hebei] embezzled several thousand taels of silver from the coffers, and instructed his bondservant to take it home. The bondservant later reported that the boat capsized in the Yellow River when he had gone half his way, so all the money was lost. In fact, he had secretly entrusted the money to his assistant. Then, the assistant, while making his way up north, was robbed and killed by bandits at Yanzhou [in present-day Shandong].

My maternal uncle was shaken by the account, and said, "Isn't that terrifying? Men didn't do it; the ghosts and deities did. Do ghosts and deities have to appear in broad daylight, holding the Mirrors of Destiny in their left hand, and the Rosters of Death in their right, giving directions to the myriad creatures to reincarnate themselves in the six realms, and then make evident the principle of retribution? This incident can be listed in the Iron Rosters of Hell."

Mr. Su said, "If the magistrate hadn't embezzled the silver, would the bondservant have defrauded him? If the bondservant hadn't defrauded the magistrate of his silver, would the assistant have the chance of cheating him? If the assistant hadn't cheated him, would he have been robbed and killed? Men did all this; the deities and ghosts didn't. If it were as you said, then the spirits sent the bondservant to take away the money because [the magistrate] was destined for retribution. They sent the assistant to take away the money because the bondservant was destined for retribution. They sent bandits to rob and kill the assistant because he, too, was destined for retribution. If the deities and ghosts were supposed to administer retribution, why should men duplicate the work? Doesn't that sound unreasonable?"

My maternal uncle said, "You are persuasive but you are distorting the truth. Listening to your ideas, however, will alert those who follow others blindly."

2. RS III:6

Fang Junguan, a female impersonator in Peking operas, was best-known in his youth for his charm and artistry, which stood him in good stead among the literati. When he grew older he took to selling antiques, and often came to the capital. Once he looked at himself in the mirror and sighed: "This is what Fang Junguan has turned into! Can you believe that he once captivated audiences with his singing and dancing?"

In a poem in which he reminisced about the past Ni Yujiang wrote:

> As he goes down in the world, his hair turning silky white,
> He remembers the old days when he beat time with clappers.
> Where has the butterfly in Zhuangzi's dream gone?
> Only a sad, withered flower is left.

The poem was in fact written for Fang Junguan.

Fang Junguan himself said that he came from a Confucian family. One day when he was thirteen or fourteen, he was attending his village school when he dreamt all of a sudden of being carried into an inner chamber. Around him were sounds of music and singing, as well as wedding candles. Looking at himself he saw that he was wearing embroidered clothes and a brocaded skirt; he also wore a headdress of jade and pearls. He looked at his two feet: they were bound, tiny and curved like bows. So he was a bride! He was shocked and bewildered, not knowing what to do. Since he was held by many hands, he was unable to extricate himself. Oddly enough, he was ushered behind some bed curtains, and seated by the side of a man. Terrified and ashamed, he woke up in a sweat.

Later in life Fang Junguan was lured by some scoundrels and sold to "the arena of song and dance." It was then that he realized that everything was pre-determined.

Ni Yujiang said, "Wei Jie of the Jin dynasty asked Yue Guang about dreams. The latter said, 'Dreams are but thought.' Probably you had such a dream because you harboured those thoughts. With those thoughts and that dream, you degenerated. From cause comes effect; the first cause originated in the heart. How can you ascribe it to pre-determined fate?"

I think that actors like Fang Junguan are the scum of the earth. Their degeneration is attributable to what they did in their former lives; they are bearing the brunt of their past actions in this life. One can't say that there is no such thing as pre-determination. Yujiang was only expressing a desire to clarify things from their root-causes.

Later Su Xingcun heard the story and said, "Xiaolan [Ji Yun] talks about cause and effect with reference to past, present, and future lives, and he wants to caution us against what may happen in the future. Yujiang talks about cause and effect with reference to one's thoughts, and he wants us to be cautious about what we think here and now. While each seeks to illustrate a different principle, I must concede that Yujiang's view warns us not to give free rein to our hearts' desires."

3. HX I:58

My nephew Yudun is my cousin Maoyuan's son. In the third lunar month of the *renzi* year [1792], Yudun assisted me in proofreading the books of the Wenyuan Treasury, and we both lived in the Huaixi Old House at Haidian.

Yudun told me about a rattan pillow painted in vermilion that Maoyuan had bought at a temple-fair in Cuizhuang some years back. One summer, whenever Maoyuan slept on it, he would hear a soft droning sound, and he thought it was an echo in his ears, appearing when he got exhausted.

After more than ten days, the sound became louder; it was as if a flying insect were stretching its wings. Another month later, it could be clearly heard outside of the pillow, heard even before Maoyuan lay down in bed. Suspicious, he cut open the pillow and a small bee flapping its wings, flew out.

On the edges of the pillow there was not the tiniest of fissures, so how could a bee leave its egg inside? If the egg were left before the pillow was painted, how come it took several years before it turned into a bee?

Some talked of metamorphosis. Well, a bee breaks out of a cocoon; it is not metamorphosed from nothing. Even if it were metamorphosed from nothing, why was it not found anywhere else but in the pillow? Why not some other pillows than this one? Without food inside the pillow, why was it still alive after two months? Would it have died if the pillow was not cut open? The reason behind all this is undecipherable.

4. LY VI:28

My great-great-grand-uncle, Master Aitang, was an eminent scholar at the end of the Ming. He specialized in philological studies of the Zheng Xuan and Kong Yingda schools. Be it summer or winter, he studied till midnight.

One night he dreamt that he came to a yamen, with a horizontal tablet which carried the characters for "literature" and "ritual." Inside there were a dozen people busy studying. He recognized all of them as old acquaintances. They, in turn, were surprised to see him. "There's still seven more years to go before you are expected here. It's too early for you to come," they said.

He then woke up with a start. Knowing that his days were numbered, he spent all his time with Buddhist and Daoist priests.

Once he chanced to meet a Daoist priest whom he could see eye to eye with. He kept him for a drink.

After leaving, the priest met Aitang's servant Hu Mende by chance and said, "Just now I forgot to give your master this book. Take it home with you."

Master Aitang found that the book contained charms and talismans for the subjugation of deities and ghosts. After giving it careful study behind closed doors, he mastered thoroughly the thaumaturgical arts, and used them in staging plays to pass the time.

Indeed, seven years later, in the *dingchou* year of the Chongzhen reign [1637], he died. He came back to life after half a day. He said, "I was punished in hell for stealing for my own use the Magic of the Five Thunders. The judge of hell is demanding that the book be returned. Burn it up quickly!" When that was done he fell dead again.

Yet half a day later he came to once more. He said, "The judge of hell checked the book and found three pages missing. I've been ordered to fetch them."

Among the ashes he discovered three pages yet unburnt. After they were burnt, he breathed his last.

All of this is recorded by Master Yao'an in an appendix to the genealogical records of our clan. Master Yao'an heard it from my late great-grandfather, who heard it from my great-great-grandfather, the person who burnt the book. Who can say there are no deities or ghosts?

5. RS III:5

The story of Gu Feixiong's rebirth is recounted in both Duan Chengshi's *Youyang Miscellany* and Sun Guangxian's *Random Words North of the Dream Marsh*. The poem relating the event is also recorded in the literary collection of his father, Gu Kuang, so it is obviously not fabricated.

Recently Shen Yunjiao, the Junior Steward, compiled a biography of his mother Lady Lu. He mentions how, just a year after her marriage, her husband Lord Zeng died, while her son Heng, born after his death, followed him to the grave when he was three.

Weeping most bitterly, Lady Lu said, "I've lived on after your father died, for your sake. Now you too have died. I can't bear to see our ancestral line terminated from this point on." When the dead body of her son was prepared for the coffin, she put a vermilion mark on his arm and made a wish: "Heaven will not put an end to my family. May this be a testimony to your rebirth."

It was the second month of the year *jiyou* in the Yongzheng era [1729]. During that month, a son with a glaring red mark on his arm was born to a member of the same clan right next door. Thereupon

Lady Lu brought him up as her own offspring. He was none other than the Junior Steward himself.

When I was Minister of the Bureau of Rites, the Junior Steward was a colleague of mine, and he narrated this at length to me. Among Buddhist writings there is, naturally, much that is wayward and bizarre. Buddhist followers exaggerated the rewards and punishments, to entice others to give alms; many untruthful accounts are propagated. Yet theories of reincarnation are really well-proven and beyond dispute. The Director of Destinies occasionally uses one person, or one incident, as a clue whereby the teaching of the spirits is revealed. The Junior Steward's story is an example of the verifiability of rebirth, which makes manifest the way in which Heaven is moved by long-suffering, chaste women. How could this be known to Confucians who eagerly spread the view that ghosts do not exist?

6. RS II:13

According to Mr. Li Youdan, one night during the final years of the Yongzheng reign, the dogs in all the homes inside the city of Dongguang began barking together quite suddenly. The noise was like tides gushing.

When panicky people emerged from their houses, they saw someone in the moonlight. He had hair reaching to his waist. He wore mourning garments, with a hemp sash round his waist. He held in his hand a huge sack, and from it came the sound of hundreds and thousands of ducks and geese. He stood erect on the ridge of one roof, and after a while crossed over to another. The next day, from wherever he stood on the roof top there dropped a couple of ducks and geese. When cooked and eaten, these did not taste any differently from fowl raised the usual way, and no one could figure out what sort of demon he was. Later, it came to pass that deaths invariably occurred in those families receiving the ducks and geese. This confirmed that he was the evil goblin.

The family of my late father-in-law, Master Ma Zhoulu, also got two ducks that night, and the same year Ma's brother, Master Gengchang, prefectural magistrate of Jingni, passed away. Mr. Li Youdan was not amiss in what he said.

From ancient times to the present, those who die are as numerous as sand. Why did the portents only appear on that particular night? Why only in that particular place? Why — in that place — only for those few families? What meaning was there behind the dropping of ducks and geese? Why ghosts and deities act the way they do is partly comprehensible, partly not. I have simply put this down in writing, without offering any comments.

7. RS IV:13

When Yishi, a Hanlin Academy clerk, went with the troops to capture Ili, he fought fiercely to break out of a seige. He was shot to death by seven spears. After two days, miraculously, he was revived. Galloping at great speed for one day and one night, he was able to catch up with the army. When Bai Xizhai and I were both at the Hanlin academy, we saw the scars of his wounds and asked how they came about.

Yishi told us that he felt no pain at all when wounded; he seemed suddenly to have fallen into a deep slumber. After a while he gradually became conscious of his soul leaving his body. Everywhere he saw wind mixed with sand, and he had no sense of direction. It dawned on him that he had died.

He felt deep sorrow as soon as he thought of his young children and his impoverished family. He was like a leaf fluttering in the wind, about to be blown hither and thither. The next moment, he thought: how little did he deserve to die such a meaningless death! He vowed to be transformed into a malignant ghost, so he could kill the enemies. Then he felt his body harden into a pillar, and the wind could not shake him. He wandered about. He was about to climb to the hilltop to seek out the enemies, when he woke up suddenly, as though from a dream, and found himself lying in a pool of blood shed during the fighting.

Sighing, Xizhai noted, "Hearing such events one feels that there is nothing to fear about dying in battle. Indeed, one could turn into an loyal official or a martyr easily. Why is everybody so afraid?"

8. RS III:21

My paternal uncle An Jieran said, "There are numerous accounts of malignant ghosts in the ancient books. Many have come to me by word of mouth.

"In the fifth month of the *guiwei* year [in the Qianlong reign (1763)], I was returning to Cuizhuang from Dijia'an, Yanshan, when I personally saw it. There was a man who seemed to be over fifty, wearing a straw hat and ramie clothing. He had tied to a willow a donkey carrying a bundle of clothing and sheets. He sat leaning against the willow. Tying up my horse, I proceeded to take a rest.

"Suddenly the man sprang up. As though defending himself with his arms, he said, 'I took your life and I will repay with mine. There's no need to beat me up like this.' For a while he struggled, then his words became less and less clear. All of a sudden, he plunged into the river, and was swallowed by the waves.

"The dozen people who witnessed this all held their palms together, and recited Buddha's name. Although there is no knowing what grievance was being avenged, the man himself did state that it was a case of 'a life for a life.'"

9. LY VI:23

When Liu Yizhai, the Chamberlain for Law Enforcement, was a Censor, he rented a house by the edge of the West River. Every night he heard the tinkling noise of clappers, which continued till dawn. The noise always came when the drum-roll at the tower was sounded at every watch. Not a human shape could be discerned, and it was so noisy that one could not get a moment's sleep. Yizhai was by nature stiff and unbending. He composed an essay condemning the nuisance. He wrote down the details, and pasted the essay on the wall in order to exorcize the trouble-makers. That same evening all was silent. Yizhai was surprised, comparing his act to Han Yu's repulsion of the alligators.

I said, "Your writing, as well as your moral stature, seem hardly comparable to those of Han Yu. But owing to your stern temper and vibrant energy, and to your lifelong abstinence from morally dubious acts, you can be fearless before the ghosts. Also, having moved to this house under rather straitened circumstances, and being too exhausted to move anywhere again, you have no choice but engage in a life-and-death struggle with them. For you, it's 'the caged beast striking out';

for the ghosts, it's 'not pressing a foe at bay.' Don't you remember the story in *Extensive Gleanings from the Taiping Reign* concerning how Secretary Zhou fought with a ghost over a house, where the ghost opted out, fearful in the face of Zhou's obstinacy?"

Patting me on my back and laughing, Yizhai said, "You are as frivolous as Wei Shou! But you know me through and through."

10. LY I:15

Licentiate Tang of Hejian prefecture [in present-day Hebei] was fond of playing tricks on others. Even today local residents still remember him as "Tang the Whistler." A tutor at the village school who liked to talk of the non-existence of ghosts once said:

"Ruan Zhan's encounter with a ghost — how could that have been true! It was just an absurd fabrication, the wild gossip of monks."

At night Licentiate Tang scattered some mud at the tutor's window and whined, striking at the door. The tutor, in fear, asked who it was. He responded: "I'm the inherent capacity of the two kinds of *qi*." Greatly perturbed and shivering all over, the tutor buried his head under his sheets and ordered two students to stand guard at the door throughout the night. The next day, he would not get up. When friends came to enquire about him, he moaned and said, "Ghosts."

Soon afterwards, when it came to be known that it was all Licentiate Tang's doing, everybody applauded. However, from that time on, demons became rampant, and not a night passed without their throwing stones and bricks, or shaking the doors and windows. At first it was thought that Tang was playing another of his tricks, but on closer look these demons were found to be real. Unable to bear the disturbance any longer, the tutor left the village school.

For when shame followed fear, the vital energies became diminished, and the opportunity was open for fox-spirits to come and assume control. That's what is meant by the saying "demons are aroused by men".

Appendix 3

The Kaozheng *Tales*

1. HX III:26

Dates are grown in my home county [Xian]. They are transported either north in lorries to supply the needs of the capital, or south in junks to be sold in the various provinces. Most natives are engaged in growing dates their whole lives.

The mists are most feared when the dates are still unripe. They shrink in contact with humid mists and become wrinkled, so that only the skin and the kernel are left. Whenever the mists come, therefore, firewood and straw will be heaped above the date trees and burnt, to produce clouds of smoke to disperse the mists. Or the farmhands will line up with their firelocks and shoot at the mists, to disperse them even more quickly. The truth is that, when the *yang* force is strong, the *yin* mists will be overshadowed. All demonic elements fear firearms.

The elderly Shi Songtao said that, whenever yellow clouds appear over the mountains of Shanxi and Shaanxi, hailstorms will come to damage the crops. If you shoot at them, toads the size of cart-wheels will fall from the sky.

When I was Commissioner of Education at Fujian, mountain elves sometimes walked on the roof at night, and the tiles creaked as they went past. When the canons at the yamen gates were fired, they would flee in great haste, and in a second it would be silent. Ghosts, too, fear firearms. When I was in Urumqi, I once shot at some malignant ghosts with a firelock, and they could not resume their original shapes afterwards. This I have discussed previously in *Record of Spending the Summer at Luanyang* [*LY* III:2]. For demons and ghosts are both of the *yin* category.

2. LY V:4

In one village, there was a newly widowed woman. A rascal bribed an old woman neighbour to help him pull the strings. At night he stole into the widow's chambers. As the two closed the doors and were about to go to bed, all of a sudden the candle flame turned green, shrinking to the size of a broad bean. An explosive sound then followed. A red light flooded the room, and there appeared a patch of light the size of a round mirror about two feet across. Inside it emerged the face of the woman's deceased husband. The couple shrieked and fainted by the bed. Other members of the household were roused; they went to see what had happened, and discovered the illicit affair.

Some wondered why, of the many widows who cannot preserve their chastity, this widow's dead husband in particular wields such power. I, however, believe that there are powerful and weak ghosts, and there are also ups and downs in men's fortune. The husband happens to be a potent ghost, and the adulterers' fortunes also happen to be at a low ebb, so the ghost can wreck destruction. There are numerous other dead persons who endure great grief in hell and are ensnared for ages by their own sins. Their spirits do not die along with their bodies.

Others suspected that demons had possessed these dead souls and caused such strange things to happen. That is possible. But demons do not arise of themselves; they are invoked by men. The *qi* of an aggrieved soul in hell sets off hidden vibrations, and the mischievous demons avail themselves of the opportunity to appear. Otherwise, why is it that the home of [the chaste woman] Tao Ying was never haunted by the ghost of Liqiu?

3. RS II:57

Peng Qi, a prisoner exile, to Changji [in present-day Xinjiang], had a seventeen-year-old daughter. Both she and her mother fell sick at the same time. The wife died, while the daughter was critically ill. Since Peng had to farm the land owned by the government, he was unable to care for his daughter. She was left to die in the forest. She moaned so sadly that those who saw her were touched.

A fellow-exile, Yang Xi, said to Peng: "You're most merciless. How can this be allowed to happen? I'd like to carry her back and have her cured. If she dies I'll bury her, and if she survives, she'll be my wife."

Peng said, "Great!" and wrote a formal note, and handed it to Yang.

Half a year later, however, the daughter got much worse and could not leave her bed. She told Yang as she breathed her last: "I'm deeply indebted to you for your immense generosity. Since my father permitted us to get married, we've lived closely together, not fearing gossip. Also I have not shied away from you. Because I've been indisposed, we haven't consummated our marriage, and I do feel guilty toward you. Should I die and not turn into a ghost, that's all there is to it. But if I should live a life as a spirit, I'll repay what I owe you." Sobbing, she died.

Yang wept as he buried her. After the burial he dreamt of her every night, and she made love to him as if she were alive. But when Yang woke up, he could not see her. He called out to her in the night, but she would not come. Yet as soon as he closed his eyes, he would see her undressing herself and lying down in bed. After this had lasted for a while, Yang could tell he was dreaming even while he was in a dream. He asked why she would not appear to him in her physical form outside of his dreams. She answered, "I heard other ghosts say that human beings partake of the *yang* element, and ghosts the *yin* element. Harm is done to man when the *yin* invades the *yang*. In sleep, however, the *yang* is restrained and one enters the *yin* mode. This enables one to remain unharmed when interacting with ghosts: only their spirits meet; the physical forms do not."

All this occurred in the spring of the *dinghai* year [1667], and by spring of the year *xinmao* [1771], four years had elapsed. I did not keep track of what ensued after returning home. The story of Lu Chong and Jin Wan [told in *In Search of Spirits*] was widely known in the past. In Song Yu's story of the King of Chu and the goddess of Mount Wu, the meetings were only occasional. An account of lovers meeting in a dream on a daily basis is rare in past literature.

4. HX II:67

Huo Yangzhong said: a painting called "Female Immortal Riding on a Deer" was hung on the wall of a traditional family home. It was signed Zhao Zhongmu (Zhao Yong, son of [the Yuan dynasty painter] Zhao Mengfu), though one could not be sure whether he actually painted it.

Whenever there was nobody home, the immortal in the painting would walk on the walls, very much like the figures on a rotating lantern. One day the owner tied a rope to the roller, hid himself and waited. Once the immortal had gone some distance, he removed the painting by pulling the rope with great alacrity. This left the immortal attached to the wall, coloured just as he was in the painting. Gradually, however, the colours faded. After half a day, they vanished altogether. It seemed that the immortal had disappeared into thin air.

Once I said, "Paintings have no material existence. Neither are they filled with *qi*, and so it seems unlikely that they can acquire spiritual life and then evolve into physical forms. I suspect the painting-demons referred to in ancient texts had taken possession of objects to make an appearance."

Later I came across Lin Deng's *Account of Wide-ranging Matters*, which recorded the story of Yuan Zhao of the Northern Wei dynasty catching a painting-demon at the Yellow Flower Temple in Yunmen. Zhao asked, "You do not have any material essence; you are created by the painter. How did you assume your present form?"

The demon responded, "The painting is the material form, and it is drawn to resemble what is real. By capturing the real it becomes imbued with spirit. This is not to mention the fact that whatever is drawn on the painting becomes the object that can be possessed by demons. That explains, your Honour, how I could respond and evolve. I am certainly guilty."

What he said seemed reasonable enough.

5. RS I:44

Jiang Baiyan said: a scholar was taking a walk on Mount Tongbo when he saw a carriage preceded by guards who appeared, judging by their caps and gowns, to be either ghosts or deities. The scholar hid himself in the woods. But the official inside the carriage, apparently of noble status, had already sighted him. He invited him out for a chat, acting in a most amicable way.

The scholar bowed and asked the man what titles or honours he had.

"I'm the mountain-deity here."

Bowing again, the scholar asked, "When were you born? I hope to spread news about you, to broaden everybody's outlook."

"Your question pertains only to ghosts of the human world, but I am a deity of the Earth. When Heaven and Earth were created, the myriad forms crystallized into being. *Qi* was gathered in these myriad forms, and vital essences were collected within the *qi*. The essences congealed to become concrete substances, which contained within themselves spiritual elements.

"Thus deities came into existence at the same time as Heaven and Earth. Only the Sages were cognizant of the origins of creation, hence the sacrificial rites to Heaven and to the mountains that they recorded in *The Book of Rites*. But the minor officials of earlier times and writers of miscellanies fabricated accounts of deities with surnames like Liu and Zhang. They alleged, too, that the Heaven-deity had lived and died. They gave the surnames of Lü and Feng to the River-deity, who they said had a wife. Confucian scholars were dissatisfied with this. So, with the advent of Zhu Xi [of the Song dynasty], there was talk of explicating the Heavenly principles, and then Zhu even refuted what *The Classic of Poetry* said about Heaven praising the Zhou kings. In this way, deities and ghosts are explained as the expansion and contraction of the forces of *yin* and *yang*.

"The mountain-demon called *kuiwang* is born of the distilled essences of woods and rocks, while the androgynous sheep called *fenyang* is born of the essences of wet earth. Why can't the primal energies, which are circulated within Heaven and Earth, accumulate and then rise up, to become the Supreme Lord? To judge by what you wear, I assume you're a literary scholar. See if you can spread my word so that the Confucians will understand why the Sages offered sacrifices to Heaven."

The scholar bowed and left. But those who heard his story unanimously thought it spurious. For me this is a deeply significant account of the origins of deities and ghosts. In truth it is a fable created by Jiang Baiyan, who puts his ideas into the mouths of deities. Why should the potent deities bother to debate with Confucian teachers?

6. GW IV:12

Wu Yunyan mentioned a certain Licentiate Qin who was not afraid of ghosts and constantly bemoaned not having seen one. One night he was taking a stroll in his villa when he heard someone behind the trees reciting lines from a Tang poem:

> Nobody knew that I came and went on my own —
> I returned only to see the moon on a vacant mountain.

The voice was melancholy and drawn out. Peering through the leaves, Qin saw a man in ancient attire leaning against a rock. Convinced that it was a ghost, he hastened to block it from escaping. The ghost, however, made no attempt to run away.

After bowing deeply, Licentiate Qin said, "We are on the different paths of light and darkness; you belong to the past, I to the present. This being a chance rendezvous, there's no need to waste words of greeting. I have come to enquire about the nature of ghosts and deities. May I ask what it is like to be a ghost?"

"Once we discard our mortal frame, we become ghosts. Like cocoons metamorphosing into butterflies, we are not aware of the process."

"Is it true that after death, the *hun*-soul ascends and the *po*-soul descends, and then both return to the primal void?"

"I have been here since I turned into a ghost. Now I appear before you in my bodily form. I never followed the generative forces of heaven and earth, ascending and descending. When my sons and grandsons offer sacrifices to me, I appear to them. Once the sacrifice is over, we become dispersed."

"Do deities exist?"

"As ghosts are real, so are deities. To use an analogy: since there are ordinary folk, there must also be governors and officials."

"Earlier Confucians said that thunder-gods and their kind are born and die within an instant. Is that true?"

"I often heard of such a theory when I was an ordinary scholar. But secretly I thought that, if each thunder-clap signalled the presence of one deity, then there would be as many deities as there were gnats. And if a deity ceased to exist when the roll of thunder was over, then deities were as short-lived as ephemera. Whenever I questioned my teachers about this, I was bitterly rebuked. After becoming a ghost, I realized that the myriad deities have duties like those of officials in the human world. They are not shadows that disappear within the twinkling of an eye. How I wish I could again challenge my teachers with what I have heard and seen! But these past teachers of mine have, I believe, become ghosts for quite some time already. They must have found out the truth for themselves, so there is no need to challenge them now.

"It seems that the Sages never advocated the theory of the non-existence of ghosts. The great Confucians fabricated this theory for fear that men might indulge in blind worship. But though one should prohibit excessive indulgence, one cannot ban worship. Though one should check sexual licentiousness, one cannot dispense with marital relationships. Though one should forbid greed, one cannot do away with money and goods. Though one should stop duelling, one cannot do away with the five types of weapons. That is why, even with their fame, with the assistance of hundreds and thousands of friends, these Confucians can only silence the general public but not convince them. Those who spread such teachings about ghosts know in their hearts that such views do not hold, but they know that if they do not hold onto such theories, they will not be considered learned men. They go against their own conscience, saying that 'this is the way things are.'

"Now you see that the earlier Confucians' attempt to combat wayward beliefs arose out of an extreme position, not out of heartfelt belief. The later Confucians' criticism of untoward ideas also arose out of pressure exerted on them, not out of deep conviction. If you believe in the Confucian theory that deities and ghosts do not exist, and challenge me on that basis, it shows how wrong-headed you are.

"Creatures of the underworld try to stay away from the living. So you should not remain with ghosts for too long. I will say no more.

You can deduce the rest." Emitting a long and protracted sound, he disappeared.

According to this account, then, the Confucians know that ghosts do exist but choose to say they do not. This ghost is as perceptive as the two ghosts of Huangshan who said that the Confucians knew that the traditional "nine squares" system of land ownership would not work but deliberately proposed that it would. If we were to regard the Confucians' view as wild and fanciful, then we would be missing the point.

7. RS I:55

Gan Bao narrated an account of Ms. Jiang, wife of Ma Shi, in his *In Search of Spirits*; she is what we call "an errand-runner for the netherworld." The Cao family of Wangqiangzhai in Wuqing [in present-day Tianjin] employed an old maid in this capacity. My late mother once asked why such people were needed, since the officials of the underworld had no lack of ghost-aides in summoning souls.

The old maid answered, "The sick bed is bound to be surrounded by human beings, and when the brightness of *yang* radiates like this, the ghost-aides have difficulty drawing close. Or there may be a really superior person, whose spirit is vigorous, or a real gentleman, whose spirit is unyielding. The aide would not dare to come close. Or perhaps there is an official in charge of military and penal affairs, whose spirit is fierce, or somebody robust and fearless, whose spirit is ruthless. In such cases, too, the aide cannot draw near. Only a living soul with a *yang* body and a *yin* spirit can remain unaffected by these circumstances, so I am inevitably called upon just in case I am needed."

This sounds reasonable, and is not likely to have been fabricated by a village woman.

8. GW I:47

One cannot tell how foxes in their magical transformations look at themselves, or at each other. I have previously discussed this in *Records of Spending the Summer at Luanyang*. But foxes are by nature adept at trickery and deception.

As for ghosts, they are formed of the residue of man's *qi*, and so they can only be as ingenious as man. Human beings cannot create something out of nothing, make small things big, or transform what is hideous into a thing of beauty. According to the various books that record encounters with ghosts, coffins are turned into palaces, into which humans can be admitted; tombs are turned into courtyards, where men can dwell. The ghosts of those who die an unnatural death, figuring in a full array of foul and odious forms, can assume beautiful appearances. Could it be that once they become ghosts, they acquire such powers? Or are they taught to do so? This is even more in scrutable than the transformability of foxes.

I remember that on my way to Liangzhou, the driver of the carriage said, pointing at a mountain pass, "Once I slept in the open on that mountain with the drivers of many other vehicles. In the moonlight we saw houses far away which were surrounded by low earthen walls. We could even see clearly the eaves of houses. The next day when we passed by, however, there was nothing there but a few tombs."

Hence such phenomena appear even in no man's land. Was the creation of funerary objects understood by the sages?

9. LX III:6

According to Cheng Yumen the Junior Compiler, a scholar was on intimate terms with a vixen, who made no attempt to cover up the truth even the first time they met.

She said, "I will not harm you through seeking to obtain spiritual nourishment, nor do I wish to make an excuse of the idea of karmic destinies. I am so enamoured of you that I can hardly contain my own feelings. To be infatuated at first sight — perhaps that indeed is destiny after all?"

She did not appear often, and she would say, "I am afraid you will fall sick from sexual over-indulgence." When the scholar had to study or write literary essays, she would leave, saying, "I do not want to be in the way when you are doing your proper duties."

For almost ten years they had an affection for each other as deep as that between husband and wife. Since it had been a long while and the scholar had no son, he asked teasingly, "Can you give birth to a son for me?"

She replied, "I cannot be sure. A foetus is created when the two essences, interpenetrating, become conjoined. At the moment of intercourse, if the *yin* essence is present but not the *yang*, or vice versa, no foetus will be produced. Even if both are there but one comes earlier than the other, the foetus will not come into being, for that which arrives earlier finds its energies dissipating instead of congealing. When the two essences arrive at the same time, neither earlier nor later, and when the *yang* element thrusts forward and gets enveloped by the *yin*, a male foetus emerges with *yang* dominant. If the *yin* element, charging forward first, is enveloped by the *yang* element, a female foetus with *yin* dominant emerges. Such is the ingenuity of the natural process of metamorphosis, something beyond man's control. Hence, a foetus can be produced with one instance of intercourse, and not be produced even with a thousand instances. We can't say for sure."

"How do twins come about?"

"When the two *qi*, equally vigorous, collide headlong, they will split into two. When they hit one another sideways, there will be more *yang* than *yin* in one foetus, and the *yin* element will be enveloped by the *yang* element. In the other foetus, there will be more *yin* than *yang*, and the *yang* element will be enveloped by the *yin*. Hence there are often twin boys and twin girls, though a boy and a girl are also simultaneously conceived."

"The essences are only activated by ecstatic pleasure. Young maidens, however, are always timid when they first get married. Yet foetuses have been conceived after the first instance of intercourse with a maiden. How can the *yin* essence be activated in this case?"

The vixen replied, "Mutual delight is experienced at the moment of intercourse. It may be tough at first, but it gets easier. Or one may appear exhausted while feeling pleased. Where there is emotional harmony, the essences will be activated, and occasionally a foetus does get conceived on the first encounter."

"If it is produced with the union of the two essences, how come conception occurs only after the discharge of the menses every month?"

"The essences are like seeds of grain, and our blood is like fertile soil. Old blood is detrimental to the essences, new blood is congenial to them, and the foetus thrives on new blood. I was once an attendant for the immortal imperial concubine, and through eavesdropping on her explanation of the origins of life and change, I have a rough idea of what it is all about. Thus, 'unlearned men and women know and do what the Sages do not know and cannot do.'"

Later, when the scholar was past thirty, his beard suddenly grew long. Quite unexpectedly, the vixen sighed and said, "Your beard is long like shiny blades. It's just unbearable. I feel frightened whenever I see you. Could it be that the karmic destiny which brought us together is over?"

At first the scholar took it as a joke, but the vixen eventually stopped visiting him altogether.

Cheng Yumen was heavily bearded, and since he was about to take a concubine, Ren Zitian had narrated the tale just to tease him. Cheng had heard it before, and after laughing at it, said, "This vixen in fact engaged in quite a bit of argumentation, the details of which you have not narrated." Hence he recounted in detail all the arguments put forward by the vixen, as described above. Since they sound sensible, I have jotted down what I can recall from memory.

10. *HX* III:33

Cai Bichang, the Prefect, said he was a judge in hell, but those who expressed their views on this doubted it. Yet Cai did foretell the date of the death of Zhu Zhujun's "eminent forebear" (author's note: In Tang times, according to *Random Words North of the Dream Marsh*, this was the term of address for deceased fathers). His mother, who predicted her own death, was accurate to the date and the hour. How can we explain that? Zhu Shijun, the Provincial Governor, narrated at length other things concerning Cai, and he is not a man given to wild statements. Gu Demao, the Director [of a section in the Ministry], also said he was a judge in hell. He later said that, because of his disclosure of things pertaining to the courts of hell, he was demoted to be a local god of the soil. That, however, cannot be verified. Once I heard him explicating the laws of hell, and what he said was already recorded in *Records of Spending the Summer at Luanyang*.

Gu's discussion of the lives of ghosts makes sense. Put briefly, ghosts are formed of man's residual *qi*, which disperses after a while. Only three types of *qi* do not disperse: the vital *qi* of the loyal, filial, chaste and righteous; the indomitable *qi* of courageous generals and brave soldiers; and the numinous *qi* of men of great talents and learning.

There are also three kinds of *qi* that do not disperse quickly. For wronged and aggrieved souls living in the yellow springs (hell) who are filled with pain, their *qi* coagulates as their bitterness hardens; for the extremely wealthy and prestigious, because they have owned a great deal, their *qi* is as resplendent as their essence is vigorous; for lovers who pine for one another and are afflicted by remorse and sorrow, their *qi* congeals because their feelings are intense. As for the fierce and ruthless, their rebellious *qi* does not disperse quickly either, but nine out of ten of them descend into hell (*niraya*), and hence they do not count. Gu spoke of all this with certainty. Could he possibly have evidence for it?

Appendix 4

The Didactic Tales

1. LY I:8

Zhou Hu, the servant of a certain Mr. Zhou of Xian county, was bewitched by a vixen. For over twenty years the two lived together as man and wife. Once the vixen told Zhou: "For more than four hundred years I've cultivated my physical form. In my previous life I owed you a debt that I have to repay now. I won't be able to redeem myself till I've served my full term, not one day less. When we are no longer tied by destiny, I'll leave."

One day the vixen appeared; she was at first elated, then sad. Weeping, she said to Zhou, "On the nineteenth of this month, it is destined that I should leave you. I've sought out another wife for you. You should deliver the betrothal gifts and confirm the marriage." She lent Zhou some money to buy the gifts. After that they were exceptionally intimate with each other.

However, on the fifteenth, she bade farewell on waking up in the morning. Zhou began to blame her for her early departure. The vixen said, tearfully, "I can't add or subtract even one day from the time predestined for us, though I can choose to leave earlier or later. I'm saving up these three days, so that we can have a chance of seeing one another again."

Several years later, true to her word, the vixen did return, and they enjoyed three rapturous days before she left. She wept as she departed, saying, "Now I'll be parted from you forever."

Mr. Chen Deyin said, "This fox-spirit has done well by stocking up what is left: in the same way one should cherish one's good fortune."

Liu Jizhen, by contrast, said, "Why leave three days behind when one will eventually be separated? Though this fox-spirit has had four hundred years of cultivation, it has not reached a state of readiness to let everything go when circumstances so demand. This is not how one should handle one's problems."

For my part, I believe that Liu and Chen each used the story to illustrate a different principle, and neither was remiss.

2. LY II:13

There was a traveller who supported himself by selling his paintings and calligraphy. He also got a concubine, of whom he was rather enamoured, at the capital. Whenever he went to a banquet, he would bring back fruits and other delicacies in his sleeves for her. The concubine also reciprocated his love.

Not long afterwards, however, the scholar was taken seriously ill and he said to his concubine, "I don't have a home, and you've nowhere to return to. I don't have any relatives, and you don't have anybody to rely on. I live on my writings and paintings. When I die, you should remarry. That is not just a matter of expediency but also reasonable. I haven't left behind any debts for you to pay off, nor can you be restrained by any parents or brothers. Do what you desire, but do not accept any betrothal gifts when you remarry. Make sure your future husband allows you to offer sacrifices to me at my grave every year, and I'll rest contented." Weeping, the concubine nodded agreement.

The new husband she married also promised to abide by the agreement, and he was most fond of her. Yet memories of her dead husband's kindness continued to haunt her and make her unhappy. Every night she dreamt of sleeping with her former husband, and she would softly whisper to him in her sleep. Her new husband, noticing this, hired a magician secretly to subdue the dead spirit with amulets and talismans.

The concubine stopped talking in her sleep, but gradually became sick. Soon she was on the point of death. Before she died, she said to her husband, beating her forehead against the pillow, "The love of my former husband is indeed hard to forget. You know it well, and I did not hide it from you. Last night I once again dreamt of him saying, 'I have long been exiled, but I have the opportunity of returning tonight. Sick as you are, why don't you leave with me?' I've already consented to his request. Can I beg you for a special favour? Bury me with my dead husband, and in all future lives I'll serve you with all my heart. I know this is a most unbecoming request but I'll let you decide."

She stopped breathing as she finished speaking. Her husband was a most generous man, and he lamented it: "The soul has gone. What's the use of keeping the body? Yang Su [of the Sui dynasty] could bring together again Princess Yuechang and Chen Deyin, who had split up. Why can't I reunite the two of them in hell?" He did as he was asked.

This happened some time in the year *jiayin* or *yimao* of the Yongzheng reign. I was eleven or twelve when I heard the story, but have since forgotten the names. I think that, when the widow remarries, she proves herself to be unworthy of the first husband's trust, and when, after the remarriage, she is only partly faithful to her second husband, she proves herself to be unworthy of his trust as well. She did not know whether to move forward or retreat.

Mr. He Zishan also said, "To die out of longing for the husband is hardly comparable to killing herself upon his death."

According to Mr. He Li'an, however: "*The Spring and Autumn Annals* admonishes virtuous men, but one should not restrain women with the principles of the educated. We should mourn the tragic experiences of this woman, and pity her for her choice."

3. LY IV:28

Mr. Shen Cangling (Shen Dan) is the younger brother of Mr. Shen Qianju. Qianju is unassuming and amiable while Cangling is generous, though both are upright and unbending. In their village a woman maltreated by her mother-in-law hanged herself. Considering that the two were families of government officials, Cangling persuaded her father and brothers not to take the case to court.

That night Cangling heard somebody sobbing first at a distance, then at the main gate, and then just outside the window. It was the woman's ghost who pleaded as she sobbed, and her words were most heart-rending. She was blaming Cangling for preventing her father and brothers from going to court.

Cangling reprimanded her, "No compensation laws pertain to a woman maltreating her daughter-in-law and killing her. You would not be appeased even if you went to court over this case. Moreover, a trial will involve a coroner's inquest, for which you'll have to be undressed. Would that not bring further insult to both families?"

The ghost continued to sob.

Mr. Shen Cangling said, "Government officials and emperors do not sue each other at court; nor do sons and fathers. Others will sympathize with you for being wrongfully killed, and reprimand your mother-in-law for her maliciousness. But for you, the daughter-in-law, to even think of suing her in court is to violate what is proper and correct. Even if you were to bring the case before the deities, they would not help you."

The ghost left quietly.

Mr. Shen Qianju said, "What Cangling said could be made known to all the daughters-in-law of the world. To tell this to the mothers-in-law would not do."

The late Master Yao'an said, "Cangling's message on filiality is directed at sons, while Qianju's message on paternal kindness is directed at fathers."

4. RS I:28

Wu Taolin, a military officer at Urumqi, said that his cousin once went to visit a friend at Jing county. One night, it happened to be raining, and he went to a deserted temple for shelter. It only had crumpled walls and desolate grass; not a soul could be found. Only the doorway gave some protection, so he went there and waited for the sky to clear.

The clouds were then dark as ink. He heard the voice of a woman in the dimness: "An aggrieved ghost bows before you and begs for some paper clothes. These white bones of hers will be eternally grateful."

He was too terrified to move but, knowing that there was no place to hide, braced himself to ask who it was.

The ghost, weeping, said, "I'm originally from this village. Once, passing by this temple on my own, I was caught by the monks and detained in the temple here. I cried and swore at them and refused to do what they asked, so they killed me in a rage. At the time I was stripped of all my clothes, and so I was buried naked. Over a hundred years have gone by. Even in hell, I still have a sense of decency. Too ashamed to meet the deities without a shred of clothing on, I've stomached my grievance and hid myself. I'm lucky enough to have met a gentleman today. If you can get hold of some coloured paper, cut it up to make dresses, and burn them up in front of the temple, then this spirit from the dark realms can cover up her body, make an appeal at the courts of hell, and then be reincarnated. I hope you'll have pity for me and come to my rescue."

Trembling, Wu's cousin agreed. The sobs then were heard no more. However, he never had the chance of visiting that place again, and so the paper clothes were never burnt. He often felt that he had reneged on his promise, leaving the ghost unavenged in hell. He continued to feel a sense of unease long afterwards.

5. GW IV:15

Gong Xiaofu, who passed the examinations the same year that I did, said: A certain man, aged over forty, had no sons. His wife was a shrew and would definitely not let him take a concubine, so he was quite dejected.

Once he chanced to come to a Daoist temple. A Daoist priest beckoned to him and said, "You're off colour and seem to be burdened with worries. Daoists are philanthropists by nature. Why not tell me what it is? Maybe I'll be of some service to you!"

Taking an interest in what the Daoist priest said, the man told him everything.

The Daoist priest responded, "Actually I've heard about it. I just wanted to ask. You should obtain about a dozen suits for ghost-orderlies, and I'll help you out. If that's not possible, get actors' suits. That too is fine."

This made the man even more perplexed. He thought, however, that the priest would not want to cheat him of his suits, which would be useless anyway. Convinced that the priest had some plan in mind, he decided to do as he was told.

That night, his wife had a nightmare. She would not wake up when she was shouted at, and she moaned most appallingly. The next day dark green bruises were found on her thighs. When she was asked about it, she would not say anything, but only sighed.

Three days later the same things happened, then again every three days thereafter. Six months later, she ordered a servant to invite some matchmakers along, saying she was going to purchase a concubine. No one would believe her. Her husband was especially hesitant, seriously concerned about consequences. She lay unconscious for days, and on waking up, asked that a concubine be bought without delay. She put the money on the table and warned a servant that he would be flogged if he failed to obtain a concubine in three days, or if he got one who was not good enough.

Obviously she was serious. Two young women were sought. She wanted both of them to stay and, that same evening, she made the wedding bed and urged her husband to climb in. The entire family was petrified and nobody understood what all this meant.

The husband, too, went through everything as if dazed. Only when he met the Daoist priest later did he realize that the priest was a master of the art of summoning souls. In the night he sent forth priests from the Daoist temple, all dressed as ghost-orderlies, while he himself sat in the hall, wearing a cap and a feathered gown. He burned amulets in order to summon the soul of the wife, who was told that his husband's ancestors and parents had brought a suit against her in the courts of hell. She was charged with a lack of filiality in terminating the ancestral sacrifices and caned with a peach-twig a hundred times. When she was sent back, she was given a date by which a concubine had to be procured. Thinking that it had all been a nightmare, the wife was at first reluctant to get a concubine. But her soul left her once every three days, as if she were conscripted. On those days when she was in a coma, her soul was hung upside down, and vinegar was poured into her nostrils. She was warned, too, that she would be consigned to hell.

Apparently, the soul-summoning arts of the Daoist priest are petty tricks, not the proper way of dealing with the situation. But there are in fact no "right" or "wrong" magical arts; it is purely a matter of how they are used. Compare this to the use of a spear. When used to rob and kill others it is the weapon of a bandit. When used in punitive expeditions it is the weapon of a king's loyal subject. The various kinds of magical arts, big or small, are at man's service. It is like hand lotions which can be used on one's hand when washing clothes, or used to defeat the Yue people. The Daoist priest has made the best use of the magical arts!

Now the shrew cannot be tamed by recourse to reason, nor inhibited by the law, and yet the Daoist priest can tame her with his magic. The sheep led by the sage emperor Yao will not move even when it is beaten from behind by the sage emperor Shun, although an entire herd will move forward when urged by a shepherd boy. Everything in this world is controlled by something else, just as each kind of medicine is counteracted by another. The sages establish their teaching through the way of the deities because they want to tame those who are recalcitrant. They have deep-seated motives. How can the Confucian teachers understand this?

6. LY I:46

Chen Guanglu (Chen Fengya) said that in Kangxi times, a student of the Imperial Academy in Fengjing was studying in his villa one day when he saw a rock amidst the grass. It was cracked and eroded, and only a few dozen words were left on it. Here and there a couple of complete statements could be discerned. The rock seemed to be a round stone tablet on a woman's grave.

The scholar's curiosity was piqued. He thought the grave should be somewhere near. He often placed tea and fruit on the rock and presented some lewd poetry.

Over a year later, he saw a beautiful girl walking by herself in the vegetable fields, holding some wild flowers in her hand. She smiled at the scholar. He hastened near her, exchanged glances with her, and then led her into the bush behind a hedge.

The girl stood still, staring right at him, as though she had something on her mind. Suddenly she slapped herself in the face, and said, "For over a hundred years my heart has been like an old well. Should I be moved now by a profligate?"

She stamped her foot on the ground several times, and disappeared all of a sudden. The scholar realized that she was the ghost from the grave.

Cai Jishi, Senior Compiler at the Hanlin Academy, noted: "In the past it was said that the final judgement on a person can be made only when the lid is laid on his coffin. This incident shows that the final judgement can't be passed even then. She was a chaste ghost, and might have fallen for the scholar due to a momentary slip." In a poem Zhu Xi has said:

> Nothing is more dangerous than human desire.
> How many people have found all their life's work undone on this point!

Very true indeed!

7. LY VI:30

Mr. Bao Jingzhi of Nangong [in present-day Shandong] said: There was a certain Licentiate Chen in his home village who applied himself to his studies in a temple. On one summer night he slept naked on the side-room. He dreamt of a deity summoning him to his throne and berating him harshly.

Chen retorted, "Several pedlars slept in the main hall. I hid myself in the side-room. Why should I be scolded?"

The deity answered, "It's fine with the pedlars, not with you. They are as stupid as deer and pigs. How can you be compared to them? As a scholar how come you have no sense of propriety?"

That is the reason why *The Spring and Autumn Annals* judges men of virtue by the harshest of standards. For the gentlemen living in this world, if they can follow the crowd, they should by all means do so; they need not seek to be different. They do not have to follow the crowd if they cannot; they need not compromise. With regard to improper acts, men of this world often point to precedents. If we put aside what is right and wrong, and instead talk about precedents, then is there nothing that has ever been done before, from ancient times till now? How can we use precedents as an excuse?

8. *HX* II: 34

In Dongguang [in present-day Hebei] there is a River Wangmang (or Husu), which dries up in times of drought, and floods on rainy days, making it difficult for one to wade across. My father-in-law Ma Zhoulu said that some time near the end of the Yongzheng reign, a beggar-woman was wading across this river. She was carrying her baby boy in one arm, and supporting her ailing mother-in-law with the other arm. Halfway across, the mother-in-law slipped and went under. The beggar-woman left her baby in the water and, making a great effort, carried the old woman on her back across the river.

The old woman reprimanded her harshly: "It does not matter that an old hag of seventy like me should die! Several generations of Zhangs have relied upon this child to perpetuate the family line. Why did you abandon him to save me? You have put an end to our ancestral sacrifices!"

The woman, sobbing, dared not utter a word, but remained kneeling. For two days the mother-in-law wailed over her deceased grandson and starved herself to death. The woman was too sad for tears and sat as though demented for several days. Then she also died.

No one knew who she was, but from the mother-in-law's curses one could tell she was surnamed Zhang. Some remarked: "Compared to the child, the mother-in-law was more important, but if the mother-in-law were to be compared to the ancestors, then the ancestors would be even more important. If the woman's husband had been alive, or if the husband had had brothers, then it would have been right to abandon the son. Since the two poverty-stricken and widowed women had only a child left to carry on the ancestral line, the mother-in-law was correct in reproaching the woman, who died only with regret."

Master Yao'an said: "The pedants lost no opportunity to rebuke others! With the swift currents gushing past, everything would be over in a split second. How can one ponder at length on the best course of action? Circumstances being what they were, abandoning the child and saving the mother-in-law would be in keeping with the just operations of Heavenly principles; it would put one's heart at ease. Were the woman to save her child and allow the mother-in-law to die, would she not feel guilty the rest of her life? Would there not then be people scolding her for abandoning her mother-in-law out of love for her son? Furthermore, since the child still had to be carried in the arm, one can raise doubts as to whether it would grow up. How much more regret there would be if the mother-in-law died and the son could not be brought up? What this woman did more than met the demands of human emotions. It was unfortunate that the mother-in-law killed herself and the woman followed her in death. That is more cause for lament! But if one were to be self-righteous and began to pontificate on the right principles, then would the dead not feel wronged and harbour grief even in the underworld? Sun Fu wrote *An Explication of the Kingly Way Discussed in the Spring and Autumn Annals.* According to him, the annals were filled with condemnation and no praise for events in a 240-year period. Hu Yin wrote *Reading the Histories and Expressing My Narrow Views.* To him no perfect men appeared after the Three Dynasties. These arguments are no doubt persuasive, but I don't want to listen to them."

9. GW IV:45

My servant, Fu Xian, was much given to reading. He could understand literature quite well, and knew a little about medicine too. Dull and imbecile by nature, he resembled the old, arrogant Confucians.

One day he strode proudly in the marketplace, and asked whomever he chanced to meet, "Did you see Wei San?" He continued strutting forward in the direction pointed out to him. After finding Wei San, he panted for a good while.

Wei asked why he was being sought out. Fu said, "Just now I saw your wife in front of the Well of Bitter Water. She was doing some needlework under a tree. She nodded off when she got tired. Your child was playing by the side of the well. He was just a few feet from it, and there seemed to be cause for some concern. However, since between the sexes there is a barrier, I did not want to wake your wife, but came looking for you."

Wei was greatly alarmed and hastened back, only to find his wife leaning against the well, weeping over her child.

Servants who read and study are to be praised. But we study to gain an understanding of principles, and through understanding principles we turn them into practical use. To swallow without digesting, so that one becomes idiotic and wayward, is harmful beyond measure. Of what worth is this kind of Confucian scholar?

10. LY III:4

Huaizhen is located about seventeen miles east of Xian country [in present-day Shandong], and *History of the Jin Dynasty* calls it Huaijiazhen.

A certain man surnamed Ma began, all of a sudden, to find spirits in his home throwing bricks and stones at night; he also heard the wail of ghosts. Fires would start suddenly even when there was nobody inside. Such disturbances lasted for over a year, and could not be halted by prayers and sacrifices. Ma sold the house and moved, but whoever rented it later was similarly preyed upon, and soon had to move elsewhere also. That being the case, no one would dare inquire about the house.

An old Confucian scholar, doubting such accounts, bought the house at an extremely low price. After consulting the almanac for an auspicious day he moved in. Strangely enough, it was quiet, and nothing unusual happened. It was generally thought that the demons were daunted by the Confucian scholar's superior virtues.

After some time some ruffians came for a visit and started a brawl with the scholar. The truth then came out: all the strange events in the house were instigated, not by real demons, but by robbers that the old scholar had paid.

The late Master Yao'an said, "Demons were no more than adepts at playing deceitful tricks. In his ability to deceive with his tricks, the old Confucian scholar should indeed be regarded as a real demon."

11. RS I:54

A man who wielded great wealth came of a reputable family. Some vile characters sought his friendship and lured him frequently to brothels, where they drank, indulged in games, and entertained themselves by singing and dancing. Within a few years the man did not even have money left for food and died, pale and starved. When he was about to die, he said to his wife, "I have come to this through the deception of my friends. I will bring a case against them in the underworld."

After half a year he appeared to his wife in a dream and said, "I have lost my case. The judge of hell said, 'Catamites and prostitutes are shameless; they earn a living by providing sensual pleasure. They cheat others of their money, and can be likened to tigers and leopards that devour men, and whales that swallow boats whole. But will tigers and leopards eat men up if men do not go into the mountains? Will whales gulp down boats if boats do not sail out to the sea? You let yourself be enticed by them. How can you lay the blame on them? However, profligate friends lay traps for beasts and will not give up till their prey is caught; fishermen suspend their bait and will wait till they catch their fish. Hence it is appropriate that in the human world there are laws, and in the underworld, karmic retribution."

I also heard that a scholar, infatuated with a vixen, became sick and died. On the day of the Pure Brightness Festival his family went to his grave and found a woman offering wine and burning paper money. Lying prostrate, she wept most bitterly.

The scholar's wife recognized this woman as the vixen and cursed her from a distance, "Wicked demon! May you be killed when thunder strikes! Why all this pretence!"

The vixen, straightening her sleeves, responded with measured calm, "The female members of our species chase after men for spiritual nourishment, but we are not permitted by heavenly law to ruin too many lives. Men chase after women out of love and desire, but over-indulgence will be harmful to them. Similarly, husbands and wives seek to please one another sexually. If they become sick or die, they are to be held responsible themselves. Ghosts and deities pay no heed to what happens in bed. Why are you blaming me now?"

These two stories serve to illuminate one another.

12. LY I:7

South of the city of Changzhou [in present-day Hebei], at Shangheyai, lived the rascal Lü Si who would not stop short of any kind of evil, so he was feared by everyone as if he were a wolf or tiger. One day at dusk, he was basking in the cool outside the village with several young scoundrels. All of a sudden they heard the faint sound of thunder, and then a storm was about to come. They saw at a distance what seemed like a young woman entering the old temple by the river for shelter. Lü told the group of scoundrels, "We can have some fun with her."

It was already well into the night, and with the gloomy clouds it was pitch dark. Lü stole quickly into the temple and gagged the woman. The scoundrels stripped her of her clothes and threatened her sexually.

Suddenly a flash of lightning shot through the window, and Lü vaguely recognized the woman as his wife. Hurriedly releasing the woman, who was tied by the hands, he asked and found out it was indeed so. Lü was filled with indignation and meant to throw her into the river.

The wife screamed, "You set your mind on raping a woman. This caused them to rape me. The principles of Heaven are clear as broad daylight. Do you want to kill me as well?"

Lü could not say another word and quickly went in search of his wife's clothes. They had already been blown into the river by the wind. Anxious and at his wit's end, he carried back the naked woman on his back. The clouds had dispersed and the moon was shining bright. There was an uproar and everyone from the village, laughing, struggled to come forward with queries. Unable to counter the questions directed at him, Lü eventually killed himself by leaping into the river.

What happened was that Lü's wife had returned to her relatives, and planned to return in about a month's time. Quite unexpectedly a fire had broken out in her family home, and having no place to stay, the wife returned earlier than scheduled. Lü was not aware of this, and hence this catastrophe.

Later the wife dreamed of Lü, who came to say, "Heavy with sin as I was, I was destined to remain in hell forever. But the magistrates of hell, on checking their rosters, discovered that in my life I had served my mother with great filial piety, and I could be reincarnated in the form of a snake. I am on my way to be reborn. Soon, your new husband will come along. You should serve your new parents-in-law as best you can. According to the code of the netherworld, lacking in filial affection is the severest of sins. Take care so you will not have to go down the soup cauldrons of hell."

On the day of the wife's remarriage, there was a long red snake at a top corner of the house. Hanging its head, it watched as though emotionally attached. The wife, calling to mind the dream she had had earlier, was about to raise her head and ask, when she heard from outside the door strains of music accompanied by drumbeats. The snake leapt a couple of times on the roof of the house and went off, quickly.

Glossary

Aitang 愛堂
An Jieran 安介然
An Zhongkuan 安中寬

Bai Juyi 白居易
Bai Minzhong 白閔中
Bai Xingjian 白行簡
baiguan 稗官
baihua 白話
baixing xiao wei xian 百行孝為
先
"Baiyuan zhuan" 白猿傳
Ban Gu 班固
bao 報
baojuan 寶卷
Baopu zi 抱朴子
baoying 報應
bazi 八字
bian 變
bian yihuo 辨疑惑

bianding 辨訂
bianwen 變文
biji 筆記
Bishu luhua 避暑錄話
Bowu zhi 博物志
boxue 博學
Boyi zhi 博異志
Boyi zhuan 博異傳
Boyou 伯有

Cai Yuanpei 蔡元培
Can tongqi 參同契
Cao Pi 曹丕
Cao Xuemin 曹學閔
Cao Xueqin 曹雪芹
chaizi 拆字
Chan Wing-tsit 陳榮捷
Changbai Haogezi 長白浩歌子
"Changhenge zhuan" 長恨歌傳
changli 常理

Chaoye qianzai 朝野僉載
Chen Baiya 陳白崖
Chen Deyin 陳德音
Chen Hong 陳鴻
Chen Liangmo 陳良謨
Cheng Hongzao 程鴻藻
Cheng Jinfang 程晉芳
Cheng Tingzuo 程廷祚
Cheng Yi 程頤
Cheng Yumen 程魚門
chengjie 懲戒
Chengshi lu 誠是錄
Chibei outan 池北偶談
"Chibi fu" 赤壁賦
Chow Tse-tsung 周策縱
chuanqi 傳奇
Chunqiu 春秋
Chunxiang zhuibi 蓴鄉贅筆
Chuogeng lu 輟耕錄
congtan 叢談
"Cui xiucai" 崔秀才

Dai Zhen 戴震
Dao 道
Dayuan 大宛
"Dinghun dian" 定婚店
Dong Han 董含
Dong Jiang 董江
Dong Qiuyuan 董秋原
Dong Yuandu 董元度
Dongnan jiwen 東南記聞
Dongpo zhilin 東坡志林
Dongxuan zhuren 東軒主人
Du Guangting 杜光庭
Duan Chengshi 段成式
Duan Yucai 段玉裁
Duyang zabian 杜陽雜編
Duyi zhi 獨異志

En Maoxian 恩茂先
Ermu ji 耳目記
ershi 耳食
Ershi lu 耳食錄
Ertan 耳談
Erxin 耳新

Fa Nanye 法南野
Fan Ni 范嬺
fanchai 燔柴
Fang Bao 方苞
Fang Dongshu 方東樹
Fang Junguan 方俊官
Fang Zhengyao 方正耀
fangbian 方便
Fei wugui 非無鬼
Feifeizi 非非子
"Feiyan waizhuan" 飛燕外傳
feng 諷
Feng Qiushui 馮秋水
Feng Tingcheng 馮廷丞
"Feng Yan zhuan" 馮燕傳
fengshui 風水
Fenmen gujin leishi 分門古今類事
fenyang 羵羊
Fu Zitang 福霽堂

Gan Bao 干寶
Gao Yue 高鉞
Gaopo yizuan 高坡異纂
Ge Dongchang 戈東長
Ge Hong 葛洪
Ge Tao 戈濤
Ge Yuan 戈源
gongsheng 貢生
Gu Yanwu 顧炎武
guai 怪
Guaiyi ji 怪異記

guan 觀
Guan Shihao 管世灝
Guan Tong 管同
Guandi 關帝
Guangwen 廣文
Guanyin 觀音
gufen 孤憤
gui 鬼
"Guiqu tu" 鬼趣圖
guiquan 規勸
guishen 鬼神
guishen nongren 鬼神弄人
"Guishen pian" 鬼神篇
Guo Pu 郭璞
Guo Tuan 郭彖
Guobao ji 果報記
Gusheng 孤賸
Guwang tingzhi 孤妄聽之

Han shu 漢書
Han Yu 韓愈
Hanlin 翰林
Hanwu gushi 漢武故事
Hanxue 漢學
Hanxue shicheng ji 漢學師承記
He Bang'e 和邦額
He Xiu 何銹
He Zishan 何子山
Heng Lantai 恆蘭台
Hong Bian 洪鞭
Hong guniang 紅姑娘
Hong Liangji 洪亮吉
Hong Mai 洪邁
Honglou meng 紅樓夢
Hou Jian 侯健
hu 狐/胡
Hu Gaowang 胡高望
Hu Shi 胡適

Hu Taichu 胡太初
Hu Yinglin 胡應麟
hua 化
Huainan zi 淮南子
Huaixi zazhi 槐西雜志
huaji 化機
Huang Fu 黃輔
Huang Jingren 黃景仁
Huang Sheng 黃晟
Huang Wei 黃暐
Huang Xiufu 黃休復
Huang Zongxi 黃宗羲
Huanyuan zhi 還冤志
huasheng 化生
"Hui zhen ji" 會真記
Huichen lu 揮塵錄
hun 魂
Hunliang 渾良
Huo Yangzhong 霍養仲
"Huofu pian" 禍福篇
huxian 狐仙
huyao 狐妖

ji 寄
Ji Lianfu 季廉夫
Ji Rongshu 紀容舒
Ji Ruchuan 紀汝傳
Ji Ruji 紀汝佶
Ji Rulun 紀汝倫
Ji Runsheng 紀潤生
Ji Yun 紀昀
Ji Zhaiyu 季齋魚
Ji Zhao 紀昭
Ji Zhuo 紀晫
jian 諫
Jiang Bingzhang 姜炳璋
Jiang Fan 江藩
Jiang Shiquan 蔣士銓

Jiang Xiangnan　蔣湘南
jianguan　諫官
Jianwen jixun　見聞紀訓
Jianwen lu　見聞錄
Jiao Xun　焦循
jie　戒
Jilei bian　雞肋編
Jin Kan　金侃
Jin Ping Mei　金瓶梅
Jin Shengtan　金聖嘆
Jin shu　晉書
"Jin Zongbing"　靳總兵
jing　精
"Jingshu lei"　經書類
jinshi　進士
jinxiang ben　巾箱本
Jishen lu　稽神錄
Jiwei zhiyi　棘圍志異
jixian　乩仙
jixie　機械
Jiyi ji　集異記
Juanshige wen jiaji　卷施閣文甲集
juren　舉人
Jutan lu　劇談錄

Kaiyuan Tianbao yishi　開元天寶遺事
Kang Pian　康駢
kaozheng　考證
Kechuang suibi　客窗隨筆
Kuangyuan zazhi　曠園雜志
kui　暌
Kuiche zhi　暌車志
kuiwang　夒罔

Lai Fangling　賴芳伶
Lanyan　蘭巖
Lei pu　雷譜

li　理/利/禮
li buke jie　理不可解
Li cheng　里乘
Li Chuo　李綽
Li Ciming　李慈銘
Li Deyu　李德裕
Li Fang　李昉
Li Fuyan　李復言
Li Gong　李塨
Li Gongzuo　李公佐
Li Jinzhi　李金枝
Li Lüyuan　李綠園
Li Mi　李密
Li Qianzhong　栗千鍾
Li Kang　李伉
"Li sao"　離騷
Li Shen　李紳
"Li Wa zhuan"　李娃傳
li wai wu wu　理外無物
Li Wenzao　李文藻
Li Youdan　李又聃
Li Yuan　李源
Li Yunju　李雲舉
Li Zhao　李肇
Li Zicheng　李自成
Liaozhai zhiyi　聊齋志異
Liehu ji　獵狐記
Liexian zhuan　列仙傳
Lieyi zhuan　列異傳
Liezi　列子
Lin Yaling　林雅玲
Ling Xuan　伶玄
Liqiu　黎丘
Liu Fu　劉斧
Liu Jingshu　劉敬叔
Liu Jizhen　劉季箴
Liu Kezhuang　劉克莊
Liu Tongxun　劉統勳

Liu Wenzheng　劉文正
Liu Xiang　劉向
Liu Xiangwan　劉香畹
Liu Yeqiu　劉葉秋
Liu Yiqing　劉義慶
Liu Youhan　劉友韓
Liu Yuxi　劉禹錫
Liu Zhiji　劉知幾
Liu Zongyuan　柳宗元
Liugong jiahua lu　劉公嘉話錄
"Liuguo nianbiao"　六國年表
Liuya waibian　柳崖外編
Long Chengzu　龍承祖
Lu Cai　陸采
Lu Jianzeng　盧見曾
Lu Jintang　盧錦堂
Lu Qi　陸圻
Lu Shuibu　陸水部
Lu Wenchao　盧文弨
Lu Xixiong　陸錫熊
Lü Dongbin　呂洞賓
Lü Liuliang　呂留良
Luanyang　灤陽
Luanyang xiaoxialu　灤陽消夏錄
Luanyang xulu　灤陽續錄
Lufei Chi　陸費墀
"Lujiang Feng'ao zhuan"　盧江馮
　媼傳
"Lunhui lun"　輪迴論
Luo Liangfeng　羅兩峰
Luo Pin　羅聘
Luo Qinshun　羅欽順
Luo Yougao　羅有高
Luyi zhi　錄異志
Lüshi chunqiu　呂氏春秋
Lüyuan conghua　履園叢話

Mao Chang　毛萇

Maoting kehua　茆亭客話
mei　魅
Mei Zengliang　梅曾亮
meipi　眉批
Meng Chaoran　孟超然
Meng'an zazhu　夢庵雜著
Mengzi ziyi shuzheng　孟子字義疏
　證
Mi Fei　米芾
Ming Sheng　明晟
Ming shi　明史
Mingbao lu　冥報錄
mingguan　冥官
"Mingli pian"　命理篇
Mingxiang ji　冥祥記
"Mu shuo"　墓説
Mutianzi zhuan　穆天子傳
muyou　幕友

nan Yuan bei Ji　南袁北紀
Ni Chengkuan　倪承寬
Nie Songyan　聶松巖
Niu Xiu　鈕琇
Nizhai　閑齋
Nuogao guangzhi　諾皋廣志
Nurhaci　努爾哈赤
Nüwa　女媧

Ouyang He　歐陽紇
Ouyang Xiu　歐陽修
Ouyang Xun　歐陽詢

Pan Deyu　潘德輿
Peng Shaosheng　彭紹昇
Pengchuang leiji　篷窗類記
po　魄
Pu Liuxian　蒲留仙
Pu Songling　蒲松齡

qi 奇/氣

Qi Xie 齊諧

Qian Chenqun 錢陳羣

Qian Daxin 錢大昕

Qian Weicheng 錢維城

Qian Wenmin 錢文敏

Qian Yong 錢泳

Qian Zai 錢載

qianding 前定

Qianding lu 前定錄

qiao 巧

Qidong yeyu 齊東野語

qijuzhu 起居注

qili moming 其理莫明

Qilu deng 歧路燈

Qingshizi 青史子

Qingsuo gaoyi 青鎖高議

Qiudeng conghua 秋燈叢話

Qiuping xinyu 秋坪新語

Qu Yuan 屈原

quan 勸

Ren Fang 任昉

Ren Lanyou 任蘭佑

Ren Meiyou 任郿佑

"Renshi zhuan" 任氏傳

Rizhi lu 日知錄

Rongmu xiantan 戎幕閑談

Rouputuan 肉蒲團

Ruan Ji 阮籍

Ruan Yuan 阮元

Ruan Zhan 阮瞻

Rulin waishi 儒林外史

Rushi wowen 如是我聞

Sanbi yitan 三筆異談

Shangshu tanlu 尚書談錄

Shanhai jing 山海經

shanxiao 山魈

Shao Dasheng 邵大生

Shao Jinhan 邵晉涵

she tan zhu 奢談助

shen 伸/神

Shen Cangling 申蒼嶺

Shen Jiji 沈既濟

Shen Qianju 沈謙居

Shen Qifeng 沈起鳳

Shen Quyuan 沈曲園

Shen Yazhi 沈亞之

Shen Yefu 沈業富

Shen Zhou 沈周

shendao 神道

shendao shejiao 神道設教

Sheng Shiyan 盛時彥

shengyuan 生員

shenli buwu 神理不誣

Shenxiang zhuan 神仙傳

Shenyi jing 神異經

Shi Huangdi 始皇帝

Shi ji 史記

Shi Jiexian 釋戒顯

shi quanjie 示勸戒

Shi tong 史通

shi yan zhi 詩言志

Shijing 詩經

shishi qiushi 實事求是

Shishuo xinyu 世説新語

"Shu'er pian" 述而篇

Shuihu zhuan 水滸傳

shuo 説

Shuo fu 説郛

Shuo lin 説林

Shuoling 説鈴

Shuoling houji 説鈴後集

shuoshu 説書

Shuoyuan 説苑

Shuyi ji 述異記

Sibu beiyao 四部備要

Siku quanshu 四庫全書

Sikuquanshu zongmu tiyao 四庫全
書總目提要

Sima Guang 司馬光

Sima Qian 司馬遷

Song Bi 宋弼

Song Mengquan 宋蒙泉

Song Qingyuan 宋清遠

Soushen ji 搜神記

Su E 蘇鶚

Su Shi 蘇軾

Suichang zalu 遂昌雜錄

Suiyuan 隨園

Suiyuan suibi 隨園隨筆

Suiyuan xibian 隨園戲編

Sun Mian 孫勉

Sun Xun 孫恂

Sun Yushan 孫漁珊

suoyu 瑣語

Taiping guangji 太平廣記

Taiping yulan 太平御覽

Taishigong 太史公

tan wuli 探物理

Tang guoshi bu 唐國史補

Tang Yin 唐寅

Tang Yongzhong 湯用中

tanhu shuogui 談狐說鬼

Tao Qian 陶潛

Tao Zongyi 陶宗義

ti 體

Tian Baiyan 田白巖

"Tiando pian" 天道篇

tianhu 天狐

"Tianwen" 天問

tiaoli 條理

tili 體例

Tingshi 桯史

tiyao 提要

Tongcheng 桐城

Waishishi 外史氏

"Waiwu pian" 外物篇

Wan Tai 萬泰

Wang Bu 王逋

Wang Chang 王昶

Wang Chong 王充

Wang Chongmin 王重民

Wang Depu 王德甫

Wang Fuzhi 王夫之

Wang Guoliang 王國良

Wang Huizu 汪輝祖

Wang Jin 汪縉

Wang Lun 王倫

Wang Mingqing 王明清

Wang Mingsheng 王鳴盛

Wang Renyu 王仁裕

Wang Shizhen 王士禛

Wang Xian 王械

Wang Yan 王琰

Wang Youzeng 王又曾

Wang Zhong 汪中

Wang Zhu 王洙

wangliang 罔兩

Wangwang lu 妄妄錄

wangyan wangting 妄言妄聽

Wei Xuan 韋絢

Wei Yuan 魏源

Wensu 文溯

Wen xuan 文選

wen yi zai dao 文以載道

Weng Fanggang 翁方剛

Wenjian yici 聞見異辭

Wenxian tongkao 文獻通考

wenyan 文言
Wu Chenyan 吳陳琰
Wu Jingzi 吳敬梓
Wu Lintang 吳林塘
Wu Shanxi 吳山錫
Wu Weiye 吳偉業
Wu Yuhui 吳玉惠
Wu Zhenfang 吳震方
wucong tuijiu 無從推究
wugui lun 無鬼論
wuhu zhizhi 烏乎知之
wuwei 無為
wuyou 五酉

xiang 享
Xiang Yu 項羽
Xianguo suilu 現果隨錄
"Xianren pian" 仙人篇
Xiao Tong 蕭統
Xiaocang shanfang chidu 小倉山房
　　尺牘
Xiaodoupeng 小豆棚
Xiaopin ji 效顰集
xiaoshuo 小說
"Xiaoyao you" 逍遙遊
Xiashan shenyi ji 峽山神異記
Xie duo 諧鐸
"Xie Xiao'e zhuan" 謝小娥傳
"Xijing fu" 西京賦
Xin Qi Xie 新齊諧
Xin Tang shu 新唐書
xingji 興寄
xingli lei 性理類
"Xingming shuo" 星命說
Xinzheng lu 信徵錄
Xiyou ji 西遊記
Xu Fang 徐芳
Xu Kun 徐昆

Xu Qing 徐慶
Xu Qiuzhai 徐秋垞
Xu Soushen ji 續搜神記
Xu Shuping 許叔平
Xu Xuan 徐鉉
Xu Yijian zhi 續夷堅志
Xu Yuanzhong 許元仲
Xu Zi bu yu 續子不語
Xuan Ding 宣鼎
Xuanshi zhi 宣室志
Xuanyan ji 宣驗記
Xuanzhong ji 玄中記
Xue Yongruo 薛用弱
Xu E 徐岳

yamen 衙門
Yan Hui 顏回
Yan Ruoju 閻若據
Yan Yuan 顏元
Yan Zhitui 顏之推
yang 陽
Yang Chaoguan 楊潮觀
Yang Shen 楊慎
Yang Shifu 楊式傅
Yang Xiong 揚雄
Yang Yi 楊儀
Yangzhou baguai 揚州八怪
Yao Mang 姚莽
Yao Nai 姚鼐
Yao Ying 姚瑩
yao you ren xing 妖由人興
Yao'an 姚安
Ye Mengde 葉夢德
Ye Shishuo 葉世倬
Yecheng kelun 冶城客論
Yeshishi 野史氏
Yetan suilu 夜談隨錄
Yeyu qiudeng lu 夜雨秋燈錄

yi 義/異
yi'an 疑案
Yijian zhi 夷堅志
Yijian zhizhi 夷堅支志
Yijing 易經
yin 陰
Yin Jishan 尹繼善
Yin Qinglan 尹慶蘭
Yin'an suoyu 蚓庵瑣語
Ying Shao 應劭
Yingchuang yicao 螢窗異草
Yingtan 影談
"Yingying zhuan" 鶯鶯傳
Yin Zhu 尹洙
Yishishi 異史氏
Yisi baibian 翼駉稗編
yiwen 異聞
yiwen zhi 藝文志
yiyu 瘞玉
Yiyuan 異苑
yong 用
Yongna jushi 慵納居士
you li 有理
youming yilu 幽冥異路
Youyang zazhu 酉陽雜俎
yu 喻/寓
Yu Chu 虞初
Yu Chu Zhou shuo 虞初周説
Yu Jiao 俞蛟
Yu Zhengxie 俞正燮
Yu Xin 庾信
Yu Ying-shih 余英時
Yu Yue 余樾
Yuan Guan 圓觀
"Yuan gui" 原鬼
"Yuan gui lun" 原鬼論
Yuan Haowen 元好問
Yuan Mei 袁枚

"Yuan shan" 原善
Yuan Zhen 元積
Yuanhun zhi 冤魂志
Yue Jun 樂鈞
Yue Shi 樂史
Yuewei caotang biji 閱微草堂筆記
Yunzhai guanglu 雲齋廣錄
Yuwen Ding 宇文鼎
yuyan 寓言

zalu 雜錄
zashi 雜事
Zashi mixin 雜事秘辛
"zashu" 雜述
Zeng Yandong 曾衍東
Zhang Du 張讀
Zhang Dunren 張敦仁
Zhang Heng 張衡
Zhang Hua 張華
Zhang Huijing 張惠璟
Zhang Jianting 張健亭
Zhang Jingyun 張景運
Zhang Mengzheng 張夢徵
Zhang Qingyuan 張慶源
Zhang Shengkang 張聖康
Zhang Tan 張坦
Zhang Xuan'er 張鉉耳
Zhang Xuecheng 章學誠
Zhang Zai 張載
Zhang Zhuo 張鷟
Zhangxun Wuji 長孫無忌
Zhao Bi 趙弼
Zhao Qigao 趙起杲
Zhao Yi 趙翼
Zhao Zan 趙儹
Zhaolian 昭槤
Zhenan 柘南
Zheng Huangu 鄭還古

Zheng Tian　鄭畋
Zheng Ya　鄭亞
zhengui　箴規
zhiguai　志怪
Zhiguai lu　志怪錄
zhiren　志人
Zhiwen lu　咫聞錄
Zhizuzhai wenji　知足齋文集
Zhong Guangyu　鍾光豫
Zhong Lu　鍾輅
Zhong Xinhu　鍾忻湖
Zhongyong　中庸
Zhongguo congshu zonglu　中國叢
　書綜錄
Zhou Ciji　周次吉
Zhou Dunyi　周敦頤
Zhouli　周禮
Zhou Mi　周密
Zhou Qi　周棨
Zhou Shuchang　周書昌

Zhou Yongnian　周永年
Zhu Gui　朱珪
Zhu Hai　朱海
Zhu Shiying　朱世英
Zhu Xi　朱熹
Zhu Yun　朱筠
Zhu Yunming　祝允明
Zhu Ziying　朱子潁
Zhuang Chuo　莊綽
Zhuang Tinglong　莊廷鑨
Zhuangzi　莊子
Zhuzi yulei　朱子語類
Zi bu yu　子不語
"Zixin"　自信
Zizhi tongjian　資治通鑑
Zong Dingbo　宗定伯
Zou Tao　鄒弢
Zu Taizhi　祖台之
Zuozhi yaoyan　佐治藥言
Zuozhuan　左傳

Bibliography

The items below indicate only texts referred to in this book; not all of them are their first editions or versions. Most of the *zhiguai* items from the *Annotated Catalogue of the Complete Library of Four Treasuries* discussed above are not included, and readers should refer to the catalogue for more bibliographical information.

Primary Sources

Changbai Haogezi 長白浩歌子. *Yingchuang yicao* 螢窗異草 (Exotic Grass at the Glow-worm Window). Taibei: Guangwen shuju 廣文書局, 1970.

Chen, Kangqi 陳康祺. *Langqian jiwen* 郎潛紀聞 (Records of Things Heard by the Lowly Official). Taibei: Wenhai chubanshe 文海出版社, 1970.

Cheng, Hongzao 程鴻藻. *Youhengxinzhai ji* 有恆心齋集 (Collected Writings at the Studio of Perseverance). 1872–1881.

Chunqiu Zuozhuan baihua xinjie 春秋左傳白話新解 (The *Chunqiu Zuozhuan*, Newly Annotated). Taibei: Wenhua tushu gongsi 文化圖書公司, 1969.

Chunqiu Zuozhuan jijie 春秋左傳集解 (*Chunqiu Zuozhuan*, Collectively Annotated). Beijing: Wenxue guji kanxingshe 文學古籍刊行社, 1955.

Dai Zhen 戴震. *Dai Zhen zhexue zhuzuo xuanzhu* 戴震哲學著作選注 (Selected Philosophical Works of Dai Zhen, with Annotations), edited by An Zhenghui 安正輝. Beijing: Zhonghua shuju 中華書局, 1980.

Dongfang wenhua shiye weiyuanhui 東方文化事業委員會, ed. *Xuxiu siku quanshu zongmu tiyao* 續修四庫全書總目提要 (A Continuation to the *Annotated General Catalogue of the Complete Library of Four Treasuries*). Taibei: The Commercial Press, 1971–1972.

Fang Xuanling 房玄齡, *et al.*, eds. *Jin shu* 晉書 (History of the Jin Dynasty). Beijing: Zhonghua shuju 中華書局, 1974.

Fang, Dongshu 方東樹. *Yiweixuan quanji* 儀衛軒全集 (Collected Writings from the Study of the Civil and Military). 1889–1894.

Gan, Bao 干寶. *Soushen ji* 搜神記 (In Search of Spirits). Shanghai: The Commercial Press, 1931.

Gong, Weizhai 龔未齋. *Xuehongxuan chidu* 雪鴻軒尺牘 (Letters Written at the Study of the Wild Goose in the Snow). Hong Kong: Guangzhi shuju 廣智書局, 1956?

Gu, Yanwu 顧炎武. *Rizhi lu* 日知錄 (Record of Daily Learning). Shanghai: Shanghai guji chubanshe 上海古籍出版社, 1985.

Guan, Tong 管同. *Yinjixuan wen chuji* 因寄軒文初集 (Essays from the Study of Taking up One's Residence, First Collection). 1879.

Han shu 漢書 (History of the Han Dynasty). Beijing: Zhonghua shuju 中華書局, 1964.

Han, Yu 韓愈. *Han Changli wenji jiaozhu* 韓昌黎文集校注 (Annotated and Collated Edition of the Literary Works of Han Yu), edited by Ma Tongbo 馬通伯. Shanghai: Gudian wenxue chubanshe 古典文學出版社, 1957.

He, Bang'e 和邦額. *Yetan suilu* 夜談隨錄 (Occasional Accounts of Conversations at Night). In *Biji xiaoshuo daguan erbian* 筆記小説大觀二編 (Comprehensive Collection of *Biji* Tales, Second Compilation), vol. 10. Taibei: Xinxing shuju 新興書局, 1978.

Hong, Liangji 洪亮吉. *Hong Beijiang shiwenji* 洪北江詩文集 (Collected Poems and Prose Writings of Hong Liangji). Shanghai: The Commercial Press, 1935.

Hong, Mai 洪邁. *Yijian zhi* 夷堅志 (Records of Yijian). Edited by He Zhuo 何卓. Beijing: Zhonghua shuju 中華書局, 1981.

Hu, Yinglin 胡應麟. *Shaoshi shanfang bicong* 少室山房筆叢 (Collected Writings from the Retreat at Mount Shaoshi). In Hou Zhongyi 侯

忠義, *Zhongguo wenyan xiaoshuo cankao ziliao* 中國文言小説參考資料 (Reference Materials on Chinese Classical Tales), pp. 25–29. Beijing: Beijing daxue chubanshe 北京大學出版社, 1985.

Huang, Zongxi 黃宗羲. *Nanlei ji* 南雷集 (Writings of Huang Zongxi). In *Sibu congkan* 四部叢刊 (Collectanea in Four Divisions), vols. 1610–1617. Shanghai: The Commercial Press, 1922.

Iizika, Akira 飯塚朗 and Imamura Yoshio 今村与志雄, trans. *Chūgoku koten bungaku zenshū* 中國古典文學全集 (An Appreciation of Classical Chinese Literature), vol. 20. Tokyo: Heibonsha 平凡社, 1958.

Ji, Shuxin 紀樹馨, ed. *Ji Wendagong yiji* 紀文達公遺集 (Posthumous Collection of the Writings of Ji Yun). Beijing, 1812.

Ji, Yun 紀昀. *Ji Xiaolan quanji* 紀曉嵐全集 (Complete Writings of Ji Yun). Beijing: Dongfang wenxueshe 東方文學社, 1935.

————. *Yuewei caotang biji* 閱微草堂筆記 (Random Jottings at the Cottage of Close Scrutiny). Edited by Wang Xiandu 汪賢度. Shanghai: Shanghai guji chubanshe 上海古籍出版社, 1980.

————, *et al.*, eds. *Siku quanshu zongmu tiyao* 四庫全書總目提要 (Annotated Catalogue of the Complete Library of Four Treasuries). Taibei: The Commercial Press, 1968.

Jiang, Fan 江藩. *Hanxue shicheng ji* 漢學師承記 (Record of Lineages in the Transmission of Han Learning). Shanghai: The Commercial Press, 1934.

Jiang, Xiangnan 蔣湘南. *Qijinglou wenchao* 七經樓文鈔 (Collected Literary Works at the Pavilion of the Seven Classics). 1920–1921.

Lüshi chunqiu 呂氏春秋 (Mr. Lü's Spring and Autumn Annals). In *Sibu beiyao* 四部備要 (Comprehensive Compilation of Works in Four Divisions), vols. 1398–1401. Shanghai: Zhonghua shuju 中華書局, 1927–1936.

Li, Boyuan 李伯元. *Nanting biji* 南亭筆記 (Random Jottings at Southern Pavilion). Shanghai: Shanghai guji chubanshe 上海古籍出版社, 1983.

Li, Ciming 李慈銘. *Yuemantang riji* 越縵堂日記 (Daily Notes at the Hall of Zhejiang Curtains). Beijing: Zhejiang gonghui 浙江工會, 1920.

Li, Dou 李斗. *Yangzhou huafang lu* 揚州畫舫錄 (Records of the Painted Boats at Yangzhou). Beijing: Zhonghua shuju 中華書局, 1960.

Li, Fang 李昉, ed. *Taiping guangji* 太平廣記 (Extensive Gleanings from the Taiping Reign). Taibei: Xinxing shuju 新興書局, 1962.

Li, Huan 李桓, ed. *Guochao qixian leizheng chubian* 國朝耆獻類徵初編 (Classified Collection of Biographies of Famous Men of the Qing Dynasty). Taibei: Wenhai chubanshe 文海出版社, 1966.

Li, Kang 李伉. *Duyi zhi* 獨異志 (Accounts of the Exceptional and Anomalous). In *Congshu jicheng chubian* 叢書集成初編 (Collectanea Assembled, First Compilation), vol. 134. Shanghai: The Commercial Press, 1937.

Li, Yuandu 李元度. *Guochao xianzheng shilue* 國朝先正事略 (Brief Accounts of the Worthies of the Qing Dynasty). In *Jindai Zhongguo shiliao congkan* 近代中國史料叢刊 (Collectanea of Historical Documents on Early Modern China), pp. 992–995. Taibei: Wenhai chubanshe 文海出版社, 1967.

Li, Zhao 李肇. *Tang guoshi bu* 唐國史補 (A Supplement to the History of the Tang). Taibei: Yiwen shuju 藝文書局, 1965.

Li, Zongfang 李宗昉. *Wenmiaoxiangshi wenji* 聞妙香室文集 (Collected Writings from the Studio of Fragrant Smell), 1835.

Liu, Fu 劉斧. *Qingsuo gaoyi* 青鎖高議 (Remarkable Opinions under the Green Latticed Window). Shanghai: Shanghai guji chubanshe 上海古籍出版社, 1983.

Liu, Kezhuang 劉克莊. *Houcun xiansheng daquanji* 後村先生大全集 (The Complete Works of Liu Kezhuang). In *Sibu congkan* 四部叢刊 (Collectanea in Four Divisions), vols. 1289–1336. Shanghai: The Commercial Press, 1922.

Liu, Shengmu 劉聲木. *Changchuzhai suibi* 萇楚齋隨筆 (Random Jottings at the Studio of Carambolas). In *Jindai Zhongguo shiliao congkan* 近代中國史料叢刊, vol. 218. Taibei: Wenhai chubanshe 文海出版社, 1977.

Lu, Changchun 陸長春. *Xiangyinlou bitan* 香飲樓筆談 (Sketches and Notes at the Pavilion of Fragrant Drinks). In *Biji xiaoshuo daguan erbian* 筆記小説大觀二編 (Comprehensive Collection of *Biji* Tales, Second Compilation), vol. 10. Taibei: Xinxing shuju 新興書局, 1978.

Luo, Pin 羅聘. *Luo Pin guiqu tu juan* 羅聘鬼趣圖卷 (The Ghost Amusement Scroll of Luo Pin). Hong Kong: Cafa Company, 1970.

———. *Wo xin lu* 我信錄 (Records of My Beliefs). In *Huaibin zazu* 懷豳雜俎 (Miscellany in Remembrance of Bin Subprefecture), vol. 3. 1911.

Mei, Zengliang 梅曾亮. *Bojian shanfang wenji* 柏梘山房文集 (Collected

Literary Writings from the Retreat at Mount Bojian). Taibei: Huawen shuju 華文書局, 1969.

Meng, Chaoran 孟超然. *Mengshi balu* 孟氏八錄 (Eight Records of Meng Chaoran), vol. 3. 1815.

Pan, Deyu 潘德輿. *Yangyizhai ji* 養一齋集 (Collected Writings at the Studio of Cultivating Unity). 1849–1874.

Pu, Songling 蒲松齡. *Liaozhai zhiyi* 聊齋志異 (Tales of Anomalies from the Studio of Leisure). Edited by Zhang Youhe 張友鶴. Shanghai: Shanghai guji chubanshe 上海古籍出版社, 1962.

Qian, Daxin 錢大昕. *Qianyantang wenji* 潛研堂文集 (Collected Prose Writings from the Hall of Devotion to Studies). In *Sibu congkan* 四部叢刊, vol. 1838–1853. Shanghai: The Commercial Press, 1922.

Qian, Yiji 錢儀吉, comp. *Beizhuan ji* 碑傳集 (Collection of Biographical Inscriptions on Stone). Jiangsu: Jiangsu shuju 江蘇書局, 1893.

Qing shi 清史 (A History of the Qing Dynasty), edited by Qingshi bianzuan weiyuanhui 清史編纂委員會. Taibei: Guofang yanjiuyuan 國防研究院, 1961.

Ruan, Yuan 阮元. *Siku weishou shumu tiyao* 四庫未收書目提要 (Bibliographies Unlisted in the *Four Treasuries*). Taibei: Shijie shuju 世界書局, 1967.

Shanghai tushuguan 上海圖書館, ed. *Zhongguo congshu zonglu* 中國叢書綜錄 (A Comprehensive Catalogue of Chinese Collectanea). Beijing: Zhonghua shuju 中華書局, 1959.

Shen, Qifeng 沈起鳳. *Xie duo* 諧鐸 (Words of Humour from an Ancient Bell). Punctuated by Wu Guoqing 吳國慶. Changsha: Yuelu shushe 岳麓書社, 1986.

Sima, Qian 司馬遷. *Shi ji* 史記 (Records of History). Beijing: Zhonghua shuju 中華書局, 1959.

Su, Shi 蘇軾. *Dongpo zhilin* 東坡志林 (Records of Eastern Slope). Shanghai: Huadong shifan daxue chubanshe 華東師範大學出版社, 1983.

Sun, Dianqi 孫殿起. *Fanshu ouji* 販書偶記 (Occasional Records of the Book Trade). Beijing: Zhonghua shuju 中華書局, 1959.

Wang, Du 王度, *et al.*, comp. *Tangren xiaoshuo* 唐人小説 (Tang Narratives). Taibei: Wenguo shuju 文國書局, 1984.

Wang, Hansheng 王寒生, ed. *Yijing qianzhu* 易經淺注 (*The Book of Changes*, Briefly Annotated). Taibei: Xinshiming zazhishe 新使命雜誌社, 1970.

Wang, Huizu 汪輝祖. *Xuezhi yishuo ji qita erzhong* 學治臆説及其他二種

(Unfounded Opinions on Learning to Govern, with Two Other Essays). In *Congshu jicheng chubian* 叢書集成初編 (Collectanea Assembled, First Compilation), vol. 45. Changsha: The Commercial Press, 1939.

―――. *Zuozhi yaoyan ji qita yizhong* 佐治藥言及其他一種 (Medicinal Words to Aid Good Governance, with One Other Essay). In *Congshu jicheng chubian* 叢書集成初編. Shanghai: The Commercial Press, 1937.

Wang, Xian 王棫. *Qiudeng conghua* 秋燈叢話 (Collected Discourses under the Autumn Lamp). Taibei: Guangwen shuju 廣文書局, 1968.

Wang, Youli 王有立, ed. *Qingdai wenziyu dang* 清代文字獄檔 (Archival Records of the Literary Cases in the Qing Dynasty). Beijing: Huawen shuju 華文書局, 1934.

Wei, Yuan 魏源. *Wei Yuan ji* 魏源集 (Collected Writings of Wei Yuan). Beijing: Zhonghua shuju 中華書局, 1976.

Wu, Weiye 吳偉業. *Wushi jilan* 吳詩集覽 (Collected Digest of Wu Weiye's Poetry). In *Sibu beiyao* 四部備要 (Comprehensive Compilation of Works in Four Divisions), vols. 2130–2140. Taibei: Zhonghua shuju 中華書局, 1965–1966.

Wu, Zhenfang 吳震方, ed. *Shuoling* 說鈴 (Bell-talk). Juxiutang 聚秀堂, 1825.

Xiaohengxiangshi zhuren 小橫香室主人, comp. *Qingchao yeshi daguan* 清朝野史大觀 (An Unofficial History of the Qing Dynasty). Taibei: Zhonghua shuju 中華書局, 1959.

Xu, Ke 徐珂, ed. *Qingbai leichao* 清稗類鈔 (Miscellaneous Notes from the Qing Dynasty). Taibei: The Commercial Press, 1966.

Xu, Kun 徐昆. *Liuya waibian* 柳崖外編 (Unauthorized Compilations of Willow Cliff). Taibei: Guangwen shuju 廣文書局, 1969.

Xu, Qiuzhai 徐秋坨. *Wenjian yici* 聞見異辭 (Accounts of Anomalies Heard and Seen). In *Biji xiaoshuo daguan* 筆記小説大觀 (Comprehensive Collection of *Biji* Tales), vol. 1, pt. 3. Taibei: Xinxing shuju 新興書局, 1960.

Yang, Yi 楊儀. *Gaopo yizuan* 高坡異纂 (Anomalies Collected at the [Residence of] High Slopes). In *Shuo ku* 說庫 (Storehouse of Talk), vol. 33. Shanghai: Wenming shuju 文明書局, 1925.

Yao, Mingda 姚名達. *Zhu Yun nianpu* 朱筠年譜 (Chronological Biography of Zhu Yun). Shanghai: The Commercial Press, 1933.

Yao, Ying 姚瑩. *Zhongfutang quanji* 中復堂全集 (Collected Writings from the Hall of Reviving the Doctrine of the Mean). In *Jindai Zhongguo shiliao congkan xuji* 近代中國史料叢刊續集 (Sequel to the Collectanea of Historical Documents on Early Modern China), vols. 51–60. Taibei: Wenhai chubanshe 文海出版社, 1974.

Yu, Jiao 俞蛟. *Meng'an zazhu* 夢庵雜著 (Miscellaneous Comments at the Hut of Dreams). Edited by Fang Nansheng 方南生. Beijing: Wenhua yishu chubanshe 文化藝術出版社, 1988.

Yu, Yue 余樾. *Binmeng ji* 賓萌集 (Records of Guests and Commoners). In *Chunzaitang quanshu* 春在堂全書 (Complete Writings at Hall of the Presence of Spring), pp. 2133–2222. 1882.

Yu, Zhengxie 俞正燮. *Guisi leigao* 癸巳類稿 (Classified Writings in the *Guisi* Year). Qiuriyizhai 求日益齋, 1833.

Yuan, Mei 袁枚. *Suiyuan suibi* 隨園隨筆 (Random Jottings from the Garden of Contentment). Taibei: Mingming chubanshe 明明出版社, 1955.

———. *Xiaocang shanfang shiwenji* 小倉山房詩文集 (Collected Poetry and Prose from the Retreat at Xiaocang Mountain). In *Jindai Zhongguo shiliao congkan xubian* 近代中國史料叢刊續編 (Collectanea of Historical Documents on Early Modern China, Second Collection), vol. 78. Taibei: Wenhai shuju 文海書局, 1981.

———. *Zi bu yu quanji* 子不語全集 (What the Master Would Not Discuss: The Complete Collection). Shijiazhuang: Hebei renmin chubanshe 河北人民出版社, 1987.

Yuandong tushu bianjibu 遠東圖書編輯部, ed. *Zhongguo lidai yiwen zhi* 中國歷代藝文志 (Bibliographies in the Standard Histories through the Chinese Dynasties). Taibei: Yuandong tushu gongsi 遠東圖書公司, 1956.

Yue, Jun 樂鈞. *Ershi lu* 耳食錄 (Hearsay Accounts). Edited by Shi Jichang 石繼昌. Changchun: Shidai wenyi chubanshe 時代文藝出版社, 1986.

Zhang, Du 張讀. *Xuanshi zhi* 宣室志 (Records from the Chamber of Expositions). In *Congshu jicheng chubian* 叢書集成初編. Shanghai: The Commercial Press, 1939.

Zhang, Yingchang 張應昌, ed. *Qing shiduo* 清詩鐸 (Qing Bell-poetry). Beijing: Zhonghua shuju 中華書局, 1960.

Zhang, Zai 張載. *Zhang Zai ji* 張載集 (Collected Works of Zhang Zai). Beijing: Zhonghua shuju 中華書局, 1978.

Zhao, Erxun 趙爾巽, *et al.*, eds. *Qing shi gao* 清史稿 (Drafts of Qing History). Shanghai: Lianhe shudian 聯合書店, 1942.

Zhaolian 昭槤. *Xiaoting zalu* 嘯亭雜錄 (Miscellaneous Recordings at the Whistles Pavilion). Taibei: Wenhai chubanshe 文海出版社, 1967.

Zheng, Huangu 鄭還古. *Boyi zhi* 博異志 (Accounts of Diverse Anomalies). Beijing: Zhonghua shuju 中華書局, 1980.

Zhu, Gui 朱珪. *Zhizuzhai wenji* 知足齋文集 (Collected Essays at the Studio of Self-contentment). In *Baibu congshu jicheng* 百部叢書集成 (Collectanea of a Hundred Categories of Works), vol. 94. Taibei: Yiwen shuju 藝文書局, 1966.

Zhu, Hai 朱海. *Wangwang lu* 妄妄錄 (Records of the Wildly Improbable). 1830.

Zhuangzi jishi 莊子集釋 (Annotated Collected Edition of *Zhuangzi*). Edited by Guo Qingfan 郭慶藩. Beijing: Zhonghua shuju 中華書局, 1961.

Zou, Tao 鄒弢. *Sanjielu bitan* 三借廬筆談 (Sketches and Notes at Thrice-Loaned Lodge). Qingdao: Guocui tushushe 國粹圖書社, 1912.

Secondary Sources — in Chinese and Japanese

Ai, Linong 艾力農. "Tantan 'shendao shejiao'" 談談神道設教 (On "Establishing Teaching through the Way of the Gods"). In *Zhongguo wushenlun sixiang lunwenji* 中國無神論思想論文集 (Essays on Agnostic Thought in China), pp. 156–174. Jiangsu: Jiangsu renmin chubanshe 江蘇人民出版社, 1980.

Bi, Shuchun 畢庶春. "Shilun *Liaozhai zhiyi* yu wu shi zhi guanxi" 試論聊齋志異與巫史之關係 (An Attempt to Explain the Relationship of the *Liaozhai zhiyi* to Shamanism and History). *Wenxue yichan* 文學遺產, no. 3 (1988), pp. 95–102.

Chen, Puqing 陳蒲清. *Zhongguo gudai yuyanshi* 中國古代寓言史 (A History of Fables in Traditional China). Changsha: Hunan jiaoyu chubanshe 湖南教育出版社, 1983.

Cheng, Yizhong 程毅中. *Gu xiaoshuo jianmu* 古小説簡目 (A Brief Catalogue of Old Fiction). Beijing: Zhonghua shuju 中華書局, 1981.

Chinese National Academy of Sciences 中國社會科學院文學研究所, ed. *Bupa gui de gushi* 不怕鬼的故事 (Not Being Afraid of Ghosts). Hong Kong: Joint Publishing, 1961.

Dong, Guoyan 董國炎, "Jiaohua zhishang yu xiaoshuo" 教化至上與小

説 (Fiction and the Supremacy of Didacticism). *Wenxue yichan* 文學遺產, no. 1 (1988), pp. 93–101.

Dongguo xiansheng 東郭先生. *Ji Xiaolan chuanqi* 紀曉嵐傳奇 (The Legend of Ji Xiaolan). Taibei: Shishi shuju 時事書局, 1978.

Fang, Zhaoying 房兆楹 and Du Lianzhe 杜聯喆, eds. *Zengjiao Qingchao jinshi timing beilu fu yinde* 增校清朝進士題名碑錄附引得 (Collated Lists, as Inscribed in Stone, of Successful *Jinshi* Candidates in the Examinations of the Qing Dynasty). Taibei: Chinese Materials and Research Aids Service Center, 1966.

Fang, Zhengyao 方正耀. "He Bang'e *Yetan suilu* kaoshi" 和邦額夜談隨錄考釋 (An Explication of He Bang'e's *Yetan suilu*). *Wenxue yichan* 文學遺產, no. 3 (1988), pp. 103–110.

Fu, Yuheng 傅毓衡. *Yuan Mei nianpu* 袁枚年譜 (A Chronology of Yuan Mei). Hefei: Anhui jiaoyu chubanshe 安徽教育出版社, 1986.

Funazu, Tomihiko 船津富彥. "En Mei no shōsetsuron-tatemae to honne ni tsuite" 袁枚の小説論 — 定前と本音について (Yuan Mei's Theory of Fiction: On His Principles and Intentions). *Tōyōgaku rōnsō* 東洋學論叢, vol. 35, no. 7 (1982), pp. 63–76.

Gao, Qihua 高琦華. "*Yuewei caotang biji* yanjiu zongshu" 閱微草堂筆記研究綜述 (A Survey of Studies on the *Yuewei caotang biji*). *Yuwen daobao* 語文導報, no. 8 (1985), pp. 10–12.

Goto, Kuniko 五嶋久彌子. "*Etsubi sōdō hikki* ni miru Ki In no gakumonron" 閱微草堂筆記に見る紀昀の學問論 (Ji Yun's View of Learning as Seen in the *Yuewei caotang biji*). *Ochanomizu Joshi Daigaku bungaku kaiho* 御茶の水女子大學文學會報, vol. 6 (1987), pp. 69–88.

Gu, Linwen 顧麟文, ed. *Yangzhou bajia shiliao* 揚州八家史料 (Historical Documents Related to the Eight Artists at Yangzhou). Shanghai: Renmin meishu chubanshe 人民美術出版社, 1962.

Guo, Licheng 郭立誠. "*Yijian zhi* yanjiu — jiantan Songdai de minsu shiliao" 夷堅志研究 — 兼談宋代的民俗史料 (A Study of the *Yijian zhi*, with Additional Remarks on the Historical Documents Related to Song Folk Customs). *Zhonghua wenhua fuxing yuekan* 中華文化復興月刊, vol. 10, no. 2 (1977), pp. 37–42.

He, Yousen 何佑森. "Qingdai Han Song zhi zheng pingyi" 清代漢宋之爭平議 (An Evaluation of the Han-Song Dispute in the Qing Dynasty). *Wenshizhe xuebao* 文史哲學報, vol. 27 (1978), pp. 97–113.

Hoshino, Akihiko 星野明彥. "En Mei to *Ko fugo* — shōsetsuka toshite

no ishiki o chushin ni" 袁枚と子不語 — 小説家としての意識を中心
に (Yuan Mei and the *Zi bu yu*: Concerning the Consciousness of
Fiction-writers). Geibun kenkyō 芸文研究, vol. 51 (1987), pp. 69–89.

Hou, Jian 侯健. "*Yuewei caotang biji* de lixing zhuyi" 閱微草堂筆記的理
性主義 (Rationalism in the *Yuewei caotang biji*). In *Zhongguo xiaoshuo
bijiao yanjiu* 中國小説比較研究 (Comparative Studies on Chinese
Fiction), pp. 145–168. Taibei: Dongda chubanshe 東大出版社,
1985.

Hou, Wailu 侯外廬. *Zhongguo zaoqi qimeng sixiangshi* 中國早期啟蒙思想
史 (An Intellectual History of Enlightenment in Its Formative
Period in China). Beijing: Remin chubanshe 人民出版社, 1956.

Hou, Zhongyi 侯忠義. *Zhongguo wenyan xiaoshuo cankao ziliao* 中國文言
小説參考資料 (Reference Materials on Chinese Classical Tales).
Beijing: Beijing daxue chubanshe 北京大學出版社, 1985.

Hu, Jiancai 胡健財. "Dai Zhen fan Cheng Zhu sixiang zhi yanjiu" 戴震
反程朱思想之研究 (A Study of the Anti-neo-Confucian Thought of
Dai Zhen). M.A. thesis, National Chengchi University 政治大學,
1989.

Hu, Shi 胡適. "Yan Li xuepai de Cheng Tingzuo" 顏李學派的程廷祚
(Cheng Tingzuo of the Yan-Li School). In *Hu Shi xuanji: renwu* 胡
適選集：人物 (Selected Works of Hu Shi: Personalities), pp. 111–
158. Taibei: Wenxing shudian 文星書店, 1966.

Hu, Yimin 胡益民. "*Yuewei caotang biji* fan lixue wenti xinlun" 閱微草堂
筆記反理學問題新論 (A New Approach to the Question of Anti-
Neo-Confucianism in the *Yuewei caotang biji*). *Wenxue yichan* 文學
遺產, no. 2 (1990), pp. 120–125.

Huang, Jinhong 黃錦鋐, *et al. Zhongguo wenxue jianghua shi (10): Qingdai
wenxue* 中國文學講話史 (10)：清代文學 (Discussions on Chinese
Literature [10]: Qing Literature). Taibei: Juliu shuju 巨流書局,
1987.

Huang, Lin 黃霖, and Han Tongwen 韓同文, eds. *Zhongguo lidai xiaoshuo
lunzhu xuan* 中國歷代小説論著選 (A Selection of Studies of *Xiaoshuo*
Theory through the Dynasties) Nanchang: Jiangxi renmin
chubanshe 江西人民出版社, 1982.

Huang, Yunmei 黃雲眉. "Cong xuezhe zuoyong shang guji *Siku quanshu*
zhi jiaji" 從學者作用上估計四庫全書之價值 (Evaluating the *Siku
quanshu* in Terms of Its Use for Scholars). *Guoli Beiping tushuguan
guankan* 國立北平圖書館館刊, vol. 7, no. 5 (1933), pp. 51–62.

Jian, Youyi 簡有儀. *Yuan Mei yanjiu* 袁枚研究 (A Study of Yuan Mei). Taibei: Wenshizhe chubanshe 文史哲出版社, 1988.

Jiang, Dongfu 姜東賦. "Ye shuo He Bang'e" 也説和邦額 (Also on He Bang'e). *Guangming ribao* 光明日報, 10 September 1986.

Jiang, Ruizao 蔣瑞藻, ed. *Xiaoshuo kaozheng* 小説考證 (Evidential Research on the *Xiaoshuo*). Shanghai: The Commercial Press, 1935.

Jin, Chunfeng 金春峰, *Qingdai jiechu de wushenlun sixiangjia Hong Liangji* 清代傑出的無神論思想家洪亮吉 (Hong Liangji, a Renowned Agnostic of the Qing). In *Zhongguo wushenlun wenji* 中國無神論文集 (Essays on Agnosticism in China), edited by Zhongguo wushenlun xuehui 中國無神論學會, pp. 272–287. Hubei: Hubei renmin chubanshe 湖北人民出版社, 1982.

Jin, Jiaxi 金嘉錫. *Zhuangzi "yu" zi zhi yanjiu* 莊子「寓」字之研究 (The Word "Yu" as Used in *Zhuangzi*). Taibei: Huazheng shuju 華正書局, 1986.

Kakinuma, Chizuko 柿沼千鶴子. "*Etsubi sōdō hikki* ni okeru shippitsu taido no henka ni tsuite" 閲微草堂筆記における執筆態度の變化について (On the Evolution of [Ji Yun's] Writing Attitude in the *Yuewei caotang biji*). *Ochanomizu Joshi Daigaku bungaku kaiho* 御茶の水女子大學文學會報, vol. 3 (1984), pp. 58–77.

Kawata, Teichi 河田悌一. "Shindai gakujutsu no ichi sokumen — Shu In, So Shinkan, Kō Ryokichi to Shō Gakusei" 清代學術の一側面：朱筠、邵晉涵、洪亮吉、章學誠 (One Aspect of Qing Scholarship: Zhu Yun, Shao Jinhan, Hong Liangji and Zhang Xuecheng). *Tōhō gakuhō* 東方學報, vol. 57 (1979), pp. 84–105.

Lai, Fangling 賴芳伶. *Yuewei caotang biji yanjiu* 閲微草堂筆記研究 (A Study of the *Yuewei caotang biji*). Taibei: Taiwan University Publications, 1982.

Lai, Xinxia 來新夏. "Qingren biji suilu: guanyu *Sangang shilue* he *Chunxiang zhuibi*" 清人筆記隨錄：關於三岡事略和蓴鄉贅筆 (Random Records of Qing *Biji*: Concerning the *Sangang shilue* and the *Chunxiang zhuibi*). *Xuelin manlu* 學林漫錄, vol. 1, no. 2 (1981), pp. 171–175.

Li, Changji 李昌集. "Zhongguo zaoqi xiaoshuoguan de lishi yanbian" 中國早期小説觀的歷史演變 (The Historical Development of the Early Views of Chinese *Xiaoshuo*). *Wenxue yichan* 文學遺産, no. 3 (1988), pp. 1–9.

Li, Jianguo 李劍國. *Tangqian zhiguai xiaoshuoshi* 唐前志怪小説史 (A History of *Zhiguai* Fiction before the Tang Dynasty). Tianjin: Nankai daxue chubanshe 南開大學出版社, 1984.

Li, Jinquan李錦全. "Zai yinguo baoying shuo de beihou" 在因果報應説
的背後 (Behind the Theory of Retribution). *Beifang luncong: Harbin
shida xuebao* 北方論叢：哈爾濱師大學報, no. 5 (1984), pp. 65–70.

Li, Mengsheng 李夢生. "Yuan Mei *Zi bu yu* qiantan" 袁枚子不語淺探
(An Overview of Yuan Mei's *Zi bu yu*). *Zhongguo gudian wenxue
luncong* 中國古典文學論叢, no. 4 (1986), pp. 256–271.

Liang Zhai 量齋. "Diyu guannian zai Zhongguo xiaoshuo zhong de
yunyong he gaibian" 地獄觀念在中國小説中的運用和改變 (The Con-
cept of Hell as Used and Transformed in Chinese Fiction). *Chun
wenxue* 純文學, vol. 8, no. 6 (1971), pp. 34–51.

Lin, Yaling 林雅玲. "Xuan Ding *Yeyu qiudeng lu* ji *Yeyu qiudeng xulu*
yanjiu" 宣鼎夜雨秋燈錄及夜雨秋燈續錄研究 (A Study of Xuan Ding's
Yeyu qiudeng lu and *Yeyu qiudeng xulu*). M.A. thesis, Tunghai University 東海大學, 1989.

Liu, Jingzhen 劉靜貞. "Songren de mingbaoguan: Hong Mai *Yijian zhi*
shitan" 宋人的冥報觀：洪邁夷堅志試探 (Song Concepts of Hell: A
Preliminary Study of Hong Mai's *Yijian zhi*). *Shihuo yuekan* 食貨月
刊, vol. 9, no. 11 (1980), pp. 34–40.

Liu, Yeqiu 劉葉秋. *Lidai biji gaishu* 歷代筆記概述 (A Survey of Random
Jottings through the Dynasties). Beijing: Zhonghua shuju 中華書
局, 1980.

———. "Qing Yu Jiao *Meng'an zazhu*" 清俞蛟夢庵雜著 (The *Meng'an
zazhu* of Yu Jiao of the Qing Dynasty). In *Gudian xiaoshuo biji luncong*
古典小説筆記論叢 (Critical Essays on Classical *Xiaoshuo* and *Biji*),
pp. 191–195. Tianjin: Nankai daxue chubanshe 南開大學出版社, 1985.

Liu, Zhaoyun 劉兆雲, comp. *Yuewei caotang biji xuanzhu* 閱微草堂筆記
選註 (Selected Stories from the *Yuewei caotang biji*, with Annotations). Beijing: Renmin wenxue chubanshe 人民文學出版社, 1982.

Lu, Jintang 盧錦堂. "Ji Yun shengping jiqi *Yuewei caotang biji*" 紀昀生平
及其閱微草堂筆記 (The Life of Ji Yun and His *Yuewei caotang biji*).
M.A. thesis, National Chengchi University 政治大學, 1974.

Lu, Xun 魯迅. *Xiaoshuo jiuwen chao* 小説舊聞鈔 (Collection of Past
Writings on Fiction). Hong Kong: Datong shuju 大通書局, 1959.

———. *Zhongguo xiaoshuo shilue* 中國小説史略 (A Brief History of
Chinese Fiction). Hong Kong: Datong shuju 大通書局, 1959.

Luo, Guang 羅光. *Zhongguo zhexue sixiangshi: Qingdai pian* 中國哲學思
想史：清代篇 (A History of Chinese Philosophy: The Qing). Taibei:
Xuesheng shuju 學生書局, 1981.

Luo, Jingzhi 羅敬之. *Pu Songling jiqi Liaozhai zhiyi* 蒲松齡及其聊齋志異 (Pu Songling and His *Liaozhai zhiyi*). Taibei: Guoli fanyiguan 國立翻譯館, 1986.

Maeno, Naoaki 前野直彬. Chūgoku shōsetsushi kō 中國小説史考 (Researches into the History of Chinese Fiction). Tokyo: Akiyama shoten 秋山書店, 1973.

———. "Lun Ming Qing liangzhong duili de xiaoshuo lilun: Jin Shengtan yu Ji Yun" 論明清兩種對立的小説理論 — 金聖嘆與紀昀 (On Two Opposed Theories of Fiction in the Ming and Qing — Jin Shengtan and Ji Yun). Translated by Wu Biyong 吳璧雍. *Zhongwai wenxue* 中外文學, vol. 14, no. 3 (1985), pp. 77–97.

Mai, Ruopeng 麥若鵬. "Chu jie 'Xianzhai' zhi mi" 初揭閑齋之謎 (Unravelling for the First Time the Puzzle of "Xianzhai"). *Guangming ribao* 光明日報, 2 July 1986.

Meng, Xingren 孟醒仁. "Ye jie 'Xianzhai laoren' zhi mi" 也揭閑齋老人之謎 (Again Unravelling the Puzzle of "Xianzhai laoren"). *Guangming ribao* 光明日報, 17 December 1986.

Miao, Quanji 繆全吉. *Qingdai mufu renshi zhidu* 清代幕府人事制度 (The System of Private Secretaries in the Qing). Taibei: Zhongguo renshi xingzhengshe 中國人事行政社, 1971.

Mou, Zhongjian 牟鍾鑒. "Zhongguo lishi shang guanyu xingshen wenti de zhenglun" 中國歷史上關於形神問題的爭論 (The Debate between "Substance" and "Spirit" in Chinese History). In *Zhongguo wushenlun sixiang lunwenji* 中國無神論思想論文集 (Collected Essays on Chinese Agnosticism), pp. 127–155. Jiangsu: Jiangsu renmin chubanshe 江蘇人民出版社, 1980.

Nishioka, Haruhiko 西岡晴彦. "Hojo kō" 狐妖考 (On Fox-spirits). Tōkyō Shinagaku hō 東京支那學報, vol. 14 (1968), pp. 59–73.

Onozawa, Seiichi 小野沢清一, Fukunaga Mitzuji 福永光司, and Yamanoi Yū 山井湧, eds. *Ki no shisō* 氣の思想 (The Philosophy of *Qi*). Tokyo: Tokyo Daigaku 東京大學, 1978.

Seo, Tatsuhiko 妹尾達彦. "Tōdai kōhanki no Chōan to denki shosetsu — Ri Ai Den no bunseki o chūshin toshite" 唐代後半期の長安と傳奇小説 — 李娃傳の分を中心として (Chang'an in the Latter Half of the Tang and the *Chuanqi* Tale: Concerning the Focus of Analysis in "The Chronicle of Li Wa"). In *Ronshū Chūgoku shakai seido bunkashi no shimondai: Hino Kaisaburō Hakushi shōju kinen* 論集中国社會、制度、文化史の諸問題：日野開三郎博士頌壽記念 (China,

Society, Institution and Culture), edited by Hino Kaisaburō Hakushi shōju kinen ronshū kankokai 日野開三郎博士頌壽記念論集刊行會, pp. 476–505. Fukuoka: Chūgoku shoten 中国書店, 1987.

Uchida, Michio 內田道夫. "Hōjō" 狐妖 (The Fox Demon). *Tōyōgaku* 東洋學, vol. 6 (1961), pp. 12–22.

Wang, Chongmin 王重民. "Lun *Siku quanshu zongmu*" 論四庫全書總目 (On the *Siku quanshu zongmu*). *Beijing daxue xuebao* 北京大學學報, no. 2 (1964).

Wang, Guoliang 王國良. "Liuchao zhiguai xiaoshuo jianlun" 六朝志怪小説簡論 (A Concise Study of Six Dynasties *Zhiguai*). In *Gudian wenxue* 古典文學 (Classical Literature), vol. 4, edited by Zhongguo gudian wenxue yanjiuhui 中國古典文學研究會, pp. 241–285. Taibei: Xuesheng shuju 學生書局, 1982.

―――. *Wei Jin Nanbeichao zhiguai xiaoshuo yanjiu* 魏晉南北朝志怪小説研究 (A Study of *Zhiguai* Stories of the Wei, Jin and North-South Dynasties). Taibei: Wenshizhe chubanshe 文史哲出版社, 1984.

Wang, Lanyin 王蘭蔭. "Ji Xiaolan xiansheng nianpu" 紀曉嵐先生年譜 (A Chronology of Ji Xiaolan [Ji Yun]). *Shida yuekan* 師大月刊, vol. 1, no. 6 (1933), pp. 77–106.

Wang, Liqi 王利器. *Yuan Ming Qing sandai jinhui xiaoshuo xiqu shiliao* 元明清三代禁毀小説戲曲史料 (Historical Documents on the Censorship of Fiction and Drama in the Yuan, Ming, and Qing periods). Shanghai: Guji chubanshe 古籍出版社, 1981.

Wang, Panling 汪玢玲. *Pu Songling yu minjian wenxue* 蒲松齡與民間文學 (Pu Songling and Folk Literature). Shanghai: Wenyi chubanshe 文藝出版社, 1985.

Wang, Tongshu 王同書. "Cong *Liaozhai zhiyi* yu *Yuewei caotang biji* de bijiao kan wenyan xiaoshuo chuangzuo de deshi" 從聊齋誌異與閱微草堂筆記的比較看文言小説創作的得失 (A Look at the Successes and Failures of Innovations in Classical Tales from a Comparison of the *Liaozhai zhiyi* and the *Yuewei caotang biji*). *Fudan xuebao* 復旦學報, no. 2 (1990), pp. 66–71.

Wang, Xianpei 王先霈. "Fengjian lijiao sixiang tong xiaoshuo yishu de diduixing" 封建禮教思想同小説藝術的敵對性 (The Opposition between Feudal Ethical Beliefs and the Art of Fiction). *Wenxue pinglun* 文學評論, no. 2 (1987), pp. 132–137.

Wang, Zhenyuan 王振源. "Ji Yun wenxue sixiang chutan" 紀昀文學思想初探 (A Preliminary Study of the Literary Thought of Ji Yun).

Gudai wenxue lilun yanjiu 古代文學理論研究, vol. 11 (1986), pp. 256–285.

Wu, Yuhui 吳玉惠. "Yuan Mei *Zi bu yu* yanjiu" 袁枚子不語研究 (A Study of Yuan Mei's *Zi bu yu*). M.A. thesis, Tunghai University 東海大學, 1988.

Xu, Tao 徐濤. *Ji Xiaolan waizhuan* 紀曉嵐外傳 (An Unofficial Chronicle of Ji Xiaolan). Taibei: Shijie wenwu chubanshe 世界文物出版社, 1981.

Xu, Zhenqian 徐鎮乾. "Shilun *Yuewei caotang biji* fan lixue de deshi" 試論閱微草堂筆記反理學的得失 (A Preliminary Study of the Merits and Drawbacks in the Attack on Neo-Confucianism by the *Yuewei caotang biji*). *Zhejiang shifan xueyuan xuebao sheke ban* 浙江師範學院學報社科版, no. 3 (1984), pp. 19–26.

Xue, Hong 薛洪. "'Xianzhai' yu 'Nizhai'" 閑齋與閑齋 ("Xianzhai" and "Nizhai"). *Guangming ribao* 光明日報, 10 September 1986.

Ya, Hanzhang 牙含章. "Kongzi xueshuo yu Zhongguo wushenlun sixiang de guanxi" 孔子學說與中國無神論思想的關係 (The Relationship between Confucius' Thought and Chinese Agnostic Thought). In *Zhongguo wushenlun wenji* 中國無神論文集, edited by Zhongguo wushenlun xuehui 中國無神論學會, pp. 272–287. Hubei: Hubei renmin chubanshe 湖北人民出版社, 1982.

Yamanoi, Yū 山井湧. "Cheng Tingzuo de qi de zhexue" 程廷祚的氣的哲學 (The *Qi* Philosophy of Cheng Tingzuo). Translated by Hu Fagui 胡發貴. *Zhongguo zhexueshi yanjiu* 中國哲學史研究, vol. 30, no. 1 (1988), pp. 71–78.

Yamashita, Ryūji 山下龍二. "Rongo ni okeru kishin ni tsuite" 論語における鬼神について (*Analects* on Ghosts and Gods). In *Nagoya Daigaku Bungakubu nijushūnen kinen ronshū* 名古屋大學文學部二十周年紀念論集 (Commemorative Essays on the Twentieth Anniversary of the Literature Department of University of Nagoya). Nagoya, 1968.

Yang, Guorong 楊國榮. "Qingdai puxue fangfa fawei" 清代樸學方法發微 (An Explication of the *Kaozheng* Methodology of the Qing Dynasty). *Huadong shifan daxue xuebao* 華東師範大學學報, no. 4 (1985), pp. 79–84.

Yang, Honglie 楊鴻烈. *Yuan Mei pingzhuan* 袁枚評傳 (A Critical Biography of Yuan Mei). Shanghai: The Commercial Press, 1927.

Yao, Mang 姚莽. "Yuewei caotang biji yishu chengjiu chutan" 閱微草堂

筆記藝術成就初探 (A First Study of the Artistic Achievements of the *Yuewei caotang biji*). *Beifang luncong: Harbin shida xuebao* 北方論叢：哈爾濱師大學報, no. 4 (1985), pp. 60–65.

Yu, Lei 余雷. "*Xin Qi Xie* yu Yuan Mei de zunzhong gexing sixiang" 新齊諧與袁枚的尊重個性思想 (*Xin Qi Xie* and Yuan Mei's Respect for Personal Character). *Zhejiang xuekan* 浙江學刊, no. 1 (1984).

Yuan, Xingpei 袁行霈, and Hou Zhongyi 侯忠義. *Zhongguo wenyan xiaoshuo shumu* 中國文言小説書目 (A Catalogue of Chinese Fiction in the Classical Language). Beijing: Beijing daxue chubanshe 北京大學出版社, 1981.

Yuzi 愚子. "Fengliu caizi Yuan Zicai" 風流才子袁子才 (Yuan Mei, the Hedonist). In *Yuan Zicai yanjiu ziliao huibian* 袁子才研究資料匯編 (A Compilation of Research Materials on Yuan Mei), vol. 1. Hong Kong, n.d.

Yuzi 餘子. *Zhanggu mantan* 掌故漫談 (Casual Talk of Past Anecdotes). Hong Kong: Dahua chubanshe 大華出版社, 1974.

Zhang, Hongsheng 張宏生. "Ji Yun zai *Shijing* yanjiushi shang de gongxian" 紀昀在詩經研究史上的貢獻 (Ji Yun's Contribution to the History of *Shijing* Studies). *Nankai daxue xuebao* 南開大學學報, no. 5 (1989), pp. 18–23.

Zhang, Shengkang 張聖康. "Shuo Yuewei caotang biji" 説閱微草堂筆記 (On the *Yuewei caotang biji*). *Nankai xuebao* 南開學報, no. 6 (1981), pp. 74–78.

Zheng, Huijing 鄭惠璟. "Tangdai zhiguai xiaoshuo yanjiu" 唐代志怪小説研究 (A Study of the Tang *Zhiguai*). M.A. thesis, National Taiwan University 國立台灣大學, 1989.

Zhou, Ciji 周次吉. *Liuchao zhiguai xiaoshuo yanjiu* 六朝志怪小説研究 (A Study of the *Zhiguai* Tales of the Six Dynasties). Taibei: Wenjin chubanshe 文津出版社, 1986.

Zhou, Jiming 周積明. *Ji Yun pingzhuan* 紀昀評傳 (A Critical Biography of Ji Yun). Nanjing: Nanjing daxue chubanshe 南京大學出版社, 1994.

Zhou, Zhaomao 周兆茂. "Lun Cheng Tingzuo de zhexue sixiang" 論程廷祚的哲學思想 (On the Philosophical Thought of Cheng Tingzuo). *Anhui shifan xuebao: zhexue ban* 安徽師範學報：哲學版, no. 1 (1988), pp. 44–51.

Zhu, Chuanyu 朱傳譽, ed. *Ji Yun shengping gaishu* 紀昀生平概述 (A Brief Account of Ji Yun's Life). Taibei: Tianyi chubanshe 天一出版社, 1982.

Zhu, Shiying 朱世英. "Lun Yuewei caotang biji zhi 'chang'" 論閱微草堂
筆記之長 (On the Strengths of the *Yuewei caotang biji*). *Wenxue yican*
文學遺產, no. 1 (1983), pp. 94–102.

Secondary Sources — in Western Languages

Abrams, M. H. *A Glossary of Literary Terms.* New York: Holt, Rinehart
and Winston, 1981.

Adkins, Curtis P. "The Hero in Tang *Ch'uan-ch'i* Tales." In *Critical Essays on Chinese Fiction*, edited by Winston Yang and Curtis P. Adkins,
pp. 17–46. Hong Kong: The Chinese University Press, 1980.

Anderson, Richard. "*Taiken*: Personal Narratives and Japanese New
Religions." Ph.D. dissertation, Indiana University, 1988.

Balazs, Etienne. *Political Theory and Administrative Reality in Traditional
China.* London: School of Oriental and African Studies, University of London, 1965.

Beckson, Karl, and Arthur Ganz. *Literary Terms: A Dictionary.* New York:
Farrar, Straus and Giroux, 1975.

Bennett, Gillian. *Traditions of Belief: Women and the Supernatural.*
London: Penguin Books, 1987.

Berling, Judith. "Religion and Popular Culture: The Management of
Moral Capital in *The Romance of the Three Teachings*." In *Popular
Culture in Late Imperial China*, edited by David Johnson, Andrew J.
Nathan and Evelyn J. Rawski, pp. 188–218. Berkeley: University
of California Press, 1985.

Black, Alison Harley. *Man and Nature in the Philosophical Thought of
Wang Fu-chih.* Seattle: University of Washington Press, 1990.

Blackman, H. J. *The Fable as Literature.* London: The Athlone Press, 1985.

Bleiler, Everett F. *The Guide to Supernatural Fiction.* Kent, Ohio: Kent
State University Press, 1983.

Blofeld, John, trans. *The Book of Change.* New York: E. P. Dutton, 1966.

Bloom, Irene. *Knowledge Painfully Acquired: The K'un-chih chi by Lo Ch'in-
shun.* New York: University of Columbia Press, 1987.

———. "On the 'Abstraction' of Ming Thought: Some Concrete Evidence from the Philosophy of Lo Ch'in-shun." In *Principle and
Practicality: Essays in Neo-Confucianism and Practical Learning*,
edited by Wm Theodore de Bary and Irene Bloom, pp. 69–126.
New York: Columbia University Press, 1979.

Bruner, Jerome S. *Actual Minds, Possible Worlds.* Cambridge, Mass.: Harvard University Press, 1986.

———. "The Narrative Construction of Reality." *Critical Inquiry*, vol. 18, no. 1 (1991), pp. 1–21.

Butler, Gary R. *Saying Isn't Believing: Conversation, Narrative and the Discourse of Belief in a French Newfoundland Community.* St. Johns: Memorial University of Newfoundland, 1990.

Campany, Robert F. "Chinese Accounts of the Strange: A Study in the History of Religions." Ph.D. dissertation, University of Chicago, 1988.

Chan, Leo Tak-hung. "Chinese Animal Fables of the Eighteenth Century: Translations from Shen Qifeng's *Words of Humour from an Ancient Bell.*" *Asian Culture Quarterly*, vol. 23, no. 1 (1995), pp. 29–36.

———. "In Dalliance with Ghosts: Humor and the Fantastic in Luo Pin's *Ghost Amusement Scroll.*" *Journal of Oriental Studies* (forthcoming).

———. "Subjugating Spirits: Yuan Mei's *What the Master Would Not Speak of.*" *Asian Culture Quarterly*, vol. 19, no. 4 (1992), pp. 40–47.

Chan, Wing-tsit. *Chu Hsi: New Studies.* Honolulu: University of Hawai'i Press, 1989.

Chin, Ann-ping, and Mansfield Freeman. *Tai Chen on Mencius: Explorations in Words and Meaning.* New Haven: Yale University Press, 1990.

Chow, Kai-wing. *The Rise of Confucian Ritualism in Late Imperial China: Ethics, Classics, and Lineage Discourse.* Stanford: Stanford University Press, 1994.

Chow, Tse-tsung. "Ancient Chinese Views on Literature, the Tao, and Their Relationship." *Chinese Literature: Essays, Articles, Reviews*, vol. 1, no. 2 (1979), pp. 3–29.

———. "The Early History of the Chinese Word *Shih* (Poetry)." In *Wen-lin: Studies in the Chinese Humanities*, edited by Chow Tse-tsung, pp. 151–209. Madison: University of Wisconsin Press, 1968.

Ch'u, T'ung-tsu. *Local Government in China under the Ch'ing.* Cambridge, Mass.: Harvard University Press, 1962.

Cohen, Alvin P. "Avenging Ghosts and Moral Judgment in Ancient Chinese Historiography: Three Examples from *Shih-chi.*" In *Legend, Lore and Religion in China: Essays in Honor of Wolfram Eberhard on His Seventieth Birthday*, edited by Sarah Allan and Alvin P. Cohen, pp. 98–108. San Francisco: Chinese Materials Center, 1979.

Dégh, Linda. *Folktales and Society: Storytelling in a Hungarian Community.* Translated by Emily M. Schossberger. Bloomington: Indiana University Press, 1969.

————. "The 'Belief Legend' in Modern Society: Form, Function, and Relation to Other Genres." In *American Folk Legend: A Symposium*, edited by Edward Hand, pp. 55–68. Berkeley: University of California Press, 1971.

————, and Andrew Vazsonyi. "Legend and Belief." In *Folklore Genres*, edited by Dan Ben-Amos, pp. 93–123. Austin: University of Texas Press, 1976.

de Groot, J. J. M. *The Religion of the Chinese.* Westport, Conn.: Hyperion Press, 1980.

DeWoskin, Kenneth J. "The Six Dynasties *Chih-kuai* and the Birth of Fiction." In *Chinese Narrative: Critical and Theoretical Essays*, edited by Andrew H. Plaks, pp. 21–52. Princeton: Princeton University Press, 1977.

————. "The *Sou-shen Chi* and the *Chih-kuai* Tradition: A Bibliographic and Generic Study." Ph.D. dissertation, Columbia University, 1974.

Dien, Albert E. "The *Y'uan-hun chi* (Accounts of Ghosts with Grievances): A Sixth-Century Collection of Stories." In *Wen-lin: Studies in the Chinese Humanities*, edited by Chow Tse-tsung, pp. 211–278. Madison: University of Wisconsin Press, 1968.

Dijk, Teun A. van, ed. *Handbook of Discourse Analysis*, vols. 1–4. London: Academic Press, 1985.

Duara, Prasenjit. "Knowledge and Power in the Discourse of Modernity: The Campaign against Popular Religion in Early Twentieth-Century China." *Journal of Asian Studies*, vol. 50, no. 1 (1991), pp. 67–83.

Dudbridge, Glen. *The Tale of Li Wa: Study and Critical Edition of a Chinese Story from the Ninth Century.* London: Ithaca Press, 1983.

Dundes, Alan. "The Psychology of Legend." In *American Folk Legend: A Symposium*, edited by Edward Hand, pp. 21–36. Berkeley: University of California Press, 1971.

Dunstan, Helen. "Review (of R. Kent Guy's *The Emperor's Four Treasuries*)." *Harvard Journal of Asiatic Studies*, vol. 49, no. 2 (1989), pp. 659–664.

Eberhard, Wolfram. *Chinese Fables and Parables: A Catalogue.* Taibei: Orient Cultural Service, 1971.

Elman, Benjamin A. *From Philosophy to Philology: Intellectual and Social Aspects of Change in Late Imperial China.* Cambridge, Mass.: Harvard University Press, 1984.

Eoyang, Eugene. "A Taste for Apricots: Approaches to Chinese Fiction." In *Chinese Narrative: Critical and Theoretical Essays,* edited by Andrew H. Plaks, pp. 53–69. Princeton: Princeton University Press, 1977.

———. "Oral Narration in the *Pien* and *Pien-wen.*" *Archiv Orientalni,* vol. 46, no. 3 (1978), pp. 232–252.

Feng, Yu-lan. *The Spirit of Chinese Philosophy.* Translated by E. R. Hughes. Westport, Conn.: Greenwood Press, 1970.

Feuerwerker, Albert. *State and Society in Eighteenth-Century China: The Ch'ing Empire in Its Glory.* Ann Arbor: Center for Chinese Studies, University of Michigan, 1976.

Fishman, O. L. *Tri kitaĭskikh novellista XVII–VIII vv: Pu Songling, Ji Yun, Yuan Mei* (Three Chinese Novelists of the Seventeenth and Eighteenth Centuries: Pu Songling, Ji Yun, Yuan Mei). Moscow, 1980.

Foster, Lawrence Chapin. "The *Shih-i Chi* and its Relation to the Genre Known as *Chih-kuai Hsiao-shuo.*" Ph.D. dissertation, University of Washington, 1974.

Frye, Northrop. *Anatomy of Criticism: Four Essays.* Princeton: Princeton University Press, 1957.

Goffman, Erving. *Frame Analysis: An Essay on the Organization of Experience.* London: Harper Colophon Books, 1974.

Goodrich, L. C. *The Literary Inquisition of Ch'ien-lung.* Baltimore: Waverly Press, 1935.

Guy, R. Kent. *The Emperor's Four Treasuries: Scholars and the State in the Late Ch'ien-lung Era.* Cambridge, Mass.: Harvard University Press, 1987.

Hammond, Charles. "T'ang Stories in the *T'ai-p'ing kuang-chi.*" Ph.D. dissertation, Columbia University, 1987.

Hanan, Patrick. *The Chinese Short Story: Studies in Dating, Authorship, and Composition.* Cambridge, Mass.: Harvard University Press, 1973.

———. *The Chinese Vernacular Story.* Cambridge, Mass.: Harvard University Press, 1981.

Hansen, Valerie. *Changing Gods in Medieval China, 1127–1276.* Princeton: Princeton University Press, 1990.

Harmon, Coy L. "Chü Yu's *Chien-teng hsin-hua*: The Literary Tale in Transition." Ph.D. dissertation, University of Arizona, 1985.

Hartman, Charles. *Han Yü and the T'ang Search for Unity.* Princeton: Princeton University Press, 1986.

Hinsch, Bret. *Passions of the Cut Sleeve: The Male Homosexual Tradition in China.* Berkeley: University of California Press, 1990.

Ho, Ping-ti. "The Salt Merchants of Yang-chou: A Study of Commercial Capitalism in the Eighteenth Century." *Harvard Journal of Asiatic Studies,* vol. 17 (1954), pp. 130–148.

Holzman, Donald. "Confucius and Ancient Chinese Literary Criticism." In *Chinese Approaches to Literature from Confucius to Liang Ch'i-ch'ao,* edited by Adele A. Rickett, pp. 21–41. Princeton: Princeton University Press, 1978.

Hom, Marlon K. "The Continuation of Tradition: A Study of the *Liao-chai chih-i* by P'u Sung-ling (1640–1715)." Ph.D. dissertation, University of Washington, 1979.

Hsu, Francis L. K. *Religion, Science and Human Crisis: A Study of China in Transition and Its Implications for the West.* Westport, Conn.: Greenwood Press, 1973.

Hsu, Immanuel C. Y. *The Rise of Modern China.* New York: Oxford University Press, 1995.

Huang, Siu-chi. "Chang Tsai's Concept of *Ch'i.*" *Philosophy East and West,* vol. 18 (1968), pp. 247–260.

Hufford, David J. *The Terror that Comes in the Night: An Experience-centered Study of Supernatural Assault Traditions.* Philadelphia: University of Pennsylvania Press, 1982.

Hummel, Arthur W. ed. *Eminent Chinese of the Ch'ing Period (1644–1912).* Washington D.C.: Government Printing Office, 1943.

Hung, William. "Preface to an Index to *Ssu-ku ch'üan-shu tsung-mu* and *Wei-shou shu-mu.*" *Harvard Journal of Asiatic Studies,* vol. 4, no. 1 (1939), pp. 47–58.

Huters, Theodore. "From Writing to Literature: The Development of Late Qing Theories of Prose." *Harvard Journal of Asiatic Studies,* vol. 47, no. 1 (1987), pp. 51–96.

Johnson, David. "Chinese Popular Literature and Its Contents." *Chinese Literature: Essays, Articles, Reviews,* vol. 3, no. 2 (1981), pp. 225–233.

———. "Communication, Class and Consciousness in Late Imperial China." In *Popular Culture in Late Imperial China,* edited by David Johnson, Andrew J. Nathan and Evelyn J. Rawski, pp. 34–72. Berkeley: University of California Press, 1985.

Kao, Karl S. Y. *Classical Chinese Tales of the Supernatural and the Fantastic: Selections from the Third to the Tenth Century*. Bloomington: Indiana University Press, 1985.

Kasoff, Ira E. *The Thought of Chang Tsai (1020–1077)*. New York: Cambridge University Press, 1984.

Keenan, David L. "The Forms and Uses of the Ghost Story in Late Eighteenth-Century China as Recorded in the *Yüeh-wei Ts'ao-t'ang Pi-chi* of Chi Yun." Ph.D. dissertation, Harvard University, 1987.

Kei, Suzuki, comp. *Comprehensive Illustrated Catalogue of Chinese Paintings*. Tokyo: University of Tokyo Press, 1982.

Kessler, Lawrence D. *K'ang-hsi and the Consolidation of Ch'ing Rule 1661–1674*. Chicago: University of Chicago Press, 1976.

Labov, William. *Language in the Inner City: Studies in the Black English Vernacular*. Philadelphia: University of Pennsylvania Press, 1972.

Lanser, Susan S. *The Narrative Act: Point of View in Prose Fiction*. Princeton: Princeton University Press, 1981.

Lau, D. C., trans. *The Analects*. Hong Kong: The Chinese University Press, 1983.

Lau, Joseph S. M. and Y. W. Ma, eds. *Traditional Chinese Stories: Themes and Variations*. New York: Columbia University Press, 1978.

Liu, James J. Y. *Chinese Theories of Literature*. Chicago: The University of Chicago Press, 1975.

———. *The Art of Chinese Poetry*. Chicago: The University of Chicago Press, 1962.

Lu, Hsiao-peng. *From Historicity to Fictionality: The Chinese Poetics of Narrative*. Stanford: Stanford University Press, 1994.

Lu, Xun. *A Brief History of Chinese Fiction*. Translated by Yang Hsien-yi and Gladys Yang. Beijing: Foreign Language Press, 1959.

Mair, Victor. "The Narrative Revolution in Chinese Literature: Ontological Presuppositions." *Chinese Literature: Essays, Articles, Reviews*, vol. 5, nos. 1–2 (1983), pp. 1–28.

Martin, Wallace. *Recent Theories of Narrative*. Ithaca: Cornell University Press, 1986.

McMahon, Keith. *Causality and Containment in Seventeenth-Century Chinese Fiction*. Leiden: E. J. Brill, 1988.

Muhleman, James V. "The *Liao-chai chih-i*: Themes and Art of the Literary Tale." Ph.D. dissertation, Indiana University, 1978.

Naquin, Susan, and Evelyn S. Rawski. *Chinese Society in the Eighteenth Century.* New Haven: Yale University Press, 1987.

———. "Topics for Research in Ch'ing History." *Late Imperial China,* vol. 8, no. 1 (1987), pp. 187–203.

Neville, Robert C. "The Scholar-official as a Model for Ethics." *Journal of Chinese Philosophy,* vol. 13, no. 2 (1986), pp. 185–201.

Nienhauser, William H., Jr., ed. *The Indiana Companion to Traditional Chinese Literature.* Bloomington: Indiana University Press, 1986.

Plaks, Andrew H. *The Four Masterworks of the Ming Novel.* Princeton: Princeton University Press, 1987.

Polanyi, Livia. *Telling the American Story: A Structural and Cultural Analysis of Conversational Storytelling.* Norwood: Ablex Publishers, 1985.

Pollard, David E. *A Chinese Look at Literature: The Literary Values of Chou Tso-jen in Relation to the Tradition.* Berkeley: University of California Press, 1973.

Propp, Vladimir. *The Morphology of the Folktale.* Austin: University of Texas Press, 1968.

Průšek, Jaroslav. *Chinese History and Literature: Collection of Studies.* Dordrecht: D. Reidel Publishing Co., 1970.

———. *The Origins and the Authors of the Hua-pen.* Prague: Oriental Institute in Academia, 1967.

Rolston, David, ed. *How to Read the Chinese Novel.* Princeton: Princeton University Press, 1990.

Ropp, Paul S. *Dissent in Early Modern China: Ju-lin wai-shih and Ch'ing Social Criticism.* Ann Arbor: University of Michigan Press, 1981.

Sambrook, James. *The Eighteenth Century: The Intellectual and Cultural Context of English Literature, 1700–1789.* London: Longman, 1986.

Scholes, Robert, and Robert Kellogg. *The Nature of Narrative.* Oxford: Oxford University Press, 1966.

Seaman, Gary. "Only Half-Way to Godhead: The Chinese Geomancer as Alchemist and Cosmic Pivot." *Asian Folklore Studies,* vol. 45, no. 1 (1986), pp. 1–18.

Smith, Richard J. *China's Cultural Heritage: The Ch'ing Dynasty, 1644–1911.* Boulder, Colorado: Westview Press, 1983.

Stahl, Sandra. "Studying Folklore and American Literature." In *Handbook of American Folklore,* edited by Richard M. Dorson. Bloomington: Indiana University Press, 1983.

T'ien, Ju-k'ang. *Male Anxiety and Female Chastity: A Comparative Study of Chinese Ethical Values in Ming-Ch'ing Times.* Leiden: E. J. Brill, 1988.

Thompson, Stith. *Motif-Index of Folk Literature.* Bloomington: Indiana University Press, 1955–1958.

Thrall, William F., and Addison Hibbard. *A Handbook to Literature.* New York: Odyssey Press, 1962.

Ting, Nai-tung. *A Type Index of Chinese Folktales in the Oral Tradition and Major Works of Non-religious Literature.* Helsinki: Suomolainen Tiedeakatemia, 1978.

Todorov, Tzvetan. *The Fantastic: A Structural Approach to a Literary Genre.* Translated by Richard Howard. Cleveland: The Press of Case Western Reserve, 1973.

Van Straten, N. H. *Concepts of Health, Disease and Vitality in Traditional Chinese Society: A Psychological Interpretation.* Wiesbaden: Steiner, 1983.

Waley, Arthur. *Yuan Mei: Eighteenth-Century Chinese Poet.* Stanford: Stanford University Press, 1970.

Waters, Geoffrey R. *Three Elegies of Ch'u: An Introduction to the Traditional Interpretation of the Ch'u Tz'u.* Madison: University of Wisconsin Press, 1985.

Weber, Max. *The Protestant Ethic and the Spirit of Capitalism.* Translated by Talcott Parsons. New York: Scribner's Sons, 1958.

Weinstein, Vicki F. "Painting in Yang-chou 1710–1765: Eccentricity or the Literati Tradition?" Ph.D. dissertation, Cornell University, 1972.

Wellek, René, and Austin Warren. *Theory of Literature.* New York: Harcourt Brace, 1949.

Wu, Fatima. "Foxes in Chinese Supernatural Tales." Parts I and II. *Tamkang Review,* vol. 17, no. 2 (1986), pp. 121–153 and vol. 17, no. 3 (1986), pp. 263–294.

Yang, C. K. *Religion in Chinese Society: A Study of Contemporary Social Functions of Religion and Some of Their Historical Factors.* Berkeley: University of California Press, 1961.

Yim, Sarah. "Structure, Theme, and Narrative in T'ang *Ch'uan-ch'i.*" Ph.D. dissertation, Yale University, 1979.

Young, Katharine G. *Taleworlds and Storyrealms: The Phenomenology of Narrative.* Dordrecht: Martinus Nijhoff Publishers, 1987.

Yu, Anthony C. "Rest, Rest, Perturbed Spirit: Ghosts in Traditional

Chinese Prose Fiction." *Harvard Journal of Asiatic Studies*, vol. 47, no. 2 (1987), p. 397–434.

Yu, Ying-shih. "'O Soul, Come Back!': A Study in the Changing Conceptions of the Soul and Afterlife in Pre-Buddhist China." *Harvard Journal of Asiatic Studies*, vol. 47, no. 2 (1987), pp. 384–395.

———. "Some Preliminary Observations on the Rise of Ch'ing Confucian Intellectualism." *Qinghua xuebao* 清華學報, new series 11 (1975), pp. 1–20.

———. "Tai Chen and the Chu Hsi Tradition." In *Essays in Commemoration of the Golden Jubilee of the Fung Ping Shan Library (1923–82)*, edited by Chan Ping-leung, *et al.* Hong Kong: Hong Kong University Press, 1982.

———. "Tai Chen's Choice between Philosophy and Philology." *Asia Major*, third series, pt. 1 (1989), pp. 79–108.

———. "Towards an Interpretation of the Intellectual Transition in Seventeenth-Century China." *Journal of the American Oriental Society*, vol. 100, no. 2 (1980), pp. 115–125.

Zeitlin, Judith. *Historian of the Strange: Pu Songling and the Chinese Classical Tale.* Stanford: Stanford University Press, 1993.

———. "Pu Songling's (1640–1715) *Liaozhai zhiyi* and the Chinese Discourse on the Strange." Ph.D. dissertation, Harvard University, 1988.

Index